LAND OF OPPORTUNITY

LAND OF OPPORTUNITY

ONE FAMILY'S QUEST

FOR THE AMERICAN DREAM

IN THE AGE OF CRACK

WILLIAM M. ADLER

THE ATLANTIC MONTHLY PRESS
NEW YORK

In memory of

HELEN AND MORTON ADLER

Published simultaneously in Canada
Printed in the United States of America

FIRST EDITION

Library of Congress Cataloging-in-Publication Data

Adler, William M.
    Land of opportunity: one family's quest for the American dream in the age of crack /
by William M. Adler.—1st ed.
    ISBN 0-87113-593-0
    1. Chambers, Billy Joe, 1962– . 2. Chambers family.
  3. Narcotics dealers—United States—Biography. I. Title.
  HV5805.C48A65 1995   364.1'77'092273—dc20   94-24315

Design by Laura Hammond Hough

The Atlantic Monthly Press
841 Broadway
New York, NY 10003

10 9 8 7 6 5 4 3 2 1

I knew that if I were caught I would go to the chain gang.

But was not my life already a kind of chain gang?

What, really, did I have to lose?

—**Richard Wright,** *Black Boy*

CONTENTS

Cast of Selected Characters　　**xi**

Introduction:　**Homecoming**　　**1**

Chapter One:　**Land of Cotton**　　**11**

Chapter Two:　**Washing Windows in a Blizzard**　　**33**

Chapter Three:　**Heaven Dust**　　**63**

Chapter Four:　**"BJ, Why Don't You Start Selling Crack?"**　　**77**

Chapter Five:　**Cool Hand Larry**　　**101**

Chapter Six:　**Moving Like Lightning**　　**115**

Chapter Seven:　**Marlow's One-Stop**　　**135**

Chapter Eight:　**"Good-bye, Dixie Land"**　　**163**

Contents

Chapter Nine: **Too Windy for Tear Gas**   193

Chapter Ten: **"We Rich, Goddammit!"**   219

Chapter Eleven: **"Fuck It, I'll Fix Him"**   241

Chapter Twelve: **All in the Family**   265

Chapter Thirteen: **A Tale of Two Cities**   295

Chapter Fourteen: **As Close As Brothers Get**   321

Epilogue: **Nothing to Lose**   359

Acknowledgments   375

Notes   381

Selected Bibliography   411

CAST OF SELECTED CHARACTERS

Billy Joe Chambers: b. 1962. Along with his twin, Joe Edward, the ninth and tenth of fourteen children born to Hazel and Curtis Chambers, former sharecroppers and natives of Lee County, Arkansas. Billy Joe left home for Detroit at the end of 1978. Unmarried, the father of seven children.

Larry (Marlow) Chambers: b. 1950. Second son of Hazel and Curtis. A lengthy criminal career began in 1969 when he and a friend stole a county-owned truck in Marianna, the seat of Lee County. Cultivated a ruthless reputation in Detroit. Vegetarian, yoga practitioner, property owner in Jamaica.

Otis Bernard Chambers: b. 1968. Twelfth child of Hazel and Curtis. Apprenticed with his older brothers during summers in Detroit while still a high school student in Marianna. His family arrived at his high school graduation ceremony in a caravan of stretch limousines.

Willie Lee Chambers: b. 1954. Fifth child of Hazel and Curtis. Served in the U.S. Army and worked for 13 years as a letter carrier in Detroit. Married to Linda Chambers, a Louisiana native. Two children, a daughter and son.

Diana Alexander: b. 1964. The mother of three of Billy Joe's children and the sister of Tony (Tiger) Alexander.

Tony (Tiger) Alexander: b. 1967. Started as an errand boy at thirteen and worked up to drop-off/pick-up man for Billy Joe.

Roderick Jerome Byrd: b. 1957. One of Larry's chief lieutenants and location scouts.

L. C. (Big Terry) Colbert: b. 1949. Lee County native. Introduced Billy Joe to marijuana dealing in Detroit in early 1980s. Murdered in 1990.

Terry (Little Terry) Colbert: b. 1965. Arkansas native, arrived in Detroit in 1983 to live with his father, Big Terry. Worked off and on for Billy Joe. Played a key role in the Chambers brothers' downfall.

Anita (Niece) Coleman: b. 1965. Billy Joe's first girlfriend in Detroit. The mother of three of his children and the niece of Elayne Coleman and Perry Coleman.

Elayne Coleman: b. 1964. Detroit police said she sold crack to an undercover officer on Labor Day, 1984. She paid a stiff price.

Perry Coleman: b. 1960. Elayne's brother. Convinced Billy Joe to sell cocaine and worked as one of his main suppliers.

Cindy Davis: b. 1972. Worked after school in Larry's houses as a cut-up girl. The sister of Janice Davis Roberts.

Arthur Derrick: b. 1953. A leading "weight dealer" in Detroit, he sold to Billy Joe through Perry Coleman. Owned a fleet of planes.

Kevin (Hollywood) Duplessis: b. 1954. East side entrepreneur.

Dennis Fayson: b. 1959. Member of Larry's wrecking crew. Arson specialist.

Jerry Lee Gant: b. 1962. Childhood friend of Billy Joe and foster brother of Big Terry Colbert.

Marshall (Mario) Glenn: b. 1962. Childhood friend of Jerry Gant and Billy Joe. Raised in Lee County township of Rondo. Recruited youngsters from home to work in Detroit. Fond of Cadillacs.

David Havard: b. 1949. Managed The Boulevard apartments. Larry offered him a job he could not refuse. Lived with Patricia Middleton.

William (Jack) Jackson: b. 1962. Raised in the same Detroit housing project as Roderick Byrd. Starred in Larry's home video. Dated David Havard's sister.

Michael Curtis Lee: b. 1966. Lee County native. Worked as a drop-off/pick-up man for Billy Joe. Fathered a child by Cathy Chambers, the third of the brothers' four sisters.

Belinda Lumpkin: b. 1970. Lived with Larry. Worked as "paymaster" at The Boulevard, the apartment building Larry controlled on East Grand Boulevard. Penchant for home decorating.

Patricia Middleton: b. 1955. Lived at The Boulevard with David Havard. Worked briefly for Larry. Played a key role in the Chambers brothers' downfall.

Kela Nealis: b. 1971. The mother of Billy Joe's youngest child.

Janice Davis Roberts: b. 1969. Recruited by her sister, Cindy Davis, to work after school as a cut-up girl.

Eric Lamar (Fats) Wilkins: b. 1969. Born in Arkansas and raised in Detroit. Worked as an enforcer and drop-off/pick-up man for Billy Joe.

Carl Lee (Mojo) Young: b. 1962. Grew up a couple of miles down the gravel road from the Chamberses. The families attended church together. A brother married a Chambers sister.

Paul Lamont Young: b. 1970. Carl Young's nephew. Raised in Detroit, he spent summers in Lee County. Operated several houses for Billy Joe on the west side of Detroit.

LAND OF OPPORTUNITY

INTRODUCTION

HOMECOMING

It was a bright, warm day in the Arkansas Delta, and Billy Joe Chambers was coming home in a Cadillac. Not just one Cadillac, actually, but a great, shining caravan of Cadillacs, five of them, each one snow white, the color of cocaine, rolling along the dusty, crop-lined roads of Lee County. It was his younger brother Otis's high school graduation that evening, and though Otis wasn't much of a student—he had made better than a D-plus in only one class, general science, his senior year—Billy Joe believed Otis deserved a procession befitting the brother of a self-made millionaire.

So the Chambers family packed themselves into these glistening Cadillacs, rented specially in Memphis, sixty miles to the north and across the Mississippi River, and now they were spending the day riding through the county like rural royalty, in air-conditioned comfort, drinking, waving, watching the cars' little color TVs. Families ambled out onto their front porches and into their beaten-down yards to catch a glimpse of the Cadillacs snaking north from the Chamberses' homeplace near La Grange—a sleepy, mostly unpaved settlement in the southernmost part of Lee County—toward Marianna on Highway 1, past the cotton and soybean fields, the small wood-frame and brick houses.

Soothed by the opulent motions of wealth and its visible display, the Chambers men peered out through the tinted glass at the humble, ragtag finery of the people who watched them pass. For Billy Joe, for Otis, it was like looking at old, sad-assed versions of themselves, cracked and faded photographs of young men without luck. But no longer. For the last couple of years, Otis, for one, had been dressing more fashionably. His friends came to expect that he would be sporting the latest basketball shoes and satin jackets; sometimes he wore lizard-skin boots or a belt buckle emblazoned with a marijuana leaf. "He used to come to school with wads in both pockets, in his socks," recalls a former schoolmate, adding: "I've seen him bust a hundred-dollar bill for a bag of potato chips." And Otis had hardly obtained his driver's license before he was behind the wheel of a new black Jeep with smoked windows. But even Otis's closest friends were startled by this glut of limousines.

Once the caravan reached the outskirts of town it turned east on Texas Street, past the projects and trailers and tar-paper shacks, past open drainage ditches where children played and mosquitoes bred, and on across the railroad tracks toward the more expansive brick homes. Here, where Texas Street turns into a winding, kudzu-choked country road, the procession passed the historical marker commemorating the birth of the first white child in Arkansas, an attraction the local chamber of commerce touts in its brochure. The limos snaked on toward Bear Creek Lake, a lovely, wooded site amid St. Francis National Forest (the nation's smallest), where they eased past the campsites crowded with out-of-state RVs and locals fishing from the banks for dinner.

It was late on an unhurried Friday afternoon, May 30, 1986, and as usual at this time of the month, few people in Marianna had any money to spend. "This is a first-of-the-month town," says Derwin Sims, a service station owner. "Without government assistance checks, this place would be a ghost town."

Just a few years earlier, the Chamberses themselves were only marginally subsisting. Now here they were, dressed to the teeth, drinks in hand, cruising around Marianna in stretch limousines that were as misplaced as ocean liners on Bear Creek Lake.

Just north of downtown, the caravan veered left back onto Highway 1. When a minute later the Chambers family and their entourage pulled into the Lee Senior High School parking lot, they were mobbed like movie stars arriving at a Hollywood premiere. Parents' cameras snapped, recording the event for posterity; teenagers squealed and pressed against the cars. The brothers failed to discourage this adulation. "They were throwing money out the windows!" says one teacher. School administrators were too stunned to move. "We all just kind of crooked our heads and froze for a minute," recalls Charles Robinson, the principal at the time.

As Otis Chambers's name was announced that evening over the tinny, barely audible public-address system, some of his classmates stood and cheered. Wearing a mortarboard and a half-moon grin (but not his gold medallions, which administrators had ordered him to remove before the ceremony), Otis strutted across the artificial-turf stage at midfield to receive his diploma. By the time Otis shook hands with the president of the county school board, the entire class and many of the onlookers in the rickety wooden bleachers were on their feet. The ovation was suited to a football star or the scion of a dynasty. And in a sense, his classmates were on to something: While they would soon join the army, or head north or to Memphis or Little Rock in search of work, or struggle to eke out a living in one of the poorest counties in the United States, Otis had a job awaiting him in Billy Joe's financial empire. For Otis, it was a little like being a Kennedy or a Rockefeller. His future was bright and shining.

As Billy Joe, five feet two and a hundred thirty-five pounds, gazed down from his spot in the bleachers, he felt as smug and proprietary as any self-made baron of industry. He hadn't finished the eleventh grade at Lee Senior High, but here he was, twenty-three years old and in all likelihood one of the wealthiest people in Arkansas. It was proof, really, that a person could achieve almost anything in this country, as long as he really wanted it and was willing to work for it.

Because it is made and sold so cheaply, crack cocaine revolutionized drug marketing. It has also extracted an incalculable human toll. Its low cost, instantly euphoric high, and tormenting aftereffects doom many users to repeat the cycle endlessly: the only salvation is more crack.

Although the crack epidemic in America has been covered extensively during the last decade, much of the reporting generates more heat than light. Most of the news media limit themselves to voyeuristic accounts of a day in the life of an addict or lurid, sensationalized stories of crack-related crime and violence. Scenes from the front produce vivid images, staples of local news: premature, twitching crack babies; young street-corner dealers and their walking-dead customers; accounts of the drug traded for sex, or for scavenged scraps of aluminum, or even for an infant; the bloody aftermath of drive-by shootings; police storming suspected crack houses like infantrymen; manacled blacks spread-eagled on the sidewalk.

In the age of crack, remarkable stories become all the more so for their commonplaceness. Stories such as these: a pregnant woman arrives at a hospital, having seizures and nearly comatose, but still clenching a rock; another arrives by ambulance with a dead newborn—she had freebased cocaine three days before giving birth; an addicted mother leaves the maternity ward after giving birth and never comes back; a man brings his one-month-old daughter to a hospital because her vagina was bleeding and later tells police he raped her while he was high on crack because she wouldn't stop crying.

In Detroit, the crack mecca of the Midwest, there are numbing statistics to confirm the anecdotal evidence of the shattering destructiveness of the drug. In 1983 B.C.—before crack—about 100 patients were admitted to treatment clinics in Detroit for cocaine use; in 1987, the year Billy Joe Chambers's business crested, the figure was roughly 4,500. Emergency-room admissions linked to cocaine rose from 450 in 1983 to 3,811 in 1987. In 1983, there were 10 cocaine-related deaths in the city; in 1987, 145 people died of cocaine-related causes. That same year, Detroit's murder rate, consistently among the highest in the nation, peaked. And half the murder victims age forty and under had cocaine in their systems.

Slam-bang stories and statistics outrage people, but for the wrong reasons. Crack is a scourge; its carnage, its devastation of family and neighborhood life have been documented thoroughly. But just as most stories about homelessness fail to mention that the federal government slashed housing subsidies, the raft of drug stories completely ignores why crack distribution is for so many a rational career choice. There often is no context to the stories; it is as if crack fell from the sky.

Short shrift is given to the devastating consequences for inner-city residents of the Reagan-Bush era's domestic spending policies, and to the collapse of opportunity during the 1980s for those at the bottom of the economic heap—especially poor blacks. Scant attention is paid to the fact that given the catastrophic unemployment rate among black youths, for many a job in the drug business is necessary for survival. Crack capitalism was there in the wealth-obsessed culture all along, in young black men like the Chambers brothers who were prepared to go along to get along only until they found that opportunity, that niche, when it might be possible to do more with their lives than survive: to shape their own fate.

There is a reasonable explanation for the crack whirlwind: the head-on collision during the 1980s of the cultures of greed and need. The decade's cult of money, its tone of rising expectations, insisted that the dispossessed aspire to the goals of the dominant culture yet denied them the means to obtain those goals legally. From the rubble of the crash between the American creed of equal opportunity and its denial in practice emerged a new breed of capitalist epitomized by Billy Joe Chambers and his brothers.

* * *

I learned of the four Chambers brothers on the front page of *The New York Times.* The piece was published in late 1988, shortly after the conclusion of their six-week trial in federal court in Detroit. Well into the article the reporter noted that the Chamberses grew up in a small town called Marianna in rural eastern Arkansas; I recall thinking that this was the true significance of the story. So many questions came to mind: What pushed these young men out of the South to Detroit and pulled them into their chosen pursuit? Was it in fact a choice? What alternatives did they have? What happens to those who risk almost certain imprisonment, if not life and limb, for wealth, but not only wealth, for control over their own lives as well?

It has been said that ghetto capitalists such as the Chamberses are vastly different from mainstream capitalists, that theirs is a "culture of poverty" with corresponding values. In truth they are not so different. Like any successful entrepreneurs, they identified a niche in the marketplace, assessed the barriers to entry, learned how to buy wholesale, mass-produce and market their product and track inventory. They studied the interrelationship of investment, operations, and financing. They taught themselves how to analyze risk, monitor cash flow, calculate gross margin. They implemented strict quality control measures, devised employee rules and regulations, benefit plans, performance bonuses, a customer incentive program. The Chambers brothers were rewarded with substantial profits. At the height of their power, they grossed, conservatively, fifty-five million tax-free dollars a year, revenue enough to rank their enterprise larger than any legal privately held business in Detroit.

But Billy Joe and his brothers were criminals. Like tobacco companies, they sold their product indiscriminately and remorselessly, without regard for the tragic consequences. And they sold, most often, to those who could least afford it: poor people who hung out on Detroit's Lower East Side, people whose dreams had been too long deferred, who suddenly found a world of success in crack pipes.

The Chambers brothers' means of obtaining and protecting their extraordinary market share extended beyond the basic techniques and tools of lawful business. The Chamberses employed a security force or "wrecking crew" to enforce discipline and gain retribution. The crew broke knees and heads, shot people, burned houses. These tactics are as necessary to success in their orbit as maintaining sufficient working capital, coining a catchy advertising jingle, and protecting intellectual property are to legitimate enterprises.

Just as Wall Street's inside traders cannot be written off as greedy aberrants, neither can the Chambers brothers be dismissed as aberrant ghetto capitalists—each took their cue from the wider society. They did not reject mainstream values; rather they embraced them in the only way they could. In yearning and looking and groping for a way out, the Chamberses did what most Americans would have said was the right thing to do had they not sold drugs: they strove for financial success. Indeed, their story should frighten not because it shows what made them different, but rather what made them so common.

Social and economic policy may be partially responsible for creating the conditions that enabled the Chambers brothers to prosper, but ultimately Billy Joe and his brothers must be held accountable for their actions. Drug dealers must be punished; there have to be consequences for illegal activities. But there also must be an understanding of the long road over which they traveled to the underground drug economy—of the searing effects of poverty and prejudice and a lifetime of groping for dignity within a social and economic system that limits and traps them from the moment of birth. In the case of the Chambers brothers, for instance, what of the wide and deep roots of racism and poverty in their hometown of Marianna? Lee County, of which Marianna is the seat, has a vise grip on virtually every statistical indicator of crushing poverty in Arkansas: the highest rates of unemployment, illiteracy, teenage pregnancy, infant mortality. More than 40 percent of the county's residents live below the federal poverty level; its per capita income of six thousand dollars places it among the ten poorest counties in the country; half of the county's fifteen thousand residents did not graduate from high school.

People move away from places like Marianna not because they want to but because they have to. As Clifton Collier, a sharp-eyed African-American journalist in a town with no room for a black reporter, told me: "Either you stay here with the certainty of nothing, or you take a chance and go to Detroit." And what of the knee-deep recession in Detroit into which the Chamberses waded in the late 1970s, the plant closings, the flight of jobs, capital, and the middle and working classes to the suburbs and beyond?

Pushed away from the South and pulled into the economic underground of the North and driven by the same aspirations for material gain as most everyone else, the Chambers brothers recognized crack as a lucrative business opportunity—their best chance at upward mobility. Shut out of the American Dream and given the choice of a lifetime of minimum-wage drudgery in the city or, worse yet, the stifling farm life back home, it is little wonder that such smart, brash, ambitious young men took the only road open to wealth and power and respect. What is surprising is that so few policy makers and drug warriors fail to make the connection between crack-dealing as a rational career choice and the lack of any other economic opportunity.

This is not to say, of course, that most young black men turn to lives of crime. But in Detroit, as in other large northern cities, modern social forces have conspired to leave poor, undereducated minorities without access to living-wage, low-skill manufacturing jobs. These jobs were supplanted by nonproducing service and information jobs, many of which required advanced degrees. By the early 1980s, blue-collar work had all but vanished from the local economy.

The shift of capital and resources away from Detroit was accelerated in the eighties, but transformative forces had been stirring for decades. Not the least of those forces, ironically, was the civil rights movement. With expanded job and educational opportunities and fair housing laws came a newly stratified black society.

Urban neighborhoods that previously and by necessity housed blacks of all economic standing were abandoned by many working- and middle-class families; the movement gave people the means and the opportunity to live where they chose, and many chose to leave Detroit for the suburbs.

Many of those left behind were increasingly isolated. The automobile plants had closed or relocated, as had the great department stores. Neighborhood institutions such as recreation centers, small businesses, churches, schools—the bedrock of the community—crumbled. By the early eighties even entry-level dead-end jobs were nearly impossible to come by; the inner-city economy was driven largely underground and entrepreneurial, and among the leading entrepreneurs, the community's new role models, were the Chambers brothers.

The story of the Chambers brothers could illustrate the final panel of the nation's sweeping postwar panorama: the Great Migration from plantation to ghetto. As had millions of others before them, the Chambers brothers moved from the Delta, the South's poorest, loveliest, most hate-filled region, to the promised land of the North—to Detroit: a raw, anguished, abandoned city in economic ruin. And like the stories of so many other uprooted families, theirs is one of survival and community and resilience, of the struggle to set themselves free from the limits they were born to. The Chamberses were a family who stuck together out of need and out of trust, who worked together every day from "can to can't" in the cotton fields, and later, around the clock, seven days a week, in the crack houses.

To understand what that fine spring day in 1986 meant to Billy Joe Chambers—that triumphant day spent cruising Lee County in a caravan of limousines, honoring his younger brother Otis with a spectacle that stunned the entire town, recalling as he passed by the weathered, quizzical faces of his childhood his own and his people's tribulations and humiliations; to appreciate what it meant to stand on those splintery bleachers during the graduation ceremonies, basking in the warmth of a hero returned—to understand that day fully, there must be an understanding of what he left behind when he fled to Detroit: the deep, lasting ways the rural Southern world he grew up in molded and scarred him, the forces of circumstance that held him back at home and that gave him the stubborn will and unyielding determination to survive and escape and succeed.

Until Billy Joe Chambers's brief and brilliant criminal career is seen in this light, in the light of someone who refused to settle for passivity and hopelessness, who tried desperately to create an identity and who sought somehow (however perversely it might seem to those in different circumstances) to give value and meaning to his life, it is impossible to see how much his success was worth and how badly he wanted it.

CHAPTER ONE

LAND OF COTTON

It was just before sunset, and sixteen-year-old Billy Joe Chambers was waiting on the porch of his family's house. The wood-frame, four-room bungalow—two bedrooms, a living room, and kitchen—was set on cement blocks about twenty yards off a country road. Surrounding the house was the tabletop flat expanse of Delta sky and earth, a merged and muted landscape particular to the region's sodden winters. In the idle fields, once sinewy cotton stalks were dormant and desolate; now, at the close of the year, there was no hint of the deep green leaves and dazzling white clumps that would emerge in the late summer and early fall. The road dead-ended two miles or so to the east, across the railroad tracks, at the limits of La Grange, a mostly black farming community at the southern tip of Lee County, about seven miles from Marianna, in the rich, alluvial Delta lowlands.

But while the dirt may have been rich, Billy Joe's parents, Hazel and Curtis Chambers, were not. They would eventually have fourteen children to raise, ten boys and four girls. (Billy and his twin brother were the ninth- and tenth-born.) Hazel and Curtis slept in one bedroom; the boys slept four to a bed in the other;

and the girls shared a bed in the living room. The windows throughout the house were without glass in the winter or screens in the summer; they were covered only by pasteboard. With little closet or storage space, clothes and other personal belongings were strewn all over the floor. The family's source of pride was its television, a black-and-white console that attracted friends and relatives from throughout the area. "We were the only ones with TV, at least the only blacks," says Larry Chambers, the second-oldest son. "Everyone was always coming over to watch."

It was shortly before Christmas 1978. School was out for the holiday, the Lee County cotton crop was picked and ginned, and things were as quiet on the porch as usual: too quiet. Each time Billy heard a car approaching from the main highway, a mile or so to the west, he thought it might be his twin brother Joe Edward's. Sit down, relax, Billy murmured to himself. But the moment he sat he'd bolt up, his ears playing tricks on him. The muffler on Joe's car was nonexistent, and, as his mother said, Joe Edward drove like the car only had two speeds—fast and faster. How could he *not* recognize it? Besides, he was familiar with the little traffic there was on Highway 121, the gravel road that ran between La Grange and Highway 1; unless, of course, it was somebody lost—say, somebody who'd made a wrong turn out of the barbecue joint at Cypress Corner—and he'd know that too.

The time was growing short; surely his brother hadn't forgotten about the ride. They weren't identical twins, Billy Joe and Little Joe, as his brother was known. Billy took after his mother, who was almond-colored; Joe looked just like his dark-skinned daddy. But the whole family has distinctly similar features: a high forehead, flaring nostrils, small, almost delicate ears, and a broad, elfin grin. And most strikingly, they are all short. Curtis, at five feet four, looms over the rest of his family. Hazel is barely five feet. Billy stopped growing at five-two, although he has filled out since his high school days.

Hazel and Curtis Chambers were both born into Lee County

sharecropping families. Curtis's father moved his family from plantation to plantation in the southern part of the county; Hazel's father sharecropped on a plantation near Marianna. By the time Billy Joe and Little Joe were born in 1962, Hazel and Curtis were renting the forty-acre farm outside of La Grange from which now, in 1978, the teenage Billy was planning his escape.

It had been a childhood of hardship. The house was without plumbing until the early 1970s. When Billy needed to use the toilet, he trudged down a backyard path to the outhouse; taking a bath meant pumping and hauling water from a well in a five-gallon bucket and heating it on the kitchen stove. The Chamberses worked hard to ensure that their children had enough food. During the day, Curtis worked a full-time job off the farm, at an electronics factory in Forrest City and later at a chemical plant in West Helena. Meanwhile, Hazel and the children picked and chopped cotton in the fields. There was usually no need for baby-sitters; the older kids simply dragged the younger ones along on cotton sacks as they made their way down the endless rows.

Sometimes, though, there was not enough food. "What kept us going was catfish out of the swamp and blackberry trees," recalls Larry Chambers. "Or else we'd be sent down the road to a white family's house, and we'd sit on the porch and wait for them to finish eating. We'd have a bucket and when they finished, they'd give what's left to us and we'd take it back home."

Blacks in Lee County had always lived off the scraps. Their lives were structured much as they were a century earlier—so that whites controlled practically their every waking moment. In 1962, the year Billy was born, blacks constituted more than 60 percent of the county's twenty-one thousand residents. Yet not only did whites control every major institution—the courthouse, the schools, the banks, the police department, the newspaper—not a single black was employed in *any* capacity in those enterprises (save for the segregated schools). Nor did Marianna's only industrial employer hire blacks. In fact, except for during Reconstruction when blacks briefly seized political power—the first sheriff of Lee County was black—the racial barometer had barely budged in the hundred years between the Emancipation Proclamation and Billy's birth.

At an early age black children learned by example and experience that the key to survival, as it had been since slavery, was subservience. Black children were taught to understand and accept without defiance the restrictions of living within a controlling white society whose conviction was that blacks were in every respect inferior and should be made to stay in their proper place. To do otherwise—to question authority, to act without deference, or to refuse to acknowledge one's inferiority—was to violate the unwritten but indelible code of racial behavior. And to do that was to invite trouble upon oneself and one's family for which no amount of hard work and other sorts of virtue could compensate.

Blacks, for instance, were never to address a white person by his or her first name alone; it had to be preceded with a titular *Mr.* or *Mrs.* or *Miss*. Whites, on the other hand, were not expected to extend to blacks a courtesy title. "By the age of ten," recalls Sterling King, Jr., the son of a minister, "the boss man's kids called my father by his first name, rather than Reverend King." The practice dates from slavery, when blacks had no last names. "We always called them by their first names no matter who they were or how accomplished or how old they were," a retired Marianna teacher says.

The minutiae of the racial code extended well beyond language. Black pedestrians were to step off the sidewalk to allow whites to pass; black motorists were never to pass white drivers on unpaved roads. A white never visited in a black person's home; a black never entered a white home through the front door. Blacks were not to look directly at whites when speaking. "It might imply a lack of imperial respect," says King, who is presently a Howard University professor. Or, if a black man and a white woman were conversing it might imply sexual interest. Such an implication, of course, could have dire consequences. For a white it might mean ostracism; for a black it might mean the loss of livelihood and home, or it might mean prison or something altogether worse. Although the lynching era, the days of "Kill a mule, buy another. Kill a nigger, hire another" had peaked decades earlier, the threat of mob violence was ever present. By the time of Billy's birth, only seven years had lapsed since a mob in Mississippi lynched a fifteen-year-old black named Emmett Till for whistling at a white woman.

Lynching may have fallen out of favor as a widespread tool of social control, but it lurked in the collective memory. The Till killing was on the mind of Calvin Smith's mother the day she took her son to McCutchen's Hardware in downtown Marianna. Calvin, a tenth-grader, had struck up a conversation with the proprietor's daughter. "All of a sudden my mother grabbed me," he recalls. " 'Don't talk to that girl—you wanna get killed?' "

The very threat of sanctions for crossing the color line—legal, economic, or violent sanctions—triggered in Calvin Smith's mother exactly the reaction that allowed segregation and discrimination and paternalism to flourish. Indeed, this was the cornerstone of paternalism: the better the system worked, the better everyone, white and black, understood and conformed to the required behavior, the less the sanctions needed to be administered. Don't rock the boat, it was said, and you won't be thrown overboard.

Paternalism in Lee County reached into every facet of citizenship, from the tightly controlled ballot box to the courtroom. Justice was dispensed to black laborers in the interest of plantation owners who could ill afford to lose their field hands to death or incarceration. "The bosses had a saying," says Geneva Robinson, who grew up on the Ford plantation near Brickeys in northeastern Lee County. "Keep yourself out of the graveyard, and we'll keep you out of the penitentiary." And so it was not uncommon for the presiding judge to find the guilt or innocence of a black defendant on the basis of a single question: "Whose nigger are you?"

Electoral politics was also handled by proxy. Farmers paid poll taxes for their tenants; they determined who would vote—and for whom. "If you were on a man's plantation, you didn't have a head of your own," recalls A. J. Atkins, who grew up on a plantation with the Chambers brothers' maternal grandparents. "He'd bring the ballots right out to the plantation, and you voted like he wanted you to vote."

Some planters, however, weren't taking any chances with black suffrage; they didn't want to encourage the habit. These planters were well aware of the ongoing registration drives in other southern states and reckoned that it wouldn't be long before the organizers for SNCC, the Student Nonviolent Coordinating Committee, found their way to the Arkansas Delta. And so black political participation, even as stifled and guarded as it was, was often discouraged. Says one woman whose family sharecropped on the forty-six-hundred-acre Felton plantation, one of the county's largest: "If 'Sonny Boy' [Felton] found some of his hands were going to register to vote, he'd threaten to throw 'em off the land."

Paternalism stretched even to the county's department of motor vehicles, from which farmers obtained driver's licenses in bulk for their field hands, most of whom were unable to pass the written test. The reasons most field hands could not read went deep into the economic life of the region. The prevailing attitude among planters toward black education was neatly summarized by a campaign slogan first uttered at the turn of the century by Governor Jeff Davis. Davis was a tub-thumping demagogue from the hills—the "wild ass of the Ozarks." "Every time you educate a nigger," Davis proclaimed, "you spoil a good field hand."

A half century later, the governor of Arkansas was still playing the race card. Seven weeks before Billy Joe Chambers was born, under the white-hot sky of a Delta summer afternoon, three hundred Lee County citizens—farmers, merchants, the courthouse crowd—waited in the sun for their governor. It was July of 1962, and as the mercury brushed ninety-four, Governor Orval E. Faubus, accompanied by his traveling Dixieland band, glad-handed his way through a sea of friendly faces and applause to the bandstand at the north end of the courthouse square in Marianna. Standing sentinel over the gathering was a great bronzed frock-coated statue of Robert E. Lee, the county's namesake. The Democratic party primary election—the only election that mattered in one-party Arkansas—was almost three weeks away and Faubus, the four-term incumbent, was on his final campaign swing through the Delta.

It had been a bruising campaign. Although he was favored to win reelection over five challengers, Faubus was locked in a close race with a liberal former governor named Sidney McMath. McMath hoped to garner enough votes to deny Faubus a majority and thereby force a runoff. Now, nineteen days before the election, Faubus was not taking electoral success for granted, even in Lee County, where voters had overwhelmingly supported him in each of his previous campaigns.

Most Lee County voters—less than a quarter of voting-age blacks were registered—appreciated the governor's famous action five years earlier, when he seemed to be on the verge of declaring another civil war by calling out the National Guard to save Central High School in Little Rock from integration. Faubus had deftly used the segregation issue to win his third and fourth terms in 1958 and 1960, but by 1962, the year after the Freedom Rides, the political winds had shifted; he had said little about the Little Rock incident during this campaign. He stressed instead his record as a self-styled populist, a fighting man of the people, a man who by implicit and explicit support for racial discrimination gave solace to those whites on the lower rungs of the economic ladder: those who most feared black competition for their jobs.

It was to economic development that Faubus would speak on this sweltering day in Marianna. He was introduced by Leonard Moody, a bespectacled insurance man and a former mayor who even in his sixties boasted a full head of bright red hair. Moody extolled Faubus to the lustily cheering crowd as a "stalwart statesman and exponent of good government." Then, to the strains of his band's rendition of "Dixie," the governor, a little man from deep in the Ozarks with slicked-back hair, a penchant for wide ties, and an indefatigable talent for smiling like an alligator while dangling a matchstick from his mouth, strode to the podium. After the requisite bashing of his chief opponent, the integrationist McMath (for whom Faubus once worked and who would later say: "I brought Orval down from the hills, and every night I ask forgiveness"), the governor growled: "The bidness climate of Lee County's better than it ever has been and you know it!" He cited his role in bringing to Marianna two years earlier its first industrial employer, Douglas & Lomason, Inc., a Detroit-based auto-seat-parts manufacturer. He concluded by calling Lee a "rich and productive county that has been good to its people."

In 1962 few Lee County blacks would have agreed with their governor. By that summer—eight years after the Supreme Court outlawed public school desegregation, seven years after the Montgomery bus boycott, five years after Faubus's military maneuvers in Little Rock, two years after the first lunch counter sit-ins in Greensboro—nothing had changed in the isolated and insulated world of Lee County, Arkansas.

Black children there existed much for the sake they always had—to produce cheap cotton. Large families—ten, twelve, or fourteen children, like the Chamberses—were the norm. "It's two more hands / For to carry a row," exclaimed the happy father of his newborn son in a Sterling A. Brown poem. By the age of five or six, as soon as he was big enough to wield a hoe, that child would work all day alongside his many siblings.

The work never really stopped. The Chamberses raised chickens, hogs, and cows for their own use. Billy Joe and the other kids helped out by mowing lawns, working other people's land, and doing domestic chores in town. "When we finished picking and chopping our cotton," says Billy's brother Danny, "we'd pick other people's."

The school-year calendar, like everything else in the children's lives, was dictated by the needs of the cotton. School was divided into "split terms" to coincide with lulls in the cotton cycle. Much of the cotton was picked by October 1, the traditional starting date for school. But many of the students were needed in the fields well into November and sometimes December; most did not enroll until around Thanksgiving. School recessed in early May, when the time came to prepare the cotton for chopping. The summer term began in early July, after the weeds were chopped from the cotton rows and before the fall picking season began.

Until 1958, when Lee County consolidated its rural schools, each of the county's rural townships had its own schools—one black, one white. In La Grange, outside of which the Chambers family lived, the black school was housed in two rooms: grades one to three in one room; grades four to six in the other. Each room had one teacher who was responsible, during any given term, for the education of fifty to sixty students of varying age and ability. Says L. E. Coleman, who served for thirty-seven years as a teacher and principal: "It didn't matter how old they were. We used to put the smarter students together with the sorry readers to help them along. That's how we got by."

To avoid the split terms, some parents in La Grange and other rural areas of the county sent their children to live in the Marianna school district, where students attended school year-round. The children would board with family or friends in town in exchange for money, or, more often, for food from the farm. Marianna's was one of the few black school districts without a split term; this was due largely to the influence of Anna M. P. Strong, the founder in 1926 and first principal of Robert R. Moton High School.

By virtue of her position as principal of Moton—around which black secular life revolved—Anna Strong served for three decades as the white-appointed leader of the black community. She was born in neighboring Phillips County, and left home at fourteen to begin her teaching career. She attended the famed Tuskegee Institute in Alabama, where she refined her puritan attitudes about discipline, work, and education. And it was at Tuskegee that she embraced school founder Booker T. Washington's belief that economic and moral uplift was the first step for blacks in their long climb toward equality. (Strong named her school for Washington's successor as principal of Tuskegee.) A pragmatist, Strong knew that blacks had their place in a Jim Crow world. And she knew that whites would support craft and vocational training for blacks but would not stand for the sort of education that could make them a serious factor in politics. Like Washington, she saw that for a black school to succeed she had to assuage white fears of an overly educated black community.

She did so by encouraging the most promising black youths—those, in many cases, whose parents were small landowners rather than sharecroppers—to leave home, to seek further educational or job opportunities in the cities. Whites appreciated her accommodationist ways and blacks were thankful for her instilling in them the skills and confidence they needed to succeed far away from Lee County. Hers was a forceful, imperious presence that imbued in teachers and students alike a mixture of devotion and fear. There was no need, for example, for a bell to signal the end of recess. Dr. Strong's office window faced the playground. She had only to raise the window and clap her long-fingered hands twice and "the whole campus would freeze," recalls Geneva Robinson, a former student.

After the county consolidated the rural schools in 1958, children from La Grange attended school in Marianna. And though the Marianna schools did not split terms, many of the rural students continued to attend only sporadically; they were needed as badly as ever in the fields. "We missed a couple of days a week or more," says Larry Chambers, who was born in 1950. Some children, like Danny Chambers, who was born the following year, missed school during the entire harvest—a period of more than three months. Although Danny attended school intermittently until the tenth grade, he missed so many classes while out doing field work that he says, "I may as well have dropped out in grade school."

Simply getting to and from school was a chore. Each morning the Chambers children left their home around six o'clock. They walked a mile up a rutted, dirt road to its intersection with Highway 1, where they awaited the school bus beneath a grove at Cypress Corner. During the rainy seasons, when the road to the main highway flooded, the children sloshed to the bus stop and remained in wet clothes and shoes all day long. And each morning and afternoon, rain or shine, frigid or torrid, as they hiked the distance to and from Cypress Corner, they were passed by a school bus carrying white children all the way to and from La Grange.

The schools themselves were also surpassed by their white counterparts. Endowed with a disproportionately low share of tax dollars, the black schools made do with inferior facilities and handed-down materials: from textbooks to typewriters to football helmets to laboratory equipment, everything black students used white administrators had already deemed expendable. "Blacks got whatever the whites were through with," says Lorraine Jones, a white who taught school in Marianna for thirty-three years, beginning in 1949. Once she complained to her principal that her students' torn and tattered textbooks were in such poor condition that they were useless. "That's okay," she was told, "we'll give those books to the niggers."

The books were useless in other ways. Absent from their pages was mention of black contributions to American life. "The books we got from Futrall [the white high school] had nothing on black history," recalls Calvin Smith, who graduated from Moton in 1961 and who is now an Arkansas State University historian and dean. "To read them was to reinforce your nonexistence."

The local newspaper further reinforced blacks' invisibility. As did most small-town papers, the weekly *Courier-Index* mirrored the ideas and values of the dominant society. By the early sixties the plantations may have been waning but their legacy of racism and paternalism showed no sign of editorial retreat. It was not that the *Courier-Index* merely ignored Lee County's majority black population; it distorted black news beyond recognition. To read the front page week after week was to read that crime was the principal occupation of those few blacks who lived in the county.

Otherwise, Page One treated community events and public affairs as if *no* blacks lived in Lee County, let alone six of its every ten residents. This sort of gross neglect, coupled with sensationalized publicity of black crime—in no criminal case was a black person's race not prominently displayed ("NEGRO IS HELD IN STABBING INCIDENT")—provided ample weekly nourishment for white fears about blacks and the perpetuation of racist stereotypes.

The newspaper's social news columns were as segregated as the waiting rooms of the local hospital: the *Courier-Index* published separate listings of "white" and "colored" admissions and births. The listings prefixed *Mrs.* to the names of married white women; married black women were denied the honorific—another relic of slavery, when whites did not recognize black marriages. All other aspects of black life were relegated to a single "Colored News" column written by blacks and concentrating on local religious and social activities. But no matter what else may have happened in any given week—a local man made good, plans announced for an upcoming horse show, a visit from a delegation of out-of-state farmers, the results of the gubernatorial primary (Faubus was renominated handily, including 57 percent of the 2,113 votes cast in Lee County)—there was always room on the front page for news of black violence, such as the lead story on August 30, 1962, the day Billy Joe Chambers was born: "COLORED WOMAN IS KILLED SATURDAY."

When Billy and Little Joe were only a year or two old, a German man showed up at their farm. His name was Fritz Schreiber, but everyone called him Mr. Fred. He told the twins he'd retired after working most of his life in a German candy factory, although he actually had emigrated from Germany when he was twenty-eight years old, in 1925. He landed in Wisconsin, where he found work in a dairy. For some reason—restlessness, a desire for the exotic, or for escape—he eventually retired to Lee County, moving

into a blue trailer on Chambers land. Stout and smallish, with rad-
ish cheeks and a healthy shock of white hair, he resembled no one
so much as Santa Claus. Mr. Fred doted on the twins, cradling
them together in his forearms, fishing them out from behind the
bed when they fell, giving them candy and apples and clothes. He
opened a bank account for them, and every year he'd throw them
a birthday party. On days the Chambers family was working the
fields, Mr. Fred would meet them at the end of the cotton rows
nearest his house to offer sustenance—fruit or candy or a drink.
And when he noticed the family's dwindling food supplies, he'd
often chip in a few bags of groceries. Other children from the community were always showing up at the German's house to claim his
time, his money, his candy. Whenever Billy would run away from
home, he'd stay with Mr. Fred. "We was his family, me and my
twin," Billy says. "We were crazy about him."

For all the lavish, grandfatherly attention Mr. Fred bestowed
on the twins, he reserved his true passion for their mother. At first
his relationship to Hazel Chambers was neighborly, morning-cof-
fee cordial. Then, in exchange for a few dollars here and there,
Hazel began washing his clothes and cooking for him. Although
he was more than twice Hazel's age—at the time he arrived he was
about sixty-six, she thirty-two—they found mutual comfort in one
another's company. Mr. Fred was worldly, educated, and relatively
wealthy—attributes she found lacking in her husband, Curtis.
Hazel was strikingly attractive; slim, with dark, flashing eyes and an
"eye-popping" wardrobe that next to the drab farm clothes most
women in the community wore, stood out, says a lifelong acquaintance, "like a show horse in a stable of workhorses." She
usually traveled to St. Louis, where her mother lived, to shop. And
she possessed, even two decades later, a vigorous sexual energy.
"She kinda had that hot-girl twitch," says the mother of three of
Hazel's grandchildren.

Sometime—it is unclear when—the relationship changed.
"I'm going to bed with the German and he's helping me out,"
Hazel bragged to friends. Even those who were not notified di-

rectly knew anyway; the people here, like extended family, knew each other's business. And secrets, especially regarding extramarital sex, and not just extramarital but interracial, intergenerational, extramarital sex, seeped like air from a punctured tire. "Sure we all knew about Mizz Hazel and the German," says a boyhood friend of one of the older Chambers brothers. He spoke on the condition of anonymity. "She was screwing him and milking him for everything." When Billy was four, in April of 1967, Mr. Fred, then seventy, declared in his Last Will and Testament that he would bequeath his entire estate to "my dear friend, Hazel Chambers."

Sometime in the late sixties, Curtis and Hazel opened a small café on their land, a juke joint called, alternately, the Blue Swan, the Tin Top Inn, or, simply, Curt's Place. They sold beer and whiskey, sandwiches and chips, and rented a jukebox and pool table. It took almost everything they earned to pay the bills, and the joint provided them with a little extra.

Its wooden, ramshackle exterior was green, with a tin roof. Inside it was dim and hot, often drowsy, sometimes raucous. "Once in a while they'd have a disturbment down there," says Barney L. Buford, a La Grange native who has known Curtis Chambers since the two were boys in the 1920s. "Mostly they'd be quiet-like." The juke joint's entrance and the doorway between its two rooms were short; tall enough for Curtis Chambers, who built it, but not for many of his patrons. The decor amounted to bare lightbulbs, a wood stove, and cracked, peeling walls. But people didn't go to juke joints for the decor.

Curt's Place brightened the flat fields and back roads of southern Lee County like a lantern against the night. It attracted not just local patrons but people from neighboring counties. "When Curtis had his joint open, you couldn't hardly get up and down the road," recalls Leonard Sims, an octogenarian and lifelong resident of La Grange. Says Billy Joe: "They came from everywhere—Helena, Forrest City. Friday, Saturday nights, there'd be cars so far down the road it'd be a shame. They'd be all packed in.

Inside, outside, everywhere. All the way to two or two-thirty at night."

It was nothing so much as a refuge, a place simply to pass the long, dull, lonely hours that came with each day of joblessness and dependence. People did what they felt like: drank, smoked, gambled, danced, shot pool and dice.

Curt's Place was strategically located. There were no other black-owned cafés nearby, which ensured steady business, and, as A. J. Atkins, who was a regular patron, says, "the closest law was in Marianna." But the sheriff's department in Lee County always made sure it got its share of the business. "Curtis had to pay off the law," Barney Buford recalls. "That way they'd look the other way if he stayed open past midnight or sold beer on Sundays or allowed gambling."

Billy found out early that there was yet another way of contributing to the family enterprise: hustling. "My daddy had us clean the place in the morning. So we'd go sweep up, find money, quarters, or whatever. And we'd shoot pool all day." At an early age, Billy was a pool shark, lightening the wallets of his father's clientele at the café. Soul and blues flowed from the Seeburg, balls clicked delicately on the worn felt, raucous laughter rang out— those evenings in the late sixties seemed set in a foreign country. His father told cocky customers, "My little boy can beat you shooting pool." Billy was too small to see over the pool table, so they carted him around on a wooden pop crate. "They'd let me break," Billy remembers. "A lot of times, I'd run the table. And my daddy would make twenty-five, thirty, forty, fifty dollars. That was big money back then."

Hazel also made big money hustling out of the juke joint. "She sold herself to anyone who paid the right price," says a La Grange man who insisted that he not be named, but who adds: "Believe me, I was in a position to know. A whole bunch of us were always there, sometimes all night if that's what it took, trying to outdo, one-up each other. Listen, Hazel Chambers ran that place like a cathouse—she was fucking out of both rooms and she didn't care who knew it. . . . If you had clothes, jewelry, or cash— or *anything* she could use—you had a date."[1] Another of Hazel's reputed regular customers was a member of the family's church, Mt. Perion Missionary Baptist, in La Grange. Hazel and he reunited on Sunday afternoons after services, according to other Mt. Perion members. (Asked one summer Sunday in 1990 to characterize his past relationship with Hazel, the churchgoer in question declined to comment.) Members of the county sheriff's department also were reputed to be regular clients, which some suggest may explain further why blue laws and gambling regulations were not strictly enforced at the Chamberses' joint.

The present sheriff, Robert (Bobby) May, Jr., was elected in 1975. "The joint was on its last legs then," May says, speaking in his wood-paneled office on the first floor of the county courthouse. On an end table next to the visitor's chair is a stack of *Playboy* and *Penthouse* magazines. On May's desk is a hand grenade, which he uses as a paperweight. The walls are covered with commemorative plaques, training certificates, and photographs, including one of the sheriff with his ("and Elvis's!") martial arts teacher in Memphis. Sheriff May, a Lee County native, says current and past deputies had "made me aware of" Hazel's activities. "Hazel taught those [Chambers] boys everything they know," May says. "She was whoring around and selling bootleg whiskey and those kids got a Ph.D. in hustling at home."

Curtis and Hazel fought constantly. Francis Chambers, who is married to their eldest son, Curtis Jr., believes Hazel deliberately provoked Curtis Sr. "She would bring home men friends to try to make him jealous. Or she would abandon the kids to go out on the

---

[1]Hazel Chambers declined numerous requests for interviews over a four-year period. She did once invite the author into her house, in the presence of a mutual friend. But she explained, politely, as she has many times since through family members and other intermediaries and on the telephone, that she did not wish to cooperate in the preparation of this book.

town or sometimes even run off to St. Louis." Hazel told Curtis she was "doing what I need to do" to survive, according to a family friend. So they fought, often with an audience that included their children and their neighbors' children.

The fighting was no war of words. "Mr. Curt whipped her near every morning," says a close friend of one of the Chambers brothers. "We'd be on the [school] bus and he'd be calling her a cunt and you'd see him rip her clothes off her back in the front yard." The brawls would usually end with a call to the sheriff's department; Curtis would be taken downtown, have a cup of coffee in jail, and be released.

After a few more years, a childhood of pool shots and scrapping, Billy Joe knew the angles of Lee County, Arkansas, all too well, how a man could ricochet like a ball from one tattered side of the county to the other, never ending up anywhere he really wanted to be. The county was beginning to seem like a nice place to be from and a nice place to go back to, but no longer a place to stay.

Billy had little reason to stick around. He had heard a lot of cabin-to-riches stories in the dreary classrooms of his childhood, but they were impossible to absorb, as mythological as those Greek and Roman gods. Lee was the nation's sixth poorest county; 74 percent of its residents lived in poverty and almost half the county's black children were undernourished or malnourished. Billy was not aware of the statistics, but he hardly needed the census bureau to tell him he was living on a dead-end road. School itself was boredom except for the girls, and there were girls everywhere. Billy was neither academically nor athletically inclined. He knew he would never win one of Lee Senior High's People's Choice awards, never glory in his own quarter-page photo in the *Trojan*, the school's annual. He wasn't Most Talented or Most Dependable or Wittiest; he didn't possess the Best Physique or Best Personality; and he certainly wasn't Most Likely to Succeed. Like two of his older brothers, he thought he might want to work for the

U.S. Postal Service. But he knew that if he sought such work at home his ambition would likely be thwarted, as was his older brother Willie's.

Willie had graduated from Lee Senior High in 1972. After serving two years in the U.S. Army in California, he returned home, hoping to work for the post office. The eldest Chambers brother, Curtis Jr., had planned to work for the post office, but injuries sustained in the Vietnam War (for which he was awarded the Purple Heart) left him permanently disabled. But Willie says he was told that no matter how well he did on the civil service test, neither the Lee County postmaster nor his counterpart in neighboring Phillips County would be inclined to hire him. "I was black, and there was just mainly no room," Willie says. So in the summer of 1974 Willie left home for Detroit. Within a year he landed a job with the post office. He held the job continuously, through rain, snow, gloom of night, and recession, until early 1988.

Billy was proud of his brother. Willie had left home, found a good, secure job that paid well in a big city. Exactly what Billy dreamed for himself. But first he would need to get out of Lee County. Willie's best friend at home, Edward Buford, had just graduated from the University of Arkansas at Pine Bluff with an industrial arts degree. Billy had always looked up to Buford, a warm, bearded fellow who was known, aptly, as Big Man. Buford had worked hard and done well in school. But even he couldn't find a job. Buford resorted to chopping cotton that summer with Billy's older brother Larry, who had dropped out of school years ago and had recently been paroled from jail. "I went to college all those years to go out there with a hoe in my hand," Buford says. "I wasn't exactly a walking advertisement for the United Negro College Fund."

In 1976, when Billy was fourteen, his parents were divorced. They had married in 1948, when Hazel was sixteen and Curtis was twenty-three. The chancery court ordered Curtis to make child support payments of forty dollars a week for the seven minor children who remained at home, in Hazel's custody. (They ranged in age from sixteen to two.) Curtis moved off the land his late aunt had deeded him six years earlier. He moved in with a brother's family in Marianna and then to a house trailer on a small, fenced lot in Marianna. And Billy lost his only place of refuge when Mr. Fred died of diabetes that same year. Hazel had him cremated. He did indeed leave everything to Hazel, which at the time of his death amounted to less than $6,500 in cash and property. After the German died, there was nothing strong enough to keep Billy on the farm.

His only older brother who had been living at home, David, nearly two years Billy's senior, had just entered the army. And Billy had long since tired of the Friday evening "entertainments" the young people in the community organized. The dances, the fish fries, the apple-bobbing contests were as dull as Sunday school. And the mischief in which he and his friends and brothers used to engage—tipping over the outdoor "shit houses," playing hooky from school to hang out in the juke joint—those activities too had lost luster since Billy had seen Detroit, a big, bold, wondrous city electric with possibilities.

He had spent the summer of 1978 in Detroit, sleeping on his brother Danny's couch, the whine of sirens becoming as familiar as the midsummer rasp of the locusts down home. He met a young woman in Detroit, a girl really; she was only twelve, and at under five feet tall and eighty-five pounds, a wisp of a girl at that. But Billy wasn't much bigger, and everyone, even strangers on the street, told them they made a cute couple. Her name was Anita Coleman, and she was as bright and pretty and pleasing as sweet corn ripening in the Delta sun. Everyone called her Niece (pronounced Nee-cee), an easing of Denise, her middle name. Billy had seen Niece waiting with some friends at the bus stop on Drexel Street, near the four-family apartment building Danny lived in. She was wearing shorts—"*short* shorts," she recalls—and Billy, feeling raffish and uninhibited in the big city, whistled at her. "He started talkin' to me and the next thing the bus had came and went." From then on Billy and Niece were virtually inseparable.

By the end of the summer Billy had no intention of returning home. "Here I was in another part of the world—Niece, the streets, my brother and all these older guys lettin' me hang . . . now that was straight-up heaven! And I called home right before school was starting up to say I wasn't comin' back and my moms, well, there wasn't any discussion. My moms *ordered* me back."

But between Niece and all the other marvels of Detroit, Billy just hadn't been able to shake the sights and sounds of the big city from his head. Now, as Christmas neared after four months back home in the green somnolence of La Grange—and not even in La Grange but on a farm outside the village—where, as he puts it, "there was nothing, absolutely nothing for me," he could stand it no longer—he would run away. Earlier in the week he had hocked his shotgun for fifty dollars at a pawnshop in West Helena, just over the Lee County line from La Grange. With those proceeds and another fifty or sixty dollars he'd saved, he had more than enough for a one-way bus ticket north. He knew with a fervent certainty that that was all he needed. "I was extra miserable," he recalls years later. "It was automatic I wasn't going back." Only a few days had passed since he sent Niece a love letter with three dollars enclosed. He asked her to change the bills and call him from a pay phone. (She had no home phone.) She never reached him. "By the time I tried," Niece says, "he was already on his way."

It was starting to get late and still there was no sign of Little Joe; he should have been home an hour ago. Billy thought about hitching into town, but he didn't want to lug that huge cardboard suitcase. And what if he didn't get a ride? No, he'd get a ride all right; almost anyone who passed would recognize him as a Chambers. But hitching, he decided, would be foolish. What if whoever picked him up told his mother, or a sibling? Again Billy made himself sit. He watched the wind gusting across the fields. It was a chilly wind, but he recalled how he used to have nothing better to do in the summertime than watch the dust-choked fields of cotton and corn for signs of a ripple—a breezy respite from the still air. He shifted to the edge of the chair, his neck craned toward the road to the west. By now he needed a hand to shade his eyes from the brilliant sunset, a waning orange hot-air balloon on the limitless horizon. Surely Joe hadn't forgotten. The weeks of planning—the sale of the shotgun, the letter to Niece, the covert packing—had come down to this evening, and now he wasn't even sure he had a way out.

Finally, with no more than a couple of minutes to spare, Joe arrived. Before he even cut off the engine, Billy grabbed the suitcase he'd been hiding and jumped in the car.

"Man, I *told* you I needed a ride into town," Billy said, irritated but trying not to show it.

"Where you goin'?" Little Joe asked.

"Town."

Joe eyed the suitcase. *"Where?"*

Billy paused a moment. "Bus station. Memphis bus."

"Memphis? With a suitcase?"

"Well, uh," Billy said, "I'm going to Detroit. Don't tell Moms. Don't tell *nobody.*"

CHAPTER TWO

WASHING WINDOWS IN A BLIZZARD

Eighteen hours is a long time on a Greyhound. After the ninety-minute trip from Marianna across the flat ribbon of Delta highway to the Mississippi River bridge into downtown Memphis, Billy took a few minutes in the waiting room to stockpile vending-machine snacks. Back on board, he was too excited to sleep. Nor was he inclined toward reading, a skill he had not fully mastered but one that he planned to improve upon in Detroit. Mostly he passed the time gazing at his reflection in the tinted window or trying to sleep. He twisted and squirmed through the long night, seeking comfort in an upright seat from a sweater wedged between the cold windowpane and his head. He wasn't much for sightseeing, for gauging the subtle changes in the countryside as the bus wound its way east and north through the small towns of the farm belt—he had seen enough of those to last a lifetime—and on through the gently rolling bluegrass and tobacco land of middle Tennessee and Kentucky, through the plains of southwestern Ohio and up into Toledo, the manufacturing gateway to Detroit.

Approaching Detroit from the south, on Interstate 75, the highway becomes noticeably bumpier, with potholes only an all-terrain vehicle could love. A witches' brew of vapors spews from an oil refinery and blast furnaces and innumerable smokestacks that punctuate the landscape like industrial exclamation points. To the east is the befouled Lake Erie, from the murky waters of which rises a pair of ominous nuclear reactor cooling towers. Spun throughout this fabric of steel and smoke and rust and water are pockets of single-family frame houses, some well kept with small tidy yards; others, with eaves sagging and paint peeling, rotting like the industries that once employed their inhabitants. Farther up the highway, where the Detroit River parts the United States and Canada, are the "Downriver" suburbs, working-class towns on the southwest edge of Detroit. Downriver is dotted with drawbridges and ore boats; it was developed in the shadow of Henry Ford's colossal Rouge River plant, which once was the world's largest manufacturing complex. Billy had been half asleep since Toledo, but what caught his eye were the glistening Ford cars, acres of them, ready for shipment and crammed bumper to bumper into an enormous holding pen, like cows waiting for slaughter. He knew he was almost home.

Billy Joe wasn't the first black man from Lee County to light out toward the Motor City. "I'm goin' to Detroit, get myself a good job," a bluesman of the twenties sang. Nor was he even the first of the Chambers siblings to migrate in that direction. Danny Chambers, eleven years Billy's senior, arrived there in 1970. Like Billy, Danny had had no grand plan for himself; he was certain only of his desire to leave the farm life behind. When he was eleven or twelve he lost one finger and half of another on his right hand in a tractor accident. And at about the same time, 1962, the year Billy was born, he saw his family forced off the land he says his parents had been promised by its owner. "The man promised it to us if we'd sharecrop it. But when the time came to turn it over he sold it to someone else and we got kicked off." The family crowded in with a relative, an elderly landowner whose forty acres on the outskirts of La Grange they would later inherit.

Danny knew that he wanted something different from the pervasive degradations of segregation Lee County–style. "As long as I was down there," he said years later in Detroit, "it was sure enough whites up here"—he holds one hand parallel to the floor and well above his head—"and blacks down here"—the other hand at waist level. "If you were country and black," he says, "you had nothing to look forward to but having kids and going to the cotton field."

Black families in the Delta had each other. Theirs was an interdependence born of necessity; survival often meant sharing food, or harvesting a sick neighbor's crop, or taking in an orphaned child, or, in the Chambers family's case, moving in with an elderly aunt. Such mutual aid fostered the strong tradition of extended family. The tradition transcended geography. When a migrant went north, he could count on help finding a job and housing from friends and relatives already established.

So it was with Danny, who in 1968 left home for a hop around the North with a variety of close and distant relations—siblings, a former aunt, a brother's mother-in-law—before settling in Detroit. Danny went to Detroit via St. Louis, where his two older brothers, Curtis Jr. and Larry, were living, along with much of his mother's side of the family. Curtis had a welding job, but he would soon be drafted and shipped out to Vietnam. Larry had also moved to St. Louis after a brief, unfulfilling stay in the federally financed Job Corps. He had finished the ninth grade back home and then, in 1967, entered the Job Corps, a War on Poverty program designed, in the writer Nicholas Lemann's words, to "do for teenagers what Head Start did for toddlers": prepare them for the job market by "putting them in rural camps for a period of intensive job-skills training."

The Job Corps had placed Larry in a camp in Casper, Wyoming. As remote as the surroundings were, he may as well have been on the dark side of the moon. Away from home for the first time, he was unsure of himself, constantly on edge. His temper, which he had always found difficult to control—and which, two decades later, would become notorious on the streets of Detroit—flared one time too many. Eight months after he enrolled, he was kicked out for fighting. "I was just a country boy up there in Wyoming with all those different groups," Larry says, "and I'm showing off, trying to be one of the guys. So I fought anyone."

In St. Louis, under the watchful eye of his elder brother, Larry attempted to straighten out his life. He sought legitimate work, but there was none to be found. "I walked and walked and walked and couldn't get hired anywhere—and I tried *everywhere*," Larry recalls. "One time I thought I had a job in a barrel-making factory, but they hired this white guy instead." Finally he found a job cleaning carpets; he even saved a little money.

Once Curtis had left for Vietnam, Larry quit his job. "I'd see guys hanging on the corner, pimping and selling drugs. And I got next to no money and can't get no job that pays and these guys are doing well, got plenty money. So you join that avenue and get some experience and see how to do it. And then you're not gonna waste your time looking for a job when you can make a nice piece of money on the street."

Larry would never again hold a regular job. Years later, having mastered the unconventional job skills of a criminal, he and his younger brother Billy would become leaders of Detroit's flourishing underground—a place where drugs weren't a subculture but *the* culture.

The younger Danny enjoyed his first taste of St. Louis city life, especially the street life to which Larry introduced him. Together they attempted a few burglaries, some successfully, some not. The first time they were caught, their father drove up from Marianna to plead with the judge for leniency. Danny, for whom this was a first offense, was given a two-year suspended sentence and placed on probation. The next time he was caught, attempting to burglarize a post office while still on probation, he was not so lucky; his stay in St. Louis was abbreviated by a federal judge. After four months at the federal prison camp in Terre Haute, Indiana, during which he obtained his high school equivalency diploma, he returned home for another year or so. In 1970, during a family reunion in Marianna, Danny's former aunt Eliza Chambers (she was divorced from his father's brother John) invited him to return with her to Flint, Michigan.

Danny stayed with his aunt's family for nearly a year before moving to Detroit, sixty miles southeast. There he lived for a year with Curtis Jr.'s mother-in-law, a handsome, sturdy woman named Wagie Farris who is a devoted student of the Bible and whose constant counsel is: "You *got* to be prayed up."

Wagie herself had only recently left Marianna. She was newly divorced after a twenty-two-year marriage that produced eleven children (she herself came from a family of sixteen), and had decided it was time to try something new. "The more I tried to make it," she says of her latter years in Marianna, "the worse off I was." As late as 1970, the year she moved north, her cash income in Marianna was derived from chopping and picking cotton for three dollars per hundred pounds—a rate that had not increased substantially in decades. The daily seven dollars and fifty cents or so she earned for field work was supplemented by the fifteen dollars a week she made "cleaning houses and changing diapers for white folks."

"I'd been wanting to come to Detroit all my life," she says. "I heard there were jobs here and I could make it." Wagie stayed with a daughter until she found steady domestic work through an agency. Late in 1970, not long after Wagie had moved into her own apartment, Danny Chambers arrived at her doorstep. "He was dressed all raggly," she recalls. "But he knew how to work. Just like his daddy. Curtis was a hard worker, he always kept a job. That's all them Chambers ever knew was work. The kids took care of the crop. They didn't sit around the house like Hazel, they worked hard."

Danny quickly found a welding job in an east-side factory. He sent word home, and soon a sister, Delois, followed, and in the summer of 1974, after failing to find work with the post office at home, his brother Willie made the move. By the time Billy Joe arrived from Arkansas for his summer vacation in 1978, Danny was making good money as a welder at a plant in Romulus, near Metro Airport. Billy was just shy of his sixteenth birthday, old enough for Danny, then twenty-seven, to treat him as a friend rather than the baby brother Danny knew when he left home a decade earlier. "I was pretty crazy about him that summer," Billy recalls. "It was the first time I had the opportunity to be with him as an adult. He took me anywhere he went, let me smoke weed, gave me spending money, sometimes twenty dollars, sometimes fifty."

By early afternoon, the day after Billy boarded in Arkansas, the Greyhound coach passed the city limits of Detroit. Out the right side of the bus was the Ambassador Bridge, a graceful span at the other end of which stood . . . Canada. All Billy had been able to see on the vast, no-rise horizon back home were cotton and corn and soybean fields, and, if he squinted, more of the same. Now, as close as his front porch was to the barbecue restaurant at Cypress Corner, was another country!

The traffic, he noticed, tightened considerably; cars and trucks and buses were clumped like salmon running upriver to spawn. The bus veered south off I-75 toward downtown on the Lodge freeway, past soaring church spires and the splendidly worn Tiger Stadium, and toward the glistening Detroit skyline. Billy felt again the rush he'd experienced months earlier, the first time he neared the city. The chrome and glass Renaissance Center, five shining towers of futuristic and foreboding skyscraper, rose in the near distance by the river like the Emerald City. The Ren Cen— one local critic tagged it a "weird urban stalagmite"—had opened only the previous year. At seventy-three stories it was seventy floors higher than the boxy Lee County courthouse—the tallest building in Marianna.

Even the billboards in Detroit were more architecturally impressive than anything Billy had seen before. At the interchange of interstates 75 and 94 (the highway that runs southwest to Chicago), stood a towering Goodyear sign. There were two others in the city, and along with a competitor's Ferris wheel–sized tire (a sort of steel-belted god of Uniroyal into which shooting arrows remains a favorite local pastime), they are the great roadside attractions of the Motor City. The Goodyear sign, an electric odometer with four-foot-high digits, proudly flashed the number of American cars built yearly. The board had blinked furiously during the 1960s and early seventies, but had slowed during the 1973 Arab oil embargo and the two-year recession that followed. Even as recently as the previous year, 1977, the sign beamed a healthy glow: total U.S. production exceeded nine million cars.

As Billy's bus cruised into the city at the end of 1978, the numbers on the sign ticked sluggishly, like an alarm clock in need of winding; Detroit would produce more than nine million cars, but only barely, and it would not surpass that figure again. Detroit's fabled industry was on the brink of sliding into a depression the likes of which it had not experienced since 1929. To maintain profits, the Big Three automakers had begun closing factories and laying off people in unprecedented numbers. In Wayne County, which includes Detroit, forty-two auto-related plants would be shuttered between 1978 and 1981. (By 1981 the Goodyear scoreboard was so anemic that the measure would be diluted to include not only domestically produced cars, but cars *and* trucks produced in the United States *and* Canada.) The industry also began shifting more and more production work abroad, to low-wage, nonunion countries, and to nonunion contractors in the American South and elsewhere.

But if the manufacturers were saved by their overseas and "outsourcing" operations, the city of Detroit was decimated. Within days of Billy's arrival, Detroit Mayor Coleman Young announced that he was laying off 348 workers in an attempt to reduce a budget deficit that earlier in 1978 reached sixty-one million dollars. The Chrysler Corporation alone would fire twenty-one thousand Detroit workers the following year, fully a third of its local workforce. And worst of all for Billy, who had already decided that after enrolling in school his first order of business would be to find an after-school job, more than *half* the city's blacks between the ages of sixteen and nineteen were unemployed. Overall, before the decade was over Detroit would lose nearly a quarter million jobs and a fifth of its population.

But none of that mattered. After those eighteen hours on the bus, Billy Joe Chambers was not thinking about the state of the economy, or about what he would do next year, or what he would do tomorrow. He could only gaze, slack-jawed with delight, at the downtown skyline. It was about one o'clock on a gray afternoon under a dim sky with the promise of snow. As the bus rolled east on Jefferson Avenue, under Cobo Hall and into its stall at the downtown terminal near the Renaissance Center, all that mattered was that he was off the farm, that everything was new, and that everything, anything, was possible.

Niece Coleman was waiting for Billy when the Greyhound pulled in. She had caught the Gratiot Avenue bus downtown from the stop near her mother's house on the fringe of City Airport—a small, mostly commuter- and private-plane strip—in the heart of the east side. Niece lived with her mother, Cynthia, in an old, rambling, four-bedroom house into which Billy was welcomed like a lost son. Niece's extended family, of which there were many— Cynthia had ten brothers and sisters, most of whom lived in the neighborhood—fairly doted on Billy. Cynthia was a welfare recipient, but with five other children the entitlements never quite provided enough to go around. And so she found ways, primarily by dealing in the thriving black market for prescription drugs, to supplement her income. "I was selling all types of different narcotics— cough syrups, pills, you name it, we had it," Cynthia says. She was generous with her earnings, often giving Billy and Niece hundreds of dollars. "I didn't know nothing about drugs at the time," Billy says, "but I knew she made good money hustling off the streets." Cynthia primarily dealt pills called "T's" and "blues." T's were

Talwin, a potent painkiller often prescribed for back ailments; they were taken together with blues (the trade name for which could not be determined), which were a sort of stabilizer.

At night, Billy played in marathon card games hosted by two of Niece's uncles, Alan and Perry Coleman. They showed Billy the finer points of poker and spades and a five-card game called tunk. "I had all this money and sometimes I'd lose hundreds of dollars a day; sometimes I'd win that much."

About six months after he moved in with Niece, Billy, still a fugitive from his family, called home one day to assure his family he was alive and well. "Didn't nobody know where I was at that period. They didn't know I was dead or what," Billy says.

His twin answered the phone. "Joe told me everyone was worried about me. They knew he knew where I was and they were all over his back to tell them." After Joe pleaded with Billy to at least call *someone* in the family, if not their mother, he agreed to call Willie. Willie was also living on the east side, not far, it turned out, from Niece. "Willie didn't know I was in Detroit and he told me to come back up and stay with him, go to school. I told him I was all right where I was."

But in truth the situation at Niece's was growing intolerable. For all of Cynthia's generosity, she was becoming increasingly difficult to live with. Not only was she selling her products, she had become a heavy user. ("I was pretty mixed-up at the time," says Cynthia, who underwent successful treatment years ago and is no longer involved with drugs.) Loud disputes were becoming commonplace, and Niece, self-possessed and determined not to let her mother's problems become her own, decided she had to move out. Said Niece: "She always looked in so much pain to me and I just reached the point where I never wanted to be around her." Niece moved in with her grandmother, Lillie Richards, and suggested to Billy that he try staying at Willie's awhile. Billy called Willie again and told him he'd be right over.

Soon, though, conflicts arose. Willie was soft-spoken and conscientious, a straight arrow who enjoyed his job delivering mail and was happy to come home after work and relax in front of the television until bedtime. Now and then he enjoyed a joint and a card game, but his was no life of revelry. Billy, on the other hand, had just passed a six-month course in street-wisdom; he had been tutored assiduously by Niece's family on the finer points of card-sharking and small-time drug dealing, and having acquired a taste for the streets, he wanted no part of the sedate life of his brother's family. Willie's wife, Linda, who had grown up in Louisiana, was devoutly religious and believed that Billy's unfettered lifestyle had no place in their home.

One day Billy and Willie got in a shouting match over a matter neither can recall. "I just remember he kicked me out," Billy says. Billy called Niece from a pay phone at a nearby motel. "He called me crying, crying, crying," Niece says.

She recalls him saying, "I don't have nowhere to stay. Willie put me out. I don't have any money."

"Hold on," Niece told him, cupping the phone while seeking counsel from her grandmother. "Take a cab over here and we'll pay for it."

All the while Billy shuttled between homes—from Cynthia's to Willie's to Niece's grandmother Lillie's—he managed to stay in school. He had enrolled after the Christmas break, at the beginning of the 1979 term, as he promised himself he would. He was in the eleventh grade at Kettering High, a mostly black and poor school that anchored an east-side neighborhood of deteriorated homes and weed- and trash-filled vacant lots. The rambling, two-story brick school was named for Charles Kettering, the father of the self-starting motor. But there were few self-starting students: the school's dropout rate hovered at 50 percent, and around three-quarters of Kettering students failed the annual high school proficiency examination. But the school had a job placement office, and its door was the first on which Billy knocked. The office arranged an interview for him for an after-school job at a shoe store within easy walking distance of Kettering.

* * *

Winter in Detroit, especially for Southerners unaccustomed to the hard freezes and prodigious snowfalls, is best experienced indoors. It was precisely the dead of winter when Billy started work at Eastown Shoes. He was hired as a janitor, putting in three or four hours a day after school. He earned about fifty dollars a week, some of which he spent on clothes. "I used to jack the rest of it off," he says. Indeed, he "never seemed to have enough cash," observes a former co-worker named William Hamilton, who loaned him money on several occasions. The store manager, a loquacious and dapper man named Wally Harkins, recognized in his newest and youngest employee a latent intelligence and charm; he occasionally had Billy fill in as a salesman. "He was bright, but not slick, a smooth talker," recalls Harkins. "He was always mannerable and respectful and he did what you asked him." Mostly, Billy was asked to perform perfunctory duties: sweep the floor and the sidewalk, empty the garbage, refill the stock shelves, wash the windows (on many a raw, bitterly cold afternoon, he would have to mix the soapy water with alcohol to prevent freezing). "I did whatever needed to be done. Some days they'd have me outside washing windows in a knee-deep blizzard. I'm like, Oh wow, are you kidding? There has to be a better way than this."

And there was. Detroit had long been a city of tycoons, the great czars of automobiles who had built their factories near the workers and installed themselves in the cool, leafy suburbs of Grosse Pointe and Bloomfield Hills. Detroit was a city for men who were willing to risk their capital in pursuit of riches, power, and society's imprimatur. Billy discovered that the eighties entrepreneur didn't need to go into cars to make his fortune. He found a role model closer to Al Capone than Henry Ford. His name was L. C. (Terry) Colbert, and like Billy, he had grown up poor and black on the margins of Lee County, Arkansas.

Terry was thirteen years Billy's senior and, as Billy would one day do, he had left home for Detroit during his eleventh-grade year. Though Billy was too young to have known Terry back home—Terry moved away in 1966—Billy was well acquainted with Terry's family. The Colberts, another large family with not enough room or money to survive without hardship, lived in the country near Rondo, a settlement no bigger than La Grange and only five miles west on the road that runs by the Chambers place. Colbert children attended school with Chambers children, and the families were related through marriage.

Billy had become acquainted with Terry during the summer of 1978, when he visited Detroit and stayed with his brother Danny. Billy had arrived with a friend from home named Jerry Gant, who was raised by Terry Colbert's mother as a foster child. Jerry spent the summer with Terry, and had stayed on in Detroit after Billy's involuntary return home. At the time, both Danny and Terry worked at Whitehead & Kales Company, a Dearborn-based firm that manufactured and modified trains to carry automobiles.

But Terry had not spent much time at work that summer; it interfered with his own burgeoning business as a marijuana dealer. Some days he would punch the clock in the morning and leave. Then, says Billy, "He'd go in the streets and deal all day." He usually returned at the end of the shift in time to punch out. On especially hectic days, he simply paid a co-worker to punch the clock for him at both ends. This scheme struck Billy and Jerry as boldly ingenious. "We be like, 'Damn! This nigger know how to live!' " Jerry remembers.

When Billy surfaced in Detroit the following winter, he persuaded Jerry to enroll with him at Kettering High. Neither had been studious back home, but Billy, especially, thought it worthwhile to obtain a diploma; he harbored aspirations of joining Willie at the post office, or if that didn't pan out, of becoming a police officer or firefighter.

Billy's days settled into a routine. Each morning he rode the bus to the intersection of Van Dyke and Harper, just around the corner from Kettering, at which were situated both Billy's employer and the apartment Jerry shared with Terry Colbert. Billy stopped in, and if Terry was there he usually invited Billy and Jerry to "Twist y'all a couple joints." Then he and Jerry walked to school, often sharing a smoke on the five-minute route. After school, Billy walked Jerry home before heading to his job at Eastown Shoes. After work, he caught the bus back to Niece's house, where he would struggle with his homework until frustration set in. "We used to sit at the kitchen table and read together," recalls Niece. "When he didn't know a word and I'd correct him he'd slam the book down and say, 'You think you know everything.' "

Jerry, meanwhile, did not have to venture outside the apartment to earn his spending money. Terry had a home office, running his marijuana business out of the living room. He stored his product there in Hefty garbage bags, and cleaned, weighed, and packaged it in one-ounce Baggies that sold for between twenty and thirty dollars, depending on the market rate. It was exacting work, pruning and sorting and measuring, and when Terry finished he summoned Jerry to clean up after him. Occasionally he would pay Jerry in cash, but more often he simply allowed Jerry to keep the "shake" that fell to the floor, which generally totaled an ounce or so. "[Terry] went through two or three hundred-pound bags every week," Jerry says. "That left a lot for me and BJ."

So much, in fact, that the two of them soon accumulated more marijuana than could be consumed personally. And so they started peddling loose joints in school. Demand was so great that the labor-intensive process of rolling individual joints became too time-consuming; they soon began selling only ounces.

Terry rewarded the boys' initiative. He began asking them to make deliveries, pick up payments. These were errands that could hardly be run via the bus, their normal mode of transportation; they needed a more efficient and less visible way around town. Terry gave them a used pickup truck, and with it, a new, unparalleled freedom. Says Billy: "We just ran the wheels off that poor truck."

Gradually, inexorably, school and minimum-wage work yielded to the drug business. Jerry dropped out of Kettering before the spring semester ended; Billy, at Niece's insistence, completed the semester and a month or two of the fall term. "Once he got into drugs, made some of that fast money, figured he didn't need any school," Niece says. He continued to work at the shoe store until January of 1980, but by then Niece was eight months pregnant, the snows were falling, and Billy could tolerate no longer the indignities of "washing windows in a blizzard."

Terry, meanwhile, was expanding his business interests. He had been laid off from the factory but his sideline pursuits left him with sizable cash reserves. With a portion of his savings, Terry opened a combination restaurant and party store, called the T&T, on the west side. "A born entrepreneur," as Billy labeled him, Terry also saw opportunity in the housing restoration business. There were thousands of abandoned, boarded-up, and burned-up houses in Detroit. Many were available from the city for five hundred or a thousand dollars. Terry formed a company to buy, refurbish, and resell the homes. He employed Billy and Jerry as utility men, some days helping out at the T&T (flipping burgers, working the register, selling weed), other times in the housing business, assisting his crew on everything from plumbing to electrical wiring to masonry.

For Jerry, the tensions that surfaced from living and working with his boss/brother periodically proved too great. On those occasions, he moved out and stayed with Wagie Farris. Wagie, confusingly enough, was the mother-in-law of the eldest Chambers brother, Curtis Jr., as well as Jerry's "aunt"—she was his foster mother's sister. "I been knowing Jerry since he was an arm baby," Wagie says, cradling her arms. But Jerry had grown into a bearded young man whose doleful eyes and hesitant manner around his Aunt Wagie belied his lust for the street life. Asked if she understood at the time that Jerry was "hustling," Wagie offered a parable. "God said you should work with your hands till you sweat from the end of your eyelashes. Well," she added, "I never did see that boy sweat none too much."

Two years passed. Billy continued working in Terry's ventures, selling weed when he could, and helping out Niece's uncle,

Perry Coleman, in a party store he had opened. Billy and Niece had a son, Billy Joe Jr., and thirteen months later a daughter, LaTonya. Billy was seventeen when his son was born, and like many teenagers he had never faced responsibility to anything larger than himself. "His attitude, his whole personality changed," recalls Cynthia Coleman, Niece's mother. "It was like he couldn't handle it. All of a sudden this boy got really nasty, really hard on Niece."

Niece was only fourteen when "Little Billy" was born. But she was now a mother, and in Billy Joe's eyes motherhood and the social ramble did not mix. Niece: "He thought I should just stay home. He was in the streets all day and night bein' the playboy. I never knew when he was coming or going." It seemed to Niece that the more their growing family needed him, the more irresponsible and unavailable he became. "A lot of times I'd ask him, 'What you gonna do with the rest of your life? Run the streets?' He wouldn't say nothin'. He'd just leave."

Soon Billy had something to consume all his time: a business venture with his brother Willie. At a shade over five feet three, Willie Lee Chambers is stocky and moon-faced, with a sly smile that creeps subtly along his lips—track lighting next to Billy Joe's ear-to-ear neon. He is shy, unassuming, frugal, and puritanical in his belief in the virtue of hard work. "Even as kids, every day was boot camp," says Ed (Big Man) Buford, Willie's closest high school friend. "He never believed in take-it-easy. He could pick your cotton all day and then if it was bright enough, he'd cut your grass at night."

By 1982, seven years of steady work as a letter carrier and his prudent way with a dollar had left Willie with a tidy nest egg. In July he paid twelve thousand dollars for two abandoned commercial buildings at the southwest corner of St. Clair and Kercheval, a bleak and ragged block on the Lower East Side. (To travel a few miles west on Kercheval is to enter another world: Grosse Pointe, a wealthy white enclave of chic boutiques and tony department stores that each holiday season is transformed into "Christmas Street.") Like the rest of the neighborhood, the intersection had seen better days. Once it was a retail center for a working-class area of modest one- and two-family houses; it had since become a derelict strip of liquor stores and boarded storefronts.

Neighborhood life once revolved around "Old Jeff"—the Chrysler assembly plant on Jefferson Avenue one block south and a dozen blocks east of Willie's new property. But the economic crisis that nearly bankrupted Chrysler in the late seventies (and would have without a government bailout) caused plant closings and widespread layoffs that had only deepened by 1982. By then the company had replaced much of its Jefferson Avenue workforce with robots, which were infinitely more versatile than humans— they could be programmed to spray paint or move engine blocks or assemble components or retrieve inventory or weld bodies (in 1982 robots executed 98 percent of the welds in Chrysler's K-car)—and cost but six dollars an hour, about a third of the expense in wages and benefits for a human autoworker. And robots could perform all of those tasks, as labor historian Steve Babson has pointed out, "without taking coffee breaks or filing grievances."

With jobs disappearing at Chrysler and the city's other industrial mainstays, the Lower East Side and the rest of Detroit fell into a depression from which it would not recover. In the winter of 1982, Mayor Coleman Young declared a "state of human emergency"; the following winter he renewed the declaration and called the city's economic situation "a crisis unparalleled since the 1930s." By Thanksgiving, 34 percent of the population, 410,000 Detroiters, received some form of public assistance.

On the Lower East Side, decades-old retailers on Kercheval and Jefferson, the city's major east-west thoroughfare, failed or relocated, and on some blocks of north-south residential streets more than half the houses and lots were vacant, creating an eerily rural feel to the center city. In the nearby neighborhood of Jefferson-Chalmers, an area in which Chrysler employed one of every four workers during most of the seventies, 30 percent of the housing was demolished between 1970 and 1977. The real estate market was so depressed that many residents burned or abandoned their homes rather than try to sell them.

The properties Willie purchased were diagonally across the street from a party store and a popular Alabama Style Chicken outlet. The site was on his mail route, and he knew well the potential for development; he had been evaluating its prospects ever since the owners had put in a mail-forwarding request months earlier. He planned to open businesses that would survive the permanent depression: in one building he would operate a party store; in the other a car wash. Above both buildings were run-down apartments that he hoped to refurbish as rental units.

Over the next six months, Willie's family and friends poured their time and resources into renovating the properties. By fall the apartments were ready. Willie and his wife, Linda, and their year-old daughter (a son would be born the following summer) moved into the unit above what would become the party store; Billy and Niece and their two children moved into one of the three apartments over the car wash. Willie opened the store in January 1983. He named it Willie's Retail Store, but it became better known as "BJ's"—for Billy Joe, who ran the store during the day while Willie delivered mail. Actually, Billy worked there practically around the clock: it closed between three A.M. and four A.M. and reopened at seven. Between his days at his parents' juke joint back home and his recent apprenticeship in Terry Colbert's and Perry Coleman's party stores, there was little about managing the business that Billy had not learned. He oversaw the video games and dispensed the usual fare: beer, chips, pop, penny candy, Pampers—plus one product line with higher margins with which he also had considerable experience: marijuana.

At first, marijuana was very much a side business; along with heroin, or "mixed jive," it was sold on the street corner in front of the store. None of the Chamberses sold jive, but the dealer, an older man named Freeman, paid them to allow his salesmen to work "their" corner. The corner became known as an open-air market where weed or jive could be purchased at any hour. Business was as brisk as the January weather, and entirely too conspicuous. On many occasions, a salesman would spot an approaching police officer and dart inside the store. "The police was always chasing them young guys in the store," Billy recalled. "They'd throw the dope behind the video games, or try to hide behind the video games themselves, and the cops would be right behind them, dragging them out of the store. Happened all the time."

The outdoor activity sparked the store's overall sales volume, but it fostered continued attention from the beat cops in the Fifth Precinct. Billy decided to reign in his eager workforce. Like Terry always told him, "If you take care of the product, the product will take care of you." From then on, weed would be sold only to people he knew, or to those who were referred by people he knew, and it would be sold, discreetly, from the store's tiny, unheated, and uncooled back room. And Billy told the jive dealers to find a new corner.

The discretionary sales policy hardly slaked demand. Customers were more eager than ever to buy Chambers pot; after all, anyone could buy a nickel bag on the street. But only those approved by Billy or his gatekeepers were admitted to the rarified air of the back room of BJ's Party Store. It was not that the weed was any finer than the stuff on the street; it was merely its invitation-only exclusivity that imbued Chambers product with a certain aura unmatched by other neighborhood dealers'.

It got so that Billy could no longer administer both the backroom business and the daily tasks of store management. He needed help.

One day in April or May of 1983 Billy paid his customary call on Terry Colbert; he needed fresh supplies of marijuana. Billy was surprised that his knock on the door at the house on Springarden was answered not by Terry but by a young man who introduced himself as Terry's son. Billy had heard about Little Terry, the eldest of Terry's three sons, but he had never met him, at least not since the two were young children. Little Terry's mother was a Marianna native; she and Terry had grown up together. Little Terry was born in Marianna when Big Terry was sixteen, shortly before Big Terry left Lee County for good. Little Terry's mother moved to Hughes, in neighboring St. Francis County, shortly after his birth. He attended school there until he was twelve or thirteen, when the family moved again, to Memphis. By the time he turned sixteen, Little Terry was a big, strong kid with broad shoulders and a full face with puffy cheeks that made him look younger than he was. He and his mother were often at odds, sometimes screaming at each other, sometimes actually fighting. Not long after his seventeenth birthday, in the spring of 1983, his mother decided that it was time for Terry's father to try his hand at parenting.

Little Terry had arrived in Detroit only days before meeting Billy. Billy, three years older and by then a somewhat prosperous and seasoned resident, took a liking to his fellow Arkansan. "Me and him went riding," Little Terry recalls of his first meeting with Billy, "and he asked me what I was doing for myself. I told him nothing rightly. And he asked me did I want to sell some weed. And I said, Yeah, no problem. He told me he'd give me three, four hundred a week selling weed for him."

Terry worked at BJ's Party Store for about three months. During that time, the spring and early summer of 1983, demand was so great that the business could no longer be confined to the back room: customers spilled out all over the store, sampling product between the aisles and in the street; wholesalers stopped by to pay tribute to the neighborhood's new retailing stars.

All the traffic made Billy nervous. Although he had managed to rid the corner of Freeman's corps of heroin dealers, he knew that when the long, sweltering days and sultry nights of summer arrived, and with the store's notoriety and burgeoning customer base, the cops would continue to keep a close eye on the daily proceedings.

The beginning of the end of the drug business at BJ's Party Store came in late June. A young man, passing time in the alley next to the store, threw a bottle at an idling police car. He and a friend darted up the alley, eluding the police. All was calm until the next morning.

Billy: "I was sweeping the sidewalk in front of the store and car wash. It was warm outside, people was everywhere. And then I looked up and saw a police car and then another. And before it was over about twenty police cars were there, in front of the store and everywhere. And they threw twenty or thirty peoples up against the side of the store, people that didn't have nothing to do with that bottle. Everybody in that little area, they snatched 'em up and throwed 'em up against the wall. Me, they saw that I was working. They said, 'You better get on inside the store before we take you to jail.' So I swept my way right into the store."

Within a week, Billy shifted the bulk of the business to a house Willie owned a mile or so west of the store. It was on Newport Street, three blocks north of the clamor of Jefferson Avenue. Newport once was vibrant and healthy, with a forest of elms lining either side of the road like wedding guests awaiting the bride and groom. Most of the street's homes had been owned and occupied by autoworkers and their families. The houses had been well maintained if modest: two-story frame structures with a pair of dormer windows poking out of the roof and aluminum awnings over downstairs window boxes and the well-used wooden porch. Each house had a driveway and a yard, and many were decorated with flower patches and framed by a chain-link or picket fence.

"It never was the garden spot of the world," recalls Richard F. Suhrheinrich, a federal judge who grew up on the Lower East Side during the late 1940s and early 1950s and who would one day preside over the trial of the Chambers brothers. "It was a transitory area, but it was a viable neighborhood, a rough neighborhood, but not in any way what would be considered rough today. We didn't lock our doors back then."

By 1983, with the post-industrial depression thrashing Detroit, Newport Street was an economic and social wasteland; many of the homes no longer had doors, let alone locks. The valiant trees remained, incongruous now, for the street was silent and skeletal and otherwise largely bereft of life. Its asphalt, scarred with potholes, sparkled with the broken glass of windows and street lamps; its houses were fire-gutted. Some homes were still standing, but just barely, teetering like a boxer on the ropes; they had lost roofs, or their walls were crumbling, or plywood boards covered their door frames and glassless windows. Many other lots had already surrendered, their foundations reduced to scattered brick and weed-conquered shards of concrete.

The shabby state of the neighborhood was of little concern to Willie Chambers. On the daily rounds of his mail route, up and down the north-south streets of what the postal service called Zone Fifteen—an area bounded to the west by Conner Avenue, to the north by Chandler Park, to the east by Grosse Pointe, and to the south by Jefferson Avenue—Willie became as familiar as anyone with the rhythms and possibilities of the Lower East Side's poorest neighborhoods. Where others—journalists and sociologists and urban planners and demographers—saw only a deep and complex blight, Willie saw beauty and investment potential.

Like a Wall Street financier on the lookout for undervalued assets, Willie Chambers was a bottom fisher, searching for bargain-basement properties with turnaround potential. "In Detroit, you always heard how bad the housing was," Willie says, "but Detroit had the best housing rates in the country. How can you complain when you can buy a two-family flat for five thousand dollars, or a big single-family house for four? You came out cheaper buying a house than buying a car. Some streets, like Newport, *none* of the homes was going for more than thirty-five hundred or four thousand. My real estate agent told me he *never* sold homes over sixty-five hundred—and he made a real good living."

Willie continues: "Newport was like any other street in that section of town: naked. It was stripped—vacant lots, grass growing up everywhere. But there were nice cheap homes there, just like they was all over Zone Fifteen." In June of 1982, just as Willie was readying to close on the abandoned commercial buildings on Kercheval, the space he would convert into the party store and car wash, he found a deal "I couldn't say no to": a "nice, neat" house at 1261 Newport. The house was one of the few in the area owned and occupied by a white couple, a sign, according to Willie, of good value. "To tell the truth, what I looked for was white home-owners on naked streets. Some whites they want to move so bad they'll almost give it away."

Willie bought the house just a month before he closed on the Kercheval buildings. He paid only four thousand dollars for the gray three-bedroom, two-story colonial with a fenced lot. Willie himself did not spend all that much time there. Over the next couple of years, he and his family would divide their time between their house on Gable Street (the house in which Billy had once sought refuge when tensions between Niece and her mother reached a breaking point) and, when it was refurbished, the apartment over the party store, where he could keep a closer eye on the business.

Although he intended to use the Newport house for rental income, his first and last tenants were members of his own family. At first, he rented it to Billy's twin, Little Joe, who had recently joined his siblings in Detroit. Joe had had a few scrapes with the law back home, including convictions for check forgery and illegal weapons possession, for which he served time in a federal prison. When he got out, Willie sent him money for a bus ticket to Detroit. Willie took Little Joe under his wing, putting him to work managing the car wash and charging him only ninety dollars a month in rent. "When you come from a big family," Willie explains, "you try to do what you can for the younger ones."

By early July of 1983, as the heat from the police intensified at the party store in the days after the bottle-throwing incident, and as Billy's marijuana business outgrew its back room, the Newport house beckoned Billy with the added space and security he needed to run the growing operation.

He also needed the space to accommodate a growing entourage. The core of the workforce was still Billy and his old friend Jerry Gant, along with a brother-in-law of Niece's named Willie (Boogaloo) Driscoll. The Newport house functioned as their business headquarters as well as their residence. Also still living there were Little Joe and his girlfriend, and, from time to time, Niece and the two kids, and another Chambers brother, David. At twenty-three, David was two years older than Billy and Little Joe. He had recently been discharged from the army.

Twelve-sixty-one Newport also served as the social center, day-care center, job clearinghouse, and nightclub for an ever-expanding and ever-changing cast: girlfriends; potential girlfriends; ex-girlfriends and their current boyfriends; children of girlfriends and ex-girlfriends; local siblings and nieces and nephews and aunts and uncles; friends and relatives and friends of friends and friends of relatives from Marianna and Memphis and St. Louis and Chicago; ex-employees, present employees, potential employees; hangers-on, ex-hangers-on. "There was always lots of us there and we was always partying—*always*," says Jerry Gant. "I mean twenty-four seven!"

Except for the innumerable cars parked in front of the house, 1261 Newport looked no different from the few other remaining houses on the block. (Theirs was the only house sandwiched by occupied dwellings; three adjoining lots across the street were vacant.) Like the others, 1261 had iron gates—"burglar bars" were one of the city's few growth industries—on the doors and downstairs windows. But Billy, for commercial and safety purposes, had customized the interior to his own exacting specifications. Inside the front door, in what normally would be the foyer, he created a dead space by building a sturdy wall out of two-by-fours, through which admittance was possible only via a second, locked iron gate. "If a person come through that door," Billy explains, "he got to face the wall we built before he wired up inside."

Their neighbors did not take an immediate liking to the Chambers brothers. It wasn't that Billy and the others were unduly noisy or otherwise inconsiderate. It was just, says Billy, that "being city people, they knew how young peoples is automatically. They knew it don't make no sense making friends with us because a young person ain't nothin' but a bunch of trouble."

But in time Billy won over both of his next-door neighbors. From the south side of the house, it didn't take the neighbors' teenage kids long to figure out one benefit of living in proximity to the Chambers brothers. "They were always sneaking over and asking us, 'Why don't y'all give us a joint?' " Billy recalls. "We'd give them one and then they'd run back through the alley and smoke it."

The turning point for his neighbor to the north came when the man noticed a girlfriend of Billy's, a white girl. "He was like, 'Man, she was TV *beauuutiful*. Now you okay with me.' " Billy says the man spent a lot of time on his porch watching television— and the parade of young women in and out of Billy's house. "He started asking me, Did I want a beer. And then he'd turn the TV he had out there toward my porch. Ask me, 'Can you see the TV?' And we started getting real cool."

His days on Newport marked Billy's first social contact with whites since he was a schoolboy in Marianna. Among his regular marijuana customers at the party store had been a pair of white students from a nearby private school. When Billy moved over to Newport, the guys started bringing over their female classmates, none of whom was older than sixteen. "What tripped me out," Billy recalls, "the girls had their own cars, and one of the girls had a eight- or a ten-bedroom house. I'm like, 'Come on, there ain't no houses in Detroit like this.' And I asked the girl, and she said, 'My daddy is a doctor' at some famous hospital. And then I start questioning all of 'em. And one says, 'Yeah, my daddy is a judge,' and 'My daddy is the police,' and this and that. They used to come over all the time. And hang with us and go out to eat together. And these little girls had money. They kept sixty, eighty dollars on them every day. I don't know were their parents giving it to them, or they were stealing it."

With all his new friends, Billy had little time for the established women in his life: Niece, then seventeen years old and the mother of his two children (another daughter would be born the following year), and Diana Alexander, nineteen, with whom he would also have a son and a daughter. "I couldn't understand the way he'd do things," says Diana. "He'd tell me to come over, and I'd get there [to Newport] and he'd be sitting on the couch with some other female. And then too I'd see Niece in the bedroom crying her little eyes out."

Says Niece: "Sometimes I'd come home and there would be another girl's clothes there. So I'd take off, never going back. But then he'd be real sweet, and he'd talk to my aunts and uncles and everyone and I'd end up over there again." Billy: "She was always running off on me. And I'd have to go see her at her mama's or her grandmama's, spend the night with her."

And so Niece would return to Newport. But it wouldn't be long before there would be another row, almost always over another woman, and again Niece would leave. At some point during their stay on Newport (it is unclear when), Billy began to abuse Niece (and later Diana) in ways that surpassed rudeness and neglect. Billy would beat Niece and lock her in the bedroom. She says that on one such occasion, a rival for Billy's affections told him " 'Niece don't love you no more.' So just like that here come Billy, hit me in the face with a skillet. He locked me in the house and told his brother not to let me out. By time I got out, my eye had started to infect. It was so swollen it was nearly shut."

Sometimes Billy would leave Niece locked up while he took the parties on the road. He bought a motor home ("A party-on wheels: beds and curtains and a couch and a table in the back and a stove and a sink"), packed in his friends, and drove aimlessly around the city, often ending up at Belle Isle, the offshore sanctuary in the Detroit River. "We got womens in there with the curtains pulled, and we're smoking weed and eating McDonald's and riding around Belle Isle—nothin' *but* fun!"

But Niece, stranded on Newport alone with the kids, was less enthusiastic about such excursions. One day she sought her revenge. Billy had returned home long enough to unlock the bedroom, and then had departed again, in a friend's car. Niece found the keys to the motor home, stuffed the kids in alongside her, and shifted the party-on-wheels into gear. This was a first: "She ain't," as Billy put it, "never drove a day in her life." Still, Niece managed to drive half a block toward Jefferson before losing control. The motor home struck five or six parked cars, some of which were grazed, others crushed. The motor home, too, was effectively totaled.

When Billy came home, he walked up the street, surveyed the damages, and like an insurance adjuster, started haggling with the cars' owners over settlement figures. "A couple of cars were so raggly I said, 'Well hey, I'll just give you a hundred dollars.' Another car been parked there about two years; he was happy to get a hundred. I think one guy's was worth twelve hundred, so that's what he got."

One neighbor whose car was demolished says he remembers that the young man—"he didn't look more than fifteen or sixteen"—who settled with him didn't dicker at all. "The whole thing took maybe a minute," says the neighbor, a slim, middle-aged man who worked as an independent mechanic. He preferred to give only his first name: Tony. "Here come this pint-sizer with a wad bigger than him. I seen him before but never to talk to. Drove a Seville. And had a twin, dark-skinned, who drove one too. One drove blue, the other gray. Asks what my car worth, it was a beat-up LeSabre, I think I told him maybe five [hundred], and he hands me a thousand, and says his apologies for the trouble."

It was such largesse for which Billy became famous. All over the east side, it seemed, everyone knew (or claimed to know) "BJ," the charismatic, bighearted young dealer. The man who managed the shoe store at which Billy worked after school in 1979 and 1980 had heard "street talk" about his former employee's new line of work. But a couple of years had passed since Wally Harkins had seen Billy. One day in early 1984 they bumped into each other at Northland Mall, in suburban Southfield. Billy was wearing a white and burgundy zippered jumpsuit. He was pleased to see his old boss—and for Harkins to see him, the picture of success: sharply dressed and accompanied by several young women, who had joined Billy for an expenses-paid shopping expedition. "He took me aside and we spoke a few minutes," Harkins recalls, shaking his head and laughing at the memory. "He told me he could get me anything I wanted, like a pound of weed."

Not only was it Billy's financial generosity and business acumen for which he was renowned; it was his popularity with women. That he abused his regular girlfriends was of little consequence on the streets. What really mattered, explains Junior Smith, a former associate of Billy's, was his "flash." "Once you flash what you got, it's no problem. When you have the cars, the money, you get the girls. They want to live like the rich people live."

And so Billy attracted a crowd of followers, of whom many believed their mere association with Billy, no matter how tangential (or, for that matter, how fabricated), would be sufficient to guarantee romantic reward. "A lot of guys like hangin' around me because of the womens," he says. "And when they talk to the womens they talk to 'em like they work for me. Some guys ask me: 'Hey BJ, just let me be around you, hang with you.' One thing we had was womens, and the fellas loved to be around them womens."

People turned to him when they needed a favor or were in trouble, and he encouraged them to do so. "He always asking, 'You need something, you need something? You got it,' " recalls Junior Smith. "When my sister's baby died, he bought my bus ticket to Mississippi for the funeral."

People treated him with respect, with a deference approaching awe. "The fellas would always come up to me and say, 'BJ, come and *talk* to this girl, or co-sign this, or check this for me, or holler at this person for me.' "

And he would. Day or night, his electronic pager beeped constantly—"ten times an hour, *every* hour, just like I was a doctor on call." Sometimes the message was business related, but more often it was a friend in need.

One night he was trying to sleep but his beeper would not cooperate. It must have flashed the same number twenty times,

Billy recalls. Finally, he returned the calls. A girlfriend answered from a pay phone at a nearby roller rink.

"BJ, *please* come up to Skateland. White Boy Rick [a rival dealer] up here talkin' trash."

Billy explained he was exhausted, that he just couldn't make it that night. Thirty minutes later, one of his crew showed up at the door. The girls had called him too, hoping he could persuade Billy to make an appearance. "Come on, BJ," he coaxed, literally pulling him out of bed. "We *got* to go up there for the girls."

Before long, a caravan of eight cars had converged on Newport Street. With a bleary-eyed Billy in the lead in a BMW, they pulled up to Skateland. "We went in there, and about fifty womens came to my table. 'This is Mary, and this is Susie, and this is Cherry . . .'

"And when we got ready to leave, the girls told us to stay inside. They want to go get the cars, bring them around in front, pick us up. They talked about that for so long: 'White Boy Rick, we *blew him out!* Didn't have *nothin'* to say once he saw y'all came up.'

"They enjoyed that," Billy says, sounding neither modest nor vain, "but it wasn't nothin' to me."

But it *was* something; such things did matter. Never before had the spotlight shone on him: not at home with thirteen siblings; not at school where he barely learned to read; not in athletics where his diminutive size hampered him. He was, as he says, "just another dusty little guy from down south." Less than five years after arriving penniless in Detroit, Billy Joe Chambers was, at twenty-one, a wealthy man, but more important, more important even than the cars and the clothes and the women the marijuana proceeds brought him, was the measure of respect and recognition he had won.

As Billy celebrated Christmas of 1983 with family and friends, dispensing good cheer and cash like a potentate, he couldn't help but be pleased; he had begun to carve out of scanty beginnings an abundant, nearly perfect life. His admirers were legion throughout the Lower East Side. He lived with a beautiful girlfriend and their two children and he caroused with countless other women. He was awash in cash, he had a loyal, almost worshipful circle of friends and employees, and in marijuana he had the perfect product to ensure continued prosperity.

But within six months he would come upon an even better retail line: cocaine, or, more specifically, its refined, smokable version—crack. Low in cost, highly addictive, crack was an entrepreneur's dream. It began to appear in major U.S. cities in the early eighties, arriving in Detroit by late 1983 or early 1984.

So in the summer of 1984, Billy Joe Chambers diversified his offerings yet again, offering customers at the party store and on Newport Street a constant supply of junk food, marijuana, and now, crack. Billy had foreseen that crack would soon replace pot as the drug of choice for users at the low end of the market. For him and his brothers, here finally was a way out of the cotton fields, a reprieve from the minimum-wage drudgery of shoe stores. Never again would Billy have to stoop so low.

CHAPTER THREE

HEAVEN DUST

Nearly every cocaine deal made in Detroit has its origins in Colombia, the sad and beautiful country at the northwestern tip of South America. Colombia is a land of high peaks, narrow valleys, impenetrable jungle, and a long, scenic coastline interrupted midway by the isthmus of Panama—the continent's overland link to Central America. Colombia is larger than the combined areas of Texas, Louisiana, and New Mexico; with twenty-eight million people, it is South America's third most populous country following Brazil and Argentina. It borders both the Atlantic Ocean (in the guise of the Caribbean) and the Pacific Ocean, and otherwise is bounded by Venezuela to the east, Brazil to the southeast, and Ecuador and Peru to the southwest. Three Andean ranges extend lengthwise through the western half of Colombia into Ecuador, where they merge into one, and stretch again in multiple ranges into Peru and Bolivia. It is in the temperate and tranquil foothills of the Peruvian and Bolivian Andes, between fifteen hundred and six thousand feet above sea level, that the coca bush, a green-leaved willowy plant, flourishes like nowhere else on earth. Though little coca is grown in Colombia, the country has become synonymous with the plant's most potent extract—the cocaine alkaloid. And Colombia has come also to be identified with the natural tendrils of cocaine—murder and mayhem. It is a beautiful country, Colombia, a land of mountains and rain forests and beaches, but it is a country awash in its own blood.

At the confluence of politics and history and geography stands the reason for Colombia's stature as the cocaine capital of the world: the country sits squarely between the major producers—Peru and Bolivia—and the major consumer: the United States. At the heart of Colombia's cocaine trade during the 1970s and 1980s was Medellín, the country's second largest city after its capital, Bogotá. Set in a river valley amid winding roads and pine forests, Medellín was the country's industrial heart, the Detroit of the Andes. Within the sprawling city of two million people were the country's principal machine shops, glassworks, steel mills, and textile factories. During the 1970s, plant closings and massive layoffs, particularly in the textile business, left a void in the economy. The void was filled by an emerging set of cocaine entrepreneurs who would come to be known as the Medellín Cartel. During the 1980s the cartel controlled most of the cocaine gushing into the United States.

The cartel, governed by four Medellín families, imported raw coca paste from Peru and Bolivia, refined it in jungle laboratories, then exported it to the United States, where a wholesale network distributed it to multiple-kilogram-level "weight" dealers, and finally, to street retailers such as the Chambers brothers. In Colombia, the cartel offered to thousands of people that which the legitimate economy could no longer provide: a living wage. The cocaine trade supplanted the country's traditional products—emeralds, orchids, textiles, and, especially, a milder drug, coffee—as Colombia's leading export.

In Peru and Bolivia untold thousands of coca farmers owed their livelihood to the Medellín-based drug traffickers. By the early 1980s, cocaine pumped almost a billion dollars annually into Peru's economy. Peru's president called it "Latin America's only successful multinational." In Bolivia at the time, the prevailing wage for traditional farm labor was five dollars a day—the rate Henry Ford had paid to lure sharecroppers out of the cotton fields of the American South seventy years earlier. But once the Colombians transformed the cocaine trade from what had been a cottage industry into a vertically integrated global pipeline, those same Bolivian farm families who for countless generations had toiled for subsistence wages, peasant families who formerly could ill afford to shod their children, were hired to cultivate, harvest, haul, and process coca plants. Overnight, it seemed, they were earning more money than they knew what to do with. Author Elaine Shannon reported that the farmers were so excessively rich that they streamed into small Andes towns with fistfuls of cash "to buy vacuum cleaners for houses with dirt floors, refrigerators, televisions and videotape decks for homes without electricity, cars they could not drive."

Nor did the prosperity end at the borders of the producer countries. In an employment program rivaling that of the New Deal's Works Progress Administration half a century earlier, the Colombian drug industry put hundreds of thousands of people to work: private armies to guard the coca plants and the jungle processing laboratories, bankers to facilitate money laundering, lawyers, couriers, builders, accountants, bodyguards, assassins, smugglers, real estate agents, pilots, retailers, even zookeepers: one of the cartel founders maintained some two hundred exotic animals at his seven-thousand-acre ranch.

At least as important to the cartel as its industrial foot soldiers was the complicity of public officials. In the producer nations as well as in such safe havens as Panama and the Bahamas, authorities from heads of state to judges to military leaders and customs agents—motivated by the potent mixture of bribes and violence—were thoroughly engaged in the business. It was as if the whole of Latin America had become a company town, afraid of reprisal for opposing King Cocaine, utterly dependent on the industry's jobs for its people and on the hard currency it provided its governments.

* * *

Cocaine became such big business in part because of United States drug enforcement and foreign policy efforts. As late as the mid-1970s, cocaine was a drug used only by the elite; the leading drug was still marijuana. At the time, the country's thriving marijuana market was supplied primarily by Mexican growers. Determined to stem the tide of pot at its source, the U.S. State Department and Drug Enforcement Administration funded a campaign to destroy Mexico's marijuana plantations. The weapon of choice was a herbicide called paraquat, which was known not only as a killer of cannabis but as a health hazard to humans as well.

Despite the medical evidence, the U.S.-funded helicopters rained paraquat on foreign soil. American pot smokers were outraged. "I submit that this is nothing less than a form of cultural genocide," a spokesman for NORML, the National Organization for the Reform of Marijuana Laws, said at the time. The campaign effectively poisoned the Mexican market (and not a few pot smokers), but it also subverted its own intent by opening the door to a new and well-organized breed of marijuana entrepreneur. "It's like trying to stab a piece of mercury with an ice pick," a customs agent complained to Elaine Shannon. "It just goes someplace else."

This time the mercury went south, to the Sierra Nevada mountains of Colombia. The Colombian marijuana fields were concentrated southeast of the Caribbean coastal city of Santa Marta. There grew a variety of Sierra Nevada strains, the most famous of which was a pale blond bud known as Santa Marta Gold or Colombian Gold; it was considered to be among the world's finest and costliest marijuana. Colombian dealers had tried for years to gain a stronger share of the American market. But the Mexicans' proximity to the States and their consequent lower costs (as with any business, the fewer the middlemen, the lower the markup), virtually guaranteed supremacy. By 1978, with the paraquat scare in full bloom, Colombia supplied 75 percent of the marijuana consumed in the United States.

The federal crackdown on marijuana had another unintended

effect: it spurred a revolution in cocaine distribution. As domestic marijuana dealers searched for a supplementary product, the Colombians, flush with rising profits and a well-oiled distribution network, obliged by applying the principles of high-volume marijuana smuggling to the far more lucrative business of cocaine.

Growing coca is as legal in the Peru and Bolivian Andes as growing tobacco is in North Carolina and Kentucky. For thousands of years, the Incas and other native Andeans chewed coca leaves as a stimulant and as an appetite suppressant. It was not until the middle of the nineteenth century that European scientists isolated the cocaine alkaloid from the leaf and began experimenting with its extraordinary properties and effects. "I prefer a life of ten years with coca to one of a hundred thousand without it," gushed an Italian neurologist in 1859.

By the early 1880s, a young Viennese doctor named Sigmund Freud was heartened by what he read of cocaine in a monthly medical journal called the *Detroit Therapeutic Gazette*. The *Gazette* was published by a Detroiter named George S. Davis, a principal in the nation's most renowned pharmaceutical firm, Parke, Davis & Company. Davis, of course, had a vested interest in new-product development. And so it was no wonder that while Davis's drug company was, in the words of one scholar, "an exceptionally enthusiastic producer of cocaine," his professional journal fairly burst with lavish praise for the curative powers of the drug. Wrote a Tennessee physician: "To say that I am surprised or astonished at the wonderful, and almost incredible effects of that new remedy as a nervous stimulant would not adequately express my appreciation of it." Freud was so smitten with cocaine as a treatment for depression, and indeed, as a general tonic, that he deemed it a "magical drug." (Although Freud never publicly renounced cocaine, several years after his initial writings he acknowledged certain of the substance's potential side effects, including, in the case of long-term users, "damage to the heart and other organs.")

Between Freud's writings and those of the *Therapeutic Ga-*

zette and other trade journals, cocaine quickly developed a reputation as a "universal panacea." It became a celebrated home remedy, extolled in promotional copy as a cure for everything from depression to nausea to impotence to alcoholism and opium addiction. In an 1885 pitch to doctors, Parke, Davis trumpeted coca as:

> . . . a drug which through its stimulant properties, can supply the place of food, make the coward brave, the silent eloquent, free the victims of alcohol and opium habit from their bondage, and, as an anaesthetic render the sufferer insensitive to pain, and make attainable to the surgeon heights of what may be termed, "aesthetic surgery" never reached before.

Cocaine, pure and cheap, was available everywhere in the dwindling years of the nineteenth century: in cocaine dens; in saloons, where a pinch of the drug was added to whiskey shots; and from traveling patent medicine salesmen, who peddled their "heaven dust" in every imaginable form: "in syrups, tonics, liqueurs, capsules, tablets, hypodermic syringes, cigars, cigarettes, and nasal sprays." Parsimonious businessmen dispensed it to construction crews, miners, and field hands to keep them toiling with little need for rest or food, a concept the Spanish conquerors of the Incas had pioneered in the Andes centuries earlier. And in Atlanta, an entrepreneurial chemist named John Pemberton stewed coca leaf extract with caffeine-laden cola nuts and carbonated water to produce a sweet, syrupy drink he called Coca-Cola. ("Not only a delicious, exhilarating, refreshing and invigorating beverage," Pemberton declared at the unveiling, ". . . but a valuable Brain Tonic, and a cure for all nervous affections.")

By the turn of the century, public opinion had swung in favor of regulating the use of cocaine and other drugs. This was largely a result of journalistic scrutiny of the patent medicine industry, of which the key ingredient, according to *Collier's* magazine, was "undiluted fraud" concocted by the "skillfulest of advertising bunco men." There also developed an increasing awareness of the hazards of drug use. Addicts were plentiful (one estimate put the figure at two hundred and fifty thousand) and more and more reports surfaced of lethal encounters with cocaine, opium, and other freely accessible drugs.

Concurrent with those revelations, and playing not a small role in the passage of the subsequent federal legislation banning cocaine, was the invocation of the traditional Southern bogeyman: the cocaine-crazed Negro. Newspapers and medical journals made repeated reference to the supposed connection of black cocaine addicts to a Southern crime wave. Although evidence of a link was lacking, for fearful whites such a fiction was fine fodder for the continuing subjugation of blacks. In 1903, a Georgia law enforcement official told the New York *Tribune* that "many of the horrible crimes committed in the Southern States by the colored people can be traced directly to the cocaine habit." He said that Atlanta seemed particularly distressed, and he encouraged litigation to prevent sales of "a soda fountain drink manufactured in Atlanta and known as Coca-Cola."

A few years later in Augusta, Arkansas, a town about fifty miles northwest of Marianna, a black man reportedly under the influence of cocaine gunned down seven whites before a posse killed him. Because it was widely held that the drug heightened black men's physical prowess to nearly immortal levels, making them invulnerable even to standard .32-caliber police revolvers, such incidents caused some Southern police departments to increase the caliber of their guns. "Ordinary shootin' don't kill him," a police officer divulged to a magazine reporting on the phenomenon.

In 1906, Congress passed the Pure Food and Drug Act, the first federal truth-in-labeling law. The Act precipitated the decline of cocaine and other drugs branded dangerous at the time by requiring patent medicines to list their ingredients and the proportions thereof. But it was not until eight years later that Congress banned the non-prescription use of cocaine with the passage of the Harrison Anti-Narcotic Act of 1914. Cocaine was pushed underground, where for the next half century or so it remained, undetected by mainstream society. (A 1939 Treasury Department report stated that cocaine use "continues to be so small as to be without significance.") But like seismic forces deep in the earth, it was there all along, and bound, sooner or later, to surface again.

It was not until the early 1970s that the tremors of cocaine rippled anew. Even then, cocaine was an extravagant luxury—"the caviar of the drug market." As recently as the mid-seventies, it sold for a thousand dollars an ounce, and "like high-quality caviar," wrote Robert Sabbag in *Snowblind*, "it most frequently embellish[ed] the diet of the avant-garde and the aristocratic." Cocaine was the exclusive province of hip urban professionals—status-seeking lawyers, doctors, musicians, actors, models, athletes, artists—for whom snorting "lines" of crystalline powder through a tightly rolled hundred-dollar bill was the ultimate high, if not the ultimate cliché.

But in the seventies, two concurrent events in South America, both of which were orchestrated from Washington, further hastened the cocaine revolution. The first was the extension of the Pan American Highway, the major north-south road through Latin America. The World Bank, the Washington-based international development lending institution, literally paved the way for cocaine smuggling by financing construction of the highway through the coca-growing regions of Peru, according to James A. Inciardi, a University of Delaware criminologist and historian of the evolution of drug use in America. The road opened shipping routes for corporate interests through the previously impassable Huallaga River valley in Peru's mountainous jungles. It also cleared a path for cocaine traffickers to transport their raw materials from field to laboratory via vehicles other than mules or llamas.

Prior to 1973, the South American cocaine trade amounted to competing mom-and-pop operations, all based in Chile. The Chilean traffickers bought the coca leaf from Bolivia and Peru, converted it to cocaine in Chile, and shipped it to the United States; Colombians were used strictly as middlemen. But soon after the CIA-sanctioned coup of 1973 (in which Chile's elected president, Salvador Allende, was assassinated), General Augusto Pinochet crushed Chile's flyspeck cocaine trade by arresting several dozen alleged traffickers. The cocaine business shifted to Colombia, where experienced smugglers, a complicit government, a withering post-industrial economy, an entrepreneurial culture, and blessed geography combined to create an ideal foundation for what would become the world's wealthiest and most powerful criminal organization.

By the end of the 1970s, cocaine was in such great demand in the United States that Colombian dealers were having trouble keeping pace. In an attempt to broaden their production base, they tried growing coca in Colombia, in the country's mostly uninhabited eastern plains. The coca leaves yielded a paste—the first step in the refining process—inferior to that of the Peruvian and Bolivian growers. Rather than export a second-rate product, they dumped the coca paste domestically. Ironically, and quite by accident, the failure to produce cocaine worthy of export would lead Colombian dealers to market this new derivative, the dire consequences of which would become known worldwide within a few years.

The coca paste, a smokable grayish sludge, was called *bazuko*. It was sold cheaply, for around fifty cents, usually in cigarette form and often mixed with tobacco or marijuana, as well as with traces of substances such as kerosene and sulfuric acid, which were used to separate the cocaine alkaloid from the leaf but which were not fully processed out. Because *bazuko* was smoked, it entered the central nervous system almost instantaneously, inducing in its users a fast, powerful, and profoundly addictive high. *Bazuko* appealed especially to street kids, of which there were many; in 1983, Colombian health officials counted more than six hundred thousand regular users under eighteen years old.

What was a huge public health and law enforcement problem for Colombia was a marketing breakthrough for the Medellín Cartel. The cartel was founded in 1981 by four experienced cocaine traffickers, including boyhood friends who grew up in the countryside outside Medellín and a career criminal named Carlos Lehder. Lehder was born in 1949 in a small coffee town south of Medellín, but as a teenager moved with his divorced mother to Detroit, where they stayed with relatives. Within a few years, he had learned English and gone to work for an international stolen-car ring. In January of 1973, he was arrested in Detroit for interstate transportation of stolen vehicles. He jumped bail and headed to Florida, where nine months later he was caught with more than two hundred pounds of marijuana. After less than two years in a federal penitentiary, Lehder was deported to Colombia.

Lehder's time in prison was not wasted. Beyond furthering his command of the language and the culture, his days were filled with conversations with fellow inmates about the logistics of cocaine smuggling. Shortly after his return to his homeland, he hatched a plan to transship cocaine from Colombia to the United States via flights from obscure Bahamian islands from which federal agents would be unlikely to detect the shipments. In just seven flights during 1978, Lehder shipped nearly one and a half tons of cocaine. Among his partners was an American citizen he had met behind bars. The cocaine was supplied by Pablo Escobar, a Colombian with whom Lehder would soon formalize his business relationship by organizing the Medellín Cartel.

By 1982, the DEA knew that Lehder, Escobar, and the others had formed the Medellín Cartel. The agency was having little luck stanching the flow of cocaine into Miami, but it managed, temporarily anyway, to limit the exports to Colombia of ether, a chemical vital to the second stage of cocaine processing: from paste to powder. To offset its dependence on imported ether, 90 percent of which was produced in the United States and West Germany, the cartel began shipping more raw coca paste to intermediate points in the Caribbean. Depending on the availability of ether, the paste would either be converted to powder in the islands or sent on to the United States for further refining.

Some of the coca paste destined for the United States was invariably diverted for local consumption. According to researchers interviewed for a cover story in *U.S. News & World Report*, it was in the Netherlands Antilles, a cluster of southern Caribbean islands east of Colombia and north of Venezuela, that experiments with coca paste first yielded the direct antecedent to crack. Residents there cooked the paste with baking soda, water, and rum; they called it "base rock," or "baking soda base" or simply "roxanne." Elsewhere in the Caribbean in the early eighties, American analysts heard repeatedly of "rock" cocaine usage. "A local cop asked about a drug that looked like a pebble, and people would smoke it and go crazy," a Miami doctor told *U.S. News*. "None of us had ever heard of it."

Rock cocaine was probably most pervasive in the Bahamas. The Bahamas had become Carlos Lehder's home base; in 1978, the twenty-eight-year-old took up residence on Norman's Cay, a small coral island named for a Caribbean pirate and located about forty-five miles southeast of Nassau. Lehder bought virtually every asset: the airstrip (which he upgraded to handle his storage and shipment operations), the country club, the hotel, the dock. Within a year of Lehder's arrival in the Bahamas, residents throughout the commonwealth's archipelago were smoking cocaine. Within a few years, as Bahamian dealers came to realize that rock cocaine was more potent and more addictive than powder—and hence more profitable—they phased out powder sales completely. Said one dying crack addict to a Bahamian doctor: "When the world tastes this, you're going to have a lot of trouble."

In the United States, meanwhile, many cocaine consumers were already smoking the drug in "freebase" form. Freebasing was a chemical process by which the coca paste, or base, was "freed" from the powder by treating it with ether. The resultant crystals were smoked, usually in a heated glass pipe. The rush, like that of *bazuko*, was immediate and powerful, but the use of ether, a flammable liquid, made the procedure complex and dangerous. Freebasing had been the preferred method of an increasing number of cocaine users since the early to mid-seventies, when it was introduced in the United States, probably by Americans who had tried smoking coca paste in South America. A 1977 study of some of the estimated four million Americans who used cocaine calculated that as many as four hundred thousand were exclusively freebasers. But after the comedian Richard Pryor nearly died from a freebase explosion in 1980, consumers and dealers began searching for a safer, less complicated way to freebase.

Their search coincided with a new wave of emigration from the Caribbean to the United States, an exodus greater, in percentage terms, than from any other area of the world during the 1980s. From Haitians fleeing the violence of a dictatorship to others escaping from homelands with annual per capita incomes of little more than a thousand dollars, the mythic promised land of America was an enticing lure for Caribbean exodusters.

Like other immigrant groups, the Caribbeans were torn between their past and their future, between the old and new, the rural and urban. They took of their culture what they could: their churches, their social institutions, their vices. Among the cultural accoutrements preserved in migration was the recipe for "base rock." The rudimentary baking soda method was a faster and easier way of making cocaine smokable than the dangerously volatile ether-based formula for freebase. In no time, base rock spread rampantly among the Caribbean immigrant underground, first in Miami, where, says James Inciardi, it "ultimately was made from powder cocaine rather than paste," and soon after in New York and elsewhere. And because few jobs were available for Caribbean immigrants (many of whom were undocumented and thus ineligible for lawful employment), it was perfectly logical for them to go to work in the burgeoning cocaine trade.

At about the same time, Colombian traffickers, catering to the growing demand, were shipping such vast amounts of cocaine to the United States—cocaine that was increasingly pure and yet ever less expensive—that the sheer number of people using and selling it rose exponentially. In 1983 a market glut forced the Colombians to drop their wholesale price some 50 percent lower than it had been three years earlier. The cost of a kilo (2.2 pounds) in Detroit fell to $22,000 during that summer from $46,000 in 1980. For the first time since cocaine was banned as a home remedy, the drug was affordable to the many as well as to the privileged few. Cocaine had once again become an integral part of American culture; by the following year, 20 percent of high school seniors would try the drug.

The glut that benefited consumers naturally caused a sharp drop in dealer profits. To counter their diminishing returns, the cocaine dealers responded to market forces by doing what any vendor would do in times of market saturation: they sought to broaden the market by introducing a new product. The product would be easy to consume, easy to hide, hard to quit, and accessible to almost anyone. It would retail for five to fifteen dollars per unit, as opposed to a hundred dollars a gram for powder. The product would come to be known by the sound it made when smoked. The name was deceptively simple and economical, like crack itself.

CHAPTER FOUR

"BJ, WHY DON'T YOU START

SELLING CRACK?"

"I remember the first time I saw crack," Billy once said. "It wasn't interesting to me, those little rocks. I just thought, I don't know who gonna pay ten dollars for *that*. I had tried cocaine once before, back I think when I was about eleven. My brothers had some powder. I came in on them and said, 'What was y'all doing?' And David told me, 'Get on out of here.' And I told him, 'Give me some.' And he let me sniff some. Asked me, 'Feel anything?' And I asked him, 'What do I suppose to feel?' He said, 'Do you feel any thing running down your throat?' I told him no, I left out, and that was the end of it.

"Weed was the only thing I did. For some reason I never liked to drink, and I never did try cocaine again after that. Never even thought about it again until Perry started bothering me about it and wouldn't stop no way."

Perry Coleman, the uncle of Billy's girlfriend, Niece, was two years Billy's senior. It was he, along with his older brother Alan, who schooled Billy in the fundamentals of street life when Billy arrived in Detroit. The two had remained close over the years, even through Billy and Niece's frequent separations. And though it did not take long for the student to outshine his teacher, Billy always cut Perry in on his marijuana deals, always made sure Perry and the rest of Niece's large extended family did not go without.

Perry's family had gone without in the past. He was the youngest son of fourteen children born to Lillie Richards, a Georgia native whose family had migrated to Detroit when Lillie was ten. Perry's father, a construction worker, and Lillie had ten children together but never married—it would have sharply reduced her welfare benefits. They separated in 1969, when Perry was nine. Lillie asked her parents to take Perry in. Lillie worked when she could, and the children's father contributed when he could, but welfare remained her primary means of support.

Perry grew up in relative splendor. As the only child at his grandparents' house, he was treated accordingly. "I was real spoiled," he recalls. "We had plenty to eat and I always kept myself clean and neat." But not all was rosy. His grandfather was an alcoholic. "He was mild-manner acting during the week," says Perry, "and then on payday Fridays he'd fall out drunk and want to fight my grandma."

But Perry's grandfather impressed upon him the value of the work ethic. Not only did his grandfather work on the Chrysler assembly line, he moonlighted as a handyman at a nearby Laundromat, where he found work for Perry as well. At ten, Perry was hired as a janitor at the Laundromat; he also worked a variety of odd jobs. "I never was scared to cut grass, push a car, take out garbage. If I wanted something, I learned how to get it."

An education, though, was something that had mostly eluded Perry; he made it only as far as junior high school, and never learned to read. And yet, he says, "They always passed me and I always got good grades. When they called on me to read, I just said nothing and they'd call on somebody else." It was in the seventh grade at Jackson Junior High that a teacher first noticed Perry's inability to read. Not long after she had shepherded him to a remedial reading class, he was bused to a new school. "It was a big school and they didn't know I couldn't read," Perry says. Within a month of enrolling, he dropped out.

He found work as a stocker at a neighborhood grocery, Frank's Beer & Wine. On the day he started, the boss asked him to fetch a case of Miller beer. Perry started to the stockroom and then broke down crying. "I couldn't tell Miller from Bud but I didn't let on when he hired me," Perry says. He sat me down and I confessed I couldn't read and he took pity on me and didn't fire me."

Early in 1978, Perry enlisted in the Job Corps with the hope of learning to read. Instead, he learned welding, a skill that he was able to put to use almost immediately. On his eighteenth birthday, in May, just as the first waves of recession jolted the auto industry, Ford Motor Company hired Perry in its Michigan Avenue plant on the city's west side. He was laid off a little more than a year later.

By then, some of his elder siblings had discovered the lure of drug money. His sister Cynthia (Niece's mother) was buying and selling "T's" and "blues" and other assorted prescription drugs on the flourishing black market; a brother sold marijuana out of a nightclub; and other friends and relatives were working the streets for heroin and marijuana dealers.

With a twenty-thousand-dollar severance check from Ford, Perry and his family in 1980 opened Lillie's Party Store at the corner of Chalmers and Chelsea. Most of the family worked there at one time or another: Lillie, her sister Betty, Perry and his siblings, Niece and Billy. The store was open six days a week, nineteen hours a day: from seven A.M. to two o'clock the following morning. Billy says that it was at Lillie's Party Store that he became acquainted with the concept of adding marijuana to the traditional retail mix.

The combination drug, liquor, and snack food emporium provided vital income for the family until the fall of 1984. In October, the state of Michigan revoked the store's liquor license for "allowing marijuana possession on the premises." By then the family had expanded its holdings. Alan Coleman, a pudgy-faced, sleepy-eyed twenty-five-year-old known still by his first nickname, Baby Boy, or simply Baboy (pronounced BAY-boy), opened a music store: Baboy's Records and Tapes. He also operated out of the shop a small real estate company, which Lillie and Betty managed, and an interior decorating firm. In addition to assisting the family in these pursuits, Perry worked whenever possible with Billy in his budding marijuana business. By the spring of 1984, Perry was urging Billy to try selling something new, something even more lucrative.

Billy wasn't interested. He already felt like he was atop the world. "I'm sittin' around happy, I got a couple weed salesmen, I got a bunch of friends, money is not no problem," recalls Billy of his days on Newport Street. "I had my own house, cars, everything. And Perry was coming over every day, borrowing money from me. A thousand, fifteen hundred, two thousand dollars, but he was paying me back. It would take him a day or two, or three days. But I always got it back."

One day Perry came over not for a loan but to counsel his former protégé.

"BJ, why don't you start selling crack?"

"What is crack?"

"Crack, man, is cocaine, and you make millions of dollars off that."

"I don't want no millions of dollars. I don't need no money."

Perry said, "BJ, I know what's wrong with you. You think you rich already. I'm gonna tell you. You ain't rich. You sell cocaine, you *really* gonna be rich. You'll have so much money, you'll *give* two, three, four, five hundred thousand dollars away."

This sort of banter went on probably a month or two. Billy made some inquiries about crack. He sought guidance from his major supplier of marijuana, a man named T.J. in his middle thirties whom Billy trusted and respected. "Is this crack all that it's supposed to be?" he asked T.J. "Is it worth getting into?"

T.J. cautioned against it. Says Billy: "He told me, 'Y'all might not know about cocaine. But cocaine is the most dangerous thing to ever mess with. I'd advise y'all not to never mess with cocaine. You'll realize this weed right here will carry you a long way.' "

And so Billy told Perry no; he'd stick with marijuana. Perry came back later that day. "I tell you what," Perry said. "I want you to loan me the money, and I guarantee I'll pay you back." Perry wanted twenty-five hundred dollars, the going rate for an ounce of cocaine. He said he could make ten thousand off a single ounce. Perry had always been good to his word; Billy loaned him the money.

During the time Billy considered the diversification question, he opened a new weed house, ten lots down the block from 1261 Newport. Perry had helped Billy set up the house: fortify it, staff it, supply it. Once Billy consented to the seed money for the ounce of cocaine, Perry suggested to him that the new location would make a fine crack outlet as well. Against his better judgment, Billy agreed to offer crack for a weekend-long trial period. Perry promptly brought in a friend, an experienced cocaine seller. After a couple of days during which Perry's friend sold less than two hundred dollars worth of the new product, Billy told Perry, "I told you ain't nobody want this stuff."

Perry told Billy to have faith, that it would take a little more time to pass the word. "Just give the guy another couple days," Perry said assuredly.

Billy agreed. "You and your guy got forty-eight hours." Billy had already mentally written off the loan as a cost of doing business. At least now he knew: T.J. was right about never messing with cocaine in the first place. Billy went home. It was the weekend before the Fourth of July and he felt like "kicking back" anyway. He would take the midweek holiday off like everyone else.

Billy returned to the sell house the next day, Monday, July 1. Perry's friend was lounging. Billy asked, "What's up, you out of weed?"

" 'Yeah,' " Billy recalls him saying. "Had this crazy eye, like a demon or a devil."

" 'Nigger, why you looking at me like that?' " Billy asked him.

" 'Man, you won't believe what I'm fixing to tell you, you're gonna think I'm lying.'

" 'What happened?' " Billy asked. "I'm thinking the money's short or he might have an extra thousand or whatever. I wanna know what I'm not gonna believe.

"He said, 'There was about fifteen thousand [dollars] worth of peoples been through here today looking for some 'caine!'

"I said, 'Ain't that many peoples in the world.'

"He says, 'Man, I told ya you weren't gonna believe me.' "

Within an hour Billy found himself scrambling all over the east side to meet demand; his plans for a relaxing Fourth were happily canceled. First he found Big Terry Colbert, his early mentor, who himself had branched out from marijuana to cocaine sales. And then Billy went to a guy he knew only as Twin, another of his onetime marijuana suppliers who he'd heard was now moving cocaine as well. "Twin knew from my weed-selling days that I had plenty money. And not only that but he knew I had every girl in the neighborhood. And he kind of admired me about that. So he was more than full to work with me."

The Fourth of July is a lazy day in Detroit, rarely intruded upon by work. Barbecues, picnics, fishing derbies, block parties, family reunions at Belle Isle, the scenic offshore park, are the order of the day. In 1984 the calendar denied working Detroiters a three-day weekend; the Fourth fell on a Wednesday. But because the holiday fell just two days after the month's welfare checks were distributed, it was cause for jubilance anyway—particularly for retail businesses. Especially elated, for example, were liquor store owners, who, as always, helpfully converted checks into spirits and cash. Also delighted at the spendthrift mood of the populace were Billy and Perry and the rest of the crew, who, like the liquor magnates, were too busy to take the holiday off.

For a million or so metro Detroiters, the Fourth was capped with the finale of the International Freedom Festival, a two-week extravaganza of parades, carnivals, music, and sporting events sponsored jointly by Detroit and Windsor, the foreign city across the river Billy most appreciated for its topless nightclubs and gigantic illuminated Canadian Club sign over the distillery. On

Wednesday night Detroiters gathered at Hart Plaza, on the water's edge at the base of downtown, for the annual fireworks display ignited from a barge in the middle of the river. In years past, Billy had usually found his way downtown to soak up the traditional spectacle ("Nothin' like firin' up some weed and watching the sky explode"), but this year he hadn't been able to spare the time. Only the previous day he had converted the Newport weed house into his first retail outlet dedicated solely to the sale of crack cocaine; for him this year's fireworks were strictly financial.

The cocaine was selling as fast as he could buy and process it, selling so fast that he didn't bother to package it in Baggies. Actually, it wasn't so much that he didn't *bother*—it was that no one had told him that that was how it was done. Billy and his friend Boogaloo, Niece's brother-in-law, were unschooled in the art and science of the crack business. They had no idea how even to convert cocaine powder into crack. "We didn't know *what* we were doing," Billy said years later, sounding not unlike a high-tech entrepreneur who got his start assembling clunky computers in his parents' garage. "It was mix and match all the way. We were so uneducated about it we were just taking a little bit—it might be a dime or twenty-cent worth—and sell it like that. We'd rock it up while the customer was out there waiting at the door. They be like, 'I want a twenty.' And we be like, 'Damn, they want a twenty *rock*.' So we'd go back there and rock it up and we'd be back there playing with it so long we thought they'd leave out on us."

For the first month or so, Billy and Boogaloo ran their business like a couple of frazzled short-order cooks. They worked the stove top nonstop, mixing two parts baking soda with seven parts cocaine and one part water. They boiled the mixture in a couple of Mr. Coffee pots. They cooked it for ten minutes if pressed; twenty if they could spare the time. They cooled it in ice water until it hardened, and then chipped it with razor blades into five- and ten-dollar rocks. Unlike many other crack dealers, they used no diluent, like "comeback," a chemical similar in texture and appearance to cocaine. "We never cut ours," Billy says. "What do they say on

TV? No artificial ingredients. That's us. That's why people liked us. They knew they was getting a quality product."

The nonstop pace paid off: on the Fourth alone, Billy netted ten thousand dollars from a single ounce of powder cocaine— Perry's economic forecast come true! Traffic congestion on the once desolate post-residential block suddenly resembled the Lodge freeway during a rush-hour accident. "The cars would be jammed up on the street so you couldn't hardly get by," Billy says. "And the peoples was coming in and out of the house like the train station or the bus station."

The single ounce they sold that day would come to seem like a drop in the bucket. "An ounce *was* a little, but it was a lot too," Billy says. "Nobody was selling keys back then; if you had an ounce you might as well have had a key." One reason no one sold kilos was the price: sixty thousand dollars, at a minimum. Another equally important reason was the lack of reputable dealers. "Finding a guy you could trust was a major problem," Billy recalls. "Because sometimes we'd buy ounces that wasn't no good. It was bogus powder. So it was a question of establishing ourselves. It was one thing to buy three or four ounces for six or eight thousand. But if you're gonna spend sixty thousand, you want to know you can trust them."

Billy had moved deliberately during his years as a marijuana dealer. He oversaw every detail, from negotiations with suppliers to quality control to customer service to security to expansion sites. And he left nothing to chance with other people. He took to heart Big Terry Colbert's directive: "Take care of the product, and the product will take care of you."

But the crack cocaine business was altogether different— drug-dealing on a scale that had yet to be calibrated. This new product was so powerful and yielded so much money so fast that Billy seemed unable to meet the demands he was making on himself. He was unprepared for the change. In the past, with marijuana, he knew how much business to expect over a three-day weekend, or a holiday, and planned accordingly. But right from the frenzied beginning of his entry into the crack business, from the day he was forced to abandon his plans for a relaxing Fourth, it seemed he would never regain the measure of control over his business and his life, the same satisfying blend of abandon and discipline he had concocted during his days as a marijuana dealer. Hard though he had worked when his lone product was marijuana, he had to work harder now. At first he had thought that the work-load would ease as he grew more successful—but the load seemed only to get heavier. Crack, Billy saw, was unlike marijuana: the sheer volume and velocity of repeat business was overwhelming. No matter how hard he worked, no matter how much he sold, he came to realize there was always more business than he could ac-commodate, always more money to hide, to spend.

And there was the looming presence of the police. While sell-ing marijuana, he had never had a lick of trouble with the law (al-though his brother Willie was arrested for possession of marijuana in April of 1984—he received a suspended sentence—and Jerry Gant was convicted of possession twice, in 1981 and 1982; he too was spared jail time in both cases). But within weeks of his entry into the crack business, the trade seemed to taint Billy with misfor-tune when it came to police encounters.

Business boomed all summer. Billy and Willie celebrated by buying a new car, a seventeen-thousand-dollar silver four-door Saab 900, for which they paid in full with a cashier's check. Up until then, Billy and his twin, Little Joe, had driven matching Cadillac Sevilles, both of which were high-mileage, comparatively clunky cars, a '76 and a '79, not the sort that spelled D-R-U-G D-E-A-L-E-R in blinking lights to ever-vigilant cops. But then again, says Billy, no matter what he or his friends drove around the east side, they could count on periodic stops and searches; for some cops the combination of a young black man and even an aging Cadillac constituted probable cause. "They seen me here or there, they pull me over, search me, throw me all over the car. That happened to everyone; we was always getting stopped for nothing. Other than that, I had never really came in contact with the police. They didn't know me or know what I did or nothing." By the middle of August, following what could have begun and ended as one more routinely humiliating traffic stop, his days of minimal contact with the police were gone forever.

He was on Mack Avenue one afternoon, on his way home to Newport in the brand-new Saab, when he spotted two white police officers eyeing him from a cruiser. "I knew they was gonna come after me, this young guy in a new car," Billy remembers. "And as I get down the street, I look in the mirror and here come the police car. So I run through two stop signs, I'm moving so fast trying to get to Newport. I start running stop signs because I just knew they was gonna pull me over. I didn't have no dope or money or gun or anything. Just didn't want to go through the harassment and I thought I could get to the house. They'd have me out there for an hour, searching me, they might even take my car."

Billy arrived at the house seconds before the police. He jumped out of the car, flung his keys across the street into the vacant lot, and had hopped up the steps to the porch when the police car screeched to a stop.

"Hey, you just get out of that car?"

"No sir," Billy replied.

"Let's see some I.D.," the officer said, waving Billy over to the car.

Billy: "I had just took care of my license, my license fresh clean, so it wasn't no problem about that. So I get in his car, and he's punching my numbers in the computer."

Just then Little Joe came tooling up the street on his motor scooter, a Honda. It didn't take him long to assess the situation. "What is you all doin' with my brother?" Joe inquired of the officers.

The officer filing the report "just kept on writing, didn't even look up," Billy recalls.

"Go ahead on," the officer advised Little Joe.

Little Joe rejected the advice. "Why y'all messin' with my brother?" he asked. "Y'all jealous of him or something?"

By then Billy wished that his brother would back off. "I'm like, Wow. I'm motioning him to get away from the car. And then the police tells him to get away from the car."

Joe would have none of it. "You can't tell me what to do," he told the cop. "I'm right in front of *my* house."

But then Joe appeared to back down. He rolled the scooter up onto the sidewalk, parked it in front of the house. No sooner did Billy think a potentially explosive situation had been defused than here came Joe back to the police car, "talking stuff," says Billy, "out both sides his mouth." This time Joe's chatter provoked a response.

The officer on the passenger side stepped out of the car and shoved Little Joe. Joe pushed him right back. Meanwhile, as the scuffle escalated into a brawl, the other officer was oblivious; he was trying to finish the paperwork. Finally, says Billy, the officer at the wheel "looks up and notice they fightin' like cats and dogs. He like, 'Oh shit,' throw his stuff up in the air, and gets out of the car. And they both start hitting on my brother. And I'm like, 'Oh, I can't let 'em do him like that.' And so I holler up to one of the girls on the porch: 'Come get in the police car and open the back door up for me.' And so she did! And I get out and jump on the policeman from the back. So now we're out there fighting the police and I got a lock on the guy from behind. He's like, 'This cat came from behind me and rushed me.' And I got him good; he can't even move. And the other guy hit his walkie-talkie and said, 'Officer down on such-and-such block Newport Street.' It wasn't seconds later and I looked up the street and there's five cars coming this way. And I holler at my brother, 'LET HIM GO, LET HIM GO!' And the backup, they get right out: 'FREEZE!' And the sergeant or lieutenant who came asked 'em: '*These* guys?' He couldn't believe it. And they said, 'Yeah.' And the guy started laughing at 'em, said, 'Man, these guys ain't three feet tall.' And so they throw me and my brother in the backseat and *we* start laughing. And one of 'em looked in and said, 'You laugh one more time and I'll crack your fucking head open.' "

The officer made good on his word. Once at the police station, Billy says he and his brother were taken not to the rear entrance, through which arrestees were normally escorted, but to the garage, well removed from the street in the bowels of the building. "Right there they start hitting us in the head with a flashlight, and hitting us in the stomach. And we're handcuffed, can't do a thing. They almost broke my jaw. They busted my eye, my whole face was swolled up, my mouth was bleeding bad. They beat my twin so bad he fell out. They drug him inside, called the ambulance for us, and we stayed in the hospital maybe four or five hours." Following X rays and instructions to see an oral surgeon within a week, the emergency room of Detroit Receiving Hospital released Billy and Little Joe to the custody of the Wayne County Jail. They were charged with assault and battery of a police officer.

The following day, after he and Joe were freed on bond, Billy began searching for a new base of operations. The police were unaware of the sell house down the block, but Billy believed the arresting officers intended to keep a close eye on 1261 Newport. He found a two-family, two-story flat on an equally forlorn stretch of Gray Street, seven blocks west of Newport, between Kercheval and Vernor. Within the week, Jerry Gant had rented the downstairs flat and Boogaloo Driscoll leased the upstairs unit.

The duplex arrangement was convenient and practical. They "rocked up," partied, and slept downstairs, sold upstairs. Like 1261 Newport, 2194/2196 Gray Street was a magnet for friends and family and hangers-on: a place to relax for a couple hours or a couple days, maybe smoke some weed, or help cook and cut the cocaine. Though the upstairs apartment was furnished sparsely—a telephone, two old couches, and an iron grate over the door were its chief flourishes—Jerry spared no expense for the downstairs flat. He bought a couple of La-Z-Boy recliners and spent two thousand dollars for two bedroom suites, "in case," he would later recall, "we met new women to take over there."

In the late afternoon of August 23, 1984, a Thursday, the Chamberses and some friends had gathered upstairs for a barbecue. There were Billy, his sister Delois, and four Chambers brothers: Willie, David, sixteen-year-old Otis, who was visiting from Marianna, and Little Joe. Also there were Joe's girlfriend Devona Hunter; Jerry Gant and his girlfriend, Bonnie Smith; and Boogaloo and his girlfriend, Wanda Booker.

As always, there was business to conduct. But the day's sales had been typically slow: a Thursday toward the end of the month (the day before payday; the week before welfare checks arrived) was a tight time for much of the clientele. The previous day had been sluggish as well. Wanda Booker, a heavyset, pregnant nineteen-year-old, had worked the door that Wednesday. Among her customers was a young black man who gave her a twenty-dollar bill in exchange for three rocks. Upon leaving the house, the customer had walked a short way down the street and hopped in the passenger side of a waiting car. He handed the drugs to the driver, who deposited them in an envelope. The driver, known to the young man as "T-Bone," was a veteran officer with the narcotics section of the Detroit Police Department. The young man, known now only as SOI (Source of Information) #403, was a paid informant, a snitch.

By eight-thirty Thursday morning, a police chemist had positively identified as cocaine the "white lumpy powder" in each of the three clear plastic packets. With the laboratory analysis in hand, officer Jimmy (T-Bone) Bohn presented his findings to a state district court judge, who promptly signed the warrant Bohn had drawn up to search the premises of 2196 Gray Street. Early that evening, as Billy Joe Chambers tended the glowing charcoal, Bohn returned to Gray Street along with eight fellow police officers and three sergeants.

The convoy parked around the corner from the duplex. Then one car, driven by the sergeant in charge, Ronald Ferguson, pulled around to Gray Street so he and two officers could provide "close-in cover." Ferguson issued thirty dollars in marked money to the cop who would attempt to make the buy, an undercover officer named Alphonso Mitchell. Just as Mitchell started up the front stairs to the top portion of the duplex, the door opened.

"What you want?" Wanda Booker inquired.

"Give me three tens," Mitchell said. Wanda disappeared for a moment and returned with three ten-dollar heat-sealed packs of "suspected" cocaine. Mitchell left without further discussion and was driven around the corner to the "meet spot." They had made the buy; it was time for the bust.

Within minutes, the dozen police officers were set. It was shortly after six-thirty; the steaks were not yet ready, but the barbecue would soon be over. Mitchell was assigned to lead the "entry team" up the stairs; directly behind him would be Jimmy Bohn, the "shotgun man," followed by Sergeant James Elliot, who would pound on the door and announce the raid (POLICE OFFICERS! WE HAVE A SEARCH WARRANT!), and six others, who would "search and secure the premises." Outside, two female officers were assigned to guard either side of the house; Sergeant Ferguson would watch the backyard to prevent escape down the back steps.

There was no escape attempt. As soon as Billy heard the police approaching, he coolly told everyone to remain calm, to keep their seats, as if he were a pilot warning his passengers of imminent turbulence. At the top of the stairs, Mitchell found little resistance; only an iron gate, which his police-model crowbar bent back as if it were aluminum. In the living room facing the open door, the party guests were motionless. "They just sat on the couch and looked at us," Mitchell later reported.

Not everyone took Billy's advice. Willie Chambers ran to the bathroom and attempted to flush down the toilet some damning evidence: a hundred and eighteen packs of "suspected cocaine," all of which were recovered, according to police records. Also seized were $2,318 in cash and fifty-three coin envelopes of loose marijuana, along with two scales and two heat-sealing machines. Willie and Wanda Booker, who sold the three rocks to officer

Mitchell, were arrested; the others were "investigated and re-leased": their names and (mostly fictional) addresses were re-corded. And, recalls Jerry Gant, they were advised to "watch our butts."

Nine days later, the DPD narcotics section, in the person of officer John Autrey, returned to Gray Street. The thirty-two-year-old Autrey, a six-year veteran of the narcotics section, had grown up on the east side, not far from Gray Street. Autrey brought with him yet another SOI to make an undercover buy from the upstairs flat. Again Wanda Booker, who had made bail, answered the door; Willie Chambers peeked from the dining room. The SOI asked for thirty dollars worth of cocaine. Wanda told Willie she needed "thirty." When Willie came to the door with the packet of crack, according to the SOI's report to officer Autrey, he had a "blue steel revolver stuck in front of his pants." The deal was done, and the SOI returned to the waiting police car.

The following day, Sunday of Labor Day weekend, Officer Autrey set up surveillance of the Gray Street house. He claimed to have seen "10 b/m [black males] enter and leave the . . . location with[in] a 10 minute time span." This, he concluded in a petition for a second search warrant, "is indicative of Narcotic Traffick-ing." The magistrate for the 36th District Court of Detroit agreed; he issued the warrant on Monday, September 3, 1984.

Elayne Coleman was up and out of her mother's house early that cool and cloudy Labor Day morning. There were errands to run and a prospective boyfriend to visit, and maybe she'd even squeeze in some shopping downtown and a little roller-skating before she drove her great-aunt to the hospital for her thrice-weekly afternoon visit. Elayne threw on a purple jogging suit, gulped some cereal, and jumped in the Cadillac she had recently bought for four hundred dollars from a sister's boyfriend. She started for downtown but U-turned when she saw the swarm of people and the streets closed to traffic: a hundred and fifty thou-sand unionists were parading down Woodward Avenue toward

Hart Plaza, where they would rally and listen to would-be First Lady Joan Mondale and AFL-CIO president Lane Kirkland denounce the Reagan Administration in the traditional kickoff to the presidential campaign.

Elayne was twenty years old, and at five feet tall and a shade over a hundred pounds, with a skin tone approximately that of the car's tanned leather upholstery, she seemed almost to disappear behind the wheel of the brown Caddy. The car was a '74, only ten years old, but it ran, she was fond of saying, "like spoiled molasses." Still, it got her around town to the places that counted: to work, and to the roller rink. For the last eighteen months or so, her homebound great-aunt had employed Elayne as a caretaker; it was a demanding job, all that cooking and cleaning and bathing and chauffeuring, and she planned to use the morning and early afternoon off to indulge herself a little. She especially looked forward to dropping by Royal Skateland, where she had worked happily as a snack bar attendant for two and a half years and where, had her aunt not needed her, she would probably still be employed. The roller rink was her home away from home: she had been skating there "seven days a week" since she was thirteen, and had gone to work there in the fall of 1980, not long after dropping out of seventh grade at Farwell Middle School.

Around noon, Elayne called her mother to tell her she was headed to a friend's house on Garland Street. Not long after arriving, she received a phone call from her brother, Alan (Baboy) Coleman, the budding entrepreneur (he had recently opened the record store) who was five years older than she. Baboy asked her to pick him up; he needed a ride to the store.

"Sure," she told him, unaware that the innocuous favor would change her life. "Where you at?"

"Gray between Kercheval and Vernor," Baboy directed. "Twenty-one ninety-six, green and white duplex, upstairs."

It took her quite a while to find the house. "He asked me to come somewhere I had never been before," Elayne recalls. "I don't know everywhere there is to go on the east side and I don't know anything about the west side. If I have a job, I know how to get there. Otherwise I'm gonna get lost."

Shortly before three o'clock, Elayne pulled up to the curb and blew the horn. "Why don't you come in for a minute?" Baboy yelled down. Once she was upstairs, he told her, "Why don't you let me run to the store and I'll be right back."

Save me a trip, she thought. "No problem," she said and flipped him the keys to the Caddy.

At that very minute a convoy of six police cars, one marked, the others unmarked, carrying thirteen officers who were armed with a battering ram, a crowbar, flak jackets, firearms, and the search warrant for 2196 Gray Street, was gathering in an alley around the corner for a siege on the duplex.

At three o'clock undercover officer John Autrey, dressed in a T-shirt, jeans, and gym shoes, used marked money to purchase fifty dollars worth of crack cocaine from a woman he later identified as Elayne Coleman. Autrey returned to an unmarked car, where he briefed his sergeant on the successful buy as they retreated to the nearby beachhead.

A few minutes later, the procession of police cars rounded the corner and parked in the alley behind 2194/2196 Gray. The raid plan called for ten of the thirteen officers to rush the upstairs flat, where Elayne, oblivious to the coming storm, killed time by talking on the phone to her mother while waiting for her brother to return with the car.

At three-fifteen, the officers, led by their sergeant, sprinted up the stairs, yelling, as they were trained to do, because it is held that making noise is safer than a sneak attack: the commotion generally causes people to freeze in their tracks. At the top of the stairwell, the sergeant banged on the door: "POLICE! . . . OPEN UP . . . WE HAVE A WARRANT!" And then, within seconds, he rendered that command moot, ordering one officer to force open the steel grate with a crowbar while he signaled another to break down the wooden door with a battering ram.

On the other end of the phone, Elayne's mother heard what

sounded like an explosion. "There was all this noise and then the line went dead," she recalls. That, Elayne says, was because "the police took the phone and stomped on it—for *real*."

The officer who had knocked down the door then picked the door up and tossed it out the window, warning Elayne, "If I see you up here again, this is what I'm going to do to you." Another officer asked Elayne who lived downstairs; he had noticed several young women through the open door of the lower flat and had cautioned them to "remain quiet."

Elayne told the inquiring officer, "I don't know nothing about no people downstairs." Then two female officers arrested, pat-searched, and handcuffed Elayne, escorting her downstairs and out the front door.

Naturally, a crowd had gathered on Gray Street. As Elayne and her captors started down the front steps toward a squad car, a neighbor, one of thirty or forty spectators drawn to the scene, volunteered: "The people you are looking for are downstairs. They all downstairs; something going on downstairs!"

Again Elayne was asked: "Do you want to tell on those people downstairs?" She repeated that she had no idea "about no people downstairs."

Fear took over the lower flat. Inside were Billy and a dozen or so friends and relatives. "Everyone wanted to know what to do," recalls Billy, who had been fast asleep in a La-Z-Boy in the living room until the ruckus woke him. "I told 'em to calm down and stay still. But everybody just started jumpin' around and hugging each other."

They had good reason to be jumpy. In the house was a substantial amount of cocaine—some five thousand rocks.

The police evidently had learned from one or another of the neighbors that Billy, whose name (if not face) was already known to east-side narcotics officers, was inside the flat. By the account of those inside, the police broke in chanting, "BILLY JOE, BILLY JOE, BILLY JOE." Says Billy's girlfriend Diana Alexander, then eighteen: "They figured out who we all was when they lined us up against the wall and I.D.'d us; one of 'em said to Billy, 'Nigger, I thought you was a old man.' "

The police had no warrant for 2194 Gray, the downstairs flat. But according to the official version of events, they didn't need one. In their Preliminary Complaint Reports, filed immediately after the raid, the officers said that Elayne Coleman was not detained upstairs, but rather had fled down a rear stairway into the basement, clambered through a partition dividing the lower flat's basement from the upper flat's, and sprinted up the steps into the kitchen of the lower flat, where she was finally apprehended.

That in-pursuit-of-a-suspect account would negate the need for a separate warrant. The official story continues: As officers caught up to Elayne in the kitchen, they peeked into the dining room, where, officer Jimmy Bohn reported, he saw "a number of people sitting at the table." On the table, he says, was "a large number of rolled-up clear Baggies" and "a large amount of money." He says he saw one of the persons at the table, later identified as Billy Joe Chambers, "grab some of the clear Baggies and run toward the bathroom with the Baggies in his hands." Bohn says he followed Billy into the bathroom and prevented him from flushing the Baggies down the toilet. "I . . . took the Baggies from the toilet and observed inside . . . some rock type substance which [I] believed to be rock cocaine."

But that narrative of how and why the police wound up in the lower flat without a search warrant is illogical and implausible. For the chase scenario to be believed, it also must be believed that despite all the noise the officers say they made during the raid, and despite the warning to the young women downstairs to "remain quiet, that [we're] raiding the upstairs flat," Billy and the others remained seated at the dining room table downstairs, with money and drugs piled high. And it must further be believed that Billy waited until Officer Bohn saw him at the table to dash into the bathroom with the dope. And not a little dope: Would Billy have attempted, as Bohn stated, to flush down the toilet 1,170 packs of crack cocaine at once with a police officer in hot pursuit? And how could Bohn cite as justification for the unwarranted search (as he did in his PCR) the "pre-purchase of cocaine from the residence," when the "pre-purchase"—if it was made at all—was made *up-stairs,* in a separate residence? And is it possible, as the sergeant stated, that among the "large amount of U.S. currency" he said he confiscated from the lower flat's dining room table was the fifty dollars in prerecorded funds the undercover officer Autrey had used to make the cocaine buy *upstairs?* To believe that is to believe that between the time of the transaction and the time of Elayne's arrest—about five to ten minutes, according to Autrey—Elayne went downstairs, dropped off the money, and returned upstairs. But if this were so, why would Elayne not also have deposited the rest of her alleged "narcotics proceeds"? According to officer Autrey, he found an additional one hundred and thirty dollars upstairs. And why, if she were truly working, could the police find only four packs of crack, worth ten dollars apiece (along with a couple of coin envelopes of marijuana), upstairs? As Billy puts it: "If she was really working for me up there, she'd at least have a thousand dollars of dope, but the poor girl didn't have nothing. And no way she would have sold fifty dollars and brought it all the way downstairs. That makes zero sense."

That so many details of the officers' respective stories neither make sense nor correspond suggest it is possible their version of events never occurred at all, that their tale of the pursuit of Elayne, of discovering drugs and money by happenstance, of witnessing Billy grab the dope and run, amounts not to altering evidence, but to manufacturing it.

Such a sizable bust, after all, came along infrequently. John Autrey, interviewed eight years to the day after the incident, recalls it as the most significant of the "minimum thousand" raids he participated in over the course of seven years in the narcotics section. "I remember this one so well because we never got five thousand rocks before. It was the largest cocaine seizure I was ever involved in."

Along with Billy and Elayne, the police arrested Billy's

brother Danny, then thirty-three, and their cousin Alvin (Frog) Chambers, a twenty-eight-year-old Flint resident, who was visiting his relatives on his day off from his job at a Chevrolet truck and bus factory. Both Danny and Alvin were alleged to have been sitting at the dining room table with Billy when officer Jimmy Bohn said he peered into the living room in pursuit of Elayne. Elayne was charged with two counts: selling less than fifty grams of cocaine and, because she was alleged to have worked with the three arrested downstairs, with possession with intent to sell two hundred and twenty-five grams or more but less than six hundred and fifty grams of cocaine; the Chamberses were charged with possession with intent to sell. In handcuffs the brothers and their cousin were made to march outside, and recite loudly, over and over, like boot camp recruits: "WE SELL DOPE, WE SELL DOPE, WE SELL DOPE . . ."

A preliminary examination was held a week later; the prosecution was unprepared—police chemists had not yet analyzed the alleged drugs confiscated—and the Detroit Recorders Court judge ordered the cases dismissed "without prejudice," meaning the charges could be reinstated when prosecutors were ready to try the defendants.

Arrest warrants were reissued in December of 1985. On March 25, 1986, Judge Ricardo J. Lubienski ordered the cases dismissed again, this time on the grounds that the defendants were denied their right to a speedy trial—it had been eighteen and a half months since the arrests.

That should have been the end of their troubles related to Gray Street. It wasn't. Two years later, the federal government sought to do what Wayne County authorities had twice failed to do: connect Elayne's alleged drug-dealing to Billy's operation. On March 1, 1988, Roy Hayes, the U.S. attorney for the Eastern District of Michigan, announced at a crowded press conference in the federal courthouse in downtown Detroit that a grand jury had returned indictments against twenty-two alleged conspirators in the "Chambers Brothers Organization." Two of those indicted were women. One was Larry Chambers's girlfriend; the other, whose sole alleged ties to the organization began and ended during a fifteen-minute period on Gray Street in 1984, was Elayne Coleman.

Billy, a week after the Gray Street raid: "We're at home [on Newport] and Terry's daddy [Big Terry Colbert] come over. And my brother Danny's begging him for some smoke. Big Terry says, 'I got a gram or a gram and a half in the car but I really don't want to go out there and get it. Now why don't you just make you some money and stop all this begging right here,' Big Terry tells Danny, and they laughing and joking and I go upstairs. And when I go upstairs he [Terry] leave out.

"Now the front door's wooden with a plate-glass window and burglar bars. But where you come in I built that other door, that wall out of two-by-fours. So Danny lets Terry out and locks the door back up like he supposed to. And I go upstairs and sit down on the bed. And there was a small quantity of dope in the house. Now from where I'm sitting I can see one of the other bedrooms and the bathroom. I don't know what I was thinking about. And then I notice somebody fly up the steps and run past. I didn't pay it no attention. Then I saw somebody else fly up the steps. And I got up and somebody said we gettin' raided. So I break to the other bedroom and raised the window up and see the police on the sidewalk with a gun. And I hear 'em downstairs, 'OPEN UP, POLICE!' One of 'em say, 'The door won't give.' And they got the front door open, but it was caught by the wall. They said, 'Just tear the door down,' and they knocked the glass out of the wood frame and said, 'They got a barricade still inside the house.' And I said, 'Oh wow, there's still some dope in here.' And everybody's rippin' and runnin' all through the house trying to find the dope. A girl finds it and takes it and flush it down the toilet. Now the police come in yelling: 'Where they at, where they at?' And they say, 'Everybody upstairs!' And they come up to me and say, 'They a bunch of midgets, just like this one right here.'

And this lady police come up to me, puts her foot in my back, handcuffs me, and drags me downstairs. Then they brought the dog in and the dog searching all through the house and he can't find anything.

"So they bring us outside—Danny, Big Terry, and me—and they say, 'Now we got another raid to do.' And Terry got a Lincoln outside, a smack brand-new Lincoln. And they say, 'We got a extra car now. And they start loading each other in the Lincoln—*fighting* with each other really to see who get to ride in it—and then one of them says to us: 'We gonna do y'all a favor today. Instead of y'all being *in* a drug raid, we're gonna take y'all to a raid and see how we operate from the outside.'

"So they locked us down in the backseat. And they lined up about nine police cars with the Lincoln in the front, leading the way. When they got to Kercheval they all kept going together in the line. When the light turned red, they all steady pushing through the light. And the Lincoln turned on Philip [four blocks east] and they stopped directly in front of this house and they hopped out and they was in the house in like two seconds. They was throwing stuff through the windows and bringing guys out. They weren't in the house ten minutes. And they found the dope, the money, the guns, everything. And they walked the guys by us, like telling them, 'See, these the guys that told on you.' Yeah, they trying to play us off against them. But the guys had common sense enough to know the police ain't gonna bring us to the house if we were the ones who told on 'em."

Although Billy was not arrested in this latest raid, he heard the message loud and clear: "We watchin' your ass." He stopped hanging around his sell houses, didn't drive much, hardly left home for weeks. And still, he says, he felt the heat. "I wasn't even harassed, because I wasn't going out, that's how low I was laying. Every time I looked out the windows the police were riding past, looking up at my house and at my cars and everything. Or they'd park down at the corner watching the house."

Finally it got to be too much. At the end of October, little more than two months after his and Little Joe's scuffle with police outside of 1261 Newport, and after the two raids on Gray and this latest scare on Newport, Billy decided he had had enough; it was time for a change, time to go home. He left Detroit in his Saab late one afternoon. By breakfast time the following morning, he sat in his mother's kitchen in Lee County, Arkansas. Except for gasoline fill-ups, he drove the nine hundred miles nonstop.

CHAPTER FIVE

COOL HAND LARRY

If the series of raids was Billy Joe's formal introduction to criminal jurisprudence, Billy's older brother Larry, who would soon join him in the thriving crack business, was already an old hand. His familiarity with the law dated to 1969. On the last day of that year, Larry and a friend named Willie Earl Weeams were bemoaning the fact that they had been in the Lee County Jail for a week.

Jail was no place to be on New Year's Eve. Larry had reached that conclusion earlier in the day, and as his family decorated Curt's Place, the juke joint his parents operated on their land outside of La Grange, with streamers and balloons and party hats and noisemakers in preparation for a blowout end-of-the-decade party, Larry was never more sure of anything in his life.

Larry and Willie Earl Weeams had been friends since childhood, and in a way they were even related: Larry's sister Delois had had a child by Willie Earl. Two mornings before Christmas, the pair of nineteen-year-olds—Larry was a month shy of his twentieth birthday—went for a joyride in a 1965 Chevrolet pickup truck that happened to belong to the county. Then Larry decided to trade in the truck for something a little flashier. Early in the afternoon, a telephone company employee named Peggy Stiles had returned to her desk in downtown Marianna, her brand-new Oldsmobile parked not in the nearby lot but on the street in front of a facing window, the better to admire it. She had left work at lunchtime to complete her Christmas shopping for her three young children. "I mean that car was *loaded* with Christmas," Peggy Stiles remembers two decades later. "Next thing I knew, this little-old boy just jumped in and took off. I screamed and some of the men took off after him in a phone company truck. He only got three or four blocks before he dead-ended in a [cotton] gin yard."

Larry and Willie Earl were arrested for grand larceny. Their Christmas was spent behind bars, but at least they enjoyed a good meal when their parents were allowed to deliver a holiday dinner. That had been a week ago, and on New Year's Eve, with no immediate prospects for freedom, Larry and Willie Earl decided to expedite the process.

Just after the new year dawned, the pair, along with a cellmate, hatched an escape plot: they stuffed a newspaper down the toilet in their jail cell. When the toilet overflowed, the inmates summoned the jailer. They asked for a mop. "When he opened the cell door to give it to us, we jumped him," Larry recalls. They tied him up with some rope they had hidden, took his .38-caliber pistol, and made their way the seven miles from Marianna to La Grange. But rather than show their faces at the big party at Curt's Place, they hid out in the Chambers family's church, Mt. Perion Missionary Baptist. By the time they managed to get word to a friend that they were on the lam and hungry, a statewide search was in progress. "I fried up hamburgers for them," says a friend of Larry's, "and then they got out of there in a hurry."

They left, penniless, in the minister's 1966 white Rambler. Swapping it for a variety of other cars and trucks, they financed their way around the state for a couple of days with a series of robberies. "We hit seven stores," Larry says, "doing fine until we got to Ouachita County."

At nine-thirty on a Friday evening, January 2, 1970, a bitterly cold night, Larry and Willie Earl were cruising down state highway 79 in rural Ouachita (pronounced WATCH-it-aw) County, in south central Arkansas. Larry was at the wheel of their most recent acquisition, a late-model white Chevy pickup. Suddenly, seemingly out of nowhere on this dark stretch of highway, a police officer appeared behind their pickup and flipped on his car's flashing lights. The erstwhile prisoners pulled over, ready to surrender. But the officer had no idea that the two were wanted men; he stopped them only to issue a citation for a broken taillight. Larry panicked, pulled out the stolen pistol, and fired once at the officer, hitting him in the stomach. Then Larry sped off. For a moment he and Willie Earl were free again. They knew they needed to turn off the highway, but which way? Left or right? Finding themselves careening down one unmarked country road after another, they finally ran smack into a dead end. They spun around, headed back to the highway. Roadblock. Turned around again. Dirt road. Dead-ended at a rice paddy. They abandoned the car in a telephone pole yard and took off on foot. "We spent the night in the paddy in twenty degree weather," Larry says. "Worst night of my life." Following an all-night manhunt, they were arrested without incident in the morning. The police officer survived. Larry was sentenced to forty years for assault with intent to kill.

But the Ouachita County Jail in Camden could not hold Larry Chambers. Five months later, he and some other restless inmates tied up the jailer, stole a car, and headed for Los Angeles, where a fellow escapee had friends. They were caught in Phoenix and extradited to Arkansas. This time Larry received a two-hundred-year sentence, to be served in the Arkansas State Penitentiary, a facility not known for its humanity, a place described by its own former superintendent that same year as "an isolated remnant of an ancient philosophy of retribution, exploitation, corruption, sadism, and brutality." Asked during congressional testimony to elaborate on the abuse of inmates, Thomas O. Murton (on whom the title character in *Brubaker*, played by Robert Redford, was based) recounted the use of the "Tucker telephone," named for one of the state's prison farms. "The inmate would be taken to the infirmary," Murton said, "stripped naked, tied down on the operating table, and one wire would be run to his big toe and the other to his penis and then either a warden or an inmate would sit down and ring him up, as they say."

Larry Chambers was incarcerated first at Tucker (est. 1916), and then at Cummins Prison (est. 1902). Larry was never "rung up," but he learned immediately of the inhumane treatment the prison offered its inmates. As a sort of orientation period upon his arrival, he was placed in "the hole," an isolation cell, for two to three weeks. A bare bulb burned all day and night; his bed was a worn, concrete floor; rats—"cat-sizers"—were his constant, sole companions. Every other day, he was fed: a guard threw him a hunk of "gruel." "It was everything they had cooked earlier in the week—meat, okra, beans, whatever they had, in this mushy loaf," Larry says. "I tried it the first day but you just couldn't eat it. I'm thinking at least it could make for good rat poison, but they wouldn't touch it." Larry emerged from the hole only to find that the food served the general inmate population was hardly more nourishing or appetizing than the "gruel." He and seven others staged a hunger strike. The action won him a transfer to Cummins, some thirty miles south of Tucker.

Shortly after arriving at Cummins, Larry escaped again, this time in a fashion that could have come straight out of Hollywood. Cummins Prison, like Tucker, was a working farm; the inmates, a cheap source of labor for the state, were required to toil in the fields. To save further money, the prison appointed inmate "trustys" to guard their fellow cons. One day Larry's crew was picking tomatoes in a field three miles or so from the prison, on the banks of the Arkansas River. The escape plan originally called for another inmate to try his luck, but at the last minute, the man decided he couldn't go through with it. Larry, with no such qualms, volunteered himself.

All afternoon, Larry and other nearby crew members took turns discreetly digging a shallow grave amid the tomato plants in a remote area of the field. By about two o'clock, his friends had interred him. The trustys apparently went along with the scheme: when they counted the prisoners, in the bus, at the prison, and at the regular eight P.M. and ten P.M. counts, Larry was not missed. Meanwhile, Larry fell asleep. "I was completely buried underground up to my face and they put grass and dirt over my face," Larry says. When he woke, rising from his grave, night had fallen. "I didn't know what time it was, but the stars were out bright," he recalls. "I got up, pushed a log out from the river bank, and floated downstream."

Near the town of Grady, he disembarked, swiped a car, robbed a drugstore. Then he drove to Pine Bluff, about twenty miles north, ditched the car, and caught a bus to Pittsburgh, Pennsylvania, where he looked up an acquaintance from prison. But his money was running low, and rather than test his criminal mettle in the North, he returned to familiar territory. On the way back home, he stopped in Wynne, a Delta town thirty miles north of Marianna. That was as far as he got: a failed attempted burglary of a jewelry store netted him five more years at Cummins Prison.

In 1976 Larry went home again. He was on the streets all of thirty days when the urge to rob again overcame him. His target this time was the post office in Helena, the seat of Phillips County, some fifteen miles south of La Grange. Three times while awaiting trial he attempted to escape from the Helena jail, and three times he was caught. He says he tried to flee because of the harsh conditions. The cell had no tap water. If he wanted to drink, he was forced to buy water from the jailers. When his money ran out, he says he had no alternative but to drink from the toilet.

Following the last escape attempt, he says he was held not in a regular cell but in a hideaway "dungeon" under the jail. As Larry described it in a writ of habeas corpus, the dungeon was a dark, dirt-floored cell with no bed and no toilet. He pleaded guilty, he said, only under the duress of being held in such circumstances. He was returned to Cummins Prison to serve a three-year sentence. Within a year, the Arkansas Supreme Court, agreeing substantially with the writ Larry filed, reversed the conviction.

Again Larry went home. It was the summer of 1977 and there wasn't much work to be found, especially for a jail-busting, cop-shooting criminal. He was twenty-seven, and for the past nine years—since his earliest attempts at armed robbery in St. Louis— he had spent all but a few months in jail. He wound up chopping cotton alongside Ed Buford, the recent college graduate who'd had no better luck finding work that summer.

There were choices to make in life in the "world," as Larry put it, as opposed to life behind bars. Where to live? What and when to eat? What to wear? How to support yourself? Life on the farm agreed with him no more than it did with his siblings. But he feared that if he returned to St. Louis he'd find trouble, and he wasn't ready for another jail term. He bounced around—to Detroit, where he lived with Willie, the family man and letter carrier; he thought his younger brother's stability might somehow rub off. He stayed three months, with no apparent effect. On returning to Arkansas, he successfully robbed a few jewelry stores across the state before he was foiled in his hometown: he bungled a burglary attempt in Marianna. The prosecutor, citing Larry's considerable record, recommended a stiff sentence. The judge, for reasons unknown to the defendant, gave Larry just three years' probation.

The judge may have considered his show of mercy a mistake. In September of 1979 Larry was caught with six firearms—three revolvers, a rifle, and two shotguns—stolen from the Western Auto store in Marianna. He was charged with burglary, possession of stolen property, and parole violation. Back he went to Cummins Prison, this time for eight months. After several months in prison, he wrote a letter to the Lee County prosecutor asking for leniency:

"I've been classified as a two time loser and therefore I must serve ½ of my prison sentence and I have 18 years left on parole as of now. If the judge in Marianna give me any prison sentence then I'll be classified as a three time loser and therefore, I'll be compel to serve ¾ of my sentence. Mr. Prosecutor, if I can obtain a 1 year sentence or a suspended sentence then I'll be eligible for Parole within 5 or 6 years . . .''

As his court date neared, Larry decided to appeal to a power higher than the county prosecutor. He wrote to the FBI, in Little Rock and Washington, advising the bureau that "the Lee County sheriffs may try to harm me in some form." Larry's tactics did not hurt: he received the suspended sentence he had requested. (Years later, he acknowledged that he never felt threatened by the local authorities; he "just wanted to let them know not to try anything.")

Upon his release from Cummins in May of 1980, Larry resumed his budding career as a jewel thief. Through trial and error, he had honed his technique to a point of near flawlessness.

"I used to go into a small-town jewelry store, *any* small-town jewelry store in Arkansas, and ask to see turquoise rings. Now of course I knew Arkansas stores didn't carry turquoise, but they'd always ask me if I'd like to look at something else. That gave me an opening to browse the entire store. I'd check which cases were wired with alarms (usually only the higher-priced stuff was wired up), where the infrared lights were, the rear exits, and also what the inventory looked like. Then I'd leave and call them to find out what time they close. They'd say five or whatever and then I'd wait again until nine and call again and make sure nobody's working late. Meanwhile, I'm checking out the town. Seeing where the police station is, where I can park my car on the outskirts, figure out my escape route. The worst thing is to go into a town and not know where to run.

"After nine I'd climb up on the roof—usually the buildings were no taller than two or three stories. The roof was usually some sort of soft asphalt with an under-layer of asbestos. I'd use a pickax and cut a square big enough to climb down through. That didn't take five minutes. First I'd clean out everything but the real expensive stuff, stick that up on the roof, and then go back for the jewelry that would set off the alarm."

For fifteen months or so, Larry made his living this way. He sold the goods to a "fence man," who in turn sold to an out-of-state fence. Larry cannot recall precisely how many jewelry stores he robbed during this period, but he takes pride that he was never caught. "How many counties in Arkansas?" he asked a visitor. "Seventy-five? I think I hit most of them. Some twice."

His string of successes continued uninterrupted through the following summer, until the day he bumped into a prison buddy in Little Rock. "This guy named Tisdale pops up and says he's making a killing forging prescriptions," Larry says. "He goes from drugstore to drugstore and picks up whatever he can get, mostly T's and blues." Tisdale invited Larry "along for the ride" one day. After a couple of scores in small towns southwest of Little Rock, the pair stopped in Benton, a town of nineteen thousand people off Interstate 30 between Hot Springs and Little Rock. After a successful visit to the Smith-Caldwell Drug Store, Tisdale directed Larry to wait in the car while he dropped into the West Side Pharmacy.

Just as Tisdale slipped out of view, a police car arrived. The officer "gave me a good hard look," Larry says. "I got nervous and took off." The police officer followed, and Larry and Tisdale wound up in the Benton city jail. Larry jumped bail and headed for the hometown of another Cummins Prison alumnus. He and his old friend broke into the post office and stole the money-order machine—a license to print money. Then, for good measure, they planned to rob the local jewelry store. Just before the heist, Larry's friend begged off. Larry was unbowed. "I robbed it anyway."

It was the fall of 1981. There were arrest warrants out for Larry in Benton for jumping bail and in Marianna for violating the conditions of the suspended sentence he received in 1980. He hightailed it to Detroit.

He was there three days when his accomplice telephoned from Arkansas. "He asked me did I have any money orders," Larry recalls. "I had told him *never* to discuss business over the phone, but he said he was desperate. Said he had cashed and spent every-thing I'd left him. Said he wanted to come to Detroit right away.

"So the guy called me when he got to Detroit. Said, 'I *got* to have some money orders.' I say, 'I told you not to talk business on the phone.' I told him to meet me at this hotel in Highland Park and he shows up with this guy he says is his uncle. Never said nothing about no uncle before. I was already nervous, but that did it. Told 'em to get lost.".

That's when the "uncle" showed Larry his badge. He was an undercover U.S. Postal Service inspector with whom Larry's ac-complice had cooperated (the phone calls were taped) in exchange for reduced prison time. Larry was charged and convicted of theft of government property and sentenced to four years in federal prison.

His first days as a prisoner were spent at the El Reno, Okla-homa, medium-security institution. He had turned thirty-two a week before arriving. He was determined to make the most of his time there—federal prisons offered a variety of activities and classes—but the long arm of the Marianna law had reached even into prison to restrict him. The Lee County arrest warrant issued in the wake of his detention in Benton surfaced in his prison file; under federal Bureau of Prisons policy he could not continue in prison classes until the outstanding warrant had been removed. In a handwritten motion to vacate the warrant, Larry told the Lee County Circuit Court that the classes at El Reno "will make the petitioner a better human being once he return back to society." He added: "The petitioner have no desire at all to return back to the state of Arkansas to live nor visit." Perhaps relieved that Larry would no longer seek refuge in or prey upon Lee County, the judge granted the motion.

Larry was not long for El Reno, anyway. Once again he took issue with the quality of the cuisine. "There were bugs in it, roaches," he says a decade hence, his mouth curling as if he could still see the offending plate. A hunger strike later, he was trans-ferred to the maximum-security U.S. penitentiary at Leavenworth, a limestone fortress capped by a silver dome jutting a hundred and fifty feet above the undulant cornfields and cattle farms of eastern Kansas.

Larry's time at Leavenworth was not without profit. It provided ample opportunity for exchanging ideas on criminal technique and refining his own. He learned from a California mobster about risk-reward ratio, and decided then and there that robbing a small-town jewelry store—even if it was "like taking candy from a baby"—was no longer worth the payoff. He cultivated friendships with such men: drug smugglers and bank robbers, embezzlers and money launderers. He was small-time next to these felons ("Guys you read about!"), and he listened with awe to stories of their exploits.

"These guys were motivational," Larry says, "like the tent preachers or TV preachers. They [the preachers] make their money off poor folks, their diamond rings and houseboats and all, but no use you gettin' none. Just suppose to put your faith in the Almighty, whether you got food on the table or not. But these guys here [at Leavenworth], their mentality was different. It was like everyone else gettin' theirs, you oughta get yours!"

Larry, of course, shared their views, and it validated his own philosophy of life to hear such convictions from accomplished professionals. Any doubt he had about resuming his criminal career (and there was, to be truthful, little) was in remission long before his release. "I ain't never been too crazy about work anyway, and I knew an ex-con getting out ain't gonna do much better than some little-old job chopping cotton or pushing a broom for minimum wage."

Physically Larry changed too. He modified his diet, becoming a puritanical vegetarian, declining any drugs or liquor, refusing even to drink coffee. He worked out regularly, lifting weights and practicing yoga, teaching the discipline to other prisoners. And he learned how to make money—above the eleven cents an hour he earned working in the prison shoe factory.

Through a variety of enterprises—gambling, gaming, and liquor sales mostly; a little loan-sharking on the side Larry earned almost fifty thousand tax-free dollars during his stay at Leavenworth. One of his favorite income-producers was a game called "Words" in which poker-faced players bet they knew the dictionary definition of a particular word. It was not unusual for Larry, who had read voraciously since his earliest days behind bars—who had read even the dictionary when nothing else (save the Bible) was available—to walk away from the table with hundreds of dollars in cash or IOUs. "Take *occidental*," Larry says by way of example. "I might lay maybe only ten dollars that I know what it means. That way I get somebody to raise me, because *he* don't know it but he thinks I don't know it either—that I'm bluffing. So next round I lay maybe fifty or a hundred [dollars], tell him what it means, hand him the dictionary with one hand, and take his money with the other."

In November of 1984, Larry was released from Leavenworth and mandatorily transferred to the Arkansas Department of Corrections, under whose custody he was to serve the final six months of his sentence. On April 29, 1985, thirty nine months after he was incarcerated, Larry walked out of the Arkansas State Prison a free man.

He went home to Lee County, where he and Billy Joe became reacquainted. The two were a dozen years apart in age; Billy was only seven when Larry was first jailed. But at twenty-two Billy had surpassed his brother in the things in life that mattered: money and women. Billy felt almost paternal about the older brother he barely knew; he was happy to help Larry get a fresh start.

Billy's recollections of seeing Larry were mostly in prison and jail visiting rooms. "Me and my twin the ones who used to go see him at Grady [Cummins Prison] with my mama and daddy. We used to go at least three or four times a year."

Billy had been home since the previous October, lying low and enjoying himself there as never before. Sure, he would return to Detroit sometime, but he was in no hurry. Life in the slow lane was fine for right now. He had come back to Arkansas with loads of cash, and whenever he needed more, his brother David, to whom Billy had entrusted the family business, wired it down. "Four thousand, five, six, whatever, David would send it," Billy says. And David took care of Billy's girlfriends. Diana and Niece and another of Billy's steadies named Ceecee all flew down to Arkansas for visits, courtesy of David. All told, David sent Billy close to sixty thousand dollars over a nine-month period.

Billy palled around mostly with his old friend Romia Hall. The two had grown up together in La Grange and had kept in close touch over the years. Romia was a frequent visitor to Detroit, and would stay either with Billy or with Jerry Gant, who was Romia's half-brother. Romia was an emergency medical technician who worked for a Marianna ambulance service. Billy found he liked to ride with Romia on his rounds so much that he began driving the ambulance as a volunteer. Billy had never before volunteered for anything and would have continued to work for free, had not Romia's boss insisted on putting him on the payroll. "He liked me," Billy recalls, "because I didn't mind driving to Little Rock or Memphis or wherever the peoples needed to go. Other people didn't like to drive that far."

Whenever Billy and Romia had a couple or three days off, they were on the road again: to St. Louis or Six Flags Over Texas or back to Memphis or Little Rock. "We *stayed* gone," Romia says. "That's what made it so great to have Billy around. I was working and he had plenty of money and it was all just real cool."

As for Larry, being home did not whet his appetite for work; it stimulated only a desire to taste for himself the fruits of his younger brothers' success in Detroit. After a month or so of relaxing and eating his mother's tasty, bug-free cooking, and especially of hearing Billy's fantastic tales of the streets and of the enormous sums of money to be made from the crack trade—a trade that didn't even exist in American cities at the time Larry went to federal prison three years earlier, but a trade in which the risk-reward ratio was acceptable—Larry was eager to join the wing of the family thriving in Detroit. Willie was still there, as were Danny and David and Little Joe. And their sister Delois, who had married an old friend of Larry's from Marianna, was in town as well. She told Larry there was a couch for him to sleep on. That was all he needed to hear.

Larry took it easy during his first months in town. He roamed during the day, to the suburban malls, beaches, parks. At night he went to jazz or rap clubs. He knew few people outside his family, and he wasn't yet comfortable socially with his brothers and sisters, so he usually went out alone. By the fall, Larry had familiarized himself with the city; he was lonely, and bored with wandering aimlessly. He decided to go back to school. "I'd learned Spanish in prison and wanted to keep at it," he says. (A year or so later he would acquire a pit bull, Pancho, which he commanded in Spanish exclusively: *¡ándale!* or *¡ven aquí!* or *¡bájate!*) He enrolled at Wayne State University in Detroit, where he also studied guitar and clarinet, instruments he had dabbled with in Leavenworth.

And he fell in love with a young woman. Her name was Belinda Lumpkin. She was fifteen; he thirty-five. Belinda had light, almost golden skin and wide, expressive eyes. She was slim and long-limbed; at five-seven or so, she was several inches taller than Larry. She lived only a block away, and her sister lived two houses down Knodell Street from Larry's. "I used to wolf whistle at her in the street," Larry says. The timeless strategem worked to perfection. He invited himself to Belinda's sister's house and impressed her and Belinda's other relatives with his suavity and his billfold. He showered Belinda with gifts; before she was old enough to drive he bought her a new sports car, a red Toyota MR-2.

Larry financed his love life with what remained of the jewelry he'd stolen years earlier in Arkansas, and with the nearly fifty thousand in cash he'd accumulated in prison. The money and the jewelry did not last long. What Larry didn't spend on himself or Belinda was consumed by his brother Danny's drug habit. The Chambers brothers all had their vices, but with the exception of Danny, a year younger than Larry, the use of hard drugs was not among them. "Crack," says Larry, "messes up your mentality, your body, it makes your soul crazy." Danny was unconcerned about such consequences. "He was just a fiend then," Billy recalls. "He was shooting up so much dope [heroin] and smoking so much crack that he took most of Larry's jewelry and pawned it."

Once his own funds were tapped out, Larry's brothers supported him handsomely. David invited him to move into the downstairs portion of a two-family house he owned at 10480 Knodell, a side street off Gratiot Avenue, the city's northeast artery. The property was among those David Chambers bought during his brief run of prosperity. The duplex wasn't much from the outside: its faux yellow-brick siding was peeling, and the rotting front porch was in need of skillful carpentry.

But the inside was clean and roomy. Both the upstairs and downstairs flats had two bedrooms, and the basement was finished; it too had two bedrooms as well as a washer and dryer. David bought it for forty-five hundred dollars. He had planned to rent it out, but upon decorating it, the house turned out so smartly that David decided to live there himself.

David moved to Knodell in the spring of 1985. Once he got around to furnishing the downstairs flat—he lived upstairs—Larry moved in. Larry had ridden the couch circuit for a couple of weeks, first at Delois's, then Willie's. He was happy to have his own place; privacy for him was a commodity in scant supply.

Billy stopped by the house regularly. "How ya doin' today?" he'd ask and hand Larry a wad of bills. It wasn't long before Larry tired of the handouts; he disliked depending on "my younger brothers for every dime in my pocket." He adds: "I was being treated like a kid, or a ex-con who couldn't support myself." Sometime around the end of 1985, he asked David for one last gift—ten thousand dollars. By then he had spent enough time around his brothers and their inner circles to learn the basics of dealing crack. "I'm ready to roll," Larry announced to David.

CHAPTER SIX

MOVING LIKE LIGHTNING

Detroit had changed in the nine months Billy Joe was away. He returned, somewhat reluctantly, only when it became apparent that his well of money had ceased gushing. When Billy had exiled himself in the fall of 1984, he left his brother David in charge of the Newport Street crack house. At the time, the house was "pumping" vast sums of money: thirty-five thousand dollars a day.

David and Billy had never been especially close; David was something of a loner, while Billy liked—*needed*—to be around—no, *surrounded by*—friends and admirers. They had only begun spending time together shortly before Billy had left for Arkansas the previous fall. At the time, David expressed little interest in the drug business. He had recently been discharged from the army and had moved to Detroit to be near his siblings. He enrolled in a technical college and from time to time would bring his classmates over to Billy's to party.

On those occasions he began to recognize in Billy something he hadn't seen before. It was something more than the liquor, the dope, the money, the latest music that Billy offered in abundance. It was that his kid brother had grown up, had developed a sense of style, a charisma, that left his friends spellbound. "Before," says Billy, "I was just me, the younger brother, that was it. But then he started coming around and bringing his friends and his college womens. They'd drink some Bud, some Miller, maybe some Hennessy, smoke a couple joints, and when they'd leave I give them an ounce." And then David's friends began asking David to invite Billy over to his place. "The girls was downright crazy about me; I'm knocking them off left and right. And he sees that, and it's like from there he starts hanging out with me more."

But David was not interested in selling dope. Not yet, anyway. He *did* enjoy the imprimatur of his famous last name. ("You ain't *really* BJ's brother, is you?") David was ex-army, a high school graduate, and not a bad student at the technical college. The post office surely would have a job; Willie would put in a word! But David never got around to taking the postal service exam; instead, he took a low-risk but relatively high-paying job as a chauffeur with Billy's organization. "He took us anywhere we wanted to go," Billy says. "He didn't know where he was taking us or what was the situation. He didn't want to. He'd drive a guy to a house, wait out there while he goes in and talks or cops or whatever, and then drop him here or there. We'd give him three, four, five hundred dollars every week. And that was it."

With Billy's departure for Marianna, David had stepped out of his kid brother's shadow. He took charge of the booming Newport Street house, and with Billy's old standby Jerry Gant, whom Billy had asked to advise David, promptly expanded, opening several new locations, hiring employees, and acquiring real estate all over the east side. With the cash flowing steadily to Arkansas, Billy believed he could depend on his brother for sustenance as long as he wished. By the summer of 1985, though, David began telling Billy he could no longer support him. "I'm not doing so good as you think," David told him. Billy never asked him where the money went; he figured it didn't matter.

When Billy returned, crack was everywhere: on every block of the east-side neighborhoods he frequented, in party stores and fast-food restaurants and on street corners, in houses and apartment buildings. The change was startling. "Peoples I never thought would be hooked was ripping and running the streets wild," he says. "And peoples I never thought would be selling crack were selling it. Everything was just different, everybody acting different."

It was the middle of July. Billy and Romia Hall had driven up from Arkansas in Billy's Jeep. Their first stop was Marlborough Street, where Billy's girlfriend Diana lived. Diana and Billy's first son, Billy Joe Jr., was a week old and Billy was eager to see him. (Billy and Niece's first child, born in 1980, also was named Billy Joe Jr.) "I'm coming up Marlborough, got my sound bumping, and I notice a bunch of peoples in front of her house. Then I see [Diana's sister] Lisa pointing, 'There go Billy!' And then Diana come right up to the Jeep and first thing she says—no hello, no nothin'—'I *got* to have some money for Pampers.' And I didn't have but eight hundred on me and I gave her five hundred."

If Billy was short on funds just then, it did not take him long to be back in the money. After giving Diana the cash for the baby's needs, he headed to David's house. David gave him one last bundle: six thousand dollars. Much of that money would go to employees of David's who claimed Billy owed them back wages. "Soon as I'm back, I got all these fellas worrying me to death," Billy says. They would see his car approaching and run out in the middle of the street.

"BJ, I haven't been paid in two months," they'd tell him, or "BJ, you owe me money."

"I owe you money for what?"

"I been working in one of your spots."

"Hey, you wasn't working for me, you was working for my brother. I wasn't even here!"

But Billy would pay them all. "Three hundred to this little guy; six hundred to another."

* * *

Billy never took another cent from David. He thought he would reunite with his original crew: Jerry Gant and Boogaloo Driscoll. But Jerry and David had become partners, and Jerry also had some houses he was operating on his own. Boogaloo, meanwhile, had succumbed to the temptations of crack; Billy could no longer count on him. Instead, Billy invited one of Diana's younger brothers, Tony (Tiger) Alexander, to join him. At five and a half feet tall, Tiger was as mangy and bony as a stray dog. He was only eighteen, but he was no novice. "I was practically born on the streets," he says. "I took bikes and shit, clothes, before I was ten. Never did learn to steal no cars though."

Tiger and Billy had been acquainted for five years or so, since Billy and Diana had started dating. For Tiger's thirteenth birthday, Billy gave him a motor scooter. He used it often to run errands for Billy. "Run get me some ice cream," Billy would tell him, or "Go see So-and-So; I need to holler at him." He had worked in other capacities for Billy over the years: delivering drugs, picking up money, selling marijuana and crack at the Newport Street house. And though Billy trusted him, Tiger found himself periodically squeezed out of a job. "Every time my sister broke up with him," Tiger says of Billy, "he fired me." And yet Tiger understood that Billy Joe Chambers was the Alexander family's meal ticket. Billy put them all on the payroll at one time or another—Tiger, Diana, their two sisters and brother, even their mother. And he lavished them with cash and gifts. "Billy was the best thing that ever happened to us," Tiger says.

There was nothing Tiger would not do for Billy. He worked twenty-four hours a day in a crack house, for days on end, if Billy was short-staffed. ("It wasn't no problem," Tiger explains. "I'm a light sleeper; you knock at the door and I'm up.") It was that sort of fealty Billy sought in selecting his other crew members. He relied on friends such as Tiger to introduce him to other streetwise young men who were at once hungry and dependable.

One such fellow was a hulking sixteen-year-old named Eric Wilkins. He stood six-four and weighed around three hundred pounds; his nickname was Fats. He had huge shoulders and a goatee. He was the sort of person whose height and bulk made him look menacing without effort. Fats was born in Little Rock, where his father still lived, but his mother had raised him in Detroit. He was a friend of Tiger's. "Fats was always asking me to let him work," Billy says. "And I always told him no; I didn't need him right then. And then he'd get Tiger to talk to me: 'He trustworthy; he'll do good.' Fats would tell me how down on his luck he was, and how he really needed a job bad. And then one day something happened, I don't know exactly what, to make me tell Tiger, 'Go get him.' "

"That's how it always be," Billy continues. "Like a fella will bring a lady over and say, 'BJ, I think you can trust her.' And once I trust her, she bring me one or two other girls or might even bring her mama over. 'BJ, my mama can do certain things for you.' And that's how I built a chain of people. Somebody knew somebody's brother or mama or daddy. They'd say, 'He cool. He don't want really much. He's not gonna worry you.' "

Within a month of returning to the city, Billy had his crew in place. Besides Tiger and Fats, there were guys named EZ and Shawn and Lamont, and two Marlborough Street neighbors of Tiger's, Tate and Fresh. "What put me on the map was that these guys was really eager to work hard and make money," Billy says. "True, I wanted to make money, but I already owned my own houses, had my own ride, a fine stereo, some of the prettiest womens in the neighborhood. And so these younger fellas, they was eager to become something, and off we go."

It was Billy's idea to start small, to open one outlet on Marlborough and one on Eastlawn, a block west of the house on Newport Billy had bequeathed to David. He would hire a few young women to cook, cut, and package the cocaine, his crew would work in shifts, and he would tend to administrative duties. It would be profitable, but low key, centralized, manageable. And by his staying small, the police were unlikely to bother him.

But the crew members were thinking on a different scale.

"They wanted to work the houses, plus open up a couple of houses for themselves," Billy says. "I found out the fellas had really got sophisticated since I was gone. So I just went along with them—they was really directin' me." Still, his crew understood Billy was the boss; according to Tiger, they wouldn't have had it any other way. "It take one brain to make money, that was BJ," says Tiger. "He knew the shots to call but he still treated you good. It wasn't like he'd come up to you like some other rollers and say, 'Fuck you, shine my shoes.'"

Billy's willingness to adjust his business plan was based largely on respect for his crew—they convinced him he hadn't yet grasped the degree to which crack had taken hold in the time he was in Arkansas. When they insisted they could move much more product than Billy envisioned—"He needed to be woke up is all it was," says Tiger, "like he was sleepin' under a rock all that year down south"—he yielded to their judgment. He gave each of them two houses of their own; each in turn opened two more houses for which each did his own hiring. Billy served as chief executive officer. He dealt with suppliers, real estate agents, automobile dealers, and, in his own fashion, oversaw accounting and payroll logs. ("It wasn't no hell of a record to keep up with," he says. "I made this much, I lost this much, I spent this much, and I add it up.")

Billy's faith in his crew's market analysis was well founded. Almost immediately, their initial two houses were grossing about ten thousand dollars daily. Within a month, with six houses operating all day, every day—"twenty-four/seven"—the operation was "pumping big-time"—between sixty thousand and seventy thousand dollars a day.

Operating six houses around the clock required constant communication. This was accomplished through cellular telephones ("Our cars all had three-thousand-dollar sound systems and phones," Tiger says), electronic pagers, and daily staff meetings. "I beep the fellas and they call me right back and I tell 'em where to meet me," Billy explains. "It might be someone's grandma's house or at Chandler Park or Belle Isle, or wherever I happened to be. It might even be twice-a-day meetings. And some days we might not meet at all. And it might be any time, because sometimes I'm moving from twelve o'clock at night till six o'clock in the morning. And after that, I'm not gonna see them no more maybe till twelve o'clock at night the next day. Or if everything's going pretty smooth, don't have no headaches or nothing, might be twelve o'clock in the daytime before I see them again."

The meetings kept Billy abreast of each house's problems, inventory, and balance sheet, and they allowed him to gauge his crew's morale. "One of 'em might make a request for more dope for his houses," Billy recalls. "And so I'd get that arranged. And another guy might say he needs some security over at his house, because there are guys robbing his customers, sticking them up in the cars. Or one guy's workers are cutting their rocks. Like we'll be knowing the rocks we're selling should be moving real hard, and they're just not." If that recurred, says Billy, he or another crew member would buy "undercover" from the salespeople in question. "I might buy three rocks and come back two hours later and buy four more and come back two or three hours later and buy three or four more. That way I got good samples; I *know* if they trying to sell you a five-dollar rock sliced in half."

Once old business was dispensed with, the meetings were part motivational business seminar—the inspirational leader imparting can-doism, exhorting his sales force to work harder, think smarter, serve the customer better. And the meetings were part boys' club—piquant comments on one or another's latest sexual conquest. Billy: "One guy might say, 'Well, I made twenty-three [thousand] yesterday'; another guy, 'I made eighteen but I finally got down with the freak I was tellin' all of y'all about!' And there might be another guy who didn't make but eight or nine and he might feel bad. So I'd tell him not to worry about it, there'll be better days."

Operating six houses around the clock also required a constant flow of cocaine. Billy's principal supplier the previous year was the fellow he knew as Twin. In 1984, Twin had come through in the pinch when Billy was searching desperately for cocaine during that hectic Fourth of July. But a year later, when Billy's new crew was in place and his new houses were operational, word had it that Twin had become another dealer unable to resist the lure of his own product. That made Twin a threat. "I didn't sleep easy at night knowing Twin was using," Billy says. "We had to cut him out of the picture. He wasn't dangerous because there was plenty of money on the streets right then, so he didn't have to stick *you* up. But after a while, you knew he was gonna stick *somebody* up. Didn't matter if you were one of the well-knowndest persons in the city."

Billy needed someone reliable, a nonsmoker, someone he would not lose sleep over. Someone like his old friend Perry Coleman.

Late in 1984 or early in 1985, Perry had begun working as an independent supplier—a wholesaler. He bought most of his cocaine in kilos from a "weight man"—a volume dealer—named Sam Curry. Curry had climbed to about as lofty a perch as possible for an African-American in the local cocaine hierarchy. He was an importer, or at least had ties to importers. He dealt with a fellow Detroiter who dealt with a Cuban in Miami who in turn dealt with a Colombian there.

Billy had no interest in dealing directly with Cubans or Colombians—no matter how much money he might save per kilo. He would buy only from people he knew; if Perry or Sam Curry wanted to deal with "the fellas in Miami," that was fine—so long as they kept him out of it. An ironclad rule held that his crew was not to introduce him to people indiscriminately. "If I didn't need to meet nobody," he says, "I didn't *wanna* meet nobody."

By the time Billy's crew "started elevating ourselves" in the summer of 1985, Perry's contacts with Curry and others were sufficient to guarantee that Billy would not have to negotiate with outsiders; that if, for instance, Curry became indisposed, or his current product was inferior, or if Perry's balance with Curry was outstanding, Perry could "cop" from any of three or four other weight dealers.

These were not theoretical circumstances. Months earlier, for instance, Detroit police had raided Curry's east-side residence. They found a kilo and a half of cocaine and, in a safe, a hundred and ninety-two thousand dollars in cash. (Also in the safe was a slip of paper with the name and phone number of a "Perry" and a notation that Perry owed Sam seventy-two thousand dollars. The name was unknown to the police; they filed it for later use.) A grand jury indicted Curry, and although he was confined only briefly before making bail, his downtime was such that Perry turned to interim suppliers.

Weight dealers on the east side generally saw one another not as rivals but as allies crucial to survival. The alliances could not be readily diagrammed; they were fragile and complicated and shifting constantly. But there were some truisms. One was that if one dealer's shipment did not arrive on schedule, he could invoke professional privilege to ensure fulfillment of his regular customers' orders. "They were a syndicate of acquaintances," says Melvin Turner, the Wayne County undersheriff. "If one couldn't get the dope in, another weight man would sell to him at cost." (These alliances eventually went awry. By 1990, every weight dealer who worked the east side during the mid-eighties was either imprisoned or dead.)

More often than not, as Curry's legal problems intensified, Perry bought his dope from a weight man named Arthur Derrick. Derrick worked with Curry; they had become partners in February of 1985, just two weeks before police stormed Curry's house in a predawn raid. Curry's business had been booming; many of the east-side dealers—from kids peddling two-dollar rocks at stoplights to wholesalers like Perry—beat a path to Curry's door. His problem was not the demand; it was supply. Because he dealt with a succession of middlemen, he faced numerous and repetitive problems, mostly regarding the seepage of his money or his cocaine along the leaky human pipeline from Colombia to Detroit and back.

So Curry invited Art Derrick to join him. Derrick himself had been in the supply business for years. He had the Latin American connections that Curry lacked, and Curry had the deeper customer base in Detroit. Curry turned over to Derrick the bulk of the day-to-day responsibilities for the business. ("It got so Sam wouldn't even touch the stuff," Derrick says.) The two made an odd couple, but a singularly well-matched one. Derrick, a white man, stood six feet and weighed a portly two hundred and twenty-five pounds; he looked like the guy on the next stool at the shot-and-beer joint. He had a bloated, pockmarked face, droopy mustache, and a graying, wiry pompadour; for a thirty-one-year-old he had not aged well.

Curry was short, and at a hundred and fifty pounds, stocky, with a light brown complexion. He was rarely spotted without flashy clothes and a bulky gold chain around his neck. His confident swagger was appropriate for a man in his middle thirties on top of his chosen profession, a man successful beyond his dreams.

Unlike the Chambers brothers or Perry Coleman or Sam Curry, Derrick's initial interest in cocaine was as a consumer. At twenty-one he owned a retail television store in Grosse Pointe Woods. He worked sixteen-hour days and earned a hundred thousand a year during the mid-seventies. It was during those years of interminable work (and income) that Derrick first experimented with drugs. It relieved the monotony, enabled him to put in the long hours. "I was using a lot of pills," he says, "and then I got into cocaine."

At first he bought it for personal use. "And then guys I started snorting it with wanted to buy a little pack. So I started selling to them in small quantities. And then you find out how much money's involved in dealing, and you just get hung up in it. Plus, when you're using it, you want it around *all the time*. I mean I was snorting a half-ounce a day. *Great* stuff too, I mean the best—right from Cali [Colombia]."

Years later, when Sam Curry was moving as much cocaine as anyone in Detroit, everyone, it seemed, wanted a piece of his action. But nobody else had the contacts Art Derrick did; his link to the product was forged a decade before cocaine was widely affordable. Heroin was the ghetto drug; cocaine, in powder form, was for the elite.

But that was B.C.—before crack. Once crack recast the Detroit cocaine market, Derrick's Colombian contacts became especially useful. "You're only as strong as your connection," goes one
of his favorite maxims. "That's it in this business, the whole thing.
I mean you have to have brains to run it here, but your brain's no
good if you can't get the stuff. Me, I knew a Colombian in Miami
with unlimited access and who could supply me as much as I
wanted. So he starts shipping, and all of a sudden everybody's calling me because I'm the guy."

Together Curry and Derrick made an effective team. Although Derrick had lost his "connec" by the time they hooked
up—the Colombian "disappeared" one day—Curry still needed
Derrick's expertise. Curry was enduring significant losses on every
shipment and he realized that Derrick knew his way along the pipeline as well as anyone in the city. Among the first concepts Derrick
explained to Curry was that skimming at each stop along the way
did not have to be a cost of doing business.

"When Sam brought me on," Derrick recalls, "I said, 'Fuck
these middlemen.' I mean we were just paying too much money
for this stuff. We were moving a lot of product and everybody else
was selling it at the same price we're paying for it. Plus, things were
coming up short. The Cubans [the middlemen] were going into
the packages on the way up. They would skim anywhere from an
eight ball [a hundred and twenty-five grams, or an eighth of a kilo]
to maybe a couple ounces. When we weighed it, we would tell
them how much it was short and take out the difference when we
paid them. They were telling us the dope shortages were the
Colombian's fault and they were telling the Colombian the money
shortages were our fault. We just got fed up with it. So we cut the
Cuban guys out."

The matter came to a head when one of the Cubans came to
Derrick for a $450,000 payment. His reply was audacious. "I told
him, 'I'm tired of fucking with you; I want to meet the main guy.
If the guy wants his money, you tell him to call me, because you
ain't gettin' it.'"

The Cuban retreated to Miami. A short while later, Derrick

heard from the Colombian. Derrick flew down to see him. "I told him what the fuck was going on," Derrick says. "And he tells me, 'We don't need this fucking guy, from now on we'll deal direct.' " Derrick's instinct was sound; years of experience had taught him "who could be fucked with and who couldn't." He adds: "If this Cuban had been a real killer, if he had a real crew, I would have been fucked. But you learn who's real over time."

By the end of 1985, Art Derrick and Sam Curry were the biggest weight dealers in Detroit. In addition to the Chambers brothers, Curry and Derrick supplied the city's other leading crack dealers. They "fed" Richard Wershe, Jr., aka "White Boy Rick," who was then all of fifteen years old ("He was almost like a son to me," Derrick says) and who is presently serving a life sentence without parole for cocaine trafficking; they fed Richard (Maserati Rick) Carter, who in 1988 was shot to death in his hospital bed, where he was recovering from earlier gunshot wounds; and they fed Demetrius Holloway, who was gunned down in 1990 while shopping in a downtown clothing store.

Derrick estimates that he and Curry *netted* a hundred thousand dollars a day for more than two and a half years. They usually sold seven to ten kilos daily; one day they sold twenty-five keys, eighteen of which Maserati Rick bought. That was a record. With the unfathomable riches came, for Derrick especially, the requisite lavish lifestyle. He conducted most of his business from the basement office of his home, a brick ranch house in Harper Woods, less than a mile from the northeasternmost limits of Detroit. The house itself was immodest for its environs—it spanned thirty-four hundred square feet. But it was the renovations that truly set it apart from the others in the largely working-class neighborhood. Derrick poured four hundred and fifty thousand dollars into refurbishings—three thousand alone for the front door. The property was enclosed by an electrified seven-foot white brick wall; in the backyard was a swimming pool with the initials AD laid in tile on the bottom. Derrick worked at an ornate desk in the basement.

The room's floor was white marble, its walls and ceiling mirrored.

Derrick lived for a rush. Selling cocaine, snorting cocaine, speed of travel, any sort of peril—all made life worthwhile. He owned a Corvette and a speedboat. What made him happiest was flying. He owned four planes: a Cessna 421 twin engine, a JetStar 420 Gulf jet, and two converted World War II bombers, one of which belonged previously to the Rolling Stones. The B-26 Liberator had picture windows and was painted black, with a silver lightning bolt along the side. Derrick himself was not a pilot. He says he could not have adequately savored the experience at the controls.

Instead he "bought the best pilots money could buy," one of whom was a retired air force pilot named Marvin Knecht. Knecht, a Texan, recalled in a 1988 deposition the first time he met Derrick. He had flown the JetStar from Houston to Detroit, where Derrick met him on the ramp at Metro Airport.

"Let's go to Chicago and have dinner," Derrick said.

Later he would direct Knecht to more exotic dining locales: Miami and Palm Springs were nice; Las Vegas a favorite. Derrick grew so fond of Vegas he bought a penthouse condominium at the Jockey Club.

During Knecht's first flight to Miami for Derrick, Knecht's co-pilot mentioned to Knecht that "Art wants to get married in the airplane."

"He can get married in the airplane," Knecht replied, "just clean it up, make it look nice . . ."

"You don't understand," the co-pilot said. "He wants to get married while it's airborne circling over Detroit."

Knecht dutifully flew Derrick and his fiancée to Miami to pick up the best man. Two days later, after the groomsmen, including Knecht and his co-pilot, were fitted for white tuxedos, the happy couple took their vows before twenty witnesses at fifteen hundred feet. Detroit City Airport reportedly closed for forty-five minutes during the ceremony. How, he was asked, was that permitted? Says Derrick: "We were good customers."

* * *

Derrick's best customer was Billy Joe Chambers. And if Billy wasn't the biggest crack dealer in Detroit by the end of 1985, says Derrick, he was well on his way—with Derrick's help. "They [BJ and crew] had a big engine, but an engine doesn't work without fuel," goes another of Derrick's maxims. "I'm the guy who fueled 'em." But Derrick is just as quick to give Billy credit. "It was a team effort," he says. "The guy could move the dope like no one I ever saw."

At first Billy was buying only a kilo at a time, for which the going rate was fifty thousand dollars. Within a month, as Billy's operation expanded to six houses, he began buying multiple kilos; by the end of the year Billy was buying from seven to ten kilos a week, at a price that had plummeted to as low as eighteen thousand dollars.

Though the two did millions of dollars of business together over nearly three years, Billy Joe Chambers and Art Derrick never met on the street. They worked exclusively through Perry—Derrick was as suspicious as Billy about meeting new faces. "I knew Perry," Derrick explains. "He was their supplier, their guy to hook up the dope. So why should I meet BJ or anybody else if I know Perry? It's just another guy you don't need to meet. If Perry had asked me to meet BJ, I'd have told him no. If I'm selling to you, why would you want to introduce me to the guy you're selling to? You'd just be cutting yourself out of it; why would you cut your own throat? I'd figure it's because you got busted and you wanted to introduce me to an agent to work yourself out of the case."

Anytime Billy gave Perry the word to buy, Perry would call Curry to talk price. Then Curry would beep Derrick. "Sam would tell me, ' "P-Boy" needs three,' Derrick says, "or however many [kilos] it was. Then I'd beep my runner and tell him to get this over to P." Each kilo was encased in thick plastic covering, almost like fiberglass, and wrapped in yellow duct tape.

As for the money, Derrick says he and Billy had an understanding. "We worked up front with them a lot. We'd give them the coke and then he [Perry] would drop the money at my house or Sam's. A lot of times it was short, but they always made good. Let's say P-Boy told us, 'Here's two hundred thou,' and we'd count and there'd be, maybe, a hundred and ninety-three—seven short. So we'd call 'em up and say, 'Hey, you're seven thousand short.' And they'd say, 'Don't worry about it, we'll make it up.' And sometimes they were over. And we'd call 'em and tell 'em that too. What it came down to was we were counting their money for them. Mostly small bills. Did you ever see eighty thousand dollars in singles? That's how the guys were paying me. I burned out a *lot* of money-counting machines."

During the latter part of 1985, Perry delivered most of the cocaine he bought for Billy to the duplex David Chambers owned at 10480 Knodell. Until then, Larry and his girlfriend Belinda had remained in residence downstairs. Larry not only lived there, but with the ten-thousand-dollar grant from David and the supplier connections his brothers had, he also converted the flat to his first sales outlet.

Late in the year, Larry and Belinda moved out of Knodell. "He was moving like lightning," Billy recalls of Larry's first days in the business. "One day I'm hearing he's over here, then he's buying a house over there, and one there, and one there. I was glad because he was straight up out of our hair."

Larry and Belinda moved to a house David owned on Buffalo Street, near Mound and Six Mile. (They were soon joined by Belinda's brother James, a straitlaced community college student who was two years older than Belinda. James was putting himself through school by working nights as a salesman at Sears in a suburban mall.) No sooner did Larry vacate the lower flat on Knodell than Billy converted it to a clubhouse, or "meet house," for his crew. It was, says Billy, "a place we could all get together and we knew we'd be safe. Nobody would bring narcotics or guns or money, so if ten police vans pulled up, they'd just be wasting their time. We just came there to talk, chill, sit on the porch, and maybe do nothin' for three or four hours."

The house also nominally became home for Billy. He had been without a home of his own for the several months he had been back in town. In fact, he had rarely slept more than two consecutive nights in the same bed. "I'd spend a couple nights at Diana's, a couple nights at Niece's, then maybe one with Ceecee, then a couple nights on Newport, and maybe a couple nights at a motel."

Even after he moved to Knodell, he would as often as not stay at one of his girlfriends' houses. Situated directly across the street, no more than fifty feet or so from the house, on a corner lot that faced Gratiot, was a McDonald's restaurant. Billy and his crew often hung out there, lingering for hours while becoming fast friends with the employees, particularly the many young women. At shift's end, the flirting would switch to the house, where uninterrupted parties became a given. And it wasn't just, say, the lunch-shift employees who would migrate from work to Billy's house upon punching out; it was everybody. Around-the-clock drinking, dancing, weed smoking. The place was overrun. Some of the women kept their civilian clothes there and washed their dirty uniforms in the basement. Eventually many of the night-shift workers wound up sleeping at the house; it made more sense than trying to catch a late-night bus home. They had the run of the house. "Once my day was over with, I'd go on back home," Billy says. "I'd call Niece and have her to come pick me up. And she'd be mad because I ain't been home for two days. Or I'd catch a cab over to Diana's. Mostly all the fellas would leave out of Knodell, and we'd come back the next day, and ten, fifteen, twenty womens still be there, sleeping on the floor and the couches."

Such frivolity was not conducive to business, and therefore held no appeal to Larry. Larry was as disciplined outside prison as he had been inside. Over the years in confinement, he had learned the dodge of concealing and controlling his emotions. He spoke in modulated tones, no matter whether angry or elated. He had a mellifluous voice—an overnight-radio jazz-show host's. And he was unfailingly polite, even as he readied to commit violence. Indeed, it was this strange combination of affability and fury that so frightened people; they never knew what to expect. Says one young woman who worked, briefly, for Larry: "He be smilin' and all friendly-like one minute and the next he breakin' a chair leg over your boyfriend's back."

Larry generally prefaced his conversations with the phrase "My friend." The greeting disarmed people; they would let their guard down believing he really *was* their friend. And he was—unless he detected a threat to his overwhelming need to control everything and everyone around him. "How are you, my friend?" he would inquire, or, "Hi, my friend, let's go for a ride," or, as he told one recruit: "My friend, you stick with me and we'll take this city *over*."

After years of imprisonment, of a caged existence where any form of disobedience, no matter how inconsequential, could result in an extended stay in the hole, Larry required an environment *he* could control. Control—absolute, total control—was the ticket to freedom. If Larry could build his own large-scale crack distribution organization, it would enable him, he believed, to become his own master, to break free from the cycle of petty crime and prison. He wanted never again to have to resort to burglary, or to working for anyone but himself, or, of course, to holding a conventional job. He vowed that never again would he be in a position where he would be subject to the whim of others.

Larry did not believe a truly successful business could be built by Billy's haphazard methods—lax attention to detail and discipline, constant parties and bed-hopping, consumption of liquor and pot, too much reliance on others—all of which caused a loss of control. Larry saw the way Billy's workers exploited Billy's easygoing nature; if someone shorted Billy drugs or money, he usually let the worker slide. "If a guy runs off with five thousand or ten thousand of my money, he's gonna lose in the long run," Billy explains. "Because he's gonna take the money, party with it, be broke, be back on the streets. And then I just mark him off, don't hire him back again."

Larry would react differently; he would make it clear that employee theft would not be tolerated. One former employee recalls one of Larry's favorite sayings: " 'You can have my woman, my car, my firstborn child, but don't fuck with my money.' He'd grin that grin, but you knew he wasn't kidding." Says Larry himself: "If a guy steals something—*starts* to steal something—drugs, guns, money, jewelry—I'd tell him I'll mess up his face with battery acid."

What made Larry so dangerous was that he frequently made good on his threats. Accustomed to a prison world ruled by force and violence, Larry applied those laws to the streets. The only way to get things done was to employ an iron will and an iron hand; control and intimidation, Larry believed, were the keys to accomplishment and wealth.

He says that early on in Detroit he "messed up a couple guys for one reason": to earn "a rep for fighting anyone anytime." And sure enough, his reputation for toughness would become mythical. A former worker named Von Williams says he, Larry, and a third employee, Doug E Fresh, were "just kickin' " one day. They seemed to hit it off, until Williams said something—he has no idea what—to suddenly anger Larry. Larry's eyes turned cold and hard. "I had heard you could look at him wrong and he'd shoot you," Williams says. Not exactly. Larry nodded to Fresh, who, Williams says, pulled out a pistol. As Williams recounts what happened, he hikes up a pants leg to expose some scarring just above the knee. He motions a visitor closer. And closer still. "Right here's where Marlow had me popped." (Marlow was Larry's street name.) Williams says two of his nieces and a sister also worked for Larry, selling out of a west-side house. "We was all kind of nervous around him."

The fearsome reputation served Larry well. It served also to protect Billy. Although the authorities would seek to link them as joint leaders of a monolithic enterprise, in reality the brothers' business relationship more closely resembled competitors than partners. Still, a Chambers was a Chambers, and right up until the day he learned the meaning of "conspiracy," Billy was grateful more often than not for the popular perception that the brothers worked hand in glove.

"His rep was that you better not cross him in no kind of way," Billy says. "And even though I'm [known as] a nice-type guy, word was you better not fuck with BJ because he's got a brother who will *fuck you up*." Larry wasn't the sort who, if he wanted to even a score, would necessarily hire a hit man. "He would just take 'em himself—hand-to-hand combat," Billy says. "Now he a little guy just like me, but it didn't matter how big the dude was. And so people put the mark on him he crazy. And that mean if he can't catch you, he'll catch your mama—*terrorize* her. So that right there will put a stop on anybody. They like, 'Wow, if things get out of hand, and he ain't dead, then he gonna come straight to my mama or my sister.' So everybody kind of added up what it's worth to mess with me and my brother, and what it ain't worth. They figured if you kill BJ, then you got to do Larry. And people just left me alone, and left him alone too."

CHAPTER SEVEN

MARLOW'S ONE-STOP

On the first Sunday of 1986, *The Detroit News* discovered crack. Its front-page story began:

> A superpotent, highly addictive—and medically danger-ous—new form of cocaine has begun turning up in Metro Detroit in a big way.
>
> Called "crack," it comes in small chunks rather than a powder. It is sometimes referred to as a "fast food" drug because it is made on short order and priced to appeal to teen-agers.
>
> "We started getting an increasing volume of calls about crack on the hot line about four months ago," Dr. Arnold Washton, research director of the nationwide 800-CO-CAINE help line, said last week. "The three areas we're get-ting the most calls from are New York, Los Angeles and Detroit.
>
> "Of late, the volume of calls from Detroit is nearly that of New York."

Headlined "ADDICTIVE NEW 'CRACK' COCAINE SWEEPS DE-
TROIT," the story was the first in either of the city's daily newspapers to mention crack. By then crack was hardly news to most
Detroiters; for more than a year the trade had dominated the economy of the east side. By early 1986, Billy and Larry had already
developed into something like folk heroes—the Lee Iacoccas of
the crack business—for street kids and even for some adults. Between them, they employed scores of east-side residents, with separate payrolls approaching a hundred thousand dollars a week. In
front of one woman's house one afternoon, an eight-year-old and
a nine-year-old were playing "BJ and Larry." "I'm Larry," declared the younger. "No you're not," the older kid said. "You're
BJ and *I'm* Larry."

By early 1986, Larry operated a handful of crack houses in the
neighborhood. He wanted to expand, but he believed that to open
individual houses scattered around the east side could become an
organizational nightmare. He was searching for a single, large outlet that could serve as his flagship; by the beginning of 1986 he had
found it.

The prewar building at 1350 East Grand Boulevard was a
handsome but tired red brick structure. Its name, The Broadmoor,
was carved in granite above the arched entrance. The elevator no
longer worked, the hallways were narrow, dark, and grimy, the
heating fickle. The building was horseshoe-shaped and four stories
high. It was managed by a man who Larry believed would likely be
receptive to payoffs—the man's sister dated one of Larry's lieutenants. An absentee landlord owned the building, and commandeer-
ing it would not require extensive tenant displacement: of its
fifty-two apartments, all but a half dozen or so were vacant.

The Broadmoor was decades past its prime. From the an-
tiquated building, though, which became known simply as "The
Boulevard," Larry and his lieutenants were constructing a state-of-
the-art crack empire so chillingly efficient it was as if they were
stealing chapters from the textbook of business culture. "They
were skilled entrepreneurs; they had every major business tech-

nique going for them," says William R. Coonce, the chief of the U.S. Drug Enforcement Administration in Detroit.

Sometime around the appearance of the first crack headline, the building manager spied a suspicious fellow in the lobby. "He wasn't dressed too clean and was kind of wild-looking," the manager, a man named David Havard, would later recall. Havard asked him what he was doing there; the reply was unsatisfactory. "I knew he was lying and I told him to get the hell out."

The next day the man returned with two others: Larry Chambers and Roderick Byrd, who was working as a location scout for Larry. Byrd, a college-educated Detroit native, dated Havard's sister; he had heard about the building from her. Havard answered the knock at the door. "We are working out of your building and we would like to hire your services so we won't have no trouble with the police and you," one of the three—Havard does not recall which—told Havard. Larry and his cohorts had just opened a "dime house"—ten-dollar rocks—in Apartment 101, down the hall from the manager's apartment.

As building manager, the thirty-six-year-old Havard earned two hundred and fifty dollars a week, plus free rent and telephone service. He had lived at The Boulevard since 1982, when he followed a girlfriend there. At the time, the building retained some luster. Its marble-tiled lobby still shone under fluorescent lights, the grounds were well kept, and fully half the units were occupied. There was little trouble even from the one tenant who sold drugs—heroin—from his second-floor apartment.

Havard had become the building's handyman shortly after he moved in. He was receiving General Assistance, state welfare payments for able-bodied adults, and needed additional off-the-books income. He painted apartments, changed the locks, shored up plumbing and wiring. He did good work, and the owner came to depend on him; soon he was promoted to building manager.

Havard had learned general maintenance skills from his father, a Ford worker. He began life on the west side of Detroit, but at the age of six or seven left for California with his mother following his parents' divorce. She died when he was eleven and his father reclaimed him and his three siblings, bringing them back to Detroit. David attended school through the ninth grade and had done handyman work ever since. He has the large, meaty hands of a plumber, a stubbly black-and-white beard, a stooped gait, and a mouth mostly devoid of teeth.

Havard quickly agreed to Larry's offer of a six-hundred-dollar weekly starting salary in exchange for allowing Larry continued use of Apartment 101 and, as business warranted, the use of additional apartments. "They told me all I needed to do was keep the building quiet, keep the riffraff out, and occasional other things like putting up gates and being on call for quick repairs or maintenance." After a couple of months on the job, Havard says, Larry "kicked me up to a thousand a week."

Two or three more months went by. One day Larry knocked again on Havard's door. It was opened by a short heavyset white woman, Havard's girlfriend. Patricia Middleton, who was thirty, had lived at The Boulevard since November of 1984, seven months after arriving in Detroit from a small town in southwestern Michigan. She and Havard struck up a romance (he and his previous girlfriend had since parted company), and in the spring of 1985, in April or early May, she moved into his rent-free apartment.

Pat Middleton was born in Indiana but raised across the state line on a farm in New Buffalo, Michigan, a town of twenty-eight hundred people near the Indiana border and the southernmost shores of Lake Michigan. Her parents divorced when she was five. She lived with her mother, who cleaned trailer homes and collected welfare to support Pat and four other children.

From an early age Pat figured she could do as well on her own. She ran away frequently, the last time to Indiana to be with a boyfriend. She was sixteen. When her mother finally found her, she placed Pat in a foster home. At seventeen she married. By the time she was twenty she had three children. By then, though, her marriage was over. Her husband was abusive, she says, and she was in no position to provide care for her children; she surrendered custody to a foster home and divorced her husband.

It was the summer of 1975. Pat Middleton was free of familial obligation, ready for a fresh start. One night she attended a traveling carnival. On a whim she asked for a job. She was hired to sell tickets and spent the summer on the road. She settled in the fall back in southwestern Michigan, in Paw Paw, where she met a man named Tom Middleton and "married his ugly butt." They stayed together nearly five years before she called it quits. "I got fed up and moved to Detroit," she says. "I had lived in small towns all my life and I wanted a big town I could get lost in."

She found an apartment on the city's west side and a job on the east side, as a waitress at a Big Boy restaurant on Jefferson Avenue at East Grand Boulevard. It made more sense, though, to live nearer her job. Her daily bus rode past the stately building at 1350 East Grand Boulevard. The afternoon she noticed the sign advertising a move-in special—1ST MO. RENT FREE, $200/1-BR— she hopped off the bus, knocked on the manager's door, and signed a lease for a first-floor apartment. Half a year later, she moved in with the manager, David Havard.

It was July of 1986 when Pat Middleton opened the door to her apartment to find Larry Chambers standing there. Larry asked if Havard was home. "I said no and he said he wanted to talk to me," she recalls. "He asked me if I wanted to make some money." Larry told her he would pay her eight hundred dollars a week to pick up money from four other houses he operated in the neighborhood. Middleton told him no, that she "didn't think I wanted to get involved." In that case, she says Larry told her, he would "arrange for David to have an accident." Middleton changed her mind.

Within the week, Middleton went to work as a courier. Between two and four times a week, she would pick up the money— always folded once and wrapped in rubber bands in hundred-dollar bundles and packaged in brown paper bags—from houses on Field, Canton, and Helen streets, and from a four-family flat down East Grand Boulevard. She aroused no suspicion: "I was white and chunky," she says. "I wore my Big Boy uniform and drove my AMC Concord. Police left me alone." On her first outing, Middleton picked up forty or fifty thousand dollars. On weekends, she picked up as much as two hundred thousand. She was assigned a route: "I would leave from 1350 and go to the other boulevard [house] and then I would go to Field and over on Helen and Canton." The workers at those locations would put the money in small paper bags and mark their house on the bags. She in turn placed those bags in a larger, brown grocery bag and put them in the trunk of the Concord. After her final stop, she would meet Larry at a predetermined drop-off point. Sometimes it would be a parking lot across from Chene Park, off Jefferson, or at any of a number of motels along Jefferson.

Two to three weeks after Apartment 101 was in business, Larry opened apartments on The Boulevard's upper three floors as well. In all, he opened outlets in five apartments: one on the first floor, two on the second, and one on the third and fourth floors. Each outlet offered a different-sized rock; three-dollar rocks were available on the first floor; five- and eight-dollar rocks from the second-floor units; ten-dollar rocks on the third; and twenty-dollar "boulders" on the fourth. (Later, the fourth-floor house was closed and moved down a flight; the climb was too much and Larry wanted an entire floor "clean" of crack to which his staff could flee if a raid occurred.)

From the beginning, the business was an unqualified success, raking in some sixty-five thousand dollars every weekday and close to a hundred thousand on weekend days. Larry borrowed some of Billy's successful marketing tools. He hired neighborhood kids to distribute handwritten coupons and fliers: BUY ONE, GET ONE FREE, or BUY NINE AND GET TENTH FREE. And he developed a customer incentive program to spur sales. He awarded to regulars who recruited a first-time buyer an amount of crack equal to the new customer's purchase.

The building operated around the clock, likely humming at any hour. During the week, business was generally slow in the morning. Traffic picked up around noon and stayed steady until about six P.M. It slackened until one A.M., when the bar closings brought a surge of customers for the next three hours or so.

On Fridays through early Sunday mornings, the place positively roared. "It was like a merry-go-round on the weekends; it was jammed all the time," says Pat Middleton. "On Fridays, there was probably three hundred or four hundred people that would come there. A lot of it was repeat, the same people, they would go off and come back and go off and come back." One regular customer always arrived in a stretch limousine. He would send his driver in to buy five hundred dollars worth at a time. Another was a bus driver who would pull over and run in; there were doctors, a lawyer, and other professionals. And there were lots of hard-luck customers: a pregnant teenager (of whom David Havard says "I'd kick her out whenever I saw her"); people with no money who were so desperate for their next hit they would seek to barter anything and everything they had. "Men would come in with clothes from their girlfriends or wives, or gold or diamonds or furniture, appliances, VCRs, cars—*anything*," recalls Havard.

Larry encouraged barter. Anything of value, no matter how harmful the consequences for his vulnerable patrons, he considered legal tender. He established these rates: a new nineteen-inch color television was worth five five-dollar rocks; a handgun no more than six rocks; an Uzi no more than twenty rocks; a black-and-white TV one or two rocks. The value of jewelry varied. "One guy gave me a almost new nineteen-inch color TV for three dime bags," Havard says. Other men would offer sex with their teenage daughters in exchange for rocks. Still another died of an overdose in the building. Havard says he did "everything I could to wake him up: put ice under his genitals, slapped him." A crew disposed of the body in a Dumpster.

*   *   *

Unparalleled customer service was a point of pride with Larry. When customers who did not wish to defer their pleasure requested a "smokehouse"—an on-site facility to sample their purchases—he added one on the first floor. (Among the habitués was Danny Chambers. Although Larry tried to keep his brother out, Danny would often linger for three or four days in the smoke-house.) He furnished it with a couch, coffee tables, and a radio. And he beneficently dispensed crack pipes and shots of rum on the house. Then, in response to male customers' demands for in-house sex and to female customers who craved crack but had no money, Larry converted an apartment to a brothel, or "pussy house." The apartment was spartan: a bed frame, box springs, and mattress.

"Didn't no matter if it was noon or midnight," says Billy, who visited The Boulevard but owned no part of the business. "You could get dope, liquor, pussy, and never leave. We used to joke about doing TV commercials. Larry wanted to call it Mar-low's One-Stop."

A customer who approached the iron gate of The Boulevard was greeted by an Uzi-toting doorman; only he could unlock the gate's deadbolt. Larry wanted his doormen to project warmth, and to treat the customer, no matter how pathetic, with respect. As he explained to one doorman: "When a crackhead comes to you and his woman is on his back, his babies don't have no Pampers, he hasn't eaten in two days, and he's about to spend his last five dol-lars on crack, you have to make him feel good about spending his money."

The customer was asked what size unit he wished to pur-chase. Like a ticket-taker at the multiplex cinema, the doorman would direct the customer accordingly: *"Dime rock? Third floor, first gate." "Nick? Right around the corner."* Once at the proper "house," the customer would slip his money through the gate to one of the two sellers. Like a waiter wheeling a sample dessert tray, the seller would produce a silvery saucer with representative rocks. Upon making his or her selection, the customer would be escorted by an armed guard to the exit or to one of the building's other houses. (Some customers were left to find their own way. They often mistook Pat Middleton and David Havard's barred first-floor residence for a crack house. Eventually, Havard tacked up a sign on the door: THIS IS THE MANAGER'S APARTMENT, THIS IS NO DOPE HOUSE.)

There were staircases at both ends of the lobby. Posted on the landings between the first and second floor at both ends were "watch-outs." Peering out the windows, they could observe the side streets, as well as the front and back of the building. Their assignment was to keep an eye out for police and "stick-up guys." There were also watch-outs stationed on the nearby street corners. All were equipped with walkie-talkies. And when Larry himself showed up, his street crew served as Larry's security detail: they "swept the block" before he got out of his car. "Made sure it was cool," says a doorman, "like he was J. Edgar Hoover."

Larry says the police were not difficult to spot. "Everyone knew they only had two raid vans, a blue and a brown one. Even the little kids on the street knew it: 'Here come the van! Here come the van!'"

Larry put his crew through mock raid practices, like fire drills or the old nuclear-preparedness duck-and-cover drills in school. He assigned roles to each of his workers; Larry usually reserved for himself the part of the bad cop. "Thing is," says a doorman called Pork Chop, "he was meaner than the polices. He had one of them big black [flash]lights like they bust you face with. He used to get off tellin' you 'Assume the position' and TV shit like that."

In the event of an actual raid, watch-outs were taught to first alert the rest of the staff and to hide all crack and firearms in the hallways or the elevator shaft, and then to shepherd everyone to the fourth floor, where no business was conducted. This was done because Larry knew if the police found the dope or guns, they could not charge anyone with possession; the goods were stashed in a common area of the building rather than on an individual's person. After the raid, the watch-outs would then retrieve the goods.

Police raided The Boulevard for the first time about two

months after it opened under Larry's management. David Havard had just walked out of the smokehouse when he heard the police yell "RAID!" He ran back in. When the door opened the first thing he saw was a shotgun. He was led to the hallway and instructed to lie on the floor, belly-up, hands outstretched. While he answered questions about where he lived and worked, why he was there, who worked for whom, and so forth, what struck him was not fear of arrest, but barely concealed laughter. All around him, practically stepping over him as if he were a drunk splayed on the sidewalk, was a steady stream of customers. Outside the building was a fleet of marked police cars; inside, Havard says, "looked like a schoolhouse, there were so many people in there."

Larry was not there, but he received word immediately via beeper. "We practiced what to do," Larry says. "A watch-out beeped [my number] and then hit 1350 (the building's street number) and then 11, the code for a raid, and I knew without even having to talk to anyone what was going down. And so I'd beep my van crew." The crew, with a fully equipped van, was always on call. Larry: "They'd pull up to the house, make sure the cops were gone, and put up new gates, clean up the place, do whatever repairs were necessary to open the place back up as quick as possible." Usually within an hour of a raid, the crew had the building reopened. After the first raid, Larry instituted combat pay for anyone caught in subsequent raids.

The jobs required sustained concentration and discipline. Employees worked twelve-hour shifts. There were normally about fourteen workers per shift: two sellers in each of the four apartments, a doorman, a couple of guards, and two to four watch-outs. On busy weekends and holidays, Larry summoned additional help. There were no breaks, but couriers delivered fast food regularly, usually from the nearby McDonald's. Neither sleeping nor drinking was permitted on the job. Larry frequently dropped by in the middle of the night to assure himself that the crew was alert and sober.

Larry rewarded the staff for the hard work. Watch-outs, many of whom were no older than fourteen or fifteen, were at the bottom of the pecking order. Even so, their entry-level jobs were critical to the unimpeded flow of commerce, and they were paid well: three hundred dollars a week. Doormen and guards earned between four and six hundred a week, and the sellers, cooped up behind locked gates, made eight hundred a week. Workers were penalized fifty dollars weekly if they were late for a shift; a second late arrival cost a week's pay. Larry's lieutenants, like Rod Byrd, who were in charge when Larry was elsewhere, received two thousand dollars weekly. Bonuses were paid to any employee who remained in the building for an entire pay period—a week.

For the employees who lived virtually in the streets anyway, the extra compensation was easy money. In Patricia Middleton they had a surrogate mother, a "den mother anyway," as she puts it. Middleton saw to it that they had enough to eat and drink, and that they wore clean clothes. "I bought trunk loads of food; I fed the kids in my apartment," she says. "Chicken, pork chops, they ate well. Marlow gave me five hundred dollars to put a second fridge in. I kept it full of pop for the kids." On laundry day, every employee would stuff his dirty clothes in a duffel bag. One worker would carry the bags out to Middleton's car, another would bring them in. And Middleton acted as the in-house banker, storing cash for anyone who asked in a lockbox in her apartment.

In addition to those who worked in Larry's crack houses, he employed a "support staff" that numbered as high as twenty-five. Some of the positions were typical of any sizable crack distributor: "cooks" to process the cocaine powder into crack and "cut-up girls" (or, as the police would come to call them, "rockettes") to carve the crack into retail-size units.

But Larry went a step further than most dealers, his brother Billy included. He recognized the need to monitor developments in the outside world that could affect his livelihood. He hired one young woman named "Baby Godmother" whose sole responsibility was to read the *Free Press* and the *News* every day for reports of drug-related indictments, arrests, murders, and so forth. She briefed Larry every afternoon, but none too thoroughly. "She was no good reader," Larry says with a laugh. And he hired "female spies" to "cozy up" to other dealers. "I had their hair dipped professionally," Larry says, "dressed them real well. I wanted to know where they [rival dealers] was opening up, who was working for them, and did they have any spies in my organization." And he hired "courtroom watchers"—two women who attended the trials of other dealers. Larry received daily briefings with particular attention paid to the testimony of government informants.

He also initiated a "job hotline," which amounted to authorizing certain employees to beep him with a special code amended for job inquiries. Larry: "Someone would call and say, 'Hey, I'm ready to work again,' and if, let's say, the house on Helen was just hit, I'd say, 'Well, the workers over there just went to jail and we have an opening there. Do you want it? How soon can you be there?'"

Saturday was payday at The Boulevard. Workers lined up in the hallway outside the manager's apartment. Inside, at the kitchen table, sat Larry's girlfriend, Belinda Lumpkin, and another man named Larry, who served as Belinda's bodyguard. Belinda was known as the "paymaster." She would arrive with an oversized leather briefcase, the kind with folding flaps trial lawyers favor. In it was the cash for the week's payroll, which usually amounted to around fifty thousand dollars, a ledger book, and photo albums containing a Polaroid shot of every employee. On the bottom border of each picture was the employee's name and work site: "Stacy, 1350." By the time Belinda was ready, there would be thirty or forty young men in line, sometimes as many as sixty. They came not only from The Boulevard but from the four other houses in the neighborhood Larry operated—the payroll was centralized.

The process took a couple of hours. Patricia Middleton stood at the door and let in the workers one at a time. The kids who worked at The Boulevard were paid first. "In-house first!" Middleton would bellow. She shut the door behind each one and escorted him into the kitchen. Belinda consulted her record, counted out loud the money, and handed it to Larry. Larry counted it and paid the worker. He always told each employee to count it then and there. One day a worker claimed he received less than he was entitled to. "You shorted me," he told Belinda. "No, we didn't short you," Belinda replied, noting that he was an hour and a half tardy one day. "You got deducted for being late."

Inevitably there were other employee-relations conflicts. Once a young man pushed a much smaller boy out of the pay line. Middleton told him to "knock it off."

"Fuck you, you fat white bitch," he retorted. Rod Byrd, Larry's chief of staff, handled the incident with dispatch. "Go on home," he told the aggressor. "You're not getting paid this week."

Conflicts were not always resolved peaceably. Toward the end of June of 1986, one foolhardy worker named Keith sought to capitalize on the heavy traffic in The Boulevard by establishing his own, unaffiliated sales outlet on the third floor. Larry was not keen on the competition. "This was a guy I tried to help," Larry recalls. Keith was in his early to middle twenties, about five feet six, and wore his hair in a Jheri curl. "He was homeless and broke and I gave him a job and a place to live right there at 1350. And he starts rolling right out of my place. I warned him three times, but he wouldn't stop."

They were on the third floor one night when the last of a series of heated arguments boiled over. Larry cornered Keith against the window at the end of a hallway. He gave Keith a choice: jump or be pushed. Keith froze; Larry grabbed him and shoved him through the windowpane. Keith was fortunate; it had poured the previous night and he landed on soggy grass. After a minute or so, he picked himself up and limped away. Larry never saw him again.

Larry's reputation for offering high-quality crack was as important to him as, say, Frank Perdue's reputation for selling tender chickens. Quality control was everything. Once a young employee violated his customers' trust by selling soap chunks in place of crack. Larry expressed his displeasure with a public flogging. He had arrived at the building that day dressed in what were commonly referred to as his "ass-kicking clothes": blue jeans, gym shoes, and a long overcoat; in the coat he hid a pistol. He announced that all his workers should follow him. He headed up the stairs, pausing near the well to pick up a broken chair in the lobby. Pat Middleton saw that he was angry and turned back toward her apartment. "No. *Everybody,*" he barked.

Larry led the group to a second-floor apartment where the boy was working. Larry took a leg off the chair and slugged the boy with it eight or ten times, striking him in the back, legs, and shoulders. The boy was screaming, begging Larry to stop. Larry responded, "That'll teach all of you and make you understand that no one will ever sell soap for crack."

Stories of Larry's ruthlessness were legend—and countless. A sampling: "Once he told a girl 'no' about something she asked him for," says David Havard. "She asked him again, and he knocked her out. Punched her right in the jaw."

"I once saw him almost kill this guy they call Shake N Bake," says a young woman who did not want her name used; she worked for Larry as a cut-up girl. "The guy insulted Marlow—called him a 'bitch'—and Marlow told his boys to beat him up. They used bats, two-by-fours, busted bottles over his head." She adds: "Another time he choked this girl off her feet." Tiger Alexander (who worked variously for both Larry and Billy): "He [Larry] used to carry a mini–steel baseball bat, and if you came up ten dollars short, he'd hit you ten times."

Larry did not always mete out the discipline himself. He employed a team of enforcers, the Wrecking Crew, when additional muscle was necessary or he simply could not be present for the prescribed beating. Terry Colbert, the fellow whose father first put Billy Joe in business, says a man who sold for Larry out of a house on Montclair Street once "came up a hundred dollars short. . . . After Marlow checked it out, he left, and five minutes later three cars pull up and beat up the guy pretty bad. His head was all busted, you know, his brain was almost about to come out of his head and they took him out in the back of the alley, threw him by a Dumpster, and just left him there." Colbert continues: "I didn't see him die, but I heard that he was dead."

At The Boulevard one day, a member of the Wrecking Crew asked David Havard if he could borrow the baseball bat Havard kept in his apartment. He explained that a salesman on the third floor was skimming money. The Wrecking Crew member went upstairs, crushed the young man's skull, walked him to a nearby store, and called an ambulance. On another occasion, Havard says he saved the life of a young woman who had sold as crack a bogus substance—and kept the cocaine for resale elsewhere. He says the Wrecking Crew had her tied up in the lobby when he walked in. He pleaded for her life. "I told them, 'Look, instead of killing her, do something for yourselves. Take her in the pussy house and make her give all of you head.'"

Viciousness came naturally to Larry, but he was as capable of an impulsive flicker of charm as he was a flash of anger. Unlike Billy, though, whose unrestrained ardor for young women resulted in multiple simultaneous short- and long-term couplings, Larry was less likely to act on his romantic impulses. (Though of course he did so when courting Belinda Lumpkin.) Instead, his charm was more likely to surface when women interested him as potential employees.

One afternoon in August of 1986, fourteen-year-old Cindy Davis was clowning around with some girlfriends down the block from her family's Dickerson Street home when Larry drove by. He was with a friend named William (Jack) Jackson. "He"—Larry— "asked us do we want to make a video," Cindy recalls. "They seemed like nice guys and we didn't have anything better to do so we got in their car and they took us to Knodell"—Larry's initial base of operations.

"A guy was there they call Buzz. He told us, 'If y'all cut this stuff up, you'll get some money.' I said, 'How much?' He told us a hundred each.

"So we stayed there, I'll say less than a hour, and they took us around to [the house on] Buffalo. And we got there and started dancing and made videos of us dancing. It was fun because everyone just sat around and tripping out. When they brought us home, they asked us did we want to keep on and did we know anyone else who could help out."

Later that afternoon, Cindy's sister Janice was killing time at home. Her summer vacation was at an end and in a few days the seventeen-year-old would be heading back to Southeastern High for her senior year. Cindy burst through the door waving a fistful of cash. "I made a hundred dollars! All I had to do was cut up some coke and put it in a few bags, cut up a few ounces, and they gave me a hundred dollars!"

"Who?"

"I don't even know their names," Cindy replied. "But they need some more cutters. Would you want to go with me?"

Around four the next afternoon, Janice accompanied Cindy and two of their friends back to Buffalo Street, to a two-story house with a basement. It turned out that one of the guys who had cruised by Dickerson Street lived there. His name was Marlow, they learned, and he shared the house with his girlfriend, Belinda. Through a side door by the driveway, the four young women went directly down to the basement. The furnishings were utilitarian: a couch, a television, and a glass table. Neither Larry nor Belinda was there, but "Jack" Jackson was seated on the couch with two other fellows. On the table were large rocks of crack cocaine.

"Hey, Jack," one of Cindy's friends said by way of introducing Janice, "we got you another worker."

"That's good. We got plenty to do today. We need twenty thousand dimes and ten thousand nickels." The girls explained to Janice the uncomplicated procedure. They gave her a supply of razor blades and five- and ten-dollar rock samples. "You roll your sleeves up. That's it. Start cutting. That's it," Janice says.

There was a little more to it. To ward off the chemical odor, the girls wore cloth "doctor masks" and to protect their fingers they wore Band-Aids or rubber thimbles. They were to count the rocks, put them in a plastic sandwich Baggie in quantities of a hundred or five hundred or a thousand, and indicate on a scrap of paper the amount therein. The Baggies were placed on the middle of the table and ultimately put in canvas bags—five thousand nickels or two thousand dimes to a bag.

Nothing was wasted. During the course of cutting thousands of rocks, there would accumulate a good amount of shavings. This excess was called "shake." At the end of the workday, says Cindy, "one girl would collect the shake and cook it up in a Vision pot with a little baking soda." Once it hardened, the girls cut that too. They worked four or five hours that afternoon and Jack gave them each a hundred dollars. "See you tomorrow," he told them as their cab arrived.

The girls returned the following day, and it was then that Janice met Larry. He came downstairs and pointed to one girl's rock pile. "Look at her, she is cutting boulders," Janice recalls Larry saying. He came over, picked up a rock, and trimmed it to his specifications. At the end of the second day, Jack told the girls, "I want y'all to start working and we will pay you by the week."

Janice says she never questioned the morality of working for a crack dealer. "I was thinking I always been broke, I always had to work." Janice had worked previously for minimum wage at a McDonald's and in the kitchen at Manoogian Mansion, the mayor's residence. "I was thinking about he [Larry] had some fast money. I don't have to work and I can still go to school and get my hair done. That's all I was thinking about."

Classes were starting, and to Janice and Cindy rock-cutting seemed the ideal after-school job. For three or four hours a weekday (and sometimes a full Saturday) they were to earn three hundred and fifty dollars a week, plus generous perks: cab fare when necessary, a meals stipend, a fifty-dollar bonus for each new worker recruited. (There were many bonuses paid. "Girls used to come up to us in school and get on their hands and knees and *beg* us to get them in," Cindy says.) Additionally, the boys in the crew were instructed to take the girls on shopping sprees at the mall from time to time. And to pay for their hair care.

Most days, the girls would go straight home after school and await a phone call from Jack. He "knew what time we got out of school," Janice says, "and most of the time, he made sure we got a way from school. And the boys would come pick us up and drop us off at home." Other days, if the girls knew the job site in advance, they would catch a cab to work directly from school. The cut house shifted with the ease of a floating crap game. It might be a duplex on Rosemary Street one day, an apartment at Newport and Forest the next, a house on Knodell or French Road off Gratiot the following. Why? "To be cautious," Janice explains. "Just in case somebody was wondering why is there a large amount of girls going in there all the time and coming back out." A place that had been a stash house one week before might now be a cut house. Or a former cut house might have been converted to a sell house. "We would never usually know where we were going," Cindy says. "We'd just go wherever."

The cut-up crew made Larry nervous. He could not keep a steady eye on them himself. He worried that the teenage girls would scare easily and snitch, or maybe they would steal and sell the rocks for themselves. He had no way of telling if a few rocks were missing from every key they cut. One day, convinced they were ripping him off, he ordered one shift of cut-up girls at the Knodell house to strip. "We was upstairs and he had 'em to take off everything but their bras and panties," says Tiger Alexander, who happened by at the time. "Then they go downstairs and work half-naked. He made sure they wasn't gonna smuggle none out."

But even such drastic measures could not satisfy Larry; he wanted to bypass the cut-up girls completely. The challenge was to come up with a means to mass-produce crack cocaine—to cook and cut the rocks in one labor-saving procedure. Larry spent days experimenting in the kitchen of his Buffalo Street house—an inventor possessed. Finally he emerged with a prototype: a two-foot by two-foot Plexiglas sheet permeated with holes drilled precisely the circumference of a five-dollar rock. The idea was to pour the heated liquid crack mixture over the sheet, allow it to cool, and then punch the prefab rocks out of each hole. Unfortunately for

Larry, the design was flawed; the liquid did not conform to the holes, it dripped through. "I never got around to perfecting it," Larry says, "but I was getting close. I even called the government about a patent."

Stuck for the time being (patent pending) with the cut-up girls, he issued them three principal rules: "Don't tell people where you work"; "Don't tell who you work for"; and, "Don't give out any phone numbers." If caught in a raid, the girls were instructed to "play dumb." "We would just say we don't know [who we worked for]," Janice says. "Big Man, give a name, Tony or whatever. That's who we were working for. This is our first time ever coming. We just came to make extra money or something."

As 1986 progressed, and as Larry and Billy built their parallel organizations ever larger, so large that the two, in Billy's words, were "easily outpumping anybody in Detroit," what drove them to grow larger still was not money or the accumulation of other tangible assets. Nor was it the power and respect and fear already accorded them boundlessly by the denizens of the east side, or, in Larry's case, even the desperate need to control his environment. And it wasn't the women, a certain type of whom they had their pick. For none of those goals, compelling as they were, had slaked their primal entrepreneurial thirst for growth—growth for the elemental sake of growing.

Nor had their success dimmed their need for recognition from the one person who mattered above all others. "Those boys more than anything . . . ," says their sister-in-law Francis Farris Chambers, gathering her thoughts, speaking quietly, whispering almost, ". . . what it was was those boys trying to outdo each other making their mama happy."

Hazel Chambers never could reconcile herself to the fact that she was the matriarch of a poor family of fourteen with no way out of poverty. A smart and stylish woman who was disinclined toward farm life, she was ashamed of the primitive conditions to which she had been shackled: no running water, no indoor toilet, so little food on occasion that she would dispatch her children to the neighbors' house for leftovers. And she was ashamed of her husband, Curtis, who was illiterate, uneducated to the ways of the world, and whom she considered, says Francis Chambers, "unworthy."

Years after they had left home, when the Chambers brothers achieved infamy and fortune, Detroiters would wonder how a couple of bumpkins from rural Arkansas could rule the city's drug trade. But friends and relatives back home never wondered. Hazel Chambers taught her boys a rule for living: Don't live by the rules. She lived an exemplary life. *"She was whoring around and selling bootleg whiskey and those kids got a Ph.D. in hustling at home,"* the Lee County sheriff had said. Whatever the qualities that made Larry and Billy Joe Chambers the way they were, many who knew the family believed they knew where those qualities came from. "All you got to know about them," the people of Lee County would say, "is that they're Hazel's sons."

Like many successful businessmen, they were driven also by competition. For each crack house Billy opened, Larry felt he had to open one nearby (and if Billy's was a five-dollar house, Larry undercut him—his rocks would sell for three dollars); for each luxury car Larry bought, Billy would buy a similar one—or two, with better stereos. "They didn't need any more *anything*," says Billy's girlfriend Diana Alexander. "But it was like they was fighting some kind of war and didn't either want to give up."

Larry tired of hearing stories of his younger brother's magnanimity: how Billy gave his friends a hundred dollars for something to eat, or how he gave everyone money for Christmas. One day Larry and a friend were driving when they happened upon a prostitute sashaying down the sidewalk. "Slow down," Larry commanded. They rolled to a stop, the woman poked her head in the window. Larry decided he wasn't interested after all. He stuffed a hundred-dollar bill in her blouse and told his friend to "get going." He added: "Think BJ would do *that?*"

This protracted sibling rivalry only started with Billy and Larry. It extended to their crew members, who competed for women, and to the women themselves, who competed for the richest boyfriends, the best cars, the most expensive haircuts, the finest clothes. One young woman who worked initially for Larry says she was lured away to Billy's organization when one of his crew members took a liking to her. "He always kept me in nice gym shoes and Guess jeans. He got me this *bad* Guess outfit," she says.

The rivalry put one of Larry's cut-up girls, Cindy Davis, in an awkward situation. "I went with a BJ boy, Ronald Rush," Cindy says. "That made Marlow's boys mad; they used to call me 'traitor.' But Ron had bought me three cars by I was fifteen going on sixteen—a Cherokee, a Fiero, and a Nova. Marlow's boys wasn't buying no girls cars." Cindy's sister Janice says that Billy offered such good benefits and high salaries that "if he told a boy to spend a week in a hole they would do it." Why? "They got paid more, that's why. I mean, if you know about them, they have better cars, everything."

Larry takes offense at the suggestion that Billy's employees were managed more benevolently than his own, and that such treatment inspired the sort of loyalty that his leadership-by-intimidation could not. "My people were well taken care of," Larry bristles, sounding every bit like an indignant Delta planter describing his tenant farmers. "They had plenty to eat, plenty money, girls, cars. They [Billy's crew] didn't like us because we was a successful, well-set organization."

"*We* was the well-set organization," Billy says. "We had the cars, we had the money, we had the womens, we had the houses. And you never saw us. And if you did see us, it was because we was going to pick up four or five more women. Every weekend we'd go somewhere: Cedar Point [an amusement park in Ohio], St. Louis, Belle Isle, go-cart riding, horseback riding. His fellas saw how we lived and they wanted to live that way. But Larry would have them out in the street ganging around and trying to take over the city and trying to become something that was really out of their reach."

As intense as the rivalry could be, when it came to family matters the brothers cast aside their differences. When tragedy struck, as in March of 1986 when their brother Joe died, Larry and Billy jointly organized the funeral services.

Billy's twin had been in prison for more than a year—first for a marijuana possession conviction in Detroit (he was en route from the house at 1261 Newport to the sell house down the block), and then, after being paroled, he was caught stealing postal money orders and food stamps. That offense landed him in federal prison. In February of 1986, he was released to a halfway house in Little Rock to serve the final four months of his eighteen-month sentence.

To ease his brother's layover in Little Rock, Billy arranged for Joe's girlfriend, Deedee Hunter, to stay in Marianna during those months. He paid for her trip from Detroit and bought his brother Otis a pickup to ferry her the hundred miles back and forth. For reasons unknown, the halfway house paroled Joe after only one month. It was Saturday, March 29, 1986.

Billy had been out all night. He arrived home just before sunrise, Easter Sunday. "I said to myself I'm gonna give my daddy a call, wish him happy Easter," Billy recalls. "Because once I go to sleep, no telling when I'm gonna get up. Easter probably be over by then!"

His twin answered the phone. "Who is this?" Billy asked.

"This is Joe."

"Nigger, what you doin' home?"

"They let me go early."

They talked cars briefly—Joe remarked how much he'd enjoyed driving Billy's new Saab around town the night before. And Joe said he would get up soon and wash the Fiero and ride around a while in that, and then ride around in the truck, and then take the family in the Saab to Easter services.

Then they talked about another favorite topic. "You at home now, how much money you need to hold you?" Billy asked.

"Look, I don't need no money at all."

"You got to need *some* money."

"As long as you broke," Joe, waxing philosophical, replied, "everything is all right. You got money, you got problems."

"Damn, that's deep," Billy said. He told Joe to put Deedee on the line. "I'm gonna ask her how much money she needs."

"Man, don't give her no money. You give womens money, they lose their minds."

"Aw man, you done went to jail and lost your motherfucking mind," Billy said. "I'm goin' to bed and I'll holler at you later."

A few hours later Billy woke to a ringing phone. It was Melvin Forney, his brother-in-law, calling to remind him of a favor Billy had promised. Melvin was facing a felony charge and Billy was to have already paid Melvin's lawyer ten thousand dollars.

Billy jumped in the car. He was driving on Chalmers, on his way to the lawyer's office, when he noticed his brother Willie heading the other way, toward Billy's house. They flashed their lights and pulled over at a 7-Eleven.

"What's up, man?"

"I just come over here to check you out for a minute," Willie said, unaccountably breaking into a wide grin. "And to let you know that Joe just got killed."

"Got killed? What you mean *killed?*"

"He dead," Willie said.

"Dead? I know you're not telling me he's dead—as in *dead.*"

"Yeah man, he's dead."

To drive from the Chambers family's house on Highway 121 to Mt. Perion Missionary Baptist Church in La Grange, it is necessary to cross the railroad tracks. On that Easter morning, there wasn't room in the Saab for everyone. Hazel volunteered to wait while Joe took his younger brothers and sister and his girlfriend. Joe and Deedee dropped off his siblings at the small white cinder block church and sped back to the house in a cloud of dust: down Young Street, the dirt road named for the large extended family that lives next to the church, and onto the paved highway. Services had already started and Joe knew his mother would be upset over being late. As he and Deedee approached the tracks, Joe figured he could beat the oncoming Missouri-Pacific train across. At the last second, he changed his mind. He slammed the brakes and skidded onto the tracks. The train's engine rammed the Saab's driver's side, severing Joe's head and dragging the car seventy-five feet down the tracks. Deedee survived.

Meanwhile, Hazel Chambers wondered what could be taking Joe so long. She saw the police drive by, and an ambulance, and the fire truck. Curious, she started toward town on foot. A neighbor stopped her.

"Mrs. Chambers, you must don't realize what just happened."

"No, what happened?"

"Your son just got killed."

The funeral was held the following Saturday. That gave the funeral home time enough to prepare the body for an open casket ("They pasted him back together like new," one of Billy's girl-friends says), and it gave Billy and Larry time to honor their departed brother with a display of pomp demanded of such circumstances. The day after Joe died, both Larry and Billy bought new cars. Billy paid twenty-three thousand in cash for a BMW; Larry settled for a sixteen-thousand-dollar Pontiac Fiero. They needed the cars for a funeral caravan from Detroit to Marianna.

Some forty friends and relatives from Detroit joined the procession. All told, they drove twenty vehicles. Fats Wilkins took his new Volvo, Perry Coleman lent his convertible Eldorado. There were "baby Benzes" and Saabs and Blazers and Jeeps, as well as two pickups in the rear carrying all the luggage. "When we got to Marianna," Billy recalls, "cars started pulling over—they thought the funeral had already started." (Rural southern tradition dictates that traffic come to a standstill during a funeral procession.) Instead, the Detroiters parked their cars in Hazel Chambers's yard. "It looked like a new-car lot," says a neighbor. For the excursion to the funeral and the cemetery, the mourners piled into ten limousines—five white and five black—Billy and his mother rented in Memphis. Some of the assembled from Detroit dressed unconventionally. Many of the young women wore "micro-minis," says one person from Lee County in attendance. "One guy's shirt was unbuttoned down to his navel and another wore a Crown Royal bag on his hip."

After a wild party at Hazel's house following the funeral, Billy put Joe's death behind him. "I just looked at it like it was meant for him to go for some reason. I knew he knew I loved him. And he knew there wasn't nothing I wouldn't do for him. It wasn't like he was going through a depression stage, down and out and all that. It was just a freak accident, it could have happened to me, so I just moved it out of my head."

To honor his brother, Billy took Joe's street name: Yo-Yo. The new name served additional purposes: it confused the police, who thought it was Billy who had been killed, and it enabled Billy's inner circle to differentiate itself from the many pretenders who claimed such exalted status. "I told my five guys and all the girls who used to hang around me my name was Yo," Billy says. "If you called me BJ, I know you didn't know who you was actually talking with, and you was definitely out of pocket."

That was Billy's tribute to the dead. To honor his younger brother Otis, who would soon graduate from Lee Senior High School in Marianna, Billy "gave him the works": another "car show" in their hometown. In late May of 1986, barely two months after Joe's burial, Billy and his entourage from Detroit arrived in Marianna in familiar fashion. Again they roared into town in a caravan, past the soybean fields and the high school and the courthouse square and the cotton gins and the Food Giant, and on down Highway 1 to the La Grange turnoff at Cypress Corner. And again they parked their cars in Hazel's yard for all to see. And this time, as word spread that "the Chambers boys are back with all their cars and a *lot* of girls," kids came from all over the county to check out the fleet, to pose for a picture behind the wheel of a baby Benz or while reclining on the hood of a gold-trimmed black Cadillac. The car show attracted not just kids: teachers, farmers, even a deputy sheriff. But it was on graduation day itself, Friday, May 30, that the thrill of seeing the conquering heroes returned home approached delirium. Once again, Billy hired limousines (and chauffeurs) from Memphis. This time he rented only five limos, all white, but they were stretch models, Cadillacs, the kind with an added axle and three doors on either side. And because this was a day for celebration ("Your baby bro only graduates once," Billy explains, "might as well do it up"), restraint eluded Billy and his brothers; they romped around town with the flurry and many of the trappings of a presidential homecoming.

No political advance team could have created such excitement. Limo sightings were reported like UFOs throughout the county. "I *swear* they were at Atkins Park," one resident insists; a fisherman at Bear Creek Lake who spotted the otherworldly cars was so excited he may as well have seen the Loch Ness monster; a convenience store clerk who sold one of the brothers a twelve-pack of beer says he was told to keep the change from a fifty-dollar bill. In the early evening, the Chamberses touched down at the high school for the graduation ceremonies—an apparition come alive. As described earlier, the motorcade's arrival at the parking lot beside the football field attracted a throng of cheering, squealing autograph hounds and shutterbugs.

All this commotion, of course, was not unintended. It translated into advertisements for themselves: for their wealth, the good life of Detroit, the swag of the drug business. Had the Chamberses paid taxes they surely could have deducted the costs of the limos as a business expense. The photo opportunities, the word-of-mouth buzz, helped make recruiting potential employees an effortless task. Rare was the Lee Senior High student who did not at least entertain thoughts of joining Otis and his brothers in Detroit. Marianna police estimated that no fewer than a hundred and fifty local youths journeyed to Detroit to work for the Chambers brothers. (That widely publicized figure was grossly inflated, says the rival sheriff's department. "It would be difficult to substantiate more than twenty-five," says Sheriff Bobby May, Jr. "And those would be undesirables anyway—fuckups.")

And though the police claimed that many of those youngsters were brought forcibly to Detroit, no evidence supports the claim. (One young woman whose parents believed Otis abducted her turned out to have run away with him.) Says Lillie Perry, Otis's ninth-grade English teacher, "These little kids jumped in those cars to get out of Marianna."

CHAPTER EIGHT

"GOOD-BYE, DIXIE LAND"

The Arkansas Delta was not always known for its hopelessness. In its formative years after the Civil War, Lee County was a magnet for blacks from the older cotton-producing states of the Deep South. Hazel Chambers's father, a small, wiry man named Haywood Cook, was a native of Macon, Georgia. He was lured to Lee County by tales of cheap land and abundant crops. Hazel's husband Curtis's father, who came from Mississippi, also expected a farmer's paradise. What the Chamberses and the Cooks found instead were families whose condition, as a Little Rock–based black newspaper put it, was "at best little in advance of pauperism"—the kind of conditions that would lead, over the next half century, to bloody rebellion in Lee County and throughout the Delta, and, ultimately, to so many people moving out of the county that its population of eighteen thousand in 1890 exceeded that of 1990 by more than three thousand people.

The westward migration toward Arkansas began during Reconstruction, when planters, desperate for field workers to replace their freed slaves, sent labor agents throughout the old plantation states. The agents offered fifteen to twenty-five dollars a month to work in Arkansas—double the prevailing wage east of the Mississippi River. And it wasn't just the wages with which agents lured newcomers to Arkansas. Just as Henry Ford's agents from Detroit would lure southern blacks to his auto factories a generation later, and indeed, as recruiters for the Chambers brothers would lure young men from Marianna to Detroit a century later, the agents spun elaborate yarns about the Promised Land. They told of the vast riches of the virgin fields and emerald forests of the Delta, where "sweet potatoes grew as large as watermelons," where "hogs were just laying around already baked," and where money could be plucked from trees like "picking cotton off the stalk."

If black immigrants to Arkansas did not find life as free and easy as advertised, they nevertheless continued to flock to the state. During the 1870s the state's black population soared to 211,000 from 122,000. Much of that growth occurred in the Delta, which, under the Reconstruction government of the late 1860s and early 1870s, afforded its black citizens considerable freedom in exercising political rights. In the push to develop Lee County following its creation in 1873, blacks were as welcome as whites to stake their claim to the county with no "finer prospect for future prosperity." In Lee and other Delta counties with black majorities, blacks held considerable local political power—serving as sheriffs, county clerks, tax assessors.

The power did not last long. The last Reconstruction legislature met in 1873 (the year lawmakers carved Lee County out of four adjoining counties), and although it enacted a civil rights law that guaranteed equal access to public facilities for all persons, regardless of race, the law was rarely enforced. And although the act would remain on the books for thirty-four years, by the 1880s white supremacy and segregation in Arkansas were once again facts of life.

But still blacks streamed into the state. As late as 1889, when some black leaders discussed the possibility of converting a portion of Oklahoma to a black homeland, a prominent black minister forecast in the weekly *Freeman* of Indianapolis: "Arkansas is destined to be the great Negro state of the Country. The rich lands, the healthy regions, the meagre prejudice compared to some states, and the opportunities to acquire wealth, all conspire to make it inviting to the Colored man. The Colored people now have a better start [there] than in any other state in the Union."

It would soon prove to be a false start. And it would be proved most graphically in Lee County. Cotton ruled absolutely; about 86 percent of the county's soil—a deep, black sandy loam, "richer," as the *Arkansas Democrat* put it, "than the lands along the Nile"—was devoted to the crop's cultivation. But the rich land could do nothing to counteract the steady demise during the 1880s of the world cotton market. With no alternative cash crops, the county's economy was enslaved to the market price, which by 1891 had tumbled from ten cents a pound a decade earlier to less than seven and a half cents a pound, barely enough to cover the costs of production.

In a letter in the *Lee County Courier* addressed to his "friends and fellow farmers," W. B. Snipes of the Spring Creek community warned of the dangers of overdependence on cotton and urged them to consider diversified crops. "Our grand old country is on the very verge of ruin," wrote Snipes. ". . . If we remain with cotton first last and all the time we will sink lower in poverty and ruin year by year and the time will not be far distant when our homes will be sold and our wives and little ones brought to want and misery. Take my advice and quit cotton before it brings you to this fate for it is not far off."

But no matter how hard and how carefully individual farmers worked their land, no matter if every single one of W. B. Snipes's friends took his advice to heart, they could no more affect interest rates or market price or the credit practices of Eastern banks than they could the weather. Devastated by rising costs and falling prices, and frustrated by economic forces too crushing to fight alone, millions of farmers joined a wildfire movement that came to be known as the Populist revolt, the greatest and "most elaborate example of mass insurgency" in American history. The movement's organizational base, in Arkansas and throughout the South, was the Southern Farmers Alliance (and later the People's Party). Like every institution in the post-Reconstruction South, the Alliance was segregated. Blacks belonged to a parallel organization called the Colored Alliance. Both groups (along with the Northern Alliance) advocated economic self-help. Each established cooperative stores at which members bought farm implements and other goods at not-for-profit prices and the lowest possible interest rates. And each founded state exchanges, which, by bypassing the "middleman," enabled individual farmers to sell their cotton at prices approaching those of the world cotton market.

But for blacks the challenges transcended economics. Not only were black and white farmers trapped by the same low prices and usurious interest rates, but blacks had the onus of the caste system to contend with. "Before the black man could worry about economic injustice," wrote the Populist historian Lawrence Goodwyn, "he had to worry about survival." And so in the spring of 1888 the Colored Alliance, which sprang from the cotton-producing country of East Texas, deployed organizers throughout the South to spread the seeds of agrarian revolt to the great masses of landless black tenant farmers. By 1890 the Colored Alliance claimed a membership of 1,200,000 in sixteen states.

The Colored and Southern alliances had many common miseries and grievances. As a white Allianceman said, "They are in the ditch just like we are." The alliances also shared certain goals, principal among them more control over the rules of commerce, currency, and credit. But Southern Alliance members depended largely upon blacks to harvest their crops—blacks who belonged to or sympathized with the Colored Alliance. Sooner or later that and other inherent conflicts of race and class would prove to be irreconcilable. The final break came in the summer of 1891, when the Farmers' Association, to which all the large planters in the

Delta belonged, agreed to pay cotton pickers no more than fifty cents per hundred pounds. Local members of the Colored Alliance called on their national leader, R. M. Humphrey, to intervene. During his travels around the South that summer, Humphrey, a white farmer and former Baptist minister from Texas, tried to organize a general strike for the upcoming harvest. The aim was to force the planters to pay a dollar a hundred.

His plan was met with skepticism. One Alliance member warned that the strike would "engender a race feeling, bitter and deep and lasting, and one which may result in riot and bloodshed!" The root of the problem was the division of class within the Colored Alliance. Many leaders of the various state colored alliances were landowners who worked their own fields and employed other blacks; a strike would be counter to their interests, and so they voted not to heed Humphrey's call. Humphrey formed a separate Cotton Pickers League, comprised entirely of black field hands who worked and lived on plantations.

But the constraints under which the Cotton Pickers League operated—a necessarily covert membership, few experienced leaders, the stifling air of white supremacy—doomed the organization and the strike from the start. On the day Humphrey had announced to the world that millions of pickers would desert the fields, only in two locales, a farm in East Texas, the birthplace of the Colored Alliance, and a remote east Arkansas county, did pickers even attempt to strike. The Texas matter was quickly resolved, according to an oblique newspaper account, and "within a week it seemed clear to all that the proposed strike was a total failure."

But the results in east Arkansas were not so clear. In all of the South's counties in which cotton grew, from the Carolinas to the Deep South plantation lands east of the Mississippi and across the big river to Arkansas and down through Texas from the piney woods to the high plains, in only one of those many counties did cotton pickers respond to the call for higher wages by laying down their long sacks and walking out of the fields.

The county was Lee, in the heart of the Arkansas Delta.

*   *   *

The Lee County of the early 1890s was for white landowners a place of high culture and refinement. Leading families sent home glowing accounts of their European travels, while the well-to-do who remained in Marianna attended plays and concerts at the opera house, enjoyed moonlit steamboat cruises on the Mississippi, and flocked to the thoroughbred horse track near town. There were elegant all-night balls. At one such gala, after a two A.M. supper, "dancing resumed and kept up until the roseate hue of the Eastern sky admonished the pleasure-seeking throng that the night was spent."

Just as the pleasure-seekers were crawling into their beds at daybreak, their laborers were leaving their two- and three-room tumbledown cabins for another back-breaking day in the searing late summer Delta sun. Whole families—women nearing childbirth any day, or women with newborns, some only two weeks old, young children and their younger siblings and their grandparents—worked together in the shadeless fields (trees would stunt the cotton) without talk or pause, the adults stooped halfway to the ground, the children crawling down the rows, each dragging from plant to plant a long white sack slung over the shoulder, a sack that by midday would be full, and would weigh a hundred pounds.

At a wage of fifty cents per hundred, there was little to show by sundown beyond an aching back, raw knees, and bloodied and blistered hands. When an organizer from Memphis arrived in Lee County in early September of 1891, it took him only a couple of weeks to enlist support for the strike. It began on September 20, when Colonel H. P. Rodgers, a leading planter, declined to grant his pickers' request for an increase in wages to seventy-five cents per hundred. Rodgers, a longtime Marianna city council member, most certainly did not want to set a precedent for a higher wage scale. He promptly evicted the strikers.

During the next few days the strikers gained momentum by spreading the news of the walkout from plantation to plantation throughout the county. The evidently fearless organizer from Memphis even gave a public speech in Marianna. But a white posse organized to quash the movement. If the strikers knew of the posse, they apparently were undeterred. On September 28, the county sheriff claimed that two striking pickers confronted a plantation manager against whom they held a grudge. The manager's body was found mutilated. (The owner of the plantation, a Memphis man, said his manager was killed by whites upset with his decision to increase wages to sixty cents a hundred.)

The white mob, reinforced by nearly three dozen well-armed men from neighboring Crittenden County, caught up with strike leaders a few days later. In a showdown at a cotton gin, which, as one reporter delicately put it, "assumed a sanguinary aspect," two strikers were killed and nine captured. Rather than endure needless delays by escorting the prisoners to the Marianna jail and then waiting a month for the grand jury to convene, the posse itself chose to dispense justice: en route to the jail, a gang of ten to twelve masked men hung all nine strikers.

The mass lynching was met by most white southern newspapers with editorial glee. "Too much praise cannot be given the officers of Lee and Crittenden counties for the prompt suppression of the trouble," declared the *Lee County Courier*. "The Negroes should be made to understand they cannot commit these outrages with impunity," the Memphis *Appeal-Avalanche* wrote, adding, in a steep plunge into understatement, "and that the penalty is very severe." Black newspapers, of course, viewed the hangings in a different light. "The ordinary fire and brim stone of hell," the Kansas City *American Citizen* opined, "will not be enough for these white devils."

Violence to the Reconstruction-era ideals of racial equality was also peaking in the years before World War I. The gains by blacks in education and in political, economic, and civil rights were virtually erased during the last decade of the nineteenth century and the first decade of the twentieth. A poll tax, a means of disfranchisement favored throughout the Democrat-controlled New

South, was ratified by the 1893 session of the Arkansas General Assembly. But the one-dollar tax only hindered black voting; it did not ban it. That was not accomplished fully until 1906, when the state Democratic party, led by Governor Jeff Davis, closed its primary to blacks. (The Arkansas Supreme Court upheld the right to an all-white primary in several decisions, ruling that the Democratic party was a private organization and not subject to the provisions of the state constitution.) The following year the rest of the law finally caught up with the custom: the legislature repealed the Civil Rights Act of 1873.

At the dawn of the century, Lee County experienced a bit of an economic boom. There still were vast forests of ash, oak, cypress, and red gum (which was marketed as "satin walnut"), deep green patches of timber to which the cotton fields stretched. Northern lumber interests hungered for the forests; they gobbled up huge tracts for a few dollars an acre, tens of thousands of acres in Lee and nearby counties. They built their own barges and railroad spurs and bought locomotives to connect their mills with the Missouri-Pacific line that ran through Marianna, the line that in turn connected with the St. Louis & Iron Mountain, the main line from St. Louis to New Orleans.

By 1910 three companies operated lumber mills in Marianna. The largest, L'Anguille Lumber Company (named for the small but navigable river that flows through Marianna), employed more than five hundred workers during peak production periods. Taken by the town's "charm" and its buzz of industry, visiting reporters gushed and marveled over the city's energetic populace. "It would shock a dead man," wrote the correspondent for the *Green Forest Tribune,* in Marianna for the 1913 meeting of the Arkansas Press Association, "to come in contact with such live wires as they have in that town." On another occasion, a Little Rock reporter predicted that Marianna's population of five thousand would soon double. "When that day arrives," he wrote in a fit of optimism, "the people of the city will look forward to the time when 25,000 will be written opposite the name Marianna in census reports."

It never came to be. Marianna's population would not rise much above six thousand, and the town's brief flirtation with prosperity ended with the return of the troops from World War I. During the war cotton sold for thirty-five cents a pound and the sawmills whined around the clock. With the men overseas, women ran most of the jobs, producing boxes for bacon and other war rations under contract to the Swift and Armour meatpacking companies.

World War I also meant new opportunities for blacks. In 1914, as the war embroiled country after country, immigrant laborers—miners, mill workers, meatpackers, autoworkers—deserted their jobs in America's northern cities to return to their native soil. Immigration to the United States ground to a halt. Suddenly, and for the first time, hundreds of thousands of southern blacks who had never known any option to field work but starvation not only began hearing of job vacancies in the North, they were *begged* to fill them.

The war could not have come at a better time for blacks in the Delta. The boll weevil, which had crossed the Rio Grande into Texas in 1892, was steadily munching its way northward and eastward across southern cotton fields. By 1912 it had reached eastern Arkansas, destroying millions of acres of cotton along the way. "Boll weevil got half the crop," one song went, "White man's got the rest." And in each of the two springs prior to the war, in 1912 and 1913, the Mississippi River's flood waters overcame Lee County's inadequate levees. The floods destroyed the already planted crops, drowned farm animals, and ruined the lives of small farmers throughout the Mississippi Valley.

Southern blacks left home in droves. Sixty-five thousand arrived in Chicago between 1910 and 1920; sixty-one thousand in New York. Of all the northern cities to which southern blacks fled, no city's black population increased by a higher percentage than that of Detroit. "Come up to Detroit and see how we make things hum!" exclaimed a fictional magnate in the burgeoning automobile industry. And come they did. Between 1910 and 1920 the city's black population swelled from six thousand to forty-two thousand—a staggering 600 percent increase. At the start of the century, there were but two auto companies in Detroit; they produced a total of two hundred cars in 1901. In 1917, the year America entered the war, Detroit manufactured a million cars. By 1920, the industry employed more than nine hundred and ninety-five thousand workers.

Alarmed southern planters did not take lightly the exodus of their labor force. Some towns passed ordinances requiring northern labor recruiters to pay a licensing fee of a thousand dollars or more. In others, recruiters were arrested and jailed. Some depots detained northbound trains. Just as these tactics failed to stem the tide of migration, so too did gentler efforts to persuade blacks that they belonged in the Southland. White-owned newspapers that not long before endorsed mob rule as a necessary means of control now wrote adamantly against lynching and in favor of a judicial system that treated blacks fairly. But there was no talk of dismantling the legal structure of segregation or of matching the northern wage of five dollars a day—three times what a cotton picker earned. Consequently, many blacks viewed with derision if not delight their former bosses' desperate but hollow reforms. The leading "race paper" of the time, the *Chicago Defender*, urged blacks to:

> Turn a deaf ear to everybody. . . . You see they are not lifting their laws to help you. Are they? Have they stopped their Jim Crow cars? Can you buy a Pullman sleeper where you wish? Will they give you a square deal in court yet? Once upon a time we permitted other people to think for us—today we are thinking and acting for ourselves with the result that our "friends" are getting alarmed at our progress. We'd like to

oblige these unselfish (?) souls and remain slaves in the South,
but to their section of the country we have said, as the song
goes, "I hear you calling me," and have boarded the train
singing, "Good-bye, Dixie Land."

The *Defender* was so intent on organizing the "Great Northern Drive" it did everything but press into the hands of able-
bodied black men train tickets along with each weekly edition of
the paper. In Lee County the *Defender* circulated widely but
clandestinely, tattered copies passed between tenant farmers like an
editorial Underground Railroad. By 1919, the *Defender* was so
influential in eastern Arkansas and so instrumental in fanning the
migratory flames that Governor Charles H. Brough complained to
the U.S. Post Office Department that such an "incendiary organ"
should be "exclude[d] from the mails." Though postal officials
granted Brough's complaint "due consideration," the paper was
never banned officially and its popularity was undiminished.
"Negroes grab the *Defender* like a hungry mule grabs fodder,"
lamented one critic. The *Defender* sought to cover every instance
of southern white violence against blacks—down to the most lurid
details of a lynching in the smallest towns. One edition noted that
the severed head of a lynching victim had been "thrown into a
crowd of Negroes on the principal Negro street." By dint of its
thorough coverage of such events as well as its letters column filled
with success stories from Chicago, Detroit, Cleveland, and elsewhere, the *Defender*'s every page was a virtual advertisement for
the good life of the North.

But with Armistice Day came the beginning of the end of the
good life. Returning white veterans pushed black migrants out of
the jobs they had claimed during the labor shortage and economic
boom of the war years. In the South, black soldiers—more than
360,000 had served their country—returned to a caste system by
which some, having been exposed to the wider world, could no
longer abide. Hardly were their duffel bags unpacked before the

jarring reminder came that whatever ideas about equality black soldiers had been contaminated with in France were to be quarantined now that they were back home.

One black veteran unable to keep his notions about equality to himself was Robert Lee Hill. Upon his return to Arkansas, the twenty-six-year-old farmer found conditions unchanged; the Delta's tenant-farming economy depended as much as ever upon the exploitation of blacks. It had been that way since the Civil War, when planters were left with nothing but their land and their credit, and former slaves with nothing but their labor. In both eras, the plantation owner or a local merchant furnished tenant-farmers with seed and supplies, for which he was to be paid back with a percentage of the crop, usually a quarter or a third. The planter resold the cotton locally or in Memphis, generally for a higher price than he paid. Any profit the tenants may have made usually went to pay off the planter or the merchant, whom they owed for the year's "furnish." By the end of the year, most tenants were further in debt than they had been the previous year. And since the crop-lien system dictated that tenants could not move off the owner's land until their debts were paid, they were held in nothing short of peonage.

Robert Hill decided the time was ripe for a change. In April of 1919 in a small settlement in Phillips County, just south of the Lee County border from La Grange, Hill founded the Progressive Farmers and Household Union of America. Many of the union's charter members were fellow World War I veterans who believed that if they could win the fight for freedom on foreign lands they could do so in eastern Arkansas. By September the union had organized "lodges" throughout Phillips County.

The entire country was on edge that summer; in cities everywhere the smolder of postwar readjustment had burst into flaming anger. More than twenty race riots erupted in 1919, the last six months of which the historian John Hope Franklin called "the greatest period of interracial strife the nation had ever witnessed."

There was bloodshed in Chicago and Washington, Indianapolis and Knoxville and Omaha. But in none of those urban riots did the violence approach that which began at a small sawmill settlement called Hoop Spur near Elaine, Arkansas. Hoop Spur was a cluster of three or four houses and a church adjacent to the Missouri-Pacific Railroad, which ran north from Elaine to Helena, the seat of Phillips County.

On the last evening of September, members of the Progressive Farmers Union met in the Hoop Spur Church, a narrow, unpainted, wood-frame structure. There final plans were laid for a mass lawsuit the union planned to bring against twenty-one landlords who had refused members the right to make cash settlements and who failed to render to the members accurate accounts for their crops. Because a previous union meeting was disrupted by unknown persons, members decided to arm themselves at this gathering.

Rumor in the white community had it that the union planned an "insurrection," similar in nature, they feared, to events headlined throughout the summer and in the previous day's edition of the *Helena World:* "OMAHA IS SCENE OF UNBRIDLED ANARCHY" and "MOB AT OMAHA TRIES TO LYNCH THE MAYOR." Though the rumor of violent uprising was groundless, it is understandable that an organization of angry black tenant-farmers seeking legal recourse was so viewed by the cotton planters. The sharecroppers, after all, were demanding fair treatment: a fair price for their labor and a share of the prosperity that the high postwar cotton prices brought to the Delta. But prosperity was not to be shared—not in a region in which tenant-farmers were denied the most fundamental rights of free speech and assemblage. To suggest any change, whether through threat of violence or legal action, could mean an end to a system that relied necessarily on exploitation. And that would be tantamount to an insurrection.

Late that last night of September, a car with three men, including a deputy sheriff, drove up to the church. A short time later one of the men, a white railroad agent, was killed by gunfire. The deputy later claimed they had stopped only to fix a flat and were fired on without warning; the union members said they returned shots intended to break up their meeting. At any rate, the sheriff was alerted and within hours a posse mobilized. By the following day more than eight hundred armed whites had arrived from throughout the region, many from various American Legion posts, Marianna's included. Local white women and children were herded onto getaway trains for safekeeping. The posse charged into Elaine, indiscriminately searching and ransacking black homes, attempting to arrest or murder everyone who had not already fled into the canebrakes. More gunfire was exchanged, more blacks and whites killed. "DESPERATE FIGHTING BETWEEN WHITES AND NEGROES" the *Arkansas Gazette* bannered in a first-day story, followed, on successive days, by: "NEGROES HAVE BEEN AROUSED BY PROPAGANDA" and "VICIOUS BLACKS WERE PLANNING GREAT UPRISING."

Governor Brough, no doubt aroused by the *Gazette*'s propaganda, placed Elaine under martial law and received permission from the federal War Department to order into town five hundred United States Army troops, equipped with machine guns, to "restore order."

It was officially announced that five whites and twenty-five blacks were killed, but the reported number of black deaths was surely deflated; whites in Helena boasted that "more than one hundred Negroes were killed." And even that figure, said the National Association for the Advancement of Colored People, understated the massacre. The NAACP's investigator reported that blacks in the canebrakes "were being hunted and two hundred fifty shot down like wild beasts."

Nearly one hundred blacks were indicted by an all-white grand jury on various charges; twelve were charged with murder. (A lone white man arrested was considered to be a union sympathizer.) Though the trials were brisk—none lasted more than forty-five minutes—they positively meandered compared to the five minutes (on average) required of the juries to return the guilty verdicts. In five days, twelve men were sentenced to die in the electric chair and eighty others were sentenced to prison terms of from one to twenty years.

With help from the NAACP, the death sentences were appealed. The Supreme Court of the United States, ruling that the defendants were denied due process, overturned each of their sentences. Wrote Chief Justice Oliver Wendell Holmes: ". . . no juryman could have voted for an acquittal and continued to live in Phillips County and if any prisoner by any chance had been acquitted by a jury he could not have escaped the mob." By 1925, after some six years behind bars, the Phillips County prisoners were freed from the state penitentiary—and released from a fate for which they had been forced to prepare by building their own coffins.

For the rest of the world the Elaine massacre and the Supreme Court decision it spawned, stood, in the early 1920s, as the latest symbol of the racist South; for blacks in the Delta it stood for something more. It stood, for a fleeting moment, as a sign of hope. For the first time since the cotton pickers of Lee County struck for higher wages two decades earlier, black tenant-farmers in the Delta took collective action against their landlords. And though many, possibly hundreds, paid with their lives, the highest court in the land had come, at last, to champion their cause. The Court said not a word about the larger issue of economic exploitation, but it rebuked publicly the state's criminal justice system—and it saved the lives of twelve black men.

For one sharecropping family living some twenty-five miles north of Elaine, in Lee County, the Supreme Court's decision was hailed as a harbinger. "Poppa told us when those boys was freed that it was a good sign," recalls Billy Joe's uncle Jesse Chambers, who was fifteen when the Phillips County men were released from prison. "Nineteen and twenty-five was the year my baby brother was born. And Poppa said it was 'specially a good sign for him. But it look to me now like he had the signs read wrong."

* * *

Jesse and Curtis's parents, Jim and Candie Chambers, had married in 1901, when Jim was twenty-one and Candie a few years younger. As were most sharecropping families, theirs was itinerant; Curtis's sister, Louise Chambers Stewart, five years his elder, recalls the number of plantations they lived on before Curtis's birth as "too many to remember." Most were located in La Grange or the nearby Third Zion community of Rondo, where Curtis, the seventh and last child, was born in a three-room shotgun shack.

Seventeen months later, in 1927, Curtis lost his mother; Candie died of a throat infection.

Thereafter, Jim Chambers raised his children with the help of a succession of girlfriends. At five feet eight, he was considerably taller than would be most of his descendants. In his middle forties, Jim had a receding hairline that brought into relief the high forehead and round face that would mark future generations of Chambers men. And, like certain of his grandsons would be, he was a notorious womanizer. "He was a man who liked women," says Leonard Sims, a La Grange native. "He usually kept some kind of woman around, but they usually wouldn't stay long."

Jim also relied on his neighbors and on Candie's sisters to look after the children. The neighbors would piece together quilts for the Chambers family and deliver "a mess of fresh meat from a hog-kill every so often," says John L. Chambers, Curtis's brother. Otherwise they survived on rabbits, known as "Hoover hogs," and on okra, canned fruit, and, especially, cows. "Called 'em walking smokehouses," says a neighbor. "Milk, butter, meat, leather. Even used the horns for a whistle." Candie's sister, Shug, who lived in Marianna, sewed clothes for the children and each fall purchased one pair of shoes for them. Called "Memphis flats," the shoes were tan-colored and durable: they lasted all year. "Aunt Shug" also boarded the older children while they attended the Moton School in Marianna.

But those kindnesses were not enough. "Living was just every day a struggle," says Curtis's sister Louise, a devout, tiny woman stooped from a lifetime of farm work. She is divorced and lives alone in a small house in West Helena, less than ten miles south of La Grange. "Daddy would have to go work or go for groceries; sometime he'd be gone the whole day and have to leave us young ones alone. One time, I couldn't be but maybe seven or eight, Curtis was crying so hard because he was hungry. I cooked him an egg but I didn't know to put any grease in the skillet—almost burned the house down. When Daddy came home and I told him what happened, he had tears in his eyes. Then he knew we needed a mother."

Jim eventually remarried. He and his second wife had three children. They continued to move often, until Jim acquired fifty acres of his own. In the early days of the Depression, he lost the land. Whether he lost it to hard economic times or hardheaded-ness—vice, actually—is unknown. "Daddy used to love to gamble and sometimes he lost. Did he lose the farm? He never would tell me, but that's how my brothers told it," Louise says.

The Chambers family wound up sharecropping on a small plantation near Cypress Corner they knew as "Dr. White's place." Dr. White furnished the family with everything—"from shack to seed"—necessary to produce the crop. In return, Jim Chambers split the crop evenly with Dr. White. The family stayed there for two or three years, by which time they were able to buy their own horse, mule, and enough tools, fertilizer, and seed to climb a rung back up the economic ladder to "thirds and fourths farming." They moved to yet another place in La Grange, where the land-owner received every third bushel of corn and every fourth bale of cotton.

For much of the 1920s, La Grange and the surrounding area thrived. The town's four sawmills operated nonstop; three Mis-souri-Pacific passenger trains made daily stops; and a gin shipped cotton seed and cotton, the price of which reached as high as thirty-five cents a pound during the height of postwar inflation. By 1929, though, the grip of the Great Depression, which started early in the Arkansas Delta and lasted longer than almost anywhere else, had tightened. The price of cotton dropped to less than seventeen cents, and by 1931 had slid all the way to five cents—less than it cost to produce a pound.

By 1931, the entire nation, of course, was locked in the Great Depression, but in Arkansas there was also the Great Drought. It had stopped raining just after cotton-planting season, in May of 1930. It would not rain again until the spring of 1931. Cotton, a dry-weather crop, withstood the drought better than other crops. But with warehouses stuffed with unsold bales from the 1930 crop, there was little market for cotton—at any price. The one-two punch of depression and drought ensured widespread destitution. One hundred and forty-three banks failed in Arkansas, many of them in rural areas. And so while the drought caused many farmers to default on their loans, the bank closures meant that farmers could neither borrow additional money toward their next crops nor withdraw whatever savings were tied up. And tenant-farmers like Jim Chambers, who were paid once a year and who depended on their landlords to furnish the year's supplies until the late fall harvest, were hardest hit of all. If the planter for whom Jim Chambers worked could not borrow money from his bank, he could not lend it, even at interest rates that ranged, in the words of one critic, "from twenty percent to grand larceny."

The federal government established a drought-relief fund, but the conditions President Herbert Hoover's administration imposed on farmers needing loans were so restrictive few farmers received anything. In Lee County, there were fifty-five hundred farmers, almost all of them wretched. Twenty-two qualified for a government loan.

President Hoover's aversion to federal relief—he felt, says one writer, that such involvement "would weaken the national character"—left relief efforts up to local Red Cross chapters. By the middle of January of 1931, the Red Cross was feeding half the Arkansas Delta's farming population. But the agency was running out of money. The chairman of the Red Cross chapter in Mississippi County, north and east of Lee County, warned Senator Joseph T. Robinson: "Actual starvation is going to stalk over the fertile fields of the county before April, unless there is further relief." But as a result primarily of Hoover's opposition, there would be no meaningful further relief from Washington. Its funds virtually depleted, the Red Cross reduced its monthly allocation for food to a dollar a person.

Congressional mailbags were filled with desperate appeals from eastern Arkansas. To Senator Robinson came this plea from a tenant-farmer: "Thousands of colored farmers . . . has had no break. They are barefooted and in thin clothes. Many has went to the county judges and the local Red Cross, they both say they has no funds . . . Don't turn us away." But the senator could do little to relieve the suffering. He referred his constituents' letters to a Department of Agriculture official, whose reply could only begin: "The Federal Government has appropriated no money for the relief of farmers . . ."

The rains finally came in April. A month later, at the end of May of 1931, Hazel, the last of Haywood and Eliza Cook's four children, was born. The Cooks lived on the O. B. Polk plantation, in the Pilgrim community in south central Lee County. Haywood was under five feet tall, but he had made a name for himself as a star player in the Saturday Negro baseball leagues around eastern Arkansas. The teams were composed of sharecroppers and sponsored by the planters. "The guy was a roadrunner," says Leonard Sims. "Stole any base he wanted. If he got on, you knew he was gonna score." (Well into his sixties, Haywood performed gymnastic flips—"front and back," Billy Joe says—to the delight of his grandchildren.)

Haywood also was a renowned drinker. His thirst for moonshine ultimately destroyed his marriage. Eliza (for whom Hazel and Curtis would name their second daughter), taller than her husband and sturdy, had little tolerance for Haywood's drinking. The couple "fought all the time, constant," says Joseph Cooper, their nephew and Hazel's first cousin. One winter morning, Eliza could stand no more of Haywood's drunken abusiveness. She decided to sober him up. She picked him up and "sat him on the cookstove like a tub of water," Cooper recalls. "Now I seen Uncle Hay run the bases, but I ain't never seen anyone run out and jump in the lake *that* fast."

When Hazel was barely school-aged, Haywood ran out on the marriage. Eliza, still in her twenties, married a man named Frank Jones with whom she would have six more children. An uncle enrolled Hazel at Moton School in Marianna. When she was in the eighth grade, she met a boy there named Curtis Chambers. He was five years older but had not spent nearly as much time in school as had Hazel. He attended only when rain kept him out of the fields and during the summer months when the crop was "laid by" and before it was ready for picking. He says he "got to either the seventh or eighth grade" but that he missed so much school he never learned to read or write.

What Curtis did was work. Even as a young child, Curtis worked all the time. "He worked when I didn't feel like it," says John L. Chambers, who is two years older than Curtis. "He even worked when Poppa didn't feel like it. I told Poppa I couldn't do no more and Curt would be out there like he wasn't even tired."

On March 14, 1948, when he was twenty-two and she was two months shy of her seventeenth birthday, Curtis Chambers and Hazel Cook married in Marianna. Curtis's father had died several months earlier, and for the first time Curtis was on his own. He and Hazel cash-rented forty acres, on which they farmed cotton, soybeans, and a little corn. After their first child, Curtis Jr., was born, the land was sold and the new owner evicted the young family. Once more Curtis moved, this time to a forty-four-acre farm outside of La Grange owned by his Aunt Virgie, another of his late mother's sisters. Virgie had moved off the land after the death of her first husband; she was remarried and living on a large farm in Rondo.

For the first time since the Depression, when his father lost the land he owned briefly, Curtis was on family-owned soil. And though it would be two decades before he would inherit the land from his Aunt Virgie, he knew from the day he first paid rent to her that this was the farm he and Hazel would raise their family on, and year after year, plant, chop, and pick their cotton on.

Although the family no longer had eviction worries, their lives were circumscribed, tedious, and lonely: an endless cycle of field work and child care and household chores, all done without the benefit of electricity or running water. Kerosene lamps, dim and dangerous, provided the sole lighting. A woodstove heated water hauled in for cooking, washing clothes and dishes, and bathing. There was no refrigerator, of course, which meant that only meat that was freshly butchered could be eaten. The cows had to be milked daily and their milk somehow kept fresh. In cooler months, this was accomplished by burying the milk jugs in the ground and keeping moist the surrounding soil. At other times, the milk jugs were cooled in freshly pumped water; the water would be replaced as often as possible throughout the day. With no fan, in the hot months the doors and window frames—there was no glass and usually no screens—remained open to permit entrance to any blessed breezes—along with dust and any manner of pests: stray animals, "chicken snakes," flies, and mosquitoes. To lessen the probability of bites meant sleeping under a "mosquito bar"—a veillike covering attached to the four-poster bed with poles cut from saplings. The canopy worked well against the bugs, but it also stilled and trapped the sultry air.

The cold and wet months were at least as uncomfortable. Though the doors were shut and the window frames covered with tin sheets, the house was so drafty, the roof and floorboards and walls so flimsy, that it "rained and snowed indoors," Curtis says. Trying to keep warm meant stoking the woodstove throughout the night. If it overheated, or if the overburdened tin chimney failed, sparks could fly and a house could burn. It happened to the Chamberses, and it happened to several of their neighbors.

The drudgery was leavened only with Saturday trips to town and Sundays spent in church. On Saturday afternoons, Hazel and Curtis and most other farm people streamed into Marianna. If they couldn't catch a ride with a neighbor, they caught the bus that ran between Helena, the seat of Phillips County, and Wynne, the seat of Cross County, north of Marianna. By late afternoon, the court-house square was a carnival of activity. Local blues musicians blew harps and picked guitars on the street; appreciative passersby dropped their nickels and dimes in a cup. On the well-tended square, a minister might feel the call to preach the Gospel. At first his audience might consist only of squirrels and the old men who seemed to live on the park benches, where they enjoyed their drink under the sheltering expanse of the mulberry trees. But a crowd would invariably gather, seekers of salvation from the cotton, refu-gees from the dice and card games at the jammed cafés and shops in the black business district across Main Street known as "Nigger Row."

"People on Nigger Row would be there like blackbirds," re-calls A. J. Atkins, the former sharecropper who was raised with Hazel's mother. In the 1940s, the strip housed a couple of juke joints, Reed's and O'Donnell's; two cafés, Elmer's and Vail's; and Williams' Dry Goods, which, in addition to a full line of general merchandise offered for a dime "all the bologna and crackers you could eat." There was a shoe repair shop; a tailor; a laundry and dry cleaners; and the Blue Heaven movie theater, which featured mati-nee heroes such as Zorro, Tom Mix, and Gene Autry.

And it wasn't just blacks who crowded the town. White fami-lies, just as eager to spend a day a week off the land, packed *their* cafés and shops and theater, the Imperial. Downtown was so jammed, says Jenny Ann Boyer, Marianna's historian, "You had to turn sideways to walk and wedge yourself between the people." In fact, recalls Curtis, there were times he lost Hazel in the swarm. "You'd have to remember what your wife was wearing and stand on the hood of a car to spot her."

By the late 1940s, there were fewer cars to stand on and less need to do so: the Saturday crowds were dwindling. The popula-tion of Lee County was as large as it had ever been at the start of the decade, but World War II brought fundamental change to the Delta, change that would signal the beginning of the end of the agricultural era and that would set in motion the second wave of the Great Migration. As had occurred during the First World War, the labor shortage during the forties opened up jobs in northern industries that previously had been closed to blacks (and women). Hazel's mother and her new husband moved to St. Louis, where he found work with a defense contractor. Hazel wanted to follow but Curtis was unconvinced life would be any better there. They would stay on the farm, he told her.

But many of their friends left. Though cotton was again fetching a high price, and yields were robust during the war and in the immediate postwar years, farm income could not compete with the hourly wages of the northern factories. Nor could a life of legalized subordination under Jim Crow compete with the opportunity World War II provided to escape to the more enlightened North. As the director of the Chicago Urban League put it: "There are two main reasons why the Negro leaves the South—to improve his economic situation and standard of living and to get the hell out of there."

Elijah (Bogie) Council, who was born in La Grange in 1918, "said my good-byes to Lee County" soon after war broke out. "After the Japanese bombed Pearl Harbor, I heard on the radio there were going to be jobs in Detroit." He boarded a Greyhound in Marianna ("There were trains too, but the Dog was cheaper"), and after working a couple of short-term jobs, he hired on as a janitor at Chrysler in July of 1942. Like many other industrial companies, Chrysler had converted certain of its wartime operations to arms manufacturing. (Detroit styled itself the "Arsenal of Democracy.") Council worked in the machine shop at Highland Park, sweeping and "pulling chips" from the machinery that produced gun valves. "I was pushing a broom and a mop, but I was making seventy-nine cents an hour. Best you could do back home was chopping cotton at seventy-five cents a day. When the man paid me my first check, I had to count it twice—seemed like too much!"

As Bogie Council discovered, and as his friends and relatives who followed him found, the dream of moving up and out of Lee County was within reach. There were jobs in Detroit, jobs that could lift them above the shimmering Delta horizon and give them a look at another world. Even if the new world meant working at the dirtiest, most dangerous jobs, the jobs whites refused to do, and even if it meant living in crowded, tenement-filled neighborhoods, the world up north, says Council, offered possibilities the cotton fields could not. "You couldn't see a future back home. You could in Detroit."

As Council and the thousands of other new immigrants sent word home of the opportunities up north, the fields of Arkansas emptied. Their message was simple: "Everyone writes back he's heeled. He's got him a job," one Arkansan related at the time. Between 1940 and 1950, four hundred and sixteen thousand people emigrated from the state, more, percentage-wise, than from any of the six other states that lost people during the decade. The greatest losses were from the black-majority, cotton-producing counties of the Delta. Almost twenty-five hundred people evacuated Lee County—a decline of more than 9 percent.

Not only did people find jobs up north. They found the other rewards of citizenship denied them at home. Bogie Council no longer had to pay a poll tax or seek approval of a plantation owner to vote; he could join a union, walk the city streets after dark without fear of encountering men in hoods. He worked an eight-hour day (plus overtime), rather than from "can to can't" in the fields. "The difference between Detroit and Marianna was heaven and hell," Council says.

As did most blacks in Detroit, Council lived in a Lower East Side neighborhood known as Black Bottom. Immediately east of downtown and Gratiot Avenue, the area for nearly a century had been the city's gateway for new immigrants: Germans, Poles, Russian Jews, Greeks, Italians. One group would arrive, and the more established would depart for a choicer neighborhood. "There was a constant moving of people outward from the center city, where the auto industry was founded," says Thomas A. Dietz, a historian for the city of Detroit. "But once the first wave of black migrants came during World War I, the pattern changed."

For the next three decades, through World War II, though the black population of Detroit swelled and swelled some more— from forty-two thousand in 1920 to a hundred and twenty thousand in 1930 to two hundred thousand by 1943—their geographical boundaries expanded hardly at all. As early as 1917, the Detroit Urban League reported that the "Negro immigrants . . . are in there so thick they can hardly move."

Blacks were confined to the sixty square blocks that became known as Black Bottom and an adjacent business and entertainment district called Paradise Valley. Rents were high for the dilapidated frame houses, most of which dated from no later than the turn of the century. Many were still owned by the immigrants who jerry-built them, and who had moved on, distancing themselves from the smoke of the factories and the crush of black migrants who had no choice but to settle in Black Bottom. To attempt to move elsewhere in Detroit was to invite organized resistance— angry mobs dressed as neighborhood "improvement associations." And so Southern blacks were condemned to an anthill of a neighborhood, a district urban planners dismissed as a "filthy, smelly, teeming slum."

That was not how Bogie Council saw it. "I felt like I was part of the country for the first time," he says. Council's flat, off Gratiot near Chene Street, was "shabby," but it had running water, hot and cold, and an indoor toilet. (By 1950, barely a third of Lee County farm families had electricity in their homes; fewer had indoor toilets.) And the neighborhood, crammed as it was with transplanted Southerners, was hospitable and vibrant. Nearly everyone had jobs: women worked as domestics, men in the auto factories. Like Council, most blacks were employed as janitors or in the foundries. Such work, declared one trade publication, suited their "aptitude and skill . . . for hot and heavy work."

The peculiar gumbo of vice and commerce and religion permeated the air like the spicy smoke of the dozens of fish and chicken shacks and rib joints that lined Hastings Street. There was no shortage of hustlers, from numbers runners to tent-show preachers to prostitutes, but neither was there a sense of desperation. "The hookers, good-sized women," the writer Betty DeRamus remembers, "would take breaks from shouting 'Turn the corner, baby' to rest on the sidewalks in wooden chairs."

There was in all this activity an easy familiarity: of Saturday afternoons in Marianna, the great crowds spilling out of the cafés. But if the sounds and sights and smells of Black Bottom occasionally fostered feelings of homesickness in Bogie Council, his regular visits to Lee County reminded him jarringly of why he left.

In many ways, it was not until World War II that the outside world first infringed upon Lee County. Until then no one much believed that what happened in the corridors of power and consequence in the far corners of the world—the world outside the county—could affect their daily lives. Even the widely publicized mid-thirties movement to organize eastern Arkansas sharecroppers, the Southern Tenant Farmers Union, dwindled before it reached Lee County. And as racial milestones were reached in distant places—Jackie Robinson's breakthrough to the Major Leagues in April of 1947, President Harry Truman's executive order banning segregation in the armed forces in July of 1948—Lee County blacks hailed those milestones as they might shooting stars: bright and fleeting and remote. They were not so concerned about the Brooklyn Dodgers or integrated foxholes as they were about having enough food, enough rain, enough children to bring in the crop. And one day, maybe, if they prayed on it, they would be blessed with electricity and running water for their homes.

But to the county's rulers, composed mainly of implacable segregationists, the relaxed racial attitudes elsewhere signaled the alarming possibility of a nascent civil rights movement closer to home. The alarm was sounded as early as 1944, when the Supreme Court of the United States ruled that all-white primaries were unconstitutional. (The Democratic party of Arkansas had no choice but to comply with the decision as it applied to the federal ballot. But the party, which considered itself a "private association," contended that the ruling did not apply to state primary elections. In 1945, the state legislature, led by the representatives of Lee and the other plantation counties, implemented a double primary. The party issued blacks a ballot listing only candidates for federal elections; it gave whites the federal ballot as well as a ballot for state elections.)

The Truman administration pressed for civil rights legislation as none had before. Truman's presidential Committee on Civil Rights issued a 1947 report calling for an end to the poll tax, for fair employment and anti-lynching legislation, and for desegregating the armed services; white southern Democrats found the report's conclusions so incendiary it may as well have been laced with gasoline.

In his 1948 State of the Union address, Truman further fanned the flames. "Our first goal," he told the Congress, "is to secure fully the essential human rights of our citizens." And when during the Democratic National Convention in July the delegates approved as part of the party's platform a strong civil rights plank, the Mississippi delegation and half of the Alabama delegation could stand no more—they walked out. Two days later they convened in Birmingham with fellow "States' Rights Democrats" from around the South.

The states' righters, or "Dixiecrats," nominated then governor J. Strom Thurmond of South Carolina for president and Fielding Wright, the governor of Mississippi, for vice president. Their goal was to garner enough electoral votes to force the 1948 election into the House of Representatives; their rhetoric was defiant. "There's not enough troops in the army to break down segregation and admit the Negro into our homes, our eating places, our swimming pools, and our theaters," Thurmond declared.

Naturally enough, support for the Dixiecrats was strongest in the South's rural black belt counties—those counties where blacks

outnumbered whites and, in theory anyway, had the greatest political potential. Of course, it was also in those counties, like Lee, that
blacks, wholly dependent on white plantation owners, were most
restricted educationally and politically.

Dixiecrat activity in Arkansas was conducted from an office
building on the courthouse square in Marianna. Already headquartered there was a statewide organization of plantation operators
and business executives called the Arkansas Free Enterprise Association. The Free Enterprise Association was established in 1944 to
battle "nefarious and insidious encroachments into the very vitals
of our American system"—unionism, communism, desegregation.
(It had fought for and won passage of Arkansas's anti-labor Right-
to-Work amendment that year.) The association's executive director was a hard-boiled local lawyer named John L. Daggett, a
member of one of Marianna's most prosperous and renowned families and a partner in Daggett, Daggett & Daggett. ("Every boy
child born in the family had to be a lawyer," one observer explains.) Daggett was a tireless organizer and fervent ideologue—
"probably the state's No. 1 labor-baiter," one eastern Arkansas
newspaper called him.

The Free Enterprise Association's principles—to "preserve,
protect, and defend the inalienable freedom of the individual and
the sacred right of local self-government"—squared perfectly with
the Dixiecrats' platform. Daggett already was the point man in
Arkansas for the ultra-conservatives; it was he who assumed leadership of the state Dixiecrat effort, running the campaign out of his
law office. He traveled throughout Arkansas, appealing to Rotarians, Lions, Kiwanians to fight for the heritage of the Lost Cause, to
resist the evil forces in control of the Democratic party, and to
enlist in the crusade against social equality by casting their ballots
for the states' rights ticket.

A month before the Democratic state convention, in late August of 1948, Daggett brought Strom Thurmond to Marianna. It
would be the candidate's only appearance in Arkansas. The *Courier-Index* heralded Thurmond's arrival as "the first time in history

that a candidate for President of the United States has visited a small town. . . . The occasion should be a tocsin call to every citizen of Lee County . . ." A nationwide radio broadcast and wire-service coverage of Thurmond's speech at the high school football field ensured that "pictures and stories under a Marianna, Arkansas, dateline were carried throughout the United States."

What the words and pictures captured was a plantation aristocracy holding on to the Old South for dear life. The speaker's platform from which Thurmond addressed the crowd was decorated in antebellum finery, with "old fashioned Colonial columns entwined with Southern smilax and magnolia branches" and a quartet of Marianna beauty queens in period costume. Thurmond's remarks complemented the set. "In the eyes of the nation," he warned, "the vote of any Arkansan for Truman or Dewey [the Republican candidate] would be saying: 'Yes, we want force laws for the co-mingling of the races in Arkansas.' Every vote for either Dewey or Truman is a vote for a second Reconstruction era."

In the end, Truman won almost 62 percent of the popular vote in Arkansas. Thurmond won only 16.5 percent statewide, but he carried Lee County with 58 percent. With Truman's election, the Dixiecrats lost their momentum and the foundation was laid for the emerging civil rights movement. Yet the movement that began in 1955 when a black seamstress refused to yield her seat to a white on a crowded bus in Montgomery, Alabama, would largely bypass Lee County—until the day sixteen years later when a young black woman walked into the Mug & Cone drive-in in Marianna to pick up a pizza she'd ordered.

CHAPTER NINE

TOO WINDY FOR TEAR GAS

It was an act as defiant as Rosa Parks's.

On June 8, 1971, a Tuesday, a twenty-six-year-old black woman named Quency Tillman ordered a take-out pizza at the Mug & Cone drive-in, a fast-food joint on the outskirts of Marianna. It was lunchtime, and Tillman had a one-hour break from her job as a social worker with the Lee County school system. The pizza was a long time in coming, and finally Tillman told the waitress—the owner's daughter—she could wait no longer. "Cancel the order," she said, "I've got to get back to work." The waitress protested that it was almost ready, and besides, "You order, you pay."

After work, Tillman went home and was told the owner of the Mug & Cone was looking for her. The owner, a retired army officer, was also a Marianna police officer. "I went up to the police department and the man promptly arrested me—put me in *jail*," Tillman recalls. The charge was "false pretense"—ordering a pizza without intending to pay. Bond was set at twenty-five hundred dollars. "They wanted my father to put our house up [for collateral] on the bond," Tillman says, still exasperated two decades later.

The police officer, a retired army captain, had confronted Tillman's brother Skippy a few days earlier. Skippy had just returned to Marianna from his second tour of duty in Vietnam. He was wearing his camouflage fatigues around town, which angered the army man to the point that the two almost came to blows over it. When the officer's daughter told him about the argument with Quency at the restaurant, he apparently decided to teach the Tillman family a lesson: that even if these outspoken young blacks had broken no Jim Crow law—the legal basis for discrimination had disappeared years earlier—by talking back to a powerful white person (or his daughter) they were still subject to sanctions.

The civil rights movement of the 1950s and 1960s that barreled broadside into the national status quo had barely sideswiped Lee County. Black leadership there remained the province of old-style ministers who preached turn-the-other-cheek acceptance ("Yes, we're being mistreated, but the Lord will take care of us") and teachers who taught go-along-to-get-along accommodation. Neither the Atlanta-based Student Nonviolent Coordinating Committee (SNCC) nor any other national movement organization with a presence in the Delta could make any inroads in Lee County. In 1965, SNCC established the Arkansas Summer Project to conduct voter registration drives in those Delta counties where "Negroes have met the most harassment for seeking to obtain their right to vote." Volunteers set up community centers in neighboring St. Francis and Phillips counties; Lee remained untouched. "Whites there didn't mind blacks voting," recalls Jan Wrede, a former VISTA volunteer in Marianna, "because it was understood by all that there was no such thing as a private ballot."

The belated arrival of the civil rights movement in Lee County corresponded—not incidentally—with the end of the plantation era. As A. J. Atkins, the former sharecropper, explains, "The years come when the wisdom of man opened up and farm equipment started doing more." And as tractors ("steel mules") and chemical fertilizers and pesticides and, especially, mechanized cotton pickers invaded the fields of the Delta, farmworkers became as obsolete as their mules and plows. (A two-row picking machine, operated by one person, could do the work of more than a hundred field hands.) People who were forced off the land crowded into shotgun shacks in Marianna—or, if they were lucky, into a public-housing ghetto. Unskilled, illiterate, and expendable, much of the former farm population survived on welfare.

Nor were there jobs in town. While much of the rest of the rural South attempted to diversify its economy through industrialization—recruitment of textile factories, auto-parts suppliers, light manufacturing—Lee County's planter-run chamber of commerce discouraged industrial development. (By the mid-sixties, Marianna had one major manufacturer, but the company had yet to hire its first black employee.) Other localities waged economic war over northern manufacturers seeking to escape the tyranny of high-wage union labor and high tax districts. They offered tax breaks and an abundant, compliant workforce hostile to organized labor. Marianna, however, assumed an isolationist stance. "We didn't want blue-collar workers coming down from the North and the farmers didn't want competition for their labor force," says Franklin Montgomery, who is retired from the Marianna Fire Department and who served a term as mayor in the early 1980s. Adds Roy C. (Bill) Lewellen, Jr., a Marianna lawyer and the region's first black state senator since Reconstruction: "Everyone knew the farmers fought the higher-paying factory jobs for fear of losing their laborers. We're suffering now for the lack of foresight in the sixties, when the farmers were living on easy street."

Though county officials escaped the national civil rights movement and, for the time being, union labor, they could not escape the attention of the federal government's antipoverty programs. President Lyndon B. Johnson declared in 1964 that the state would become one of the central battlegrounds of his new War on Poverty. "What is bad in the nation, in the president's view, is worse in Arkansas," the *Arkansas Gazette* surmised at the time. Sixty percent of Arkansas families made less than four thousand dollars a year; nationally only 30 percent earned so little.

What was bad in Arkansas was worse in Lee County. A 1968 study named Lee the sixth poorest county in the nation. The median family income there was less than two thousand dollars; black men earned an average of seven hundred and five dollars annually. Nearly half the county's houses were still without indoor plumbing. Its black infant mortality rate of fifty-three deaths per thousand babies was more than twice the national average and three times higher than the mortality rate of white babies in Lee County.

Such statistics compelled the government's newly created Office of Economic Opportunity (OEO) to fund a health-care demonstration project in Lee County. Its premise was radical—and sensible: that patients should have control over their own health. Policy for the comprehensive clinic would be set by a board elected by the very people it served: poor people, poor *black* people. Who better understood the problems poor people faced in obtaining adequate health care than the people themselves? The center would be staffed primarily by a doctor, a nurse, and five other inductees in VISTA, or Volunteers in Service to America, a domestic version of the Peace Corps administered by the OEO. In August of 1969, the seven VISTA volunteers arrived in Marianna to lay the groundwork for the Lee County Cooperative Clinic.

The county's prominent citizens warmly welcomed the volunteers. "They initially thought we were a group of charitable do-gooders, there to drive people to the welfare office, that sort of thing," says Daniel Blumenthal, who as a twenty-seven-year-old newly minted physician was the first doctor in the nation to serve in VISTA. Blumenthal had never lived in a rural area. He grew up in St. Louis, attended medical school in Chicago, and served his internship in New Orleans. What he saw in Lee County sickened him. "In the rural areas the delivery of medical care had fallen way behind the progress in cotton-picking and mechanized planting," he says. "Medical care was still being picked by hand. You saw infectious disease. You saw intestinal parasites—*worms*—that you might expect to see in Latin America but not in the United States."

Health care was provided to poor blacks in the way everything else was allocated. "If you lived on a plantation and your kid was sick, you would ask the plantation owner to pay for a doctor's visit," Blumenthal says. "If the owner refused, or if you didn't live on a plantation, you would go without." As one resident put it at the time: "If you ain't got no money, you don't see no doctor. You just have to suffer it out."

Blumenthal was nearly as sickened at the attitude of the medical establishment. There were four doctors serving the county's twenty-one thousand people. All were white, all practiced in Marianna. (They were especially inaccessible during inclement weather, when the gravel and dirt country roads were hazardous and sometimes impassable.) One doctor was eighty-one and semi-retired; one was sixty and relatively inactive; one told Blumenthal, "The exchange of money is necessary to establish the proper relationship between doctor and patient"; another was the head of the local John Birch Society and said "these people" spend all their money on whiskey and cigarettes. He advised Blumenthal to establish a venereal disease program because that was "the main problem with colored people here." All but one had segregated waiting rooms.

The VISTA workers' honeymoon in Marianna would not last long. "Not knowing the purpose of the VISTA program, the people of Lee County had no objection at first," County Judge Haskell (Hack) Adams said at the time. However, once "the people" understood that the clinic threatened the existing health-care delivery system, once they understood the clinic would be controlled by poor blacks, and that the clinic's patients could address some of their basic needs without relying on white-controlled institutions, it was let known the VISTAs were welcome no longer. "We got to see that their idea of social change didn't fit ours," Adams explained.

Within a few weeks of his arrival, the Lee County Medical Society—the four doctors practicing in Marianna—voted to deny Dan Blumenthal membership, which meant he also was denied privileges at the twenty-seven-bed Lee Memorial Hospital. The doctors were disturbed at reports that Blumenthal dispensed not only medicine but a sense of empowerment; it was said he had "agitated" local blacks to demand more rights. The octogenarian Dr. Mac McLendon told a Memphis reporter: "He's going to the churches and telling Negroes all they have to do to get what they want is to rear up. That's enough for me."

It was enough for most other whites as well. The fracas brought the town press coverage unmatched since Strom Thurmond stumped there in 1948 for the Dixiecrats. "The situation at Marianna," editorialized the statewide *Arkansas Gazette*, "offers the economic, political and civic leadership . . . an opportunity to show that Lee County is more committed to the proposition that the poor need VISTA's services than it is to fighting the perfidious federal government or to putting down the Negro." *What poor?* replied a Marianna farmer named T. H. Barker in a letter to the editor. "Lee County did not acquire this poverty status until a group of bureaucrats decided that we should wear this label."

Barker's antipathy toward VISTA was not unusual among whites in the county. (Among its foes, the acronym came to stand for "Vipers In Subversion To America.") The White Citizens Council, in which T. H. (Buddy) Barker was instrumental, circulated petitions for the project's withdrawal in restaurants, churches, and public buildings. The council, an affiliate of a loose regionwide confederation the journalist Hodding Carter once described as "the Ku Klux Klan with a clipped mustache," coordinated a letter-writing and telegram campaign to state and federal officials.

But the political reach of the clinic far exceeded the grasp of its opponents. With the governor's blessing, the OEO in January of 1970 awarded an initial grant of almost forty thousand dollars.

The grant enabled the clinic to lease space downtown in a five-room house (no commercial landlord would lease to the clinic) next to a funeral home on Liberty Street. (For the first few months of its existence, the "clinic" was limited to house calls; Dr. Blumenthal operated out of the trunk of his Ford Mustang.) In early 1972, despite the noisy objections of the White Citizens Council—in one two-day period, Senator John L. McClellan received more than 150 telegrams urging him to "kill" a prospective federal grant to the clinic—the OEO awarded the clinic an additional $1,200,000. The money was to be used to construct a permanent building, to increase the clinic's staff to forty-six persons, and for a fleet of vans and trucks to transport patients. Suddenly the establishment had a federally nourished King Kong on its hands; the clinic's annual budget of six hundred thousand dollars exceeded that of the county.

It is true that until the VISTA workers—the "bureaucrats"—began organizing the community, poor blacks were voiceless and powerless. But the assault on the county's paternalistic white supremacy was indigenous: it sprang from local blacks—subjects turned citizens—emboldened by the successes of their community-controlled clinic. Though they knew from daily life what the VISTAs knew in theory—that health and medicine were inextricably linked to poverty, to lack of education, and to a social structure that denied blacks control over their own lives—these forces were as much a part of the landscape as the flat sky, the levee, and the cotton itself. For the clinic organizers to begin to change such forces would require moving social mountains more than a century in the making.

And it would require a visionary leader. In its first administrator, a Lee County native named Olly Neal, Jr., the clinic found one. Neal had graduated from Moton in 1958 and gone to college in Memphis, where he became a founder of the campus sit-in movement. He was a natural organizer: forceful and articulate and fearless. He was big and blunt and possessed a voice so booming it

could render a bullhorn superfluous. Despite the occasional desegregation breakthrough, Neal grew discouraged with his fellow students' apathy. "People should have been committed," he has said.
"Negroes in Memphis weren't committed to anything."

Neal quit school in 1961 and moved to Chicago. He worked
as a letter carrier for several years until the army drafted him. Following two years in Vietnam he returned to college in Tennessee,
this time at a small, black, conservative school in the town of Jackson, eighty miles northeast of Memphis. In January of 1969, the
school's science building exploded. Neal's radical reputation made
him a leading suspect in the bombing. He was convicted only of
disorderly conduct and inciting a riot, fined fifty-three dollars, and
expelled from school.

A nonprofit organization in Memphis affiliated with St.
Jude's Hospital hired him to supervise a feeding program in a poor
neighborhood. During a visit home in February of 1970, Neal
heard that VISTA was organizing a health clinic in Marianna.
When the clinic opened its doors on Liberty Street the next
month, Neal was its administrator. From the beginning, Neal
made it clear that he and the board of directors elected from the
community would control the operation. "I didn't want a situation where everyone would say, 'Well, he's there, but the white
folks are runnin' the thing.' I wanted black folks to be able to say,
'Well, you just gotta admit, shit, we runnin' that one.' "

From the very start, the clinic was an unqualified success.
Neal and the board set non-medical policy: the hours of operation,
the fee scale, and so on. And in direct response to the expressed
needs of the community, they developed an array of health-care
services: prenatal care, parasite screening, family planning, psychological counseling, dentistry. "We are not convinced that the specific medical services we provide are going to solve anyone's
problems," Neal said not long after the clinic was founded. "Oh
sure, we can relieve pain and suffering for a while. But the individual must learn that he often can be in control."

Neal and the others saw health care as more than freedom

from disease or illness. Simply put, they believed that if a patient could control, say, his hypertension, or diabetes, or the frequency of his children's upper respiratory ailments, he could learn to respect himself. And that self-respect would carry over. "If we could organize around health care," Neal asks, "why not around other parts of our lives?"

They began with politics. In the summer of 1970, a group of mostly young black activists, some of whom, like Olly Neal, were Vietnam veterans or had lived elsewhere and returned home, began discussing the particulars of mounting a serious challenge to white officeholders. One of the group was Sterling King, Jr., the minister's son who had served overseas in the Peace Corps and registered voters in Mississippi. At first, King recalls, "we had to meet in people's homes because of the fear of meeting in public places." The group settled on a name, Concerned Citizens of Lee County, and a full slate of candidates, headed by a man named Thomas Ishmael, who would run for the chief executive office, county judge, against the four-term incumbent, a leading foe of the clinic.

Because whites controlled the county Democratic party, the Concerned Citizens' slate ran as Republicans—an otherwise moribund party. (To this day, most black candidates for local office run as Republicans.) As Republicans, they could set their own, cheaper filing fees and appoint their own poll-watchers and a member to the local election commission. The three-member commission oversaw the polling process and counted the ballots. It was composed of one Democrat, one Republican, and a second member of the majority party—the white-ruled Democrats.

But a black appointee to the election commission did not guarantee black voters and poll-watchers freedom from harassment and intimidation. At some precincts, for instance, sheriff's deputies wearing guns looked over the shoulders of black voters. At one polling place, a white police officer listed the license plates of cars driven by blacks; at another predominantly black precinct, voters were forced to wait outside in a cold rain. And when R. C. Henry, a black teacher who served as a poll-watcher, complained to the county sheriff of other practices that violated the Arkansas Election Code, he says the sheriff replied: "Damn the book. I run this town."

Although 60 percent of the sixty-six hundred voters were black, and although the Republican candidate for governor, Winthrop Rockefeller, carried Lee County, Thomas Ishmael, the Republican candidate for county judge, lost the election by eight hundred votes. Many believed the election was stolen from Ishmael. Whether this was so cannot be documented; the ballots no longer exist. Thomas Ishmael, for one, believed some of the ballots ceased to exist *before* they were tallied. "Some of my votes were in boxes that fell into the Mississippi River on the way to being counted," Ishmael said not long before he died.

But the loss galvanized the black community. Six months later, on the second Tuesday of June of 1971, the owner of the Mug & Cone arrested Quency Tillman following the dispute over a two-dollar pizza. The incident, humiliating as it was, would not have caused a ripple in a time not long past. But in the wake of the raging battle over the health clinic and the elections, such treatment of a young black woman could no longer be tolerated; the arrest was too much to bear. The forces that bubbled underground for years finally, inexorably, erupted.

Word spread quickly of the arrest. By the following day, the Lee County Concerned Citizens had presented a handwritten list of twenty-three demands to the Marianna–Lee County Chamber of Commerce. If the demands were not met within forty-eight hours, whites were told, the Concerned Citizens would call a boycott of all downtown white businesses. These were the demands.

Blacks in the Following Places.
1. Black in the Health office.
2. Black in all Drug Stores.

3. Black in Court house.
4. Telephone office.
5. Banks.
6. Ark. power Light
7. Water Dept. Office workers.
8. Full time check out girls in grocery store.
9. Blacks in City Government choosen by the Black people's choice.
10. Some blacks hired in all public offices.
11. I. the Tax Assessor's office.

   II. County Clerk's office.

   III. Revenue Department.
12. In the school system we want teachers hired on merit and not because of race, creed or color.
13. Students to receive fair treatment and graded fairly.
14. Students kept in school and not put out unfairly.
15. Black teachers not to be demoted.
16. No more police brutality and insults.
17. Black principals to continue to be principals and *not* assistants.
18. Black advisory council should be selected by Black citizens and not by "City Fathers" by 6-10-71.
19. Mr. A. L. Johnson [principal of the formerly black high school], based on education and experience, be appointed principal of Lee High School [the new, integrated facility] by 6-10-71.
20. All charges against Miss Quency Tillman be dropped by 6-10-71 and *all* monies paid in connection with her arrest and her brother (who bailed her out) be returned.
21. One of the two banks hire Mrs. Willie Howard or Rabon H. Cheeks by 6-10-71.
22. That 2 Black policemen be hired by 6-10-71, and that these Black policemen be approved by the Concerned Citizens of Lee County, Masons, Eastern Stars, and the Lee County Council on Human Relations.

23. We expect to see an announcement relative to this in the
     Courier-Index 6-10-71.

The chamber of commerce ignored the demands. The newspaper printed no list of grievances; no effort was made to meet or
negotiate with the Concerned Citizens. Early Friday morning, a
parade of pickets gathered on Poplar Street, in the heart of the
shopping district. They were issued instructions and leaflets and
sandwich-board signs and began circling the businesses along Poplar, Main, and Court streets—the periphery of the courthouse
square. They marched peaceably but their very presence, their organized protest, their leaflets—ATTENTION! BROTHERS AND SIS-
TERS! STAY OUT OF THE DOWNTOWN STORES BEGINNING AT 8:00 A.M.,
FRIDAY, JUNE 11, 1971—announced emphatically that the era of si-
lence and submissiveness was over. Their signs underscored the
point. HELP YOURSELVES, KEEP YOUR MONEY IN YOUR POCKET, NO
SHOPPING; WHITE PEOPLE HAVE MONEY IN THEIR VEINS, BLEED 'EM,
NO SHOPPING; I'M BLACK, I'M PROUD, HOW ABOUT YOU? NO SHOP-
PING.

From their office at 35 East Main (in what remained of the
once thriving block of black businesses), the Concerned Citizens
exercised tight control of the boycott. They arranged free transportation to out-of-town stores, helped consumers unaccustomed
to paying their bills by mail fill out checks and money orders, address envelopes. If patronage of a downtown store could not be
avoided—if, for example, an ill person needed a prescription
filled—he or she would be issued a special credential, like a hall
pass in school.

Defiance of the boycott was not tolerated. A minister who
preached opposition awoke one night to find his house engulfed in
flames; someone had firebombed it. One retailer complained that
"all my good colored customers out in the country, they've been
threatened so bad they're scared to even come to town to pay what
they owe me, much less buy anything."

The boycott's effect was apparent immediately. Black shoppers, whether intimidated or supportive, were rarely seen down-town. Many whites, fearful of confrontations with picketers, also limited their downtown shopping. Some stores held half-price sales, another moved its stock and employees to a sister store in West Helena, others closed. "It's made a ghost town out of Marianna, killed it, dead," the owner of the Western Auto store said at the time.

A month into the boycott, the picketers were gone, save for the two principal organizers, Rabon Cheeks and Prentiss Neal. (Neal was a younger brother of the clinic administrator, Olly Neal.) One afternoon while they stood on a street corner distributing leaflets, Hack Adams, the county judge, drove up—and onto the sidewalk. He claimed his truck's brakes malfunctioned, causing the truck to swerve toward the leafleteers. To Cheeks and Neal it was no accident; the judge intended to run them down.

The pair marched over to the police station to file charges. The chief told them no arrest warrant would be issued. "Go see the sheriff." Off they went to the county courthouse. The sheriff said, "Go see the prosecuting attorney." As the pair was leaving, in rushed Hack Adams himself, pistol drawn. "You niggers, get out of here," he reportedly said. "I run the courthouse. I will kill the whole pack of you lying sons of bitches."

Judge Adams was restrained, and later arrested. But by then, the pretense for a nonviolent standoff had disappeared. Early one morning a week before Adams's trial, three stores in a downtown shopping center burned. "It was definitely arson," the commander of the local office of the state police said. That same day, a gunshot hit a patrol car driven by a sheriff's deputy. Though the Concerned Citizens issued a statement "deploring" the acts, the fire sent an unmistakable signal that no longer would blacks turn the other cheek. "What we tried to communicate, instead," Olly Neal once said, "was, 'If you will sit and talk with us, that's what we want to do. But if you go the violence route, it will be returned in kind.' "

* * *

On August 5, 1971, Hack Adams had his day in court. The city was taut with emotion; the governor, tipped to a possible riot, had ordered in a squadron of state police to keep the peace. An evenly divided crowd of blacks and whites packed the municipal courtroom. The trial was over in fifteen minutes. Judge Adams pleaded no contest to charges of assault and possessing a deadly weapon. He was fined ninety-five dollars.

Outside afterward, the plaintiffs, Prentiss Neal and Rabon Cheeks, held an impromptu press conference. A group of about twenty white men, most brandishing baseball bats, gathered nearby. A reporter for the *Arkansas Democrat* asked Neal if he had been threatened since the charges were filed against Adams. The white mob pressed closer. Neal answered that he had heard the Ku Klux Klan had a fifteen-hundred-dollar bounty on him.

One of the whites swore at Neal. The reporter turned to the white spectator. "Is it true you would like to kill this man?"

"It's not him we want," the reporter was told, "it's you."

"You reporters are the ones causing all the trouble," another volunteered. Still another kicked him in the butt, warning, needlessly, "You'd better get out of town fast."

(The state's editorial cartoonists and columnists had a field day with the developments. Wrote one editorialist: "Since the Game and Fish Commission has failed to announce it, I would like to disclose to hunters that it is now open season on all newsmen in Marianna.")

Later that morning, as bat-wielding whites continued to roam the square, the state police disappeared. "They told us they were 'going fishing,' " recalls Harold Meins of the White Citizens Council. "The implication was: 'Do what you want to do.' "

Though boycott leaders had made themselves scarce, their lawyer, a white man named Al J. Daniel, Jr., and his wife watched from across the street, snapping Polaroids. When one of the camera-shy mob noticed the couple, he led a group toward them. They surrounded Daniel, a twenty-seven-year-old from a Little Rock civil rights firm. While one man grabbed his neck and his tie, others took turns pummeling Daniel. Once he regained enough of his faculties to register a complaint with the police department, Daniel described the beating, mentioning that most of the mob brandished baseball bats. Carrying a baseball bat was not against the law, the officer replied. "Well, off the top of my head, I didn't know whether it was or not," Daniel later admitted. "But I sure didn't think any ballgame was going on."

Later that afternoon, after the big-city lawyers and reporters had retreated, the White Citizens Council issued a "BULLETIN" to the boycotters: "If you want Marianna to be a battle ground, you Can get it!" It went on: "You can look for the same medicine as you got a taste of today every time leaflets are passed out. No more food stamps will be signed by white people as long as this is going on! THIS IS OUR LAST WARNING! All you Red-Blooded Whites Come to The Aid of Your Town!"

A follow-up bulletin, air-dropped the next day from crop dusters, announced to "The good black citizens of Lee County" that "THE BOYCOTT IS OVER." It was signed: "The Good White Citizens of Lee County."

But the Good White Citizens had yet to meet a single demand (since raised to forty-one) presented by the Concerned Citizens. Though a cease-fire was negotiated, the boycott would remain in effect for nearly another year. The truce held for five months—until the anniversary of the birthday of Martin Luther King, Jr.

January 13, 1972, dawned cold, a cold unusual to the Delta. By 8:15, the temperature was barely above freezing; the water in the mud holes of the Lee Senior High football field had a thin layer of ice. Marianna's new school consolidated the old black and white high schools; it had opened in 1969. But most well-off whites in Lee County, as in much of the South, countered court-ordered integration by sending their children to private school. Consequently, though only 58 percent of the county's population was black, blacks comprised 80 percent of the public school population. And like all major local institutions, the school administrators—the principal, the superintendent, and the president of the school board—were all white.

A week earlier, student leaders had petitioned the principal to commemorate Martin Luther King's birthday with an assembly. They had asked to hold the assembly the following day, a Friday, January 14. The principal refused, explaining that the only birthday observed in Marianna schools was Jesus Christ's. The superintendent seconded the principal's decision. "If we let them set aside a special day for Martin Luther King, what would we say to the white students who might want to hold a day for Robert E. Lee?"

(Such insensitivities filtered down to the teachers. One former student remembers her eleventh-grade English teacher referring to James Weldon Johnson as the well-known "Nigra" author. Another said that during the 1968–1969 school year, the term just prior to mandatory desegregation, she was one of five black students in an otherwise white school. She recalls that upon her arrival each day in English class, the teacher sprayed her and the other blacks with disinfectant. "Then she sprayed the seats with Lysol when we left.")

Inside Lee Senior High that Thursday morning in early 1972, the first bell had just rung. A couple hundred students were gathered in the hallway near the principal's office. In the principal's outer office were a dozen students. "We want to talk to you about our petition," a spokesman explained to him.

"Fine," the principal replied. "I'll be glad to talk to five of you as soon as the halls are cleared and the students are back in class."

The students rejected the offer. At 8:21, the principal told the students they had ten minutes to either be in class or leave the campus. "No! No!" they shouted back. At 8:31 he told the teachers to lock their classrooms. "Don't let anyone in or out."

A few minutes later the sheriff arrived. At 8:50, he reiterated the principal's order: Go to classes or go home. He gave the students five minutes to disperse—or face arrest. At 8:55, a team of law enforcement officers began arresting students and loading them on school buses. Before one bus was fully loaded, the students still in the hallways streamed outside into the parking lot. By then, reinforcements—state troopers, the fire department, and the local civil defense unit—had arrived. After a conference between school administrators and student leaders failed to resolve the "sit-in," at 10:16 the sheriff commanded the fire department to turn its high-pressure hose on the students. By then, the temperature was in the mid-thirties.

The tactic worked. Most students, although tripping over one another, fled unharmed except for the drenching; others were less fortunate. Some were beaten with nightsticks or slapped or kicked. One student needed three stitches to close a head wound; another was treated locally for head injuries and then transferred to a Little Rock hospital. Asked later about the wisdom of dousing the students on a day so intemperate, Hack Adams replied: "We had no choice. It was too windy to use tear gas."

Police charged 117 students with disrupting classes, a misdemeanor offense.[1] The incident so outraged parents that they added the entire school system to the ongoing boycott. For the remainder of the spring term—more than four months—three thousand of the school district's five thousand students stayed away from school.

The truce was over. The night of the demonstration, despite a citywide curfew, someone firebombed the home of a white deputy sheriff. Ten days later, Harold Meins, the White Citizens Council president who owned the Holiday Sands motel and res-

---

[1]A visiting municipal judge found fifty students guilty and thirty-four innocent; he dismissed the cases of thirty-three defendants for lack of evidence. Those convicted were fined two hundred dollars, with a hundred dollars suspended, and sentenced to six months in jail with four months of the sentence suspended, and the entire jail sentence suspended if the offending students "were enrolled in school by September 1 and behaved themselves."

taurant, called the Marianna Fire Department. "I've got a short in my sign," he told the dispatcher, referring to the electric wiring in his road sign. "I think it may catch." Every fire truck in town was dispatched to the scene. Meanwhile, downtown, a blaze started in the black commercial district of Main Street, directly behind the fire station. By the time it was brought under control, seven storefronts had been reduced to their brick foundations. Officials said the fire started in the office of the Concerned Citizens—the boycott headquarters.

It was open season again in Marianna. Harold Meins says he heard from a black busboy that the boycotters planned to retaliate by setting his restaurant afire. From his motel switchboard, Meins triggered the White Citizens Council's emergency response network. First he called a pilot who flew crop dusters. "Cotton pickers wanted at the Holiday Sands," Meins told him, codespeak for "help needed." The pilot immediately strung a red banner from the rear of his plane. This alerted farmers to call the switchboard. In this manner, Meins recruited some seventy men armed with all sorts of weapons—from a slingshot to high-powered rifles—to camp in and around the property. "We weren't going to kill them, just capture them," Meins says of the would-be arsonists. (No attempt was made to burn the building.)

With both sides stockpiling firearms and firebombs, with death threats telephoned back and forth, with sniper bullets glancing off cars and whizzing through houses, it's a wonder no one died. But it was understood that if harm was done to either camp, retaliation in kind would be forthcoming. To the menacing calls Harold Meins says he received at his business, he told his switchboard operator to respond: "If you kill Harold, Olly Neal's a dead nigger."

The logistics of killing Neal, the clinic administrator who whites suspected was the behind-the-scenes mastermind of the boycott, preoccupied the White Citizens Council. Once Meins attended a meeting at which he says "a man from out of state" presented a plan to "take out" Neal for twenty-five hundred dollars.

"They wanted me to write a local man a check; he could cash it and pay the contract guy." Another time, Meins says he was shown bombs intended for Neal's house and the clinic. Both plans were aborted, Meins says, because "we decided to wait until the niggers drew blood."

In late July of 1972, thirteen months after initiating it, the Concerned Citizens of Lee County voted to end the boycott. Though none of the group's specific demands was addressed, the Concerned Citizens believed they had made progress, that there had been a "definite change in the attitudes of whites as related to blacks." Twelve businesses had closed—more than a third of the downtown retailers. The real estate market, commercial and residential, had atrophied. Whites complained that the boycott "ruined" Marianna, but the losses hardly affected most blacks. As Quency Tillman put it then: "If they want to go out of business, let them; I ain't got no business to go out of."

Billy Joe Chambers was nine years old when the boycott ended. By the mid-1980s, when Billy was returning periodically to Lee County to recruit employees and flaunt his success in Detroit, little had changed economically or socially. The color line still suffused almost every aspect of life. There were no blacks behind the counters at the businesses that rimmed the courthouse square, none in the fire department or on the board of the chamber of commerce. No blacks belonged to the Marianna Country Club or the Rotary or Lions clubs. None attended the private Lee Academy. (Asked why no blacks were invited to enroll, a parent of Lee Academy students named David Cahoon, a lawyer and former prosecutor, says: "We wanted our kids to go to school with people who bathed every day and who weren't on welfare.") And those whites in the "private-school circle" who attended football and basketball games at the nearly all-black Lee Senior High customarily sat in the visitors' section.

That individuals as well as institutions remained anchored to traditional race relations could be seen in the details. When white women drove across town to pick up their black maids, the maids sat in the backseat. A prominent white minister's wife says it would not be possible for her and her husband to host a black couple for dinner at their house: "We might lose our jobs." A white man, a self-professed "moderate," says a movie theater could not survive because of competition from cable television and video movies, and "because of integration people wouldn't feel comfortable there."

Segregation continued in the 1980s to so permeate the order of life that it transcended life itself: no blacks were buried in the city-maintained cemetery.

Nor had the political seeds sown during the seventies borne fruit. Blacks had gained so little political power that some were still afraid to register to vote. "They figure that if they get registered, then their boss will find out, and then they're messing around in white folks' business and they will lose their jobs," one man said in a 1988 federal court deposition. Though blacks had won seats on the county school board and the Marianna Board of Aldermen, no black held countywide office. The county judge, a sallow-eyed water sportsman named Kenneth Hunter, explained to the *Arkansas Democrat* in 1988 why blacks were unqualified to do so. "It's taken a while for them to get people smart enough that they could run the office if they got it."

For all of its problems Marianna retained plenty of small-town charm. While uniformity had enveloped much of the nation like a creeping fog, most national arbiters and purveyors of culture and commerce ignored Marianna. There was no interstate highway, no Golden Arches, no national newspaper or shopping mall or motel chain or multiplex cinema. The regulars who gathered for coffee each morning at Sparks' Drive-In or Waid's Kountry Kitchen (PLATE LUNCHES, STEAKS, FRESH CATFISH) thought as much about leaving their keys in the car as they did about breathing. A call from a pay phone in Marianna was still a dime; service station attendants still pumped gas and checked under the hood; Johnson's Grocery, a third-generation family business, still offered credit and still delivered; and the courthouse crowd still went home at noon each day for dinner.

The facts of life in Marianna were delivered weekly by the *Courier-Index*. Besides the ritual coverage of births, deaths, weddings, and the machinations of local government, the paper hailed the new books obtained by the public library and trumpeted the good news from Strong Middle School: "FOUR HOMEROOM CLASSES HONORED FOR NO DETENTION HALL REFERRALS." The monthly city council meetings, held in the municipal courtroom, were brief, informal affairs—one alderman spent an entire meeting meticulously cleaning his fingernails with a pocketknife. There were often no spectators, save for the *Courier-Index* reporter who roosted in the judge's chair above the council members. Among the matters the mayor introduced during one fifty-four-minute session were the possible placement of a new stop sign and the havoc wreaked by the previous night's hailstorm. The entirety of one alderman's Parks and Recreation Committee report consisted of this: "I think we're gettin' along real fine." After the council adjourned at 8:30 or so that night, downtown was as quiet as a cemetery, the loudest noise the plink of june bugs ricocheting off the streetlights.

On the surface, race relations in Marianna were as amiable as the council meetings. But under the quiet landscape and the cordial talk floated a latent sense of boundary, a line over which neither race usually ventured to step. Dropping the subject of race relations into a conversation with most of the powers-that-be was like asking about a long-suppressed family secret—it just wasn't an outsider's business. A banker who moments before was extolling the benefits of small-town life bolted from his own office so suddenly it was as if he had witnessed a robbery of a Brink's truck. (He returned a minute later, apologetically explaining that there had occurred an unspecified "minor emergency" and that the interview was over.)

Mayor Martin Chaffin also found the subject of race too troublesome to discuss. Chaffin was in his middle fifties, with a tanned, rectangular face, silver hair, and tortoise-shell aviator-style glasses. He left Marianna after high school and did not return until 1978. He dressed like the retired Sears manager he was: plaid shirts, khaki pants, and sensible brown walking shoes. He was elected mayor in 1982 and reelected in 1986 to a four-year term.

Talking about his dream for a revived Marianna, the mayor customarily punched the air with excitement. "Sure we bottomed out economically, but our attitude *has* [punch] changed. We're more positive. Now we're saying *can-* [punch] *do* [punch]." Asked finally about racial tensions in town, Chaffin dodged the question like a motorist swerving to avoid a pothole. "You're gonna find criticism on anything," he says, and then, before grinding to a halt, adds, "I try to dwell on the positive. We're in the center of a sportsman's paradise, you know."

In the center of the center of the sportsman's paradise was the courthouse square, Marianna's commercial hub. Along with the boxy stone courthouse, the law firms, and the municipal offices that bordered the square were mom-and-pop retailers: a jeweler, an upholsterer, a small-engine repair shop, a video rental outlet. There was also the black-owned Marianna Funeral Home, half of whose business was "ship-in" from the North. The south end of the square, which once housed a small discount department store, had lost its eminence; in its stead sat several sadly bereft store-fronts, a thrift shop, and, on the corner of Main and Poplar, a tap dance studio. Still keeping vigil over all this activity was the towering statue of Robert E. Lee. At the base of the twenty-five-foot monument was this inscription: NO BRAVER BLED FOR A BRIGHTER LAND. NO BRIGHTER LAND HAD A CAUSE SO GRAND.

There were in the middle 1980s traces of the Marianna of the Confederacy. The chamber of commerce distributed a brochure during those years entitled "The Marianna Advantage." "Welcome to The City Beautiful" it began, and depicted a Marianna of magnolia-shaded streets and splendorous antebellum homes graced by wraparound porches and expansive lawns. Though cotton was dethroned long earlier, it would be only slight caricature to have drawn Marianna through the eyes of the vestiges of the plantation aristocracy as a world of happy darkies singing all day in the snow-white fields. "Our people are content here," says a wealthy farmer's wife who rents a row of tumbledown houses to poor black families. "If they weren't, they'd move."

Many of Lee County's fifteen thousand residents could hardly have afforded to move if they wanted to. Lee remained the poorest county in Arkansas, and among the ten poorest in the nation. Its population had declined another 18 percent—the highest percentage lost of any of Arkansas's seventy-five counties. The county's unemployment rate hovered among the two or three highest in the state; at times it topped 20 percent. And though the official unemployment rate for young black males was a steady 40 percent, the reality was far grimmer. "I can't think of eight black teenagers who are employed," Bill Lewellen, the state senator who was then a Marianna alderman, said in 1988.

Even if there were more employment opportunities, most residents would have been restricted to low-skilled, low-paid positions. Only one in five black adults in the county was a high school graduate, and half the adult population was functionally illiterate. One of every three public school teachers failed a 1985 statewide basic skills test—the worst rate of any of the state's school districts. The teachers' test results were reflected in their students' performance: Lee County students in two of three grades tested had the state's lowest average achievement test scores. The results reinforced the pointlessness of school. At a goal-setting workshop for eight graders, two students told their teacher they saw no need to stay in school past junior high. "We can make more money now on the street."

But school-age children found it no easier outside the classroom. There was no summer jobs program, no public swimming pool, no organized recreation. Black kids were excluded from Little League baseball; whites played on the private Lions Club field at the country club. "Our kids have nothing to do, no money to spend, nowhere to go, day after day," says Pinky Hill, a black woman who started a youth group. "They can chop cotton or they can hang out at a beer joint."

It was in front of a beer joint, Jesse's Place, that James McKinney was hanging out one endless Tuesday afternoon when a guy driving a brown Dodge Colt pulled up. James was a tall, gangly seventeen-year-old of engaging presence and polite demeanor; he had been expelled from Lee Senior High School for fighting with a pregnant girl. It was May of 1986. He had no job, no plans for the summer or beyond. He was living with his aunt, who booted him out of the house whenever her boyfriend spent the night, and so he made a habit of sleeping in the car. She refused to clothe him; after his final pair of pants wore out, he took, unsuccessfully, to shoplifting. And now he was on the streets for the long, hot Marianna summer.

James did not recognize the driver immediately. His name was Marshall Glenn, but James knew him as "Mario." He didn't recognize Mario because Mario always drove a black Cadillac Fleetwood with gold trim. On this day, Mario's Cadillac was in the shop. (Mario cherished all things Cadillac. He usually wore a black golf cap with the distinctive Cadillac crest-and-wreath logo, as well as a gold necklace and gold ring adorned identically. He was one of the few customers in Jesse's Place to carry an alligator-skin briefcase, and he was one of fewer still to produce from such a briefcase a cellular phone.)

Mario was living in Detroit. He had dropped out of the ninth grade some years earlier, and after having no success in the local job market—he couldn't even find work chopping cotton—he had left home at the age of twenty-two in 1985. His close friend Jerry Gant, the fellow with whom Billy Joe had begun his career by peddling loose joints in the hallways of Kettering High in Detroit, had invited Mario to join him in Detroit.

Mario asked James if he wanted to make some money. "He showed me a mound of money and then he peeled off a hundred-dollar bill and sent me to the store to get three pops and a Twinkie," James recalls. "So I brought him back the stuff and the change and he gave me forty dollars just for going."

Mario asked James if he'd like to make some more money. "I knew he was in with the Chamberses, but I asked him how much," James says. "He told me at least fifteen hundred a month." On a Friday night three days later, James met Mario back at Jesse's Place. With Mario were enough other recruits to fill five cars.

The caravan drove the fifteen hours straight through to Detroit. James rode with Mario, Mario's girlfriend, and another fellow. They took James to a brick apartment building on Shoemaker Street, just off I-94 on the east side, where he would be stationed for the next two weeks—a crack dealer in training.

They went to an upstairs apartment open for business. "There were two guys in there and Mario told me to watch them so I could learn how to do it," James says. The two young dealers were natives of Marianna. They left, as James McKinney had, as the Chambers brothers had, as countless others have for generations, because if their future in Detroit seemed uncertain, their future in Marianna held little *but* certainty—in the words of the local black journalist Clifton Collier, "the certainty of nothing."

CHAPTER TEN

"WE RICH, GODDAMMIT!"

Eleven days before Otis Chambers graduated from Lee Senior High, the nation's top federal narcotics officers convened in suburban Washington, D.C. Gathered around a U-shaped table at a conference center in Alexandria, Virginia, were some thirty-five of the United States Drug Enforcement Administration's highest-ranking officials: agency administrators, desk officers, international attachés, and SACs. It was Monday, May 19, 1986, the first day of the three-day semiannual meeting of the SACs, or special agents in charge, the chief executives of the DEA's field offices around the globe. It was customary for each desk officer (the cocaine desk, the marijuana desk, the heroin desk) to report on the latest intelligence culled from SAC reports, but this meeting would be devoted almost exclusively to the cocaine desk—to exchanging notes for the first time on the latest scourge of the streets, the cocaine derivative that had come to be known as crack.

From Detroit came Special Agent in Charge Robert J. De-Fauw, a fifty-two-year-old career narcotics agent. DeFauw had begun thirty years earlier as a Vice and Rackets Squad officer with the Detroit Police Department; since 1961 he had worked for the

DEA and its forerunner, the federal Bureau of Narcotics. After stints overseas during the 1960s and 1970s, DeFauw returned to Detroit in 1981 to head the two-hundred-employee regional DEA office. (The region included four states, the western portion of Pennsylvania, and Ontario, Canada.) Ruddy-faced and blue-eyed, with a silvery pompadour, DeFauw was a Marine Corps veteran and an old-school cop who bemoaned the lack of discipline—unpolished shoes, unkempt uniforms—he found prevalent among younger police officers.

DeFauw's presentation to his counterparts began with the highlights of his agents' successful efforts to break the "Golden Crescent" heroin connection between some Arab-Americans in Dearborn, west of Detroit, and their associates in Pakistan and Afghanistan. He then spoke of the possible revival of Young Boys Incorporated, a Detroit heroin distribution gang whose leaders were imprisoned in 1983. Finally he talked about the "tremendous influx and wide availability" of crack cocaine on the streets of Detroit. Then, one by one, the SACs based in some of America's other major cities—Los Angeles, New York, Baltimore, Miami, Boston—reported similar findings.

Much of the remainder of the meeting focused on how to address the crack problem without promoting the drug and, says DeFauw, "without telling every kid in town how to make it." Of that period, he says: "We knew cocaine was coming in ad infinitum from Colombia. And we knew we couldn't stop it at the source; cocaine was a natural resource there and we couldn't deal with corruption at every level of their government.

"Since we couldn't attack the source, we decided to make our stand here. But everything was against us. The faucet was on and we couldn't turn it off. It was coming in by air, land, boat. The supply was absolutely unlimited, the price was dropping, and the Detroit economy was in the toilet. Kids in the ghetto who couldn't get jobs or couldn't *get to* jobs—they didn't have transportation out to the suburbs—could rock up cocaine and sell it on any street corner."

DeFauw returned to Detroit convinced that the problem had to be attacked at the street level. But how? It was impractical to lock up every "street-corner dealer"—the jails and courts were already overburdened, and many of the dealers were subject only to prosecution under the law for juveniles. He did what officials often do when confronted with a problem for which there was no simple solution: he launched a public relations campaign. DeFauw met with civic leaders, educators, and chiefs of police from towns in surrounding areas. He told them of the DEA's "three-pronged approach": enforcement, eradication, and education, and he pledged federal cooperation with state and local law enforcement efforts. He sent agents and celebrities into Detroit high schools and middle schools to urge students to "just say no" (First Lady Nancy Reagan's infamous mantra), and he sought to convince the public that their help was vital to ridding Detroit of crack cocaine.

The cornerstone of the strategy was a telephone hotline: 1-800-NO-CRACK. Detroiters were invited to report suspected drug activity; DeFauw especially encouraged rival dealers to "give up" their competitors. By July, the hotline was operational. Six agents, rookies mainly, worked eight-hour shifts fielding calls on a half dozen incoming lines day and night. The phones rang steadily—more than fifteen hundred times that first month. "No crack," the operator-agent would say, "may I help you?" And further questions: "Does someone live in the upstairs? Are there people going in and out all day? How are the buys made? Are there cars parked out there?"

The tips poured in to the DEA's third-floor office in the Federal Building, good, verifiable tips: A man wearing Jordache jeans and driving a 1980 GMC car is selling between one P.M. and six P.M. daily; a group of thirty teenagers, stationed at all four corners of an east-side intersection, is selling ten-dollar rocks. But there were no follow-up plans, and many of the tips languished. "Truthfully it was bullshit," says Thomas McClain, one of the rookie agents assigned to the hotline. "I wasn't real impressed with the DEA at the time. All we had was notepaper. No forms, no method of organizing the information, nothing. We filed the paper in Xerox boxes, half-assedly. Then I started putting color-coded stickers on return calls, but that was the extent of it. There was no thought given to what to do with all these people phoning in. The only thought given was to the public relations value of it."

McClain had started with the Detroit field office in November of 1985. He was a "white boy from the suburbs" of Pittsburgh with the sort of former schoolboy football player's body that might be described as burly if not for his baby face. Though he ventured to eastern Pennsylvania to attend college, he otherwise had lived the whole of his twenty-eight years in the Pittsburgh area, including three years of law school. "Going to Detroit," he says, "was like going to Islamabad."

He had not intended to work for the DEA. Federal agencies were recruiting new law school graduates. He and three classmates signed up for the FBI. But McClain failed the bureau's blood pressure test and wound up in drug enforcement. "I was young and single," he says. "I thought the DEA was pirates and sailing ships in strange countries." Instead it was three months of training in the heat of a Georgia summer, a two-month interim job back in Pittsburgh, and a permanent assignment in the city his colleagues unfailingly reminded him was the "murder capital" of the United States. At graduation, he was ceremoniously handed a diploma and a revolver. "They gave everyone six bullets for your gun and six bullets for your pouch," he recalls. "And to the guys going to Detroit, they gave you the box of fifty rounds."

McClain's early disillusionment with the DEA was so great that he strongly considered leaving the agency to resume his law career. The Michigan bar examination was scheduled for the last Tuesday and Wednesday of July. When the hotline began at the start of the month, McClain was assigned the graveyard shift—midnight to eight A.M. He didn't mind the odd hours. The phones were quieter then. He was able to grab four or five hours' sleep on the pullout couch in the office—enough to concentrate for the rest of the night on his studies for the bar exam.

* * *

The nation was in an uproar over the spread of crack. Len Bias, a twenty-two-year-old basketball star, had died of an overdose in the middle of June of 1986, two days after the Boston Celtics signed him as their first-round draft choice. Barely a week later, National Football League player Don Rogers, a defensive back for the Cleveland Browns, dropped dead of an overdose. Surveys showed cocaine use and cocaine-related crime and deaths had risen to unprecedented levels; in Detroit, the number of deaths attributed to the drug would rise from ten in 1983 to a hundred and seven in 1986. A Baltimore study found that between 25 and 50 percent of all homicides, and at least 75 percent of all property crimes, were cocaine related. Lurid stories on the dangers of crack—the "most dangerous substance on earth" it was often called—found a home on the front pages of American newspapers and the covers of American magazines.

The intense news coverage of the deaths of Bias and Rogers prompted public outcry over the spread of crack. Such outcry, as it often has, prompted Congress to do what it does best—hold hearings. In the middle of July, two weeks after the NO-CRACK hotline started, two U.S. House committees held a joint hearing on "the Crack Cocaine Crisis." Invited to appear was the commanding officer of the Narcotics Section of the Detroit Police Department, Inspector Joel Gilliam.

Gilliam told the members of Congress that as recently as September of 1985—ten months earlier—crack "wasn't even in the streets of Detroit, and now it constitutes eighty-five percent of our enforcement effort." He said that one major difficulty of fighting crack is that the problem "does not have a face on it. It is everybody and it is nobody. It is 'them' out there doing it." He continued: "What we have attempted to do is put a face on the problem. Right now, who are the drug pushers? It is kind of hard to fight a shadowy adversary . . . if you cannot at least come up with some kind of description of who he is or who it is."

Even as Inspector Gilliam was testifying in Washington,

back in Detroit Tom McClain of the DEA had a "face"—a large-scale crack dealer, a living, breathing adversary. McClain didn't know much about him. He drove a white Jeep, he might be from Arkansas. But "night after night," McClain says, he and the other agent-operators would talk to people, "good people, ladies and gentlemen, and the same name kept popping up: 'BJ.' "

The resounding response to the hotline demanded further action and organization. By the first of August, the DEA and the Detroit Police Department had agreed to jointly support a new task force to follow up on leads the hotline generated. The No-Crack Crew, as it came to be known, was composed of seven DEA agents and five police officers and a sergeant. The crew was a combination of young federal agents such as McClain with limited street experience and DPD narcotics officers who were veterans of tens of thousands of raids between them. With the exception of a black female, the crew members were all white men; most had worked together for more than a decade and were U.S. Army or Marine Corps veterans. They had come to believe that the narcotics section, if not the entire police department, had lost its sense of mission, had given up on the city. Some members of the crew believed the narcotics section had been eroding as the department itself had evolved over the past thirteen years from a predominantly white force to an integrated one.

The change began with the 1973 election of Coleman Young, the city's first black mayor. The police department had been a white stronghold, a bastion of racial discrimination that six years earlier had provoked the bloody four-day riot that devastated large portions of the city. Coleman Young altered the police department forever. He abolished a police unit called STRESS ("Stop The Robberies, Enjoy Safe Streets"). The unit, organized in 1971, was made up of white undercover officers posing as drunks and derelicts in black neighborhoods. In the two and a half years STRESS existed, its crew shot and killed twenty-two people, all but one of whom were black. And Mayor Young instituted an affirmative action hiring policy. By the end of 1976, half of the Detroit Police Department's commanders were black, and the department had its first black chief. By 1979, 38 percent of the department's uniformed officers were black—seven times the percentage of a decade earlier.

The cost of affirmative action was an ugly and substantial backlash. As black police officers began to outrank whites, as whites were denied promotions, some white officers, some members of the No-Crack Crew, believed the department, and the people of Detroit, suffered. "Detroit was a great city to work narcotics before blacks started being bosses," says Greg Woods, an officer who comes from a family of police officers. "But I am a racist. I'll be honest, I am. Fuck them niggers."

If not all of Woods's colleagues shared his extremism, most did believe that Narcotics had lost its heart, that their superiors were more concerned with feathering their own nests than with fighting crime. "We'd have to use our own money to make [undercover] buys," Woods says, "because the nigger commanders were busy spending Secret Service funds"—marked money—"on their car telephones." If Detroit is to make a stand against cocaine trafficking, another DPD narcotics officer told Tom McClain of the DEA, "You're gonna have to do it. The department can't handle it. Most guys are loyal only to themselves. They just want to do raids and get on TV."

The No-Crack Crew thought themselves defenders of the old school. They were low-tech and proud of it. "To be a narcotics officer you don't need a computer; you gotta learn the difference between reality and bullshit," says Officer Gerard (Mick) Biernacki, who joined the narcotics section in 1973. "And then you gotta have a crew that likes to work and has brains and doesn't get real excited and blow it." The crew was on the job seven days a week, sixteen hours a day. "Had to be to keep up with the bad guys," DEA agent Richard J. Crock explains. "Normal police work," Biernacki says.

They first reformed the hotline procedures. Complaint forms

were drafted and a filing system implemented to replace the note-pads and looseleaf sheets boxed in chaotic piles throughout the office. On the forms were to be noted the address of the suspected crack house, whether there were weapons within, whether there were bars on the door, the price of the rocks, the name or the street name of the suspected dealers, the make, model, color, and license plate numbers of the cars they drove. And from the scattered remains in the boxes, the crew exhumed and sorted the early complaints. Together with the new, standardized forms, they logged and filed the tips by geographic area: Lower East Side, near west side, and so on. Most of the information seemed to implicate small traffickers. But there was that one name—"BJ"—that "kept popping up."

Early one morning during the first week of August, within days of the formation of the crew, a woman named "Pat" called the hotline. She was afraid to give her full name but said she had just moved out of an east-side apartment building at 1350 East Grand Boulevard. She said the building, The Broadmoor, had been overrun at the beginning of the year by a man named "Marlow." "He's big," she said. "He's got five apartments in my building" as well as several other east-side houses. "And he's got a brother," she added. "They call him BJ."

On August 20, 1986, a Wednesday, Pat Middleton met for the first time with Tom McClain and Mick Biernacki of the No-Crack Crew. Biernacki was a hulk of a man with a USMC tattoo on one arm. He had served with the corps in Da Nang. In his thirteen years as a narcotics officer, he says he participated in more than twenty thousand raids; he was shot "only once." He had dealt with thousands of informants, not all of them reliable. One thing he had learned was to "never give your hand away to anyone new because you can't trust who they're being sent by. The Chambers knew we were working them and they could have set somebody up by giving them, say, ten thousand dollars to act like an informant and find out what we know. So you don't give your hand up to anybody. Especially if they're acting like they're dumb or goofy. You let 'em out at the next corner. I don't need them."

McClain and Biernacki picked up Middleton on a side street off Jefferson Avenue. Biernacki was driving his unmarked surveillance van with tinted windows. "When you pick up a new informant like that, you just listen," Biernacki continues. "And the last thing you do before you drop them off is you play taxicab. You ask her where do I turn and she says, 'Turn right, it's the second house.' You copy down the address, and lo and behold when you get back she's right on the button. It's one of the [hotline] complaints. So you let them do the talking and try and verify it later."

The first place to which Middleton directed the officers was 1350 East Grand Boulevard. From there they drove by another half dozen houses she said her boss, "Marlow"—Larry Chambers—operated. As the tour ended, Biernacki had Middleton fill out the forms certifying her as an official police informant. She began meeting with the officers regularly after that, once a week at first, and then every other day and sometimes daily.

Based on the initial information Middleton and other informants provided, the crew formed two surveillance teams. Over the next few days, working twelve-hour shifts, they followed cars they believed belonged to BJ or his associates from one house to another. The cars made numerous trips between a house on Wade the crew had raided previously to one on Glenfield to another on Gable; at every stop, according to the surveillance reports, money or a "large clear plastic baggie" was exchanged between black males. On Friday, the crew hired informants to attempt to make undercover buys at the Glenfield and Gable addresses.

Neither informant had any luck. At Glenfield, the salesman told the would-be customer, a stranger, he could sell him no rock unless someone the salesman knew would vouch for him.

"I've been copping cocaine from the joint on Wade but it just got cracked," the informant replied.

"It's back up," the seller said. "We just dropped some rocks off this morning over there. Just ask for Shug."

Over on Gable, meanwhile, the informant reported that no dope was being sold but that there was assorted "paraphernalia"—"the type used to rock cocaine up."

That information was enough to satisfy a magistrate that there was "probable cause" to issue search warrants for the two addresses. The plan was to simultaneously raid the two houses. At 1:30 on Monday afternoon, August 25, police officer Mike Cowling and his crew broke down the side door at 12575 Glenfield. At the same time, several miles away, officer Mick Biernacki's crew walked in the open front door at 13424 Gable, the residence of Willie Chambers.

On Glenfield the crew found seven people, only two of whom they arrested—the others were under eighteen. They also seized $2,822 from a clothes chute in the basement, one coin-envelope of "suspected cocaine," a couple of scales, four firearms, two boxes of plastic sandwich bags, a beeper, and assorted jewelry: gold chains, necklaces, rings.

On Gable the only person present was Linda Chambers, Willie's wife. The officers found none of the "paraphernalia" their informant reportedly saw three days earlier, but they did report finding a large Ziploc bag of "suspected cocaine" in the kitchen. They also confiscated $114 in cash, nine hundred-dollar savings bonds, a small jewelry store full of gold rings and chains, and a brand-new white Jeep—the vehicle BJ had been seen driving—registered to Willie Chambers.

Shortly after 1:30 that Monday afternoon, the phone rang in Fats Wilkins's Jeep. Billy Joe Chambers, riding shotgun, picked it up.

"What's up?" It was a neighbor of Willie's.

"I'm just calling to let you know Willie's getting busted."

"Getting *busted?*"

Billy needed to get word quickly to his Glenfield crew. He called a girl named Tammy who lived around the corner from Glenfield, "thirty seconds from her door on Wilfred."

"Go tell the fellas on Glenfield Gable got raided," Billy instructed. "And do it right now, don't wait a minute, don't wash your face, don't comb your hair, don't do nothing."

She called Billy back a minute later. "Vans and police cars all over the driveway at Glenfield," she reported. "They busting that house too!"

Billy understood why Glenfield was raided. He knew about the hotline of course—everyone did—and he figured someone tipped the police to all the traffic there. "Our cars was there all the time," he says. "Willie used to stop by there, Otis, I'm there, Fats is there." But why raid Willie's house on Gable? Billy didn't live there, didn't sell from there. The only thing he could figure was that the police mistook Willie for him. (Willie had been arrested in the first raid at the duplex on Gray Street, in August of 1984.) In that way, he saw the raid on Gable in a positive light. The police had missed their target; none of his crew had snitched. "Everyone knew where I stayed," Billy says, meaning that any of his crew could find him at one or another of his girlfriends' houses. "They knew Diana lived on Marlborough. They knew Ceecee lived on Hardy, they knew Niece lived with her grandmama on Evanston. So I'm thinking: Why not these houses? Why Willie's? I knew they hittin' at me, but they ain't hittin' the nail on the head yet."

The day after the raids, the No-Crack Crew convened, as they did most mornings, at their unofficial headquarters, a Polish coffee shop on Chene Street, just south of I-94. Tom McClain had found the raids -the preparation, the anticipation, the execution —grueling. "I was never so psychologically exhausted," he recalls. "The cops were used to it, but I wasn't." Until that breakfast, in fact, McClain sensed that the DPD guys, blue-collar, ex-Marines, native Detroiters, clannish, had already dismissed him—the boyish, degreed suburbanite—as a "suit"; he was on the crew all right, but not "one of us." "They were hard-drinking, quick-shooting, tough, tough cops," McClain says. "Guys who would get drunk, go in an alley, and shoot rats for fun. To them I was some snot-nosed college boy." But as the crew compared notes from the parallel raids, McClain mentioned a couple other findings from the house on Gable: a funeral notice for a young man named Joe Edward Chambers, who had died in March, five months earlier. The notice said that Joe Chambers had eleven brothers, among them Billy Joe, Larry, and Willie. McClain also found a wall calendar bearing the logo of the First National Bank of Marianna, Arkansas. As McClain presented those early clues to what he was beginning to think might be a major interstate criminal organization, it was as if he had begun also to initiate himself into the closest of fraternities. "This chicken-shit lawyer may have something," Officer Mike Cowling said.

Tom McClain looked up Marianna in the atlas and placed a call to the sheriff of Lee County, Bobby May, Jr. The sheriff told the DEA agent that he was well aware of the "Chambers bunch," adding: "We're country law enforcement officers but we didn't exactly just get off the watermelon truck." He said his department had started an investigation "a couple of years ago" following a tip from the local Western Union operator. The operator had called a friend of hers in the department, Deputy Stanley Barnes.

"Stanley," she said, "I know I'm not supposed to say anything, but I couldn't help noticing . . ." She went on to say that a high school student named Otis Chambers and his mother, Hazel, were patronizing Western Union suspiciously often. Initially it was maybe a couple times a month that one or the other stopped by to pick up a wire transfer—in amounts of five hundred or a thousand dollars. Then the pace picked up. Several times a week Hazel or Otis (and later, friends of Otis's) would retrieve as much as five thousand dollars. The money always was wired from Detroit.

Barnes reported the tip to Bobby May, who asked the Western Union operator to keep a log of Chambers family transactions and to be sure to save the receipts. Then Barnes called the narcotics section of the Detroit Police Department. "Somebody there took down the information, but it was some time before we heard from them again," Barnes says.

In the summer of 1986 Detroit finally did call back, in the

person of Tom McClain. Bobby May reiterated the Western Union connection and also told him: "We know they're doing all their dirty work up there. They're always coming home to flaunt their money, showing up in new vehicles. We're watching the family closely, but they haven't sold any drugs in Lee County and it's no crime to wire money back and forth or ride around in a limo." Still, he cautioned McClain, "I'd handle them like I'd handle a rattlesnake."

In mid-September of 1986, Jerry Gant and a boyhood friend from Lee County named Carl Young were shooting pool and listening to music in the basement of a house Jerry owned on Martin Street, on Detroit's west side. Jerry and Carl were the same age, twenty-four, but they had gone their separate ways since the beginning of high school. Jerry had dropped out in the ninth grade and moved to Detroit (where his foster brother, Big Terry Colbert, introduced him and Billy Joe to the drug business); Carl had stayed home and graduated with the Lee Senior High class of 1982.

Carl eventually became a truck driver in Texas. When the job ended in early 1986, an older brother—Carl was one of twelve children—found Carl a job in Detroit delivering auto parts. When Jerry Gant heard "Mojo"—Carl's old nickname—was in town, he invited him to stop by. On the morning of Wednesday, September 17, Carl telephoned Jerry to say he had a delivery to make on the west side that afternoon and that he could come by afterward.

Carl unhitched the trailer from his semi at an auto-parts place on Michigan Avenue sometime between two-thirty and three o'clock. He arrived at Jerry's house shortly after three-thirty. Around four P.M., as the two old friends were hanging out in the basement, they heard a sudden commotion upstairs. Glass was flying, the front door was crashing down, and a small army was invading. "POLICE OFFICERS, WE HAVE A SEARCH WARRANT!"

Jerry and Carl momentarily froze in horror. Then they ran: Jerry straight up to the kitchen and Carl to the top of the rear stairs, where he found himself in the attic. "When I got to the attic there was nowhere to go, so I just dove into the insulation," he later recalled.

Police officer Mike Cowling, shotgun drawn, was the first of ten agents and officers in the house. As he hurried from the front door to the kitchen in the rear of the house, he heard footsteps at the rear stairs. He climbed the stairs to the attic, where he found Young hiding in the loose-blown insulation. Nearby, Cowling spotted a clear plastic shopping bag, which contained several "disks" of cocaine base. Under a nearby dresser, Cowling discovered an arsenal of weapons, mainly assault rifles and automatic handguns. The No-Crack Crew confiscated the cocaine, nine guns, $1,295 in cash, and Jerry's car, a 1984 green Saab, in which was found slightly more than two grams of cocaine. Carl and Jerry were arrested, charged with possession with intent to distribute four hundred and fifty grams of cocaine.

That night Carl saw himself on the evening news; the No-Crack Crew had invited along a favored crime reporter to chronicle their exploits. The reporter, Chris Hansen, worked for the top-rated local newscast; he would come to work closely with the authorities on the Chambers case. *The Detroit News* also ran a story, under the headline "RAIDED CRACK DEN 'WAS ALWAYS BUSY.' " The story pointed out that the "rundown house" was across the street from Chadsey High School. It said police "smashed what they described as a major cocaine laboratory manufacturing crack to sell to students," adding that the police claimed "they found four hundred thousand dollars' " worth of cocaine.

The claim was false. The police confiscated four hundred and fifty grams of cocaine, slightly less than half a kilo. By police officer Mick Biernacki's own reckoning, "Out of one kilo you can make fifty thousand nickel rocks"—a quarter of a million dollars. So the amount of cocaine seized on Martin Street could yield, at most, little more than a hundred and ten thousand dollars. This is not to suggest that such a sum is insignificant. The point is that the bust *was* significant; the puffery serves only to depreciate the No-Crack

Crew's work. The falsehood also served to burnish the police department's reputation for a willingness to sacrifice the truth for the greater good of convicting drug dealers. It is a charge some officers do not necessarily deny. "We might have mixed up a few numbers now and then," one officer, who asked for anonymity on this matter, said with a wry smile. "But what the fuck difference does it make? I mean, who are the good guys here and who are the bad guys?" Asked whether the "mix-ups" could have extended to the sworn affidavits officers made to obtain search warrants, and whether those mix-ups might have included false information or fictitious informants, the officer's smile disappeared. "Print that shit and you're fucked," he said.

The successful Martin Street bust and the accompanying overblown news coverage gave the crew license to ratchet their investigation up a notch. With all the hotline callers citing "BJ," with Pat Middleton's statements linking Larry's operation at The Boulevard with BJ, with the dual raids on Gable and Glenfield, with the recently uncovered "Arkansas connec," the No-Crack Crew, says Tom McClain, was "convinced the Chambers were big, but we couldn't prove it. Martin"—the Martin Street raid— "helped give us the confirmation we needed." (This was despite the legal setback prosecutors suffered: charges against Jerry Gant in state district court were dropped because a title search had traced the house to another owner.)

The raid also yielded more evidence of the organization's network in Arkansas. Police learned that both Jerry and Carl were born in Lee County. And through a subpoena issued to Michigan Bell for the past several months' phone bills to the Martin Street house, they learned that since the middle of July, there had been 204 calls placed to or from Marianna and other eastern Arkansas exchanges.

Within days, McClain and his fellow special agent Dick Crock were at the door of the office of the United States Attorney, the top law enforcement official in the eastern judicial district of Michigan. They wanted to expand the reach of their task force into other federal jurisdictions—the Internal Revenue Service, the Bureau of Alcohol, Tobacco, and Firearms, the Immigration and Naturalization Service, the Customs Service. To bring on representatives from those agencies, to expand what had been an informal DEA-DPD task force into a federally funded Organized Crime Drug Enforcement Task Force required Justice Department approval. The timing was good. A newly released DEA report cited Detroit as one of twelve American cities where crack was "readily available." Attorney General Edwin Meese, who also headed the National Drug Policy Board, had indicated he would soon recommend to Congress that it authorize supplemental appropriations to the DEA for just such task forces. The assistant U.S. attorney who supervised the drug unit signed off on the task force, but, says McClain, the federal system was "slow as molasses, and they didn't consider it a priority. We weren't getting the *oomph* out of them we needed."

The No-Crack Crew's patience with criminal procedure wore thin. Especially irksome was the Fourth Amendment to the Constitution, which dictates that people be "protected against unreasonable searches and seizures," and that police must have "probable cause" to obtain a search warrant. The Chambers brothers were so nimble that pinning down their operations long enough to obtain and execute a warrant was proving difficult. "This was a noncivilized place and we had to work within the cumbersome Fourth Amendment in a circumstance where martial law would have been appropriate," Tom McClain says. "The Chambers were masters at manipulating the Fourth Amendment. They established different places to buy [cocaine], store it, cook it, cut it and package it, and sell it. And for each stage, they'd have a dozen different places they could go to—and they were fast. A lot of raids, we'd miss the chicken and get the feathers."

One such raid occurred at an east-side motel. At one-thirty on a Friday afternoon in the fall of 1986, a DEA informant called

Special Agent Kenneth Johnston to tell him that if he hustled over to Room 327 of the Regency Inn, at Harper and Conner, he could intercept a "load of eight to ten pounds of cocaine" that a certain BJ Chambers was to buy. The source said the load would be moved quickly.

Forty-five minutes later, Johnston, with seven other agents and police officers in tow, knocked on Room 327. No answer. Citing "exigent"—urgent—"circumstances," they used the manager's passkey to get in, where they indeed found four kilos of cocaine in the dresser. The bricklike packages were six inches by five inches by four inches and wrapped in fiberglass matting and yellow tape. They were marked "Reina Condor" and "EU Reina." *Reina* means queen in Spanish; *EU* is the Spanish abbreviation for *Estados Unidos,* or United States.

The agents waited in vain for three hours for the room's registrant to return. At five-thirty, agent Johnston heard from his source that word of the seizure "was on the street." It was a nice haul: the four keys would have sold for about eighty thousand dollars wholesale and a million dollars retail. But with no suspects, no way to connect the bust to Billy Joe Chambers, the authorities again missed the chicken and got the feathers.

The first Friday of October of 1986 marked the beginning of "No Crack Week" in Detroit. The highlight of the week was a DEA-sponsored anticrack rally at Cobo Hall, the downtown sports arena. Three thousand middle school and high school students were bused in for the ninety-minute concert and pep rally. As armed undercover federal agents looked on, the crowd danced in the aisles to the music of rap star General Kane, who took care to announce that "Crack is the devil himself." A popular radio disc jockey advised the students to "Crack a book and get hooked on life." Nancy Reagan sent a telegram, wishing everyone well. The master of ceremonies was Lem Barney, former Detroit Lions football player and a member of the NFL Hall of Fame. "Dope has only one deadly enemy," Barney told the students. "It's the word *no.*" (Years later, in the spring of 1993, Barney himself would be arrested for possession of marijuana and cocaine.)

The night before the rally, Art Derrick, Billy's main supplier during that period, learned of the event from a TV newscast. He had a flash and called Perry Coleman, the middleman.

"P-Boy!" he cried with the exuberance of a man inspired. "I see Mayor Young and Isiah [Thomas, the Detroit Pistons basketball star] are coming out with No-Crack Day tomorrow. Tell your boys to put the rocks on sale two-for-one!"

In September, Larry Chambers had gone on a buying spree. Over the course of eleven days he bought two cars and two houses. He paid thirty-six thousand dollars for a Camaro and a Mercedes (both used), and he paid thirty-six thousand for two houses, one on Knodell Street, and one on Albion. The Knodell house was a few lots down from the duplex he shared briefly with his brother David not long after he arrived in Detroit. Larry had been using it for some time alternately as a central cook house, stash house, and cut house. The house on Albion Street was to be his new home. In early October he moved in with his sixteen-year-old girlfriend, Belinda Lumpkin, and her brother James, eighteen.

Like other houses Larry and his brothers bought, 17204 Albion was unexceptional from the outside. He installed burglar bars on the windows and doors, a chain-link fence around the backyard, and a satellite dish on the roof, but otherwise made no cosmetic exterior renovations. Inside, though, Larry spent some forty thousand dollars to transform a common, eighteen-thousand-dollar middle-class residence into his and Belinda's vision of a decorator's showcase.

The three-story, three-bedroom brick house was stripped, repainted, carpeted, and stocked with top-of-the-line appliances, audio and video equipment, and modern furniture, including a glass-top dining room table, a black and gold-trim coffee table, and an Italian top-grain leather sectional sofa. All of the furnishings were bought new especially for the house. The bathrooms, upstairs and down, were adorned with marble—the floors, sinks, and tubs—and with a great deal of gold. The basement was finished with wood paneling; its principal attraction was a wet bar, well stocked, with blinking lights that framed the mirrored wall behind it.

Larry cared less than Belinda for the fine things in their home. To him the significance was more symbolic: the house showed in tangible ways the great distance he had traveled from past deprivations. How, for instance, he had gone from an overcrowded rural dwelling without running water to gold bathroom fixtures; or from sharing a lumpy mattress with any number of his brothers to barrackslike prison dormitories to a deluxe king-sized bed with his lovely, eager-to-please girlfriend.

Larry was so delighted with his new home that he produced a video tour, adding his own voice-over and distinctive cackle. "This is the basement bar, serving wine, whiskey, beer, orange juice, grapefruit . . . heh, heh, heh, heh . . . This is a twenty-four-karat-gold faucet . . . heh, heh, heh, heh . . . This is the living room, excuse me, the dining room. Now we are going upstairs . . . This is the television room . . . ."

By early October, Larry, Belinda, and James were just settling in to their luxurious digs. One day DPD officer Greg Woods, the self-described "racist" member of the No-Crack Crew, happened by his in-laws' place of business, an east-side glass company. "I stopped in," Woods recalls, "and they told me about this big order a young black girl paid in cash. They got the receipt, told me the name Belinda Lumpkin, and gave me the address of the place. That's how we found out about Albion and hit it."

Officer Mick Biernacki had a very different and most likely false story he told to obtain the search warrant, invoking an informant who "had just been present inside" 17204 Albion and who saw Larry arrive with a "large amount" of suspected cocaine. In any case, a magistrate signed the warrant at 2:50 P.M. At four o'clock, the raiding party arrested Larry, who was home alone, in the TV room upstairs. They found no drugs, no guns, and very little cash: a hundred and eighty-one dollars. But the furnishings were so posh, the house so elegant, that rather than wreck the premises, as was their usual practice, the crew elected to preserve everything, to inventory the items, and to call in the forfeiture unit of the Wayne County prosecuting attorney. (Under Michigan law, if there is probable cause to believe that money or other property was "derived from illegal trafficking in controlled substances," the assets are subject to seizure.) "It was all brand-new stuff, tons of it," recalls Frank Heaney, the forfeiture unit officer who was summoned to the scene. "Most items still had the price tags on."

As remarkable as were the furnishings, the evidence the raid produced was not particularly incriminating—except for one other extraordinary finding: a cache of Larry's homemade videotapes.

Some nouveau riche tycoons erect statues in their own honor, or name opera halls or airliners after themselves. Larry Chambers commemorated his newfound wealth by shooting home videos. He bought a Panasonic camcorder sometime during the summer of 1986, shooting footage of the camera-mugging Chamberses and their friends in a variety of recreational pursuits: back in Lee County they tool around in all-terrain vehicles, tote rifles, wear bandoliers across their chests, and line dance in a cotton field. On a trip home from Detroit, they are shown rocking out across the Mississippi River bridge at Memphis. And at his new home on Albion Street, Larry demonstrates yoga positions on the floor of the basement and giddily presents the guided tour.

Most provocatively, Larry taped his lieutenant, William (Jack) Jackson, in Detroit in the kitchen of the house on Buffalo Street Larry lived in prior to moving to Albion. (It was in the basement of that house that the sisters Janice and Cindy Davis and their friends worked as cut-up girls.) It is a video portrait of gleeful incredulity, of dollar fever worthy of a game show contestant. Jackson joyously shakes a laundry basket full of cash. "Money, money, money!" he exclaims. "We rich, goddammit! Fifty thousand here, ain't no telling how much up there. I'm going to buy me three cars tomorrow—and a Jeep!" Jackson later asks Larry, who is not on camera: "Should we give these ones away, man, since we've got five hundred thousand dollars?"

"Well," Larry replies, a statesman of finance, "I'll tell you what we can do. We can give it to the poor."

They deliberate and decide that the money, floating from the basket like fabric softener, should go to the oppressed of South Africa. After all, Jackson reasons, "We still got about a million upstairs."

The No-Crack Crew confiscated eight videotapes. Though the footage is not consistently riveting—much of one tape, for instance, lingers on a still life of Larry and Belinda's matching cars—in aggregate the tapes portray Larry in all his humanity: the vain egotist, the unrefined intellectual, the orthodox materialist, the disciplined entrepreneur, the dark humorist, the rank sexist, the schoolyard bully.

The police were most interested in the tape of William Jackson; it came to be known as the "Money, Money, Money" video. When they first saw it, recalls Officer Biernacki, "We had to play it and replay it and replay it. And when we stopped laughing we wondered whether he'd [Larry] be stupid enough to go outside and show us where he was. And he did! He went outside and started filming his cars and his house on Albion and then came back to the house on Buffalo." Beyond its entertainment value, the tape enabled the No-Crack Crew to make a stronger case to the prosecutors and the magistrates whom they were asking to authorize the search warrants. "It showed the AUSAs [assistant U.S. attorneys] the amount of money coming in on a daily basis," Biernacki says. "After that, our work became a little easier."

Two days after the Albion raid, the No-Crack Crew hit paydirt again. During a raid at the Knodell Street duplex, which Larry then was using as a cook house, they arrested four men, including William Jackson, the star of Larry's infamous video. And on an otherwise bare wall near the archway between the living room and the dining room, officers found a handwritten poster Larry had tacked up outlining his organization's guiding principles and a set of dos and don'ts. The poster listed rules, violations, and dollar fines. "D.O." and "P.U." stood for drop-off and pickup, and "D" for drugs. "Riding dirty" meant driving with dope in the car.

1 Stealing among the group — 300

2 Fighting among the group — 100

3 Neglecting one's house — 100

4 Failing to follow instructions — 100

5 Revealing secrets about the organization — 500

6 Playing loud music while picking & dropping — 50

7 Bringing strangers to the house — 500

8 2 must ride together at all time — 100

9 When you are riding dirty you do not stop at your friends or family house — 400

10 Lying for another worker — 500

11 Causing confusing among the members — 200

12 Speeding while D.O. your P.U. — 100

13 All money must be P.U. before 6 a.m. in the morning — 200

14 You are on call 24 hours

15 If you hire a worker and he/she run off you must pay for the lost

16 One does not ride with money and D. at the same time — 300

17 One must not ride with all the D on them when they are D.O. — 300

Comments:

One will be promoted & graded according to his work and conduct.

If you are planning on getting rich forget about you girlfriends & family

You will not have too much time for parties or concerts

You shouldn't wear chains, Fila's, gold, etc.

Hard work & dedication we will all be rich within 12 months

Your success are going to depend on how well you follow instructions

CHAPTER ELEVEN

"FUCK IT, I'LL FIX HIM"

Billy: "In 1986 and even into 'eighty-seven, we wasn't big, but people said we was. What made us big was Larry, because he had a place [The Boulevard] that was outpumping anybody in Detroit. And so people on the streets automatic put us—me and Larry—as a tag team. So *my* name was extra big. Plus, they say I got places making fifty, sixty, seventy thousand [a day] like Larry pumping. And that's where the cops got their information from."

Nobody provided the police with more information than Terry Colbert, the young man who had worked for Billy years earlier at BJ's Party Store. Terry was born in Marianna and raised in nearby Hughes, Arkansas, and then Memphis. He was the fellow whose father, Big Terry Colbert, had introduced Billy to the drug business and who had been Billy's first supplier—of marijuana as well as cocaine. Back in the spring of 1983, when Billy was running his fledgling weed business out of the back room of the party store, he had hired Little Terry, then seventeen and a newcomer to Detroit, as a salesman. Terry lasted only a few months on Billy's payroll. By July of that year, when Billy moved himself and his business headquarters to the house at 1261 Newport, he told Terry his services were needed no longer.

Little Terry never again would draw a salary from Billy (he was paid about three hundred and fifty a week at the store), although he sometimes ran errands or did other odd jobs, even, as he later claimed, dropping off and picking up money and drugs. But Terry became a user. He changed from an easygoing if unreliable young man to—as many who knew him put it—a "fiend." "The man started smoking his lights out," says Billy. "He stopped functioning properly, stopped thinking properly. He started robbing motherfuckers, snatching purses, any little thing for money. He was ripping off his own daddy all the time to where it got so bad his daddy threatened to kill him. And Terry knew he wasn't kidding."

Terry was trapped. He couldn't quit crack and he couldn't sell it; none of his friends or family trusted him to work in the business. "Here's his daddy doing great selling cocaine, marijuana, heroin, LSD," Billy says. "And here I got houses, money, girls—so do his uncle and young brother. And he sees this, *wants* this, and the only thing he got is crumbs off our table: a girl or two, a old mail Jeep I gave him, a little pocket money here and there."

The money usually wound up again in Billy's pocket, via his crack houses. "I was using every day, constant," Terry remembers. "But I knew all those people who had it so I never had to worry about it. I was going through four, five hundred [dollars] a day, easy."

If Terry scored enough free rock, he slept at a pay-by-the-week motel, usually the Cabana on Harper. If he couldn't make the rent, he crashed at one or another of Billy's houses, where he begged the workers, "Can't I just get a dime or a twenty?" or "Can I wash your car?" or "Can I answer the door?" He went without sleep, he says, "all day, all night, sometimes three and four days straight." Billy tried to avoid him, but Terry would wait for him to show up somewhere—for days on end. "Or he'd run up to me at McDonald's and ask me for money," Billy says. "I'd give him what I had in my pocket: sometimes three or four hundred; sometimes twenty, thirty dollars."

Terry had no one else to turn to. His father shunned him; his mother, an alcoholic who was separated from his father and who could neither read nor write, was consumed by her own problems. "That's a lot of pressure on a young guy like Terry," Billy says. "He can't handle it. He sees the drugs defeating him, we're defeating him, his own mama and daddy defeating him. He's been crushed like a jellybean. Now he's living mad, and he wants that shit stopped."

"Me and Billy was always tight," Terry says. "Then because I was smoking he starts neglecting me, like I'm a nobody. I said, 'Fuck it, I'll fix him.' "

In October of 1986, Terry Colbert walked into the Fifth Precinct of the Detroit Police Department and volunteered his services in its investigations. He told Mick Biernacki, who as a member of the interagency No-Crack Crew was summoned to meet with Terry, that he had never used crack. And he said that until he had been fired, he sold it for Billy Joe Chambers.

Biernacki had the good sense to take Terry on as a registered informant. Their first meeting lasted an hour. They rode around in Biernacki's surveillance van while Terry directed him past ten or so houses he said Billy operated. Some of the locations were the same ones Patricia Middleton had pointed out in earlier expeditions. For his efforts that day Terry was paid either fifteen or twenty dollars. Asked later what he did with the money, he replied: "I went and bought me some crack with it."

Among the places Terry pointed out that first day was a house on Kresge Street, a side street a block east of Gratiot Avenue and across the avenue from the Chamberses' Knodell Street haunts and from the McDonald's Billy frequented. Terry told Biernacki that Billy used 9302 Kresge, a brown house with artificial brick siding on a fenced corner lot, as his headquarters. He said he himself had been a "drop-off and pickup man" for Billy and that he and the others—Fats Wilkins, Jerry Gant, and guys named Peanut, Karate, and Lamont—reported to Billy at 9302 Kresge.

Kresge was Billy's headquarters. The house was owned by

Perry Coleman, Billy's longtime friend, supplier, and the uncle of his first girlfriend in Detroit, Niece. Perry had purchased Kresge as one of eight or nine rental properties in June of 1985. Until the fall of 1986, a girlfriend of Perry's had lived there. When she moved, Perry suggested to Billy it might make for a good meet house. He charged Billy five hundred dollars a month.

At noon on Monday, November 24, 1986, Biernacki and three other police officers set up surveillance. A sample entry in their log: "12:56 p.m. P.O. [James] Tishuck obs. 1986 Mercedes Benz red in color w/ gold trim 86/MI 14852D park in frt. of target location . . . B/M 5-7, 150 lbs blk jerri curled hair, wearing long blk ct, gold framed sun glasses. carrying drk colored brief case and wht plastic bag entered target location."

The officers kept an eye on the house for four hours that afternoon. They returned the next morning at eight, and left twenty minutes later to obtain a search warrant. The warrant stated that an informant inside the house the previous day (unnamed, but presumably Terry Colbert) witnessed "certain Lieutenants in the Cocaine Organization arrive carrying brown paper bags filled with US Currency in every denomination . . ." It also said that the informant had been used "on 114 separate occasions," a figure that strongly suggests once again that the police were not above hyperbole. (Terry Colbert had only very recently signed on as an informant; it is inconceivable that he could have been used so many times already.)

Shortly before two-thirty P.M. on the Tuesday before Thanksgiving of 1986, a member of Billy's crew, sixteen-year-old Paul Young, pulled up to the curb at 9302 Kresge. He hadn't planned to go in, only to drop off a friend before heading home to shower and change clothes; he had been working at another house all night and day. Then he had to go pick up a friend from his girlfriend's house. But he remembered he was low on cash, and went in to ask Billy for a loan. The house was filled with the usual fellows, their girlfriends, and assorted others—nineteen people in all. Paul found Billy in the kitchen, but before he could even ask him for some money, another associate of Billy's walked in. Paul deferred to the older man, Kevin (Hollywood) Duplessis.

Paul waited in the dining room, idly playing a tabletop video game with Tiger Alexander (the nineteen-year-old brother of Billy's girlfriend Diana) and with some girls Tiger wanted Billy to meet. Billy had fired Tiger recently—he was always firing Tiger—and Tiger had come over to plead for his job. "But I knew how to get it back," he says. "Just bring Billy some fine females." At about 2:35, a girl named Kim strolled in from the living room, smoking a joint. "Police outside, y'all," she said. So nonchalant was her tone that nobody paid her any attention; Paul says he didn't bother looking up from the video game. "It was like, 'Oh, that's nice, Kim; now pass the joint.'"

Just then, Paul recalls, his friend Lamont ran through the house screaming, "There's a raid!" That was their only warning, Paul says. "No police yelling, 'Police, open up!' like they say in court they yell. That's bullshit. They don't yell anything; you don't get a chance to open the door. All you hear is 'Detroit police' and your door falling."

As the door came down everyone dashed for the upper staircase. "A girl tripped near the top of the stairs and the rest of us behind her dominoed," Paul says. "I thought that was it for me and Billy. We were the last ones up." Somehow, they made it upstairs in time to pile on the couches in one of the bedrooms and to stash their beepers under the cushions. Billy reminded everyone to give their alias names and he told them to say they were there watching *Scarface*, the movie in the VCR at the time. (The 1983 film, starring Al Pacino, chronicled the ultraviolent rise and fall of a Cuban refugee turned cocaine trafficker; it was one of their favorites.)

The officers lined everyone up against the wall to photograph and question them. All were asked their name, address, and date of birth. Tiger Alexander was among the first questioned. "This cop asked me what they always ask you. 'Who let you in the house?' I told him I didn't know. Then he asked what was I doing there? I told him, 'Watching *Scarface*.' He pulls out the video and hits me in the face with it." How hard? "It knocked me down and the tape broke. Then he asked me, 'Do you have any complaints?' I told him 'No, sir.'"

Paul Young said his name was Lamont McCarter—his middle name and his mother's last name. Billy said his name was David Johnson; he gave a phony birthdate as well. The officer questioning Billy also asked him: "Where do I know you from?" Billy said he couldn't imagine. "Have you been in a drug raid before?" Billy told him no. The officer pulled Mick Biernacki over, who was busy taking pictures. "Do you know this one?" he asked. "Nope," Biernacki said. Then Biernacki stared hard at Billy. "Tell BJ we know who he is," he warned, "and tell him we're on his ass and he's going down real soon."

While the question-and-answer session continued, one of the concealed beepers went off. It was Paul's. A DEA agent grabbed it.

A Marianna native named Michael Lee was the only person arrested upstairs. (Two others, Hollywood and Fats, were apprehended in the basement and the kitchen respectively.) Michael Lee was handcuffed behind his back and then, according to Paul Young and others, he was pushed down the stairs. "[DEA Special Agent] Richard Crock made sure we saw what happened," Paul says, "and told us: 'Your little time for games and parties is over now. This is your only warning. So take the warning and get the fuck out of here. I don't want to see any of you stop. All I want to see is assholes and elbows when you all hit that door.'"

As Crock spoke, Paul found himself at the top of the stairs. "I had just seen Mike get thrown down and I'm thinking I know this motherfucker gonna push me too, I know he gonna push me." Crock saw Paul hesitate. "What the fuck you waiting on?" Paul didn't answer; he flew down the stairs. Toward the bottom he stumbled. He looked up from the floor to see "this cop who's every bit of six-seven or six-eight and gotta be near three hundred pounds. God*damn*. He looked like Herman the Monster. I just put my head down and kept running."

Billy's crew met up across the street at McDonald's after they were released. They could not go much farther; the police confiscated six of their cars. "We're standing there and here come the police in a convoy down Gratiot," Paul says. "They're taking our cars to the Ninth Precinct and they've got the windows down, the radios all the way up, some of them on the telephone, holding the phones up. And they see us in McDonald's parking lot looking like, 'Damn, there go my car'—really rubbing it in."

Later that afternoon, Paul finally made it over to his friend Rich's girlfriend's house—he was to have picked him up hours earlier. When he got there, Rich was not pleased. "Oh, you wanna play games now, huh?"

"What you talking about?" Paul said.

"You know, motherfucker. When I called you on your beeper I got called back and they said, 'This is the DEA; may we help you?' "

Seven days after Billy narrowly avoided arrest on Kresge Street, the No-Crack Crew again let him slip from their clutches. During an evening raid at 9432 Hayes Street, a two-story brown brick house reputed to be Billy's latest headquarters, the crew entered the house to find fourteen youths—seven girls, none of whom was older than sixteen, and seven young men, of whom Billy, at twenty-four, was the eldest. They were gathered around the television in the living room, watching a nationally syndicated Geraldo Rivera special entitled "American Vice: The Doping of a Nation." The live show featured a pair of drug raids, with Geraldo and his camera crew along for the ride. (And in a life-imitating-live-TV spectacle, on hand at Hayes Street with the No-Crack Crew was its ever-present WXYZ Channel 7 news team.)

Officers seized fifteen thousand dollars in cash, a "large baggie" of "suspected cocaine," two new Jeeps and an old Trans Am, and a sawed-off .22-caliber rifle. They also found handwritten leaflets, about the size of three-by-five cards, advertising: GOOD $10 BOULDER CRACK SOLD OUT BACK DOOR. Three of the young men were arrested. The juveniles were cited for curfew violation, but none was detained for longer than it took to issue tickets at the Ninth Precinct. Everyone else was released, including Billy, whose *nom de raid,* David Johnson, again went unchallenged.

For every dollar and every car the No-Crack Crew confiscated during their many raids—the raid on Hayes Street, the last of 1986, was the twenty-eighth on alleged Chambers-related houses since the crew formed in early August—it was widely believed that many more eluded seizure; that trunkloads of cash were shipped regularly out of the city in vehicles purchased and registered in Michigan, but spirited away to Arkansas. Those assets were valuable to local prosecutors and police eager to offset budget shortfalls and as further evidence of a large-scale criminal organization.

In the middle of December an assistant prosecuting attorney in Detroit wrote to the commanding officer of the narcotics section of the Detroit Police Department, Inspector Joel Gilliam. (It was Gilliam who earlier that year had testified before Congress on the difficulties of fighting crack.) "It has been brought to my attention," A. George Best, the point man on the Chambers case in the prosecuting attorney's office wrote, "that large amounts of U.S. currency and numerous vehicles are being transported out of the City of Detroit to the 'home base' of [the Chambers brothers], that location being Marianna, Arkansas.

"I believe," Best added, "that the assets located in Arkansas are seizable as drug proceeds. . . . In order for those assets to be identified, located and seized, investigation needs to be done in Arkansas." Best requested that Gilliam dispatch to Marianna at least three of his narcotics officers—Biernacki, James Tishuck, and Mike Cowling. Best said he needed their help to "create an 'expense picture'" of the Chambers family. They would gather property and land-sale records and conduct surveillance of the Chambers homestead. They would also be asked to provide "photographic evidence" of vehicles and other property.

Gilliam approved the request. Shortly afterward, a half dozen members of the No-Crack Crew (the DEA approved the trip for several of its agents as well) set off in a van for Arkansas. Accompanying them, as usual, was Chris Hansen, the Channel 7 reporter, and his cameraman, Chuckie. It was a tight squeeze. "We had just enough room for a tote bag each," recalls Mick Biernacki, "and the rest was beer." A couple of supervisors also went, Biernacki says, "but they got to fly down, of course."

They stayed in Memphis, at a Holiday Inn. Although it was wintertime, it wasn't the Arctic air they were accustomed to in Detroit. "We hung out around the pool a lot," says Officer Greg Woods. "It was a good time—a lot of power drinking. Hansen picked up the tab for the champagne."

Once the crew roused themselves from poolside and piled in the van for the seventy-five-minute drive southwest to Lee County, they had a terrible time pinpointing their target. They were afraid to tip local authorities to their mission, so asking directions to the Chambers family's house was not an option. They did pay a courtesy call on the Marianna Police Department.

"We told 'em," Biernacki says, " 'We're guys from Detroit down here just looking at something that might have showed up on some cars,' is all."

"No problem," they were told. "You need maps?"

"Like dummies, we said no," Biernacki recalls. "I was driving, Dick's [Crock, of the DEA] in the front seat, we got the cameraman, Chuckie, and Chris, but of course he's combing his hair all the time. We're driving and driving and looking and all we had was rural route whatever the hell it was. We're driving around for three hours or so. Everybody's getting mad. I says, 'Dick, we *gotta* ask somebody. I can't find this place.' We're on this road and we turn around in some driveway and I see the mailbox that says CHAMBERS. And on the side of the house are Mercedes and BMWs and Jeeps. And we look at each other and say, 'Do you believe this?'

"And there's Hansen going nuts with his hair spray and getting his cameras out."

* * *

At 10:35 on the morning of Thursday, December 18, 1986, Assistant United States Attorney Thomas Ziolkowski convened a panel of grand jurors on the ninth floor of the Federal Building in downtown Detroit.

"Ladies and gentlemen," the government prosecutor began, "I'm here on a new matter that is being opened for you today for your consideration. I'm with the drug unit, Controlled Substance Unit here in the U.S. attorney's office, and we're investigating several targets as far as their involvement or alleged involvement in narcotics distribution, specifically cocaine and crack cocaine in the City of Detroit. Some of the people we are going to be looking at: Larry Chambers, C-h-a-m-b-e-r-s; Billy Chambers, Otis Chambers, Kevin (Hollywood) Duplessis; and there will be some other ones. . . .

"What we are looking at are some violations of Title 21, which is a drug law. . . . Specifically what we are looking at is conspiracy to possess with intent to distribute, and conspiracy to distribute cocaine [in other words], the actual selling . . . on the street." Ziolkowski told the grand jury that conspiracy here means not merely "distributing the cocaine"—that is a separate crime—but "agreeing" with at least one other person to distribute the drugs.

He added that his office also was investigating Larry and Billy for their alleged "supervisory" roles in a "continuing criminal enterprise"—a separate, greater offense under Title 21. A CCE, Ziolkowski explained, consists of at least five people who get together to commit "three or more unlawful acts," and who make "substantial income" from the acts."

Around the time the grand jury was meeting, Larry Chambers was bending a friend's ear about ways to hide and spend his substantial income. One idea he had, according to Morris Hampton, a friend who installed burglar bars on Larry's houses, was to "build an underground house, store his money there, and come out like Batman." Morris thought the plan unfeasible. He suggested that Larry use his money to travel. " 'See the world,' I told him. He asked me where I'd go. 'Hawaii,' I said. So he said, 'That'd be nice, man.' Then he said, 'What about Jamaica?' He'd seen their tourist bureau ads on TV."

Sometime between Christmas and New Year's Eve, Larry, Morris, and five others—Larry's sisters Delois and Cathy, his brother Danny, his girlfriend Belinda Lumpkin, and her brother James—left for a weeklong trip to Jamaica. They stayed at the Americana Hotel in Ocho Rios. "We had a ball, we really did," Morris says. They had long leisurely dinners, danced at nightclubs, strolled on the pristine beaches. Larry brought his camcorder. He taped the group gazing at cruise ships in the harbor, shopping at the outdoor marketplace, cavorting and singing alongside a strolling female guitarist. During a tour of a shantytown, Larry handed the camera to his guide while he sampled fresh coconut milk. *"Perfecto,"* he proclaimed.

Larry enjoyed himself so much he decided to make Ocho Rios his permanent vacation spot. The climate was agreeable, the people friendly, his assets untouchable. On a subsequent trip with Belinda and James Lumpkin, Larry gave his traveling partners five thousand dollars to put in their carry-on bags—enough for a down payment to a builder on a new sixty-thousand-dollar house and land in a subdivision about two miles from the Americana. The property would be titled in James's name, a ploy Larry had used in Detroit on various cars and houses purchased with his money.

Larry also planned to invest in legitimate businesses in Jamaica. He and Belinda flew down frequently; there were direct flights from Detroit Metro and for the first few months of 1987 they went as often as every other week. He says he became friendly with the mayor of Ocho Rios, who provided Larry with a driver and introduced him to the police chief and members of the business community. He spoke with them about opening a water-slide amusement park and a chain of video stores. The Jamaican officials apparently were taken with the wealthy American entrepreneur, and with certain of his traveling companions. "Every time I went back to the States the mayor told me, 'Bring me back American girls!'"

While Larry celebrated New Year's Eve in Jamaica by dining and dancing with friends and family aboard a cruise ship, back home in Detroit his organization had sprung a couple of major leaks. One of the cut-up girls, seventeen-year-old Janice Davis, had decided over the Christmas break to quit work. She was a new mother and had started attending church again; she was trying to stay in school and keep her life on course. But the easy job, the short hours for the long dollar, was tempting. "Here is four hundred dollars for nothing," Janice put it. And those perks were great: the employer-paid hair care, taxi rides, and shopping expeditions. "They were treating us pretty good," she later told the grand jury. Still, she never could shake the idea she worked for some dangerous people. "I used to be scared of everybody," she said. "That's why I stopped."

No one hassled her when she told them of her decision. "They just told me not to tell if I ever got caught," she testified. Her friends and sister, who continued as cut-up girls, told her she was crazy for leaving. "You missing out this good money."

"Not me," she answered. "I be too scared." She found secretarial work at a tuxedo shop in suburban Warren. It paid minimum wage, but she liked answering phones and doing computer data-entry. "It was a good job." And it was legal.

Some time after Janice quit the organization, she bumped into Belinda Lumpkin in a parking lot at a shopping mall, where Belinda threatened her. "Nobody never got wrong with me until now," Janice testified. The two had been friends. "We used to hang out together."

"What's this I hear about you going to the police on the Chambers?" Janice says Belinda asked her. Janice denied that she snitched, telling her, "I wasn't going to the police about no Chambers." Belinda advised Janice "to get on [your] knees and start worrying about [your] baby." Belinda added: "You don't know who you're messing with and you better watch yourself."

* * *

There was one other key defector. For nearly five months after Patricia Middleton called the No-Crack Hotline, she teetered acrobatically between two masters. She worked for Larry Chambers, making eight hundred dollars a week ferrying cash to him in the trunk of her 1978 AMC Concord. And she met regularly with Mick Biernacki and other members of the No-Crack Crew, keeping them abreast of Larry's movements. One morning in January of 1987, her tightrope act crashed with startling finality. She had spent the night with her boyfriend, David Havard, at David's sister Darlene's house. In the morning, after David and Darlene were gone (Pat was baby-sitting Darlene's six-year-old niece), there came a knock at the door. Standing there were Larry Chambers and Rod Byrd, his top lieutenant. Byrd was dating Darlene.

"I asked them if they wanted to come in," Pat says. She figured they were looking for Darlene. "They said no and just stood there." Then Larry pulled a gun. He "put it to my head and said if I talked to Biernacki again he would 'blow my fucking brains out.' " Pat Middleton says she was too scared for words. "I stood there and peed in my pants."

No matter the extremes to which Larry went to coerce loyalty, the fact was that the organization he'd assembled and held together by intimidation was, by early 1987, unraveling. The authorities had sketched for grand jurors a broad-stroked portrait of a monstrous two-headed drug ring. Below the powerful heads, Larry and Billy, their brothers Otis and Willie were depicted as next in command. Under them, the monster divided in two: Larry's lieutenants, including Belinda Lumpkin and Rod Byrd, and Billy's, among whom were Jerry Gant, Marshall (Mario) Glenn, the Cadillac-enthralled recruiter, and Carl Young, the trucker and childhood friend of Billy and Jerry's. Feeding the beast were the alleged suppliers: Kevin (Hollywood) Duplessis and Perry Coleman.

There were faces still to be filled in, other supposed recruiters, suppliers, lieutenants: co-conspirators not yet identified. And the designated heads of the continuing criminal enterprise had not yet been ensnared in the requisite three separate raids. Those were details to be drawn over the coming weeks and months, fine lines needed for indictment. By early 1987, the panorama prosecutors were painting was by no means fully realized, but like a Polaroid snapshot in the seconds after the film is ripped from the camera, it was emerging: slowly, clearly, and inevitably.

Early in the last week of February of 1987, Billy fitted a key into the door of Room 5 of the City Airport Motel. For the past three months or so—since the close shave on Hayes Street—the room had been home for Billy. The room itself was charmless: two beds with lumpy, sagging mattresses, a mildewed carpet, an intermittently working television. That the entire two-story, blue-and-white structure, on Gratiot around the corner from the commuter airport, could best be described as drab was beside the point. The point was that this was Billy's crew's new hangout—an expansive headquarters that had assumed the festivity of a college dorm after final exams.

Billy didn't live there alone. He and his crew rented twenty rooms—the entire ground floor (save for four rooms the manager kept for his family). For the privilege of exclusivity, Billy paid six hundred dollars a night. "We let 'em rent out the upstairs on Friday and Saturday nights, but the rest of the time they wasn't renting to nobody else," Billy says. "And that was good with them; they didn't want nobody else there once we got there.

"Everybody stayed there. Like if somebody went home and they didn't want to be at home no more, they'd come there. They even brought their friends, because everybody had their own room with two beds. So one girl might bring her sister and two of her girlfriends. Me and Kela [Billy's new girlfriend] stayed there all the time. We was even there Christmas. *That* was a party for real. Lots of peoples getting sloppy drunk in the hallway, screaming and all."

Around seven o'clock on the evening of February 23, a few of the guys and their girlfriends were standing around the hallway, "laughing and tripping." Otis was there, as was Anthony Wilkins, who was a classmate from Marianna better known as "23," and

Fats Wilkins and Michael Lee and a guy named Tate and a girl named Halas and her sister, Celina. Billy had returned to the motel about half an hour earlier, tired from a full day of business. More of the crew would have been there, but some of them had just that morning bought themselves cars, some vintage 1978 and '79 Trans Ams. They had been gone all day, rounding up the titles and tags. When they arrived back at the motel, around six, their girl-friends told them they wanted to try out the new cars. The guys said no. Upon Billy's arrival, the girls appealed their case to a higher authority. "All the girls running up to me telling me they in love with those raggly-ass cars outside, and 'The fellas won't let us drive them, won't give us the keys,' like they got new BMWs or something. So I just said, 'Fellas, why don't you let the girls drive the cars?' So some of the fellas left with the girls, other guys just gave 'em the keys."

That's when Billy told the others to keep it down; he needed a nap. But the mood in the hallway was buoyant; Billy would get no rest. He figured he might as well join them. A minute or so after he stepped out of Room 5, he noticed a guy running down the hallway, waving frantically toward the hall door and some other unseen person or persons.

"Somebody yelled, 'Damn, here go the police,'" Billy re-calls, "and the next thing I know all these polices is steady jumping through the door. We broke and ran, and Fats fell. And Otis fell over him. And they got up and were running for the back door and I just stepped in my room. And then I thought, Shit, it don't make no sense stepping in here. So I stepped back out in the hallway, and I'm looking at them kicking in all the doors. And they come up to me and do me like they do everybody: hit me in my stomach, in my jaw a couple times, knocked me on the floor, kicked me a few times. That was it. They asked me my name. I told 'em David Johnson."

But this time the police knew whom they had.

"You think we're fucking stupid?" asked one of the officers. "You're BJ Chambers."

* * *

Otis Chambers and his girlfriend, Chenine Currie, were burning up Arkansas Highway 79 in a new white Corvette. The seventeen-year-olds were on the last leg home from Detroit, just twenty-two miles north of Marianna, when Chenine rolled through a stop sign in Hughes, Arkansas, a farming town of two thousand residents. It was late one afternoon in April of 1987. The infraction caught the unblinking eye of Hughes Police Chief Herbert Neighbors, who was on traffic duty in his cruiser along with Officer Monroe Scofield.

Chief Neighbors flipped on the blue lights and pulled over on the shoulder behind the Corvette. He asked Chenine for her driver's license; she didn't have one. She said her name was Tammy White and that she was twenty-three. Neighbors arrested her and told Officer Scofield to take her and Otis to the police station. Neighbors, meanwhile, drove the " 'Vette" back to the station. There he asked Otis who owned the car. "He said that he borrowed it from a friend to come from Detroit to see his people in Marianna," Neighbors recalls. Neighbors searched the Corvette. In a compartment behind the rear seat on the passenger side he found a thirty-gallon dark green trash bag. In the bag were sixty bundles of money, a total of $59,624. Otis and Chenine said they knew nothing about the money, didn't even know it was in the car.

The car was traced to a Chambers brother-in-law who lived in Texas. As for the cash, according to Billy (Otis declined to be interviewed), Otis planned to store it safely at home, far from the reaches of the Detroit police. "He was just gonna put the money up, so when he got back to Detroit and needed some he could call home and say, 'Hey, send me five thousand.' "

Chief Neighbors called the FBI. A quick background check of Otis led the bureau to Tom McClain of the DEA, who advised that his agency was in the midst of a "sensitive investigation" of the Chambers family. He asked that an "in-depth interview of the subjects not be attempted," and that the car and money "be held for proof of ownership."

Hazel and Curtis Chambers came to Hughes to post bond for

the minor traffic offenses. The Hughes Police Department retained the car and the money. The FBI concocted a plan to learn something about the source of the money. If the money did not belong to Otis or Chenine, it belonged to someone—someone who was bound to be angry at Otis for losing it. Special Agent Scott Battershell showed up on Curtis Chambers's door "under guise of concern for welfare of his son," as Battershell put it in an internal report.

Curtis, though, did not bite. He was "reluctant to provide information," Battershell wrote. "He suggested the money in his son's possession was meant for him as repayment for a debt." Curtis Chambers was a reasonable man. He understood human nature, knew why the agent was interested in the cash. You return the money, he told the G-Man, and I'll "split" it with you.

The IRS ultimately seized the money and the car. But Herbert Neighbors was not without reward. His department kept half of the nearly sixty thousand dollars and he would later fly to Detroit at government expense to testify about the incident. It was his first and only plane flight. "Otis Chambers and this ol' gal, they were just mules bringing the money south from Detroit," says Neighbors, a nineteen-year law enforcement veteran, "but it was the biggest highlight of my career."

Six days later in Detroit, Billy and Michael Lee were "chillin' out" in the kitchen of a house on Hamburg Street. They were seated at the table, watching a game on television when, Billy says, "something hit the door real hard: BOOM! It didn't panic me and it didn't panic Mike because we weren't doing nothing. But the door wasn't giving, so one police knocked the front windows out with a shotgun. And he climbed in, looked at us just sitting there, and he screamed, 'GET UP!' And we looked at him, like, Get up? What for? And he screamed it again, and the other cops outside heard him, and they started diving through the window too like, Damn, what's going on? And I'm still sitting there and he puts the shotgun to my head, and I say, 'Okay, man, you want us to get up that bad, we'll get up.' "

The police offer a vastly different account of the raid. In testimony in Detroit Recorder's Court, and later in federal court, the "shotgun" officer, Kenneth Surma, said that as he entered the house he saw Billy drop a heat-sealed packet of cocaine down a heating vent in the living room. Surma testified that he instructed another officer, Keith Terry, to go down to the basement to retrieve the Baggie. Terry corroborated the story. He said he found the Baggie at the bottom of the vent, in the ceiling of the basement.

"That story was strictly something to make their case," Billy says. "There wasn't anything in the house, just a trigger-happy cop going crazy with a shotgun. Surma said I threw the cocaine down the vent in the living room. But I never got up out from the kitchen table until he put the gun to my head. I guess he figured while they ramming the door three or four times, I'm out there in plain view trying to unscrew the vent and put something down it." Billy was found guilty of possession of two-tenths of a gram of cocaine—the equivalent of about three five-dollar rocks—and put on probation for two years.

The day after the Hamburg Street raid, a Friday, Little Terry Colbert was at Job Corps school when his brother came to him with sobering news. "Be careful, because Billy Joe Chambers has a contract on you, because he thinks you're a snitch."

"Where did you hear this from?"

"Never mind," his brother replied. "Just be careful."

Terry left school and checked into Junior's Motel, at Mack and St. Jean, a regular haunt. He ran into a guy named Charles who told him: "BJ is putting contracts out on people he thinks is snitches."

The world was closing in. Terry left the motel for his father's house on Coplin Street. "Stay the fuck away from me," Big Terry told his son. "I don't want to deal with problems and you are a problem."

Terry picked up his girlfriend and went back to Junior's

Motel. They hid out until he could make contact with the No-Crack Crew. At ten-thirty on Sunday morning, Terry met police officer Mick Biernacki and DEA special agent Dick Crock at the Ninth Precinct. The authorities took his statement and placed Terry in "protective custody" at the Red Roof Inn in suburban Plymouth. There he would remain for nearly three weeks, until the federal grand jury investigating the Chambers brothers was ready to summon him as its first civilian witness.

By May 20, 1987, when Terry Colbert solemnly swore to tell the truth to the grand jury, the investigation had been assigned to an assistant United States attorney named Lawrence J. Bunting. Larry Bunting was no buttoned-down prosecutor. He was a hefty man with graying hair, aviator glasses, and an ever-present cigarette. Bunting was comfortable around cops. He enjoyed going on raids, liked seeing firsthand the "rollers"—as he called drug dealers—in their native environment. Bunting told the jurors the "minimum charge" he would seek against the Chambers brothers would be a continuing criminal enterprise, "and it may end up being a RICO"—a case brought under the Racketeer Influenced and Corrupt Organizations Act—"investigation."

Then Bunting asked Terry a series of questions seeking to establish his credentials as an expert witness. Terry said he and Billy "were sort of raised up together down south." He said he met Billy again in 1983, after they both had moved to Detroit, and that his father, Big Terry, was supplying weed and cocaine for Billy. He said he himself had worked on and off for Billy, and that Billy currently operated "over about two hundred or more" crack houses. Terry also said that Billy had already retaliated against him. "Last week," he said, "a couple of BJ's boys, they jumped on my brother and beat him up real bad, messed his eye up and got a deep gash on his eye." Bunting asked his witness whether the assailants explained to his brother why they beat him up. "Yeah," Terry replied. "They said, 'We can't find your brother but we got you. When you see your brother, tell him we are going to get his ass.'"

Minutes after his chilling and useful testimony the DEA paid Terry Colbert two thousand dollars. In an internal memo, Special Agent Dick Crock wrote that he made the payment because "a murder contract is in existence" and that Terry was "unable to retrieve any of [his] personal possessions from [his] place of residence." Crock also wrote that he offered Terry the "opportunity to apply for the U.S. Marshal's Witness Protection" program, but that he declined.

Terry Colbert didn't need protection from Billy Joe Chambers; he needed money. If it took holing up in an isolated motel for a few weeks, if it took dancing to whatever tune the prosecutors called, including lying under oath, he would do it, "as long," he admitted years later, "as I was gettin' paid." Terry knew neither guilt for lying nor responsibility to his friends and family; he knew only craving for cocaine.

"Billy didn't know I was talking," Terry says. "I was still hanging around all the time. I was smoking so much that whatever bullshit the cops asked me, I said yes this, no that—whatever they wanted. I guess I never was thinking it would go so far."

The Hamburg Street bust was the second of three overt acts the grand jury would need to charge Billy with supervising a continuing criminal enterprise. (The first came three years earlier, in the Labor Day 1984 raid of the duplex on Gray Street. There police said they chased Elayne Coleman from the upper flat to the lower, where they say they caught Billy flushing cocaine down the toilet.) Now, in the summer of 1987, the authorities hoped to complete the investigation. They had worked the case night and day for a full year and still there were no indictments imminent. And there were other big cases demanding their attention. With their principal wells of information, Patricia Middleton and Terry Colbert, dry, they needed a new source of intelligence. They needed, it was agreed, a plant.

Romia Hall picked up the phone ringing at his trailer home on Texas Street, on the south end of Marianna.

"Whatcha know, nigger?" It was Billy calling his best friend. Romia was the emergency medical technician with whom Billy had worked during his months in exile from Detroit in 1984 and 1985.

"I'll be down for the Fourth," Billy advised.

A few days later Billy and family rolled into town. Waiting for them were DEA Special Agent Tom McClain and three members of the narcotics section of the Detroit Police Department. The law enforcement officers had arrived on July 2 to meet with local and state police, who were convinced the Chambers family was "the major source of cocaine in eastern Arkansas."

During a morning-long briefing at the regional headquarters of the Arkansas State Police in Forrest City, the Detroit officers heard from Marianna police chief Mark Birchler. Birchler, a native of southern Illinois, was a fast-talking likable man of thirty-three with an open, pleasant face, a beer gut, and a bent for self-promotion. He and a state police sergeant told their counterparts from Detroit that they had been conducting a long-term investigation. They had learned that one local supplier of cocaine was a man named Jesse Woodson, the proprietor of the Big Boy Lounge on Mississippi Street in Marianna. The lounge, better known as Jesse's Place, was the site from which a five-car caravan of young recruits had left for Detroit a year earlier. Woodson, the local police said, was a close friend of the Chambers family.

Local police had already prepared some two hundred arrest warrants. They planned to start serving the warrants, with the aim of developing witnesses against the Chamberses. At two-thirty that afternoon they picked up an acquaintance of Billy's named Melvin Brown. He was wanted on an assault-and-battery charge. Melvin told police that Billy had invited him to go to work in Detroit, but that he had declined because he had a new baby and because he had heard that police there beat workers caught in raids. Rather than face extended jail time, Melvin agreed to a deal: introduce an out-of-town informant to Billy so that the informant might infiltrate the organization. Two and a half hours after he was arrested, Melvin Brown was released from jail to "lay the groundwork for the introduction."

The informant was a thirty-five-year-old Detroiter named Morris Killingham. Killingham was a two-time felon and an experienced snitch: the DPD's narcotics section had employed him in that capacity for five years. He and Melvin Brown were introduced and given their cover story: they were to pose as cousins, and to say that Killingham lived in Chicago, where he had sold crack, and that he was now looking for work in that field in Detroit.

On Friday, July 3, while they waited for Billy to arrive in town, Melvin took Killingham to Romia Hall's house. Romia wasn't home, though, and they left. Killingham went to his motel, a small, run-down place called the Sands, the lone motel in Marianna. The Sands was known mostly for its blue-movie channel and as a place where a little crack could be scored. Melvin eventually ran into Billy, who had arrived that evening in a white stretch limousine. According to Killingham, who three months later told his story to the grand jury, Melvin told Billy he had a cousin from Chicago who "had some coke he wanted to get out of Arkansas."

"I'll be in town later on tonight and then I'll talk to him," Billy reportedly replied.

At three o'clock in the morning Melvin Brown dropped by Killingham's motel room. Killingham said that Melvin told him that Billy "still would like to meet me but he was running back and forth and they were partying and getting high." Later that Saturday morning, Killingham testified, Melvin and Killingham finally ran into Billy in the parking lot of the Family Dollar Store. Billy was in Marshall (Mario) Glenn's black Cadillac.

Melvin made the introductions, telling Billy that Killingham "wanted to come back and work with them." Killingham quoted Billy: "He said, 'Well, I don't know if I'll be taking anyone else back up, but if I do I want younger kids—fifteen, sixteen, and seventeen.' " Killingham added that Billy explained he preferred juveniles because they "would be less trouble if anything happened with the law."

That, apparently, is as close as Killingham came to planting himself in the organization. Billy, though, says the entire story is fabricated. He says he made a point of keeping a low profile in Marianna (although the white limo hardly discouraged attention). "I'd stay at my daddy's house in town, and ride around with Romia and my brothers and that's it. No outsiders ever hung with me. I might hang around Jesse's Place a little. Shoot a few games of pool, drink a beer, but that's about it. You can be damn sure nobody never approached me about no job in Marianna. There wasn't no way in the world somebody could get close to me. That was just totally fake. It's something that you just can't do. You *got* to know somebody or go through somebody. Once a guy says, 'Hey, he's cool,' then you *might* do it. But how can you walk up to somebody you don't know and say, 'Hey, I wanna sell some dope for you'?"

The Chambers brothers were back in Detroit by Monday night. On Tuesday, Otis stopped by one of Billy's houses on the west side, a house owned by Little Terry Colbert's uncle (and Big Terry's brother), Tommie Colbert. Big Terry, three years older than Tommie, had invited Tommie to Detroit to work with him. And he gave Tommie the house, a three-family flat.

Sometime in 1986 Tommie rented the house to Billy for use as a crack outlet; it was one of the few west-side houses Billy operated. By the middle of 1987, by Tommie's reckoning, Billy had fallen behind in rent payments. Tommie and Otis, who functioned occasionally as Billy's agent, argued repeatedly about the money before the holiday weekend. Now that Otis was back from Arkansas, Tommie demanded the arrears immediately.

On this torrid Tuesday afternoon, the two resumed their heated dispute, their voices spilling out into the street. Little Terry, who the authorities maintained feared for his life, was there, as he often was, because there was plenty of crack to filch. Otis finally stalked out. After a half hour of ominous peace, Otis returned. With him were five or six others, including Karate, a big brooding man, and Peanut, who was toting an Uzi submachine gun. As the argument resumed, Otis looked hard at Little Terry and said, "You know, I don't like you no way." That was the enforcers' cue. While Karate lit into Terry with a baseball bat, Peanut punctuated the walls with bullet holes.

Terry made a run for it, leaping out the window. Otis and his crew darted around the house. "There he goes, right there," Otis shouted. "Shoot him." Peanut fired, wounding Terry twice above the right knee. As far as Terry was concerned, he had just barely escaped death. An ambulance rushed him to Detroit Receiving Hospital. For the rest of his life he would have a scarred leg; soon he would have his revenge.

CHAPTER TWELVE

ALL IN THE FAMILY

For one local television station, mired like the others in the low ratings of summer, a time when Detroiters take to the outdoors while they can, the Chambers family was like Christmas in July. In the year the No-Crack Task Force had been operating, it had executed some forty raids on alleged Chambers-owned or -operated crack houses. On most of those raids (and on the first excursion to Marianna) the task force was accompanied by reporter Chris Hansen of WXYZ-TV, the local ABC affiliate. Hansen was born in Chicago and grew up in Michigan. He landed his first on-camera reporting job while still an undergraduate at Michigan State University in East Lansing. After college he worked for a station in Tampa, Florida, for a couple of years. In 1984, when he was twenty-four years old, WXYZ summoned him home.

Even before the No-Crack Crew had formed, Hansen was doing stories on the drug's proliferation in Detroit. In August of 1986, as the crew geared up, Detroit Police narcotics commander Joel Gilliam suggested to Hansen that he profile the novel state-federal task force. "I basically lived with them for the course of the eighteen-month story," Hansen says. (He grew so close to the No-Crack Crew that a number of them attended his wedding.)

The fruit of Hansen's labor—of a year spent on call twenty-four hours a day with the cops, of trudging along behind them from raid to raid in a bulletproof vest, of hanging out afterward in cop bars and coffee shops, of virtually trading his press card for a deputy's badge—was a five-part story on the Chambers brothers.

The series featured lots of hyperbolic footage, replete with you-are-there shots of cops busting down doors and sweat-stained post-raid interviews. It also featured the broadcast premiere of Larry's confiscated home videotapes—the tapes the No-Crack Crew had seized the previous October in the raid on his Albion Street home. The series aired each weeknight of the last week of July of 1987, during one of the quarterly "sweeps" months, the crucial ratings periods on which television stations base their advertising rates. "The ratings were huge," Hansen says.

The station aired promotional spots on radio and television for several days before the series was to begin. Billy Joe Chambers was one of the listeners whose news appetite was whetted.

"We were just riding around in Fats's Jeep, me and the fellas, and they had a tape player in the ride like always," Billy recalls. "But I liked to listen to the radio because I got tired of listening to the same old tapes over and over. So I took the tape out, and we was listening to the music on the radio and a commercial break came on. And the announcer said, 'We got an exclusive video of a large drug family in Detroit, and we want to tell you they're *big,* and we got a series coming on starting Monday for five days on Channel Seven.' "

Billy says he had no clue about which drug family would be featured. "We knew they were filming us because when they put us up against the wall [during raids], the cameraman would swing the camera down and shoot us from floor level. But we didn't know what for, probably just so they'd make our I.D.

"So when I heard the radio talking about a drug family, I said, 'Man, damn, we got to know these peoples if they're *that* big.' And then we talked about who gonna know 'em. Because Fats knew more peoples than me. He and the fellas grew up in

Detroit, and they went to school with So-and-So's brother, or his nephew, or they talked to his sister before. So everybody was gonna meet back at my house that Monday on Wilfred, and we'd have a little reefer and something to drink. And we all there, waiting for it to come on, and then it did, and the announcer said: 'And let me tell you, these peoples here is *big* in Detroit in the drug business and they name is Chambers.' "

At least Billy had an inkling that watching the news would be worthwhile; Larry had no such warning. He was fixing himself a late dinner that night with the television blaring from the living room. "I hear [anchorman] Bill Bonds talking about a notorious gang called the Chambers brothers," Larry remembers, "but I wasn't really paying it no attention. Next thing a voice sounded so much like Jack [William Jackson], I thought he was in the house. Then I realized that it was Jack on TV and I just started laughing so hard I couldn't stop."

The Chamberses and their associates weren't the only ones taken by surprise. On Wednesday morning, July 29, after parts one and two of the series had already been broadcast, the federal grand jury investigating the Chambers case convened to hear further testimony. Asked by assistant U.S. attorney Larry Bunting whether there were any questions before he called the first witness, one juror asked: "If this is supposed to be a secret, why was it on TV last night?"

"That's a very good question, ma'am," Bunting replied, adding, "The first I knew that something like that was going to happen was Saturday evening." Bunting said he was watching the late news on Channel 7 when he heard the anchor say, " 'There will be a new and exciting series starting Monday at eleven o'clock,' in which they were going to detail the operations of a dope family."

Bill Bonds was the cantankerous and popular lead anchor for "Channel 7 Action News at Eleven." He was no drone of a newsreader, no blow-dried happyface indistinguishable from that of any other local market. (In fact, he wore a variety of toupees.) He was

Detroit's own: a fifty-five-year-old guy who grew up in a west-side working-class neighborhood; the city's version, as a *Wall Street Journal* profile put it, "of newsman Howard Beale of the movie 'Network,' who was mad as hell and wouldn't take it anymore."

It was hard to ignore Bill Bonds; many tuned in for the shock value. In a "special report" on AIDS two years earlier, he said some gay people were "groin terrorists" who were trying to spread the disease through "zipper warfare." Another time on the air he challenged the mayor to a boxing match. And he was famed for his booze-fueled temper off camera as well. "The newspapers get on Bill for getting into bar fights," a WXYZ colleague commented, "but what the hell is wrong with that? That's what Detroit is about. This is a tough town."

Bonds liked to remind viewers that his first job in broadcasting, at a radio station, paid "a buck an hour." Now he was a showman making almost a million dollars a year, but he wore his blue collar as prominently as his hairpieces. He revered hard work, hated greed, despised what drugs were doing to the city he loved. It could be heard in his voice: an anger, a resentment toward the "crooks" and "thugs" who would tear down the city. Here I am, he implied on any given issue; are you with me?

Bill Bonds welcomed viewers to the Monday, July 27, 1987, newscast: "Good evening, everybody. Tonight we're going to show you something we don't think you've ever seen before on television. We're going to give you an inside look at the lifestyle of one of this area's drug families. They are called the Chambers family, and let me tell you, they have made an incredible fortune selling cocaine and crack at the hundreds—that's the hundreds—of dope pads that they control in this area.

"They make enormous amounts of money. As a matter of fact, just today alone, their profits will probably add up to between ten and thirty thousand dollars—just for today.

"Their wealth, however, is surpassed only by their arrogance. An incredible arrogance that led them to make their own home television videotape movies. A team of Detroit and federal drug agents are now very close to busting the family and putting an end to their business once and for all. And for nearly a year, Channel Seven's Chris Hansen has been investigating this family, this gang, and tonight he has the first in a series of exclusive close-up reports which we call 'All in the Family.' "

Hansen, lean and sandy-haired, with a slightly nasal voice, spoke over home footage of the Chamberses: "Imagine four brothers, several of their relatives and friends together forming an extended family, which according to police runs half of the cocaine and crack business in Detroit . . .

"Imagine one Detroit police narcotics crew with federal agents raiding the family's dope pads and investigating the family almost exclusively for nearly a year . . .

"Imagine no longer. It is true. You are about to get closer to a drug gang than you probably want . . ."

Minutes after part one aired, Willie Chambers burst into Billy's house. "Damn, man, you see that shit on TV?"

On his heels was Larry, who stopped by with William (Jack) Jackson, the star of the "Money, money, money" home video filmed in Larry's kitchen on Buffalo Street. Jack had raced over to Larry's house within a couple minutes of the broadcast. Jack was scared to death. "What y'all gonna do?" he asked. "Are we gonna get up together and go somewhere?"

"No," Billy told him, "we ain't going nowhere, we ain't running."

Billy felt he had nothing to worry about. Larry had filmed him driving a van on the highway and scooting around on an all-terrain vehicle at his mother's house, but how incriminating could that be? He knew, though, that Jack had reason to fear. "He left town that night," Billy says, "and I knew we'd never see him no more."

William Jackson was a couple of weeks shy of his twenty-fifth birthday when he vanished. He and Larry had met through a mutual friend a year earlier, in the spring or early summer of 1986.

Larry and the friend were talking on the street when Jack wheeled up on his signature ten-speed bicycle. "He overheard me saying I gave someone five hundred [dollars] for a [crack house] rental," Larry recalls. "He said, 'You don't have to pay that much; I can get 'em for fifty to seventy-five.' So he started working for me and we got tight."

Jack had been floundering for the better part of a year, since quitting a job as a cement-finisher. He was making good money on that job, thirteen or fourteen dollars an hour, but not as good as some of the other employees. "The owner was this Italian guy who was paying whites seventeen and eighteen an hour," Jack says, "and he didn't show me the same respect he showed them."

Jack's mother had raised him alone in a house on the Lower East Side. (He never knew his father, who lived in Jack's birthplace of Brooklyn, New York, until he was eighteen.) He was smart and well spoken, but he started acting out in middle school. His mother took a leather strap to his backside so often that by high school "it didn't hurt no more." He dropped out of eleventh grade.

Jack was "fascinated" by Larry. "He had everything, every kind of fancy car," Jack says. "Meeting him was the turning point in my life."

The true turning point, actually, was the night he stumbled into the starring role in the video. "Biggest mistake I ever made," he allows. "I'd had a few drinks and some marijuana." It was about eight-thirty or nine on a summer night, "hot hot out." Jack and a fellow named "G"—Gary—were riding around, shirtless, when they stopped in on Buffalo Street. "I come in and there's Larry talking to some guys. And he had that video camera strapped on his shoulder. I see that lump sum on the table and start acting the fool."

As high as Jack was that night, he knew that he had incriminated himself. He decided to take the tape. But how? He was stumped. "I tried putting it in my shorts, but it was too obvious," he recalls. Finally he stashed it in the brown bag out of which he had been drinking a "forty"—a forty-ounce bottle of Colt malt liquor. Then he drove out to Belle Isle and threw it off the bridge into the Detroit River. "Figured that was that."

A year later, though, Jack was passing the time of day when he saw himself on a teaser for that evening's newscast. "I had forgotten about it because I thought I threw it in the water," he says, never dreaming that he mistakenly grabbed another of Larry's tapes. "I'm sitting there like, That's me, but *how?* My heart was beating like a cartoon and my mind was blown, that it was."

He says he figured he and the "brothers" would be indicted any day. "And I knew if they tried me with them, I'd be hung." So he ran, spending the next four and a half years on the lam.

On Tuesday night, for part two of the series, a crowd again gathered at Billy's to watch Bill Bonds further acquaint them with his viewers. "Talk about laughing all the way to the bank," Bonds began. "Wait till you see the home videos we're going to show you tonight. Wait till you see the evidence of the arrogance that we're talking about and the ha-ha-ha attitude.

"Good evening, everybody, there is overwhelming evidence tonight, and we have it, that a cocaine empire is operating in Detroit, and it is, for the most part, run by just one family: the Chambers. And according to information gathered in a huge city and federal investigation, this Chambers family and their associates are probably responsible for more than fifty percent of the cocaine and crack sold in our city. A drug dynasty so entrenched, so big, so powerful, it has taken Detroit and federal narcotics agents almost one full year to even come close to shutting down this incredible multimillion-dollar operation. And during that year, Channel Seven reporter Chris Hansen has also been investigating this arrogant and very powerful drug family. A family which went as far as to make home videos of themselves and their operations and their attitude . . ."

Hansen's segment began again with William Jackson's joyful star turn and included the raids of Jerry Gant's house on Martin

Street and of Larry's mega-house, The Boulevard. Then Bill Bonds speculated, probably correctly, about what many viewers must have been thinking. "You're probably wondering, Look, if those people at Channel Seven and the police and the feds have so much evidence on these people, this family, why are they not locked up behind bars?

"Well," Bonds explained, "here's part of the answer. While the people we have identified are facing local drug charges, they have come up with bond and they're out of jail and they continue, we are told, to allegedly operate. That's why a bigger federal case is being put together right now. When that is finally put together, these alleged kingpins could be off the streets for a long, long time."

On Wednesday there followed yet another damning clip of Jack in the kitchen on Buffalo Street. In his lead-in, Bonds offered his own interpretation of the footage. "Nothing like a little home video to let you know what people are really like," Bonds began. "And you're about to see money and power that ninety-nine and nine-tenths percent of us will never have—the money and the power derived from what we are told is the biggest single drug family operating in metropolitan Detroit tonight. . . . And this family is certainly not shy about their business and the way they do it. Let me tell you, they *flaunt* it."

Hansen's piece opened with a shot of loose bills scattered upon a smoked-glass kitchen tabletop, and then cut to Jack, shirtless and smiling. "This is all the evidence they'll need to send our asses to Jackson [site of the state prison of southern Michigan]," he said.

On Thursday the scene shifted to Marianna. Bonds's introduction to Hansen's on-the-road-with-the-cops report again emphasized to the many hard-pressed Detroiters the staggering amount of cash involved.

"And you think you have problems," Bonds said. "How's this for a problem? So much money you don't know what to do with it, and you can't spend it. Imagine making so much money from running Detroit's biggest cocaine crack ring that you can't keep all the money in Detroit or even the state of Michigan. So much money that really what you have to do to take care of the problem is take a lot of cash out of the state. Such is the case this evening of the Chambers family . . . Detroit and federal drug agents have been tracking this family for almost a year and a half now, and the trail led them to a place called Marianna, Arkansas."

"It's a small town," Hansen says, over a shot of the city's name painted on a railroad overpass, "about an hour west of Memphis, Tennessee." The scene shifts to wet, wintry farmland. "Cotton is what they grow down here, but Detroit narcotics officers and federal agents say Detroit drug money is what the Chambers family launders here."

Billy found anticlimactic the final segment, on Friday. It focused on other drug dealers, particularly "White Boy Rick" Wershe, the eighteen-year-old "reputed baby-faced coke kingpin" and his alleged ties to the Chambers family. But if that installment was a letdown, Channel 7 made up for it the following Monday. According to Bonds, the "tremendous reaction" to the series fairly demanded that the station rerun, "without interruption," Larry's home videos.

"Why show you this?" Bonds asked his audience after repeated showings of the tapes. "Well, virtually everybody we know who should know tells us that at the bottom of all this terrible violence in Detroit, where so many kids under seventeen have been shot and killed, is drugs. And it is getting worse, it is not getting better. This past weekend, thirteen kids, seventeen and under, shot in Detroit, one of them killed. Since January, two hundred and fifty-six Detroit kids shot in Detroit. As one adult put it this weekend, a mother: 'Our kids are catching hell, they're getting killed, blown away over drugs.'

"Tonight we showed you some of the people responsible."

The implicit television indictment revealed to Billy what the authorities knew of him and his brothers; he learned the scope of the investigation, how far along it was, its primary targets, that the Detroit cops had been to Marianna, even that the police had Larry's videotapes. What surprised Billy most, he says, was the distorted depiction of himself. "They made something else out of me. They had me and Larry working glove-in-hand running this drug empire. I knew if they was so stupid to think we ran half the dope houses in Detroit there wasn't no use being too worried about it."

Still, Billy knew that *Chambers* had become a household word in the city; he told his crew to lie low. "We virtually stopped selling, period," he says. "Some of the fellas were doing a little on the side, but mostly we was chillin'. They was on us so tight," he says of the police, "we had to change our ways. It wasn't nothing anymore to know the police was down the street watching our house or talking to people we knew or dropping off a subpoena. They was always there. It was so much shit happening to us Ray Charles could see it."

On the heels of the Channel 7 miniseries the federal grand jury intensified its investigation. In August, Larry Bunting and Tom McClain, the DEA lawyer/special agent, reviewed for a newly impaneled grand jury the state of the case. Bunting reminded the jurors of the secrecy requirement of the proceedings. He said that the case posed "a lot of potential danger . . . for the people out on the street. And any of the names that come up here . . . should never pass outside the room for obvious reasons: there is a wrecking crew . . . out to kill people."

Tom McClain said that the Chambers organization included "a few hundred individuals." He said that its leaders were Billy ("a rather good marketing man") and Larry, and that "our latest information is that they are now running very similar parallel organizations.

"Within the last year," McClain added, "since we've been investigating them, our information has been that Larry and BJ have split and run different organizations, and come back and combined either their whole organizations or certain parts of the

process, and split again and come back two or three times throughout the year." McClain said also that three other brothers were
involved—Willie, Otis, and David—and that another, Billy's twin,
Little Joe, had died in "a car wreck with a train" on Easter Sunday
of 1986. Willie, who worked for the U.S. Postal Service, "doesn't
appear to be directly involved in the crack business," McClain told
the grand jury. "We think he's a step back or a step above." Otis
"is involved in doing enforcement action, either beatings or very
possibly killings. . . . And in moving large sums of money in and
around the Detroit area and from the Detroit area to other locations." David is "mostly involved with Larry, oftentimes running
and overseeing the process of changing powdered cocaine hydro-
chloride into the crack." McClain said that the No-Crack Crew
found David Chambers during one house search. "Since that
time," he said, "we haven't seen too much of him on the east side.
We believe he may be running a similar organization or a block of
these organizations, possibly on the west side."

David Chambers, then twenty-seven and two years Billy's
senior, was no longer in the business; he was barely alive. If
McClain's intelligence was stale, he was to be excused: it wasn't
until after Billy returned from the Fourth of July weekend in Marianna that he learned his brother was dying.

"I didn't know he was sick," Billy says. "The day we was
leaving [for Arkansas], I was calling around to see if everybody
ready. And my sister told me David said he feels so bad he don't
believe he can make it. I said, 'He got to be joking with you because he knows we're gonna have a damn good time when we get
down there.' So we had to leave without him. And then we hadn't
been down there but a short while when my sister called talking
about how David looks so bad like he's about to die. So when I got
back to Detroit I went and saw him in the hospital. He's just laying
in the bed.

"I'm in there just so cool, bullshitting with him so much—
I'm really the bullshitter in the family. I'm like, 'Nigger, get up out

of the bed, why you faking?' I'm just saying whacked-out shit like that. And he be laughing every time I come in. My mom pulled me out of the room and let me know to stop playing with him."

"Do you know what's wrong with him?" Hazel Chambers asked softly.

"No, what's wrong with him?"

"He got the AIDS."

Billy says neither he nor any of his brothers were tested for the AIDS virus. "There's no telling how long he had it. It was really sad, seeing him suffer in the bed like that. He couldn't move around, couldn't take care of himself. That was the worst part about it." Billy says David told him, "You the best brother I got," and gave him title to the six houses he owned. Billy's sister, Eliza, was a registered nurse in Texas. She flew to Detroit to care for David during his last couple of months in the hospital. On September 12, 1987, in Marianna, Hazel and Curtis Chambers buried a son for the second time in eighteen months.

Throughout the fall, Larry Bunting led a parade of witnesses before the grand jury. One juror asked him whether the Chambers brothers were "aware" of the investigation. "Unfortunately they are," he answered. "They are aware of it in general terms because of the repeated raids at different locations. . . . But in addition to that, there was the TV-cast on the investigation, not authorized, of course, by myself."

Billy also had firsthand information from his many friends called before the grand jury. "I knew who was going downtown because I was paying most of their cab fares down there," he says. "They told me when the feds came to their houses and left subpoenas. They told me what they was asking 'em and who else they saw down there [at the courthouse], waiting to go inside to testify." But Billy says he never told a witness what to say. "That's one thing common sense tells you you can't do—stop a person from talking."

*　*　*

On a Wednesday morning early in September of 1987, three young women—the eldest was twenty-one—appeared separately before the grand jury. The first was Cynthia Abbott, a seventeen-year-old senior at Denby High School. She was a friend of some of Otis's girlfriends, a beauty, and Billy fell for her the moment he met her. They had dated for about five or six months. "She always said she made BJ look good," recalls Sharena Jasper, Cynthia's best friend of the time. "She loved him," Sharena says, "but she was talking to other boys too." Despite his own many romantic entanglements, Billy could not abide Cynthia's flirtatious ways. As he had with at least two other girlfriends—Niece Coleman and Diana Alexander—Billy resorted to beating Cynthia when she angered him. "I know he hit her so bad she had stitches in her head once," Sharena says. "I saw her in the hospital."

Was it out of fear or loyalty that Cynthia Abbott lied to the grand jury? Asked if she knew Billy Joe Chambers, she said: "I know of him. I don't really know him. But, you know, I know him." She told jurors she hears "from other people, you know, about him all the time." From whom? "Lots of people, you know. Like sometimes, I be at school, I hear his name. Or I'm out on the streets walking, I hear his name a lot of times." She did concede that she was one of fourteen people caught during the raid on Hayes Street (when the police interrupted the Geraldo Rivera live-drug-bust special). But, she said, she had no idea who most of the people in the house were, and that although she recognized Billy and Otis Chambers there, she had no idea how they made a living.

More forthright was the next witness, Celina Hurt. Celina, a twenty-one-year-old, worked as an aide at a nursing home. She said she had met Billy a year or year and a half earlier, late one night ("around four in the morning") at the house on Knodell. "We were just enjoying some music," she recalled, "[having] a nice time." She said that she had seen Billy several times since—at a skating rink, at a party on Philip Street, and at a house on Glenfield. She figured he did "what everybody else was doing—the dope thing." In fact, she confided, it was at the Glenfield house, in the basement, that she worked briefly as a cut-up girl. (Celina, like the others who testified before the grand jury, was granted immunity from prosecution.)

Police had detained Celina the previous February during the raid at the City Airport Motel. She was there that evening to see one of Billy's crew members.

"What for?" the prosecutor inquired.

"What you usually do in a hotel," she said. "No offense."

Cynthia Abbott and Celina Hurt did not testify voluntarily. Theirs were two of the many names police collected during raids. Though the young women had been ruled out as likely targets for indictment, the authorities hoped that the constraint of a federal subpoena might squeeze them tight enough to cough up a few pertinent facts. If the grand jury was disappointed with the results thus far that morning, it would be compensated with the revealing testimony of the day's final witness.

Her name was Janice Davis Roberts, the former cut-up girl who had defected the previous February. (She had since married a man named Charles Roberts, whom she described as a drug dealer.) On this day, some seven months removed from her last contact with Larry and Belinda, the eighteen-year-old described in absorbing detail her life as an assembly line worker in the crack trade. She told about getting into the business through her sister Cindy, whom Larry and Jack Jackson had recruited on the street; about Jack's supervisory methods; how she'd know which house to work at on a particular day ("We would get a call when we got home from school. . . . And the boys would come pick us up and drop us off at home"); about the performance bonuses and the shopping trips; how to prepare for a raid; and how Belinda threatened to harm her baby.

Toward the close of her forty-five-minute appearance, Janice said she could not understand how Belinda would have known about her cooperation with the police. She said she suspected Larry kept a police officer on the payroll. "They got a police working for them who will let them know where the house is getting ready to be busted," Janice said. "[That's why] a lot of times when the houses got busted they didn't find anything."

After Janice Roberts left the grand jury room, some of the jurors expressed their concerns about her allegations of payoffs to the police. A juror asked Larry Bunting, who had conducted the questioning all morning, whether it was "feasible" that the police "may be involved in this, not on the right side." Asked another: "Wouldn't it be a shame if you go through all this, after many years . . . and [the] Chambers[es] . . . are set free?"

"That would be a shame, and it will not happen," Bunting declared.

"But these people are on the same side," a juror persisted.

Bunting explained that there are two mechanisms for uncovering police misconduct: the Internal Affairs Division of the Detroit Police Department and the FBI's public corruption unit. "And I can assure you," Bunting added, "that they are vigilant."

And beyond that, he seemed to be saying, there is an impenetrable wall of rectitude: ourselves.

"I have been in law enforcement for about twelve years now," Bunting elaborated. "Every time somebody gets caught, they always figure they can buy their way out by paying off somebody, and everybody is crooked. And some people sit around and talk about, 'How is it that Billy Joe has been on it this long?' And so they will say, 'Well, he must have paid off the cops, or he must have paid off somebody.' So just because some people say they have bought a lawyer or a judge or a cop doesn't mean that it's in fact the case.

"But this investigation . . . is not going to be derailed . . . unless they buy all of us, and I don't think they are going to do it to you, and I know they are not going to do it to me."

The grand jury met biweekly throughout the fall. Meanwhile, though the raids had slowed—the No-Crack Crew was busy closing in on two of the Chamberses' alleged main suppliers, White

Boy Rick Wershe and Art Derrick—other branches of the task force, notably the IRS, were amassing evidence to bolster their case. Agents combed Detroit banks, auto dealers, jewelry stores for clues to the Chamberses' assets and tax liabilities. Among other findings was information linking Hazel Chambers to a new Jeep purchased for thirteen thousand dollars in cash in Detroit. The Jeep was bought on May 22, 1986, and registered to Hazel. Her sons gave it to her in celebration of Otis's graduation from Lee Senior High.

On December 1, 1987, federal agents took it away. With a search warrant in hand, Tom McClain of the DEA joined a pair of Detroit-based IRS agents, Little Rock–based IRS agents, and an agent of the Bureau of Alcohol, Tobacco, and Firearms at Hazel's newly remodeled home on Highway 121 outside La Grange. Nobody was home when they arrived at ten A.M. An hour later Hazel drove up in the black 1987 Jeep Wrangler. Tom McClain presented her with the warrant and told her he was "seizing the vehicle as proceeds of narcotics sales."

McClain had grown to like the small-town kindnesses of Lee County. It was his second trip there in less than six months, and apparently the locals had not forgotten his face. "We were legendary," he says. "People on the street I didn't know said, 'Hi, Tom.' " (He developed a fondness for Memphis, too, where the agents stayed and ate and drank, and where he found time for romance: he and one of the IRS agents, Cynthia Stock, had their first date on Beale Street, the renowned blues music district; the couple eventually married.)

By December the No-Crack Crew was back on the Chambers case full-time. White Boy Rick Wershe had been jailed in October, caught in a rental car with eleven pounds of cocaine. (The car had been rented by a niece of Mayor Coleman Young's who was Wershe's lover.) In January of 1988, a Detroit Recorder's Court jury would find White Boy Rick guilty of possession with intent to distribute a total of more than seventeen pounds of pure cocaine; he would be sentenced to life in prison without parole.

Art Derrick, too, was all but finished. The flamboyant supplier (it was he who kept a penthouse in Las Vegas and who once exchanged gunfire with Cuban middlemen in the basement of his house) to both White Boy Rick and the Chamberses would be arrested at his palatial home on March 1, 1988. Police confiscated the house, fifty thousand dollars in cash, a hundred thousand dollars worth of jewelry, a new Corvette, a 1985 Cadillac Seville, and his fleet of aircraft. He struck a pre-indictment plea bargain with prosecutors and was sentenced to ten years in federal prison.

Thirty-five minutes after Hazel's Jeep was seized in Arkansas, a Detroit police narcotics crew raided Willie Chambers's residence on Buffalo Street in Detroit. With them, ever faithfully, was Channel 7's Chris Hansen. The warrant stated that Billy and Otis were moving cocaine and money between that house and the nearby house on Gable Street owned by Willie. Although the officers found neither cocaine nor any sign of Willie's younger brothers, they found a small amount of marijuana—one joint and less than a gram of loose weed. The bust of a bust was no impediment to a good news story. While the television camera rolled, Willie was arrested, handcuffed, advised of his constitutional rights, and led to a squad car. "All for show," Willie says. "They got pictures of me in the car and let me go, soon as he finished filming, just like that." As he tells it, it was as if once Chris Hansen got his story for the evening news, he turned to the actors in uniform and yelled "Cut!" The DPD's Preliminary Complaint Record would tend to support Willie's assertion. "The subject was released at the scene pending charges," it stated.

A week before Christmas, Janice Roberts testified again before the grand jury. Although she had long since stopped working for Larry, she was still familiar with various aspects of the organization. She told the jurors she was living with her husband, Charles Roberts, at the Skyview apartments near City Airport. Charles worked as a drop off/pickup man for her sister Cindy's boyfriend, Ronald Rush, who in turn worked for Billy Joe Chambers. Ronald and Cindy spent a good deal of time at the apartment. Cindy kept Janice abreast of activities; Janice in turn passed on the information to the authorities, who by now were paying Janice for her knowledge.

Among the persons the prosecutor asked Janice about was a friend of hers named M. C. Poole. Until recently—until around Thanksgiving, when Larry had reason to believe Poole stole fifty thousand dollars from the headquarters safe—Poole had been a drop-off/pickup man for Larry. Now, though, Poole was lucky to be alive. He had used the windfall to buy himself some early Christmas gifts: a Jeep Cherokee and a few gold rope necklaces. Larry cared for neither the brazen theft nor the showy way Poole spent the money. Larry: "My beeper was steady jumpin' three zeroes"— the code for "smoking" Poole. "Guys were *begging* me: 'Lemme smoke him.'" Momentarily overcome with the spirit of forgiveness, Larry says he decided to let Poole live but that he was informed to consider himself banished forever from the organization.

Then Poole did something truly foolish. After he'd been fired, he continued on his cash pickup rounds at several of Larry's houses. As if nothing had changed, Poole carted off the sellers' proceeds, left them receipts, and was on his way.

Now Poole was showing up Larry. Larry offered the hit to a salesman named Derrick Poole (no relation). Derrick had worked for Larry since the beginning of 1987. He sold eight-dollar rocks out of a second-floor apartment at The Boulevard, and in August he was transferred to a house on Sheridan Street. There he was coupled with a worker who Larry heard was selling plaster chips in place of crack. Larry, Jack Jackson, and a man known as "Cripple Mike" showed up to put a stop to that scheme. The three of them traded blows upon Derrick Poole's co-worker with a wooden two-by-four, a television set, and a lamp. Then, while Derrick watched, they dragged the man from the living room to the kitchen, where they poured hot grease on him. Then Larry returned to the living room, picked up the two-by-four, and belted Derrick across the head.

That encounter had occurred several months earlier, and now, in late November, Larry sought to make amends with Derrick. He came to the house Derrick shared with his aunt to offer Derrick three thousand dollars to kill M. C. Poole. Unknown to Larry, the aunt overheard their conversation from behind a partially closed door. Derrick told him he would have to decline the offer.

Larry found another would-be assassin, but the gunman's aim was imprecise. Poole was shot four times: in the back, stomach, thigh, and in one of his shoulders. After a brief hospital stay, he returned to his house on Lakeview, on the Lower East Side, alive and limping.

On the Sunday after Thanksgiving, Larry told Rod Byrd, his right-hand man, to "finish the job." Byrd summoned a member of the Wrecking Crew he knew wouldn't flinch. "Byrd told me he'd give me a thousand [dollars] to kill M. C. and five hundred to burn his house," says Dennis Fayson. Fayson and Byrd were both raised in the Brewster housing project, a red-brick city unto itself just north of downtown and west of the Chrysler Freeway. Brewster, one of the nation's first experiments in public housing, was dedicated by Eleanor Roosevelt in 1935. For years it thrived as a prideful, cohesive community. By the 1970s, though, as jobs disappeared from Detroit, broken homes replaced intact families as the rule. Brewster was lawless, violent, drug saturated—"Baby Saigon," residents called it. Selling drugs was the principal means of ascent for many of its young residents. In Dennis Fayson's family, for instance, his younger brother and two cousins sold heroin and cocaine years before Dennis went to work for Larry Chambers. Dennis proudly says of his brother, "He put himself through college doing stickups and selling dope."

Dennis, the eldest of four children of a schoolteacher, looked the other way when it came to drugs. He made it as far as the eleventh grade, and then embarked on a radio broadcasting career. He worked as a disc jockey at a community radio station—he has a commanding, sonorous voice—and built enough of a following that he was in demand as a deejay at private parties, cabarets, clubs. It was during those moonlighting jobs, in the middle and late seventies, that he had his first taste of cocaine. "Women were intrigued by my voice," Dennis says. "They used to hear me on the radio and then when they met me they couldn't believe it was me. They'd ask me, 'What you want, baby?' *Everybody* was doing cocaine. I'd work this party and that party and here's a snort here and a snort there and pretty soon all you want all the time is that upward feeling cocaine gives you."

Dennis managed to keep his habit in check. He enrolled in broadcasting school and began working in the office of a downtown entrepreneur who sold real estate and women's apparel. ("It was a prestigious job," he says. "I wore a coat and tie to work.") The businessman encouraged Dennis to study for his real estate license, which he was "fifteen or twenty hours short" of obtaining when his career plans went up in the blue-flamed smoke of a crack pipe.

Dennis had married in 1977, when he was eighteen. When the marriage broke up in 1984, Dennis moved to Austin, Texas, where he had relatives working in construction. The economy there was fairly booming (the state bird was the construction crane, went the joke), and Dennis found no shortage of work. And although he was not smoking as much cocaine—the quality of rock wasn't as good as in Detroit and the price was higher—he fell in with a crowd that manufactured and sold methamphetamine, an injectable form of speed known as "bathtub crank." ("I was shootin' the shit out of the stuff," he says.) For the next three years, he divided his time almost evenly between the two cities, depending on the availability of work, crack, and crank.

In the summer of 1987, with the Texas economy in free fall, Dennis returned to Detroit. A girlfriend of his was a regular customer of Larry's house on Hardee Street. "I started scoring from there too and pretty soon I met Byrd," Dennis explains. They hadn't known each other at Brewster. Byrd thought Dennis was from Austin; he called him "Tex." "But then we figured out we knew people who knew people [from Brewster]," Dennis says.

One day Dennis was at a gas station next door to the Hardee Street house. He was high and the attendant "tried to beat me out of ten dollars; he figured I didn't know the difference. So I stabbed the dude." Byrd heard about Dennis's exploit, told Larry, and they soon offered him a job on the Wrecking Crew. "I was a paid pit bull," Dennis says. He was six feet tall and a hundred and ninety-five pounds, with massive shoulders, a tiny, angular head, and eyes that when he smoked cocaine turned as hard as Larry's—so hard that "my chick used to tell me, 'Baby, you get so evil I look in your eyes and see death.' " His right forearm was adorned with a tattoo: a skull smoking a joint.

Larry normally insisted on a drug-free workforce; his contempt for crackheads (save for his brother Danny) bordered on the pathological. But with Dennis Fayson he felt an affinity for a user he had not before experienced. Upon meeting him, Larry enthused: "My friend, I hear you can wake up, throw six rocks in the pipe, and be ready to beat up the world."

In September of 1987 Larry asked Rod Byrd to put Dennis to the test. A sixteen- or seventeen-year-old kid had tried, for reasons unknown, to burn down one of Larry's houses. Byrd told Dennis and a co-worker named "Black" to "hammer" the youthful offender. Black found the kid, kidnapped him at gunpoint, and brought him to a house at Van Dyke and Kercheval. When Dennis arrived, the kid was bound to a chair with rope and had a hood over his head. Black and Dennis led their victim across an alley to a vacant garage. They grabbed his wrists, held them to the concrete floor, and pummeled his hands with hammers. Then they hammered his feet, his knees. The kid lost consciousness. They hammered his ribs. They left him in the garage. Dennis says he heard later the injuries left the young man paraplegic, never to walk again. Dennis says he felt bad about the beating, but that "I did it because it was part of my job and I wanted to move up in the organization and I wanted a [Ford Mustang] 5.0."

It was just a few weeks after Dennis returned to Detroit that the "All in the Family" series aired. He was impressed that even after Larry's home videos became "the talk of the city," Larry and

Byrd managed to stay in business. "I thought they had a lot of nuts," Dennis says. "Rambo [Dennis's nickname for Larry] was a role model for every kid on the east side. It was exciting to be down with him, just the name carried power; it was like a passport."

When he wasn't needed to wreak havoc on people or property, Dennis worked the door in several of Larry's houses. He excelled in that job, he says, because when he wasn't high he was a "people person." He developed a loyal clientele who found him agreeable to most any form of payment: TVs, guns, food stamps. (Other workers were immovable: cash transactions only.) He did not feel he made all that much money—five hundred dollars a week was his base salary—but he received bonuses for the higher-risk Wrecking Crew assignments. He also was given ten or twenty dollars a day "lunch money." Instead of the cash, he always took his per diem in rocks, "because I had food stamps from customers to buy me potato chips and soda water."

Working the door enabled Dennis to feed his daily five-hundred-dollar habit with minimal out-of-pocket cost. Larry was known for his generously sized nickel rocks. Most were so large, Dennis says, that he could shave a "big nick" nearly in half and the customers "would hardly never complain."

In October, Byrd learned that the owner of a house the organization was leasing had gotten greedy. Byrd had been paying the man a hundred and fifty dollars monthly to use the house for crack sales. Then he heard the homeowner had rented it concurrently to another dealer. "We might as well burn it down," Byrd told Dennis. Dennis "put two rocks in my pipe, hit it, and went to burn the house." He entered through the back door into the kitchen, ignited a blanket from the stove top, and walked around the first floor, setting afire the drapes and living room furniture.

When Larry decided, on that Sunday after Thanksgiving, that the time had come for M. C. Poole to pay with his life for the senseless crack house robberies, Larry and Byrd turned finally to Dennis Fayson, who had long since proved his merit as a hit man and arsonist. "Byrd told me to firebomb M.C.'s house," Dennis recalls. "He wrote down the address on Lakeview, told me to memorize it and swallow the paper." Byrd gave Dennis seven or eight nickel rocks: "enough to get me evil." Dennis hired a friend to drive. They stopped to buy gasoline for the job. He smoked a couple of rocks and finished off a bottle of Wild Irish Rose, his favorite cheap wine. The friend parked around the corner from Poole's house. Dennis smoked a couple more rocks. He poured the gas into two wine bottles. ("I always used Wild Irish Rose, like it was good luck." And he liked the taste. "People ran it down, but we drank it mixed with Kool-Aid and lime juice or lemon in a blender. It was like a Slurpee.") He stashed the bottles and some rags under his coat and made his way to Poole's backyard. He would "mix the cocktails" there, pitch one onto the back porch, and run around to the side yard to heave the other through the living room window. As the porch went up in flames, though, Dennis heard babies crying inside. The job went unfinished. M. C. Poole had again escaped alive.

Larry had been living on the west side since late July, since the "All in the Family" series drew gawkers to his once luxuriously appointed house on Albion Street. (He had refurnished the house more modestly after the October 1986 raid in which police, Larry says, "snatched it all but the kitchen sink—only 'cause we didn't have no gold in the kitchen.") He had also shifted his business headquarters, from the various single-family houses on the east side to an apartment in the Brewster project. He stayed there several months, until some residents he had paid to keep quiet threatened to squawk. In late September or early October of 1987, Larry moved his base of operations into a private apartment complex called the Skyview. The complex consisted of four three-story tan brick buildings at the intersection of Conner and East McNichols, near the edge of City Airport. The Skyview had become a mecca for dealers; word had it that management looked the other way. Larry liked that the massive parking lot provided a measure of anonymity the residential side streets of Detroit could not, and that the buildings required a key to enter, which afforded an extra layer of security. He rented three one-bedroom apartments, Units 106 and 203 in the Conner building and Unit 49 on the McNichols side, across the parking lot. (As was his practice, none of the leases was in Larry's name.)

For two months or so at the Skyview, Larry says he was "rollin' like Nolan—sailin' smooth and movin' more shit than U-Haul." There was no police interference, no hassles from neighbors, and only minor personnel conflicts. In early December, though, the smooth sailing hit a riptide that nearly sank the business.

Diagonally across the hallway from Larry's basement Apartment 106 was Apartment 111: Janice Roberts's home. Larry was aware she and her drug-dealing husband lived there, but he says he had no idea that she was cooperating with the authorities. (Yes, he had heard rumors from his girlfriend, Belinda, much earlier in the year that Janice had snitched, but there were rumors about lots of former employees. And Janice and Belinda seemed to have patched things up.)

But Janice was cooperating. "I'm back friends with Belinda now," Janice told the grand jury. "She has been coming over. I gave them [the No-Crack Crew] her license plate number of her new car." During a meeting with agents on Thursday, November 19, she mentioned that Larry was headquartered in the apartment across the hall from hers; the information netted her a hundred dollars that day. (The DEA paid Janice a total of eight hundred and sixty dollars between November 19 and December 17 of 1987, the day of her final appearance before the grand jury.) Beginning the following Monday and for the rest of November and the first three days of December, the task force maintained a surveillance van in the parking lot of the Skyview.

On Thursday morning, December 3, the surveillance team watched as Larry entered the Skyview with an unknown associate. They had a search warrant for Apartment 106. The warrant recounted that "During the last week, two SOIs [sources of information] . . . state that Larry Chambers aka Marlow is presently using [the] apartment . . . for storing both cocaine and money." As Larry led the man, a customer from out of town, downstairs to Apartment 106, the agents donned their bulletproof vests and prepared to execute the warrant. Inside 106, there was a good deal of paraphernalia, cocaine and cocaine residue in pots and pans on the stovetop, loose rocks, and so forth. The scene made Larry's customer nervous. "My guy didn't feel safe," Larry recalls, "so I took him upstairs." Larry and his customer had just walked into Apartment 203 when the phone rang. It was his lieutenant, Albert (Baldy) Rucker, calling from Apartment 49, across the parking lot. Baldy could see from the window a squadron of police cars pulling up to Larry's building. "He saw the agents coming and called to warn me," Larry says.

The raid team forced open the door to 106: no Larry, but a good haul. They found eight hundred rocks, almost half a kilo of powder, tally sheets, a scale, a couple of beepers, and seven hundred dollars in ones. And they noticed a money order, dated November 16, 1987, for rent on Apartment 49.

Off the raiding team went across the parking lot. Without a search warrant they entered Apartment 49, where a federal agent named George C. Dahl later claimed Baldy Rucker, nineteen, was found with a loaded, sawed-off shotgun "beneath" his feet. (Dahl, of the Bureau of Alcohol, Tobacco, and Firearms, asserted that Rucker was "observed running" from one building to the other and was "pursued" to Apartment 49, which would have negated the need for a warrant. But his statement, written the following June when Rucker was a federal fugitive, wanted, among other charges, for the firearm violation, contradicted a police report written the day of the raid. Officer Mick Biernacki wrote that another officer and "Agent Dahl apprehended subject Rucker *in the hallway.*")

For the couple of weeks following the raid, Larry had trouble sleeping. Now, on the morning of Saturday, December 19, after a long, late night of work, he awoke early, around six. He couldn't fall back to sleep, so he headed over to his latest headquarters, the Sunrise apartments, a red brick three-story building on East Outer Drive. The Sunrise, according to Billy, was another haven for dealers, *weight* dealers, a place "mostly for their girlfriends to stay and sit on their money and their drugs."

Larry had used Apartment 308 there "as a backup unit" for some time—it was a five- to ten-minute drive from the Skyview, depending on traffic—but it wasn't until the recent raid that he abandoned for good the three Skyview apartments. He arrived at Building C of the Sunrise around 6:50, more than an hour early for his regular eight o'clock meeting with his lieutenants. He wandered around the one-bedroom apartment a while, "wondering what to do with myself until eight." There was a portable television in the living room, a few sleeping bags on the floor, a large oval-shaped table, and about ten chairs. ("We cut up the dope and took naps is all we did there.") At seven, as he poured a glass of orange juice, he heard the pounding on the door: "DRUG AGENTS, OPEN UP." Oh Lord, they got me again, he thought. Then he had the presence of mind to grab a dish towel, dust his prints off his gun, and throw it in a kitchen cabinet. He ran to the bathroom and waited to be arrested.

The agents had been on surveillance at the Sunrise all week, working from four A.M. until noon. They noticed, says Mick Biernacki, that Larry and his lieutenants "started changing their habits. They began changing their times for moving money around. If we were on surveillance at five-fifteen in the morning hoping they'd leave by six as usual, we found we'd be sitting around till eight till their cars started to move. And it wasn't the usual route they drove. They'd go through an alley, down a side street. They were cleaning themselves. So that's when we switched over to airborne—helicopters.

"A chopper lets you stay way behind him on the ground," Mick Biernacki continues, "a mile or even two miles if you want to, while your pilot calls off the streets from the air. The choppers we got are very quiet, muffled. And we got some helluva pilots."

The agents had been tipped to the new location and to Larry's eight A.M. staff meetings by a twenty-year-old cousin of Jack Jackson's whom Larry had fired the previous month "for stealing money and not showing up on time." ("What really got him mad," Larry says, "was I took his car back.") When Larry arrived, the six agents on duty gave him a few minutes to get settled inside and then pounced on him.

They handcuffed him in the bathroom and brought him out to the living room. A search of the premises turned up more than five thousand rocks and Larry's blue steel .357 Magnum revolver, loaded. As the agents were beginning their paperwork, they heard a couple of approaching voices in the hallway discussing the night's revenues. While one officer quickly propped up the door against the frame (the battering ram had knocked the door off its hinges), another, DEA special agent Dick Crock, put a gun to Larry's head. "If you warn them I'll kill you," Crock advised, his white, pearl-handled automatic pistol nestled against Larry's temple. Larry kept his mouth shut.

As word of the arrest spread over the course of the weekend, a concern approaching hysteria engulfed the east side. "Seem like the whole neighborhood knew by a day after Larry went down," recalls Dennis Fayson. "The dope fiends were panicking and I was worried who was gonna pay me and whether we were gonna have enough rocks to stay in business tomorrow." On Sunday, their regular payday, none of Byrd's workers was paid. The following day, Monday, December 21, Byrd stopped by the house where Fayson was working. He brought with him five thousand dollars worth of rocks. "He told us he had met with BJ and Larry on Sunday [in the visiting room of the Wayne County Jail] and that Larry's workers could work for him [Byrd] or BJ and that either way we'd get our Christmas bonus. I told him I'd sell these and let him know when I decide."

Well before Larry was arrested, Dennis says he "could see it coming on the wall." To protect himself ("self-preservation is the first law of nature," he says) he had begun stealing dope and money in ever-larger quantities, "trying to build me a little nest egg." He felt this was justified because the organization underpaid him for his treacherous work. "For the shit I done he should have given me more money," Dennis says, adding: "Byrd used people, he used me, and once Rambo"—Larry—"went down, I decided I was gonna kill his [Byrd's] ass, put him in the river, and go on back to Texas."

On Christmas Day, Dennis was standing in the backyard of one of Byrd's houses, about to commence with armed robbery. His timing could not have been worse. "I was fixing to jump one of his workers" when police arrived to raid the house. Dennis was arrested and transported "downtown." The question of whom to work for, Billy or Byrd, was moot. Now, with the feds bandying about words like conspiracy and numbers like twenty-five to life, the former disc jockey had an altogether different decision to make: whether or not to sing.

After sweating out his options in jail, after meeting with a court-appointed "funky-ass lawyer looking like Olive Oyl who didn't give half a fuck" about his case, after deciding "I wasn't gonna do no twenty-five for the little I got paid," Dennis Fayson agreed to cooperate. On December 30 he met with Tom McClain of the DEA. He acknowledged to McClain that his duties included numerous beatings and burnings and that he "worked the door" at a variety of crack houses. He explained that he worked for Rod Byrd, who was a lieutenant for Larry. He said that Byrd initially discouraged him from smoking crack. But once Byrd understood that only when Dennis was high would he "perform violent acts," Byrd encouraged his habit.

Dennis discussed some routine aspects of the operation. He said that the drop-off men delivered five hundred dollars worth of crack at a time. The seller was to hide a hundred dollars worth on his person and the remainder in the house. If during a raid a seller was able to conceal some or all of the rocks, the seller was rewarded with a bonus amounting to half the value of the rocks saved.

Sometime after his meeting with Dennis, Tom McClain appeared in a public detention hearing for another alleged co-conspirator. During the course of his testimony McClain mentioned that Dennis Fayson was cooperating with the government. At the time Dennis was housed in the federal prison in Milan, Michigan, in protective custody. McClain let slip Dennis's name in open court even though it had been established, McClain later acknowledged, that it was "within the [Chambers] organization's power to order and commit the murder of a person in the custody of the United States Marshals Service."

Fayson was hustled to a waiting van and taken to a remote jail in rural Shiawassee County, about twenty-five miles west of Flint. He was placed in solitary confinement. "I had no idea what was going on; why are the feds taking me out in the woods? I thought they were gonna kill me."

The following day he got word of McClain's testimony—word that the "whole world" knew he snitched. "Oh my God," he said, "I'm a dead man."

CHAPTER THIRTEEN

A TALE OF TWO CITIES

After Larry went down, Billy could feel the heat of the investigation bearing down upon him, a heat as relentless and unforgiving and heavy as a late summer afternoon in the shadeless cotton fields of his youth. Billy had two strikes against him: the arrest in the duplex on Gray Street in 1984 and the 1987 arrest on Hamburg Street. One more and the case the government had worked for eighteen months would culminate in a massive indictment. Federal prosecutors were convinced they had enough evidence already to indict the Chambers brothers and dozens of others on conspiracy charges, an offense that carried a maximum sentence of twenty years. But to further charge Billy as well as Larry with supervising a continuing criminal enterprise—an offense that carried a possible life sentence and that required, among other things, proof of at least three criminal acts committed "in furtherance of the criminal enterprise"—they needed once more to catch Billy in the act of possession with intent to distribute.

But Billy didn't know that. He knew nothing about a continuing criminal enterprise or a conspiracy, the charges federal prosecutors were preparing to present to the grand jury. "I still didn't know what the fuck an indictment was," he recalls. What he knew was that the "feds wouldn't rest until they got me. They had ran me so bad in the streets I didn't give a fuck if the end *was* near."

It was the last day of January of 1988. Larry had been in residence in the Wayne County Jail since his arrest. He was being held without bond; he would remain in custody pending trial. At a hearing a month earlier, assistant U.S. attorney Larry Bunting and DEA special agent Dick Crock reviewed for the federal magistrate Larry's criminal record, dating to his first offense in St. Louis in 1968.

"Does he have," Bunting asked Crock, seeking to elicit compelling evidence for the defendant's continued detention, "based upon your information, does he have a total of twenty-three prior felony convictions?"

"That's correct."

"Including assault with intent to kill?"

"Yes, sir."

"Escape from prison?"

"Yes, sir."

"Burglary and grand larceny?"

"Yes, sir."

"A violation of parole?"

"That's correct."

"Okay. Armed robbery?"

"Yes."

A month had passed since Larry's arrest, and then a week, and then another, and Billy was still on the street. On this day, Sunday, January 31, while most of the nation settled in to watch the Super Bowl, Billy, who was no fan of televised sports, decided to treat some friends to an early evening showing of the hit movie *Fatal Attraction*. They were to meet at his friend Poo's house on Beaconsfield.

"I promised the girls I'd take 'em to the show," Billy says.

"When I got over to Beaconsfield, they didn't have no weed rolled up yet. And they had a weed roller there. There were about nine of us: six girls and three guys. And I sat down at the dining room table to roll the weed up and every time I twisted up a joint, they'd grab it off the table. That's why it took me so long. Otherwise we would have been gone already. I'm sittin' there steady twistin' when the police kicked the door down. They said they found me carrying seven ounces of dope in one hand, a thousand-some dollars in the other hand, and a gun up under my arm."

Billy was taken for "processing" to the Fifth Precinct house, where he and Officer Ralph Unger conversed in the interrogation room. According to Unger, Billy told him he did not want to go to jail, and made Unger an offer: "How about if I get you one kilo and that way nobody gets hurt too bad?"

Billy spent the night at the precinct house and was taken downtown for arraignment the following morning. He remained in the county jail while his attorney appealed for a reduction of the two hundred and fifty thousand dollar cash bond. By the end of the week, the lawyer had prevailed upon the magistrate to decrease the bond by ninety thousand dollars. Otis hustled the cash downtown—sixteen thousand dollars (10 percent of a hundred and sixty thousand)—and Billy was sprung, for the time being.

Billy had a new steady girlfriend, Kela Nealis. She was slight and light-skinned and short: about Billy's height. And she was nine years Billy's junior. They met one day when Billy was leaving his girlfriend Diana Alexander's house. He spotted Kela down the block chatting with Tiger Alexander, Diana's brother and his crew member. Billy asked Kela if she needed a ride somewhere.

"Who is *you?*" she replied.

"I'm BJ."

"*You're* BJ? You know my mama then."

"Who is she?" Billy asked.

"You know her," Kela explained, "the lady with the scar over her eye."

Kela became pregnant in May of 1987, the month she turned sixteen. It would be her first child. Billy had already fathered three children with Niece Coleman, his first girlfriend, and three with Diana. Now, in early February of 1988, the baby was due in a few weeks. Kela and Billy were living together on Gitre Street. It had been a difficult pregnancy and Kela was in considerable pain. She needed Billy at home, if only, he says, to "have someone listen to her whine." He didn't mind though, because he was not anxious just then to "test my luck" any further in the streets. "So I was virtually around the house all the time," he says.

On Friday, February 26, 1988, the federal grand jury indicted Billy Joe Chambers, his brothers Larry, Willie, and Otis, and eighteen other persons. The U.S. attorney had planned to hold a press conference announcing the indictment that day, but three of the four Chambers brothers, along with most of the other defendants, were not yet in custody. In order to ensure that none of them fled, prosecutors waited until Tuesday afternoon, after police and federal agents had rounded up the lead defendants, to unseal the indictment.

On Saturday, February 27, a son, Sanchez Joe Chambers, was born to Kela and Billy. Mother and child stayed in the hospital until Monday night. At five minutes before ten on Tuesday morning, the first of March, Billy and Poo pulled up in a gray Ford Tempo to Otis's house on Nottingham Street. Kela had sent Billy out for supplies: Pampers, a crib, a baby carrier. While he was out, he figured he'd pick up a few other items. He was carrying a lot of cash, about thirteen or fourteen hundred dollars. "I didn't want all that on me because we was getting ready to cop some weed and liquor too," he says. He told Poo to stop at Otis's. He would drop off most of the money there, attend to his shopping, and pick up the wad of cash on the way home.

On the way inside, Billy noticed two men lurking in an unmarked car across the street from the house. He figured the house was under surveillance. "I kind of tipped my finger to the guy,"

Billy recalls. "Didn't nobody say anything, but just to let him know I seen him."

Billy and Poo were in the house for about five minutes. They emerged with Otis, and the three drove away, Poo at the wheel, followed by the surveillance team. At the intersection of East Outer Drive and Dickerson—about half a mile from Nottingham Street—Poo was stopped at the traffic light. The unmarked car pulled in front of him. The undercover officers jumped out and announced to Poo and his passengers that they were under arrest. Billy figured it was "more of the same general harassment" to which he had grown accustomed. "They handcuffed us all together: arm to arm to arm," Billy says. "I thought they'd take us down to the Ninth [Precinct], slap us around, slam our beepers down, take my seventy or eighty dollars, and let us go. But then so many police cars showed up it was a shame. That's when I knew something was totally unusual."

Tom McClain hurried over from the Federal Building to the Ninth Precinct at Gratiot and Gunston. He positively identified Otis and Billy and read and explained to Otis his Miranda warning. Otis said he understood his rights and wished to remain silent. Then McClain handed Otis a copy of the warrant for his arrest. Otis said he did not understand the warrant.

"This charge means that the government says it can prove that you, your brother Billy Joe, and a number of other people have been selling crack in Detroit," McClain explained. "We will give you a copy of the indictment when we get you to the Federal Building."

"How many people is on the list?" Otis asked.

"Do you mean how many people are included in the indictment?" McClain replied.

"Yeah."

"Oh, I don't know, Otis, how many do you think we could have included?"

"Oh," Otis said, "about four hundred."

* * *

McClain served Billy with the warrant and informed him of his Miranda rights. Billy too said he preferred to remain silent. And then: "We knew the indictment was coming. We knew you guys wouldn't quit and we have policemen who are our friends who tell us when our name is mentioned around the police stations."

"Why didn't you run?" McClain asked.

"To where?"

"Another state or another country."

"Then I'd be a fugitive. That ain't no way to live," Billy said. "How much time do you figure I'm facing, thirty or forty years?"

"Life, Billy," McClain replied.

"Yeah, okay, that's what I figured."

At 10:55 A.M. police arrested Willie Lee Chambers, the fourth indicted brother. He was on the job in his blue-gray U.S. Postal Service uniform, delivering mail at 12868 St. Louis Street. By 12:15, three others had been rounded up: Elayne Coleman, the young woman whose role in the conspiracy was limited to supposedly having sold fifty dollars worth of crack to an undercover officer four years earlier; Romia Hall, who was arrested at his trailer home in Marianna and charged with recruiting for the organization; and Roderick Byrd, Larry's top lieutenant.

Shortly after one that afternoon, March 1, 1988, the United States attorney for the eastern district of Michigan, Roy C. Hayes, Jr., stood behind a lectern sprouting a forest of microphones. He was on the ninth floor of the Federal Building, a landmark ten-story prewar structure of shining black marble and sandstone that straddles Fort and Lafayette streets for a full block. There amid a backdrop of law books ("our Perry Mason collection") and flags (an American, a Michigan, and a newly minted U.S. attorney design) in the cramped law library of the U.S. attorney's offices, Hayes readied to address a crush of reporters convened for a press conference. There were perhaps twenty chairs in the room, and sixty people, including reporters, camera operators, and, alongside and behind Hayes, representatives of the local, state, and federal law enforcement agencies that comprised the joint No-Crack Task Force. William Coonce, the special agent in charge of the Detroit office of the DEA, was there, along with Detroit chief of police William L. Hart and the heads of the local offices of the Bureau of Alcohol, Tobacco, and Firearms, the IRS, the INS, and the Marshals Service.

Hayes spoke first. In a prepared statement, he announced that the federal grand jury had returned an indictment against twenty-two persons "involved in a major narcotic trafficking operation, centered in the Metropolitan Detroit area, and known as the Chambers Organization." (An early version of the indictment listed forty defendants, says Tom McClain, who drafted the document. "But [the U.S. Department of] Justice said that was too many to try at once, that we'd be in trial for six months.")

The front page of the fifteen-count, twenty-seven-page indictment listed the alleged co-conspirators in apparent starring order, beginning with the four brothers. The indictment charged them and a supporting cast of eighteen with a variety of crimes, including conspiracy to sell cocaine, evasion of taxes, and possession of illegal firearms. The complaint also stated that four of the defendants were "involved in" three unrelated murders, though the indictment charged none of them with murder. And Billy and Larry were also charged with supervising a continuing criminal enterprise. "This is the most significant case I have ever seen come down in this judicial district in terms of the impact on the community," Coonce of the DEA told reporters. "Hopefully, this will be a message to the kids out there that this is what is going to happen to you despite the fact that you can make these kinds of profits."

Police Chief Hart said the indictment would curb the flow of drugs in Detroit. "You're working on the real cause of the problem if you can put these people that supply in jail," he said. Four years later, in the spring of 1992, Hart himself would be convicted of embezzling more than two million dollars in police funds intended for undercover drug operations. He would be sentenced to ten years in federal prison.

Roy Hayes offered the numbers that make reporters salivate. He said that federal and state agents seized sixty-eight vehicles; jewelry worth half a million dollars; two hundred and fifty weapons; and half a million in cash. At its peak the organization purchased ten kilos of cocaine every other day, operated some two hundred crack houses, supplied another five hundred houses, employed five hundred workers, and grossed up to three million dollars a *day,* according to the federal authorities. It seemed that Billy and Larry would have been able to bail out Chrysler themselves. "Somebody making that much, I'd give him five Corvettes trying to be his friend," Billy says, ridiculing the estimate.

The authorities later admitted the figures were based on largely anecdotal evidence. Nevertheless, says Hayes, "They became the dominant crack distribution network in the history of this town." Hayes said the Chambers brothers were so alarming in size, so power drunk and money hungry and vicious that he himself would prosecute the case—the first time in six years a U.S. attorney in Detroit would go to trial personally.

The indictment sparked a firestorm of publicity: "U.S., DETROIT POLICE TEAM SMASHES CRACK DRUG RING" thundered the Gannett paper in Detroit; "CASH LURED ARKANSANS TO CRACK" echoed the Gannett paper in Little Rock. Ten of the twenty-two defendants were Marianna natives; another's father grew up there. By the day after the indictment, reporters from Detroit and Little Rock and nearby Memphis were hurriedly dispatched to Marianna. Not since the tense days of the boycott sixteen years earlier (and a quarter century before that, the Dixiecrat uprising) had the town received such media scrutiny. Like hunters in a game preserve, reporters and camera crews stalked the hallways of Lee Senior High School, hoping to bag any ham of a schoolkid with an opinion on the Chambers gang. "Here they come, in limos, Jeeps, all full of women," one student recalled of the glory days, "stereos blasting music and sounds like you've never heard. You could hear them coming blocks away."

Townspeople felt under siege by "the media." They were outraged by the grossly distorted images of themselves they saw on television and in the newspapers, and appalled that they were powerless to do anything about those images. Most believed that Marianna had been unfairly portrayed as a drug haven; that for the sins of four brothers and a few of their friends outsiders had mercilessly ridiculed and persecuted their town. "Those stories were written to shock white people," says Bill Lewellen, the state senator who was a Marianna alderman at the time. "The fact is that our problems are no different than any other town's. If you take a kid from anywhere else with no income and no means of making a living, he's gonna do the same thing."

Not everyone in town was averse to the publicity. Police chief Mark Birchler made himself available for self-serving quotes seemingly on a round-the-clock basis. (He even hosted a *Detroit News* reporter as his houseguest.) Birchler was the equivalent of a bit player taking credit for a hit show's success, yet the big-city press lapped up his portrayal of small-town-cops-get-their-men as a key factor in the Chambers brothers' demise. "I would see Michigan vehicles, BMWs, brand-new vehicles that were just not typical of Marianna," Birchler told the *Arkansas Democrat*. "I started gathering intelligence." He said he eventually planted two youths undercover who were "instrumental" in bringing down the organization. A story in *Time* concurred. "In February," the magazine reported, "tips from disaffected Marianna youths led to criminal indictments in Detroit . . ."

But as the sometime-rival Lee County Sheriff's Department sees it, Birchler was more concerned with "filling up his scrapbook for the grandbabies someday," as one deputy puts it, than with police work. "Mark's first involvement," says Sheriff Bobby May, Jr., "was when the DEA and Detroit police did a raid on Hazel's house. It was a real cold day and the agents called our office asking for coffee. Our deputies were down there already and I told them to call the city police. And Chief Birchler brought them coffee. *That's* how he got involved."

The *Time* story, part of a cover package on "Kids Who Sell Crack," came on the heels of the indictment. The lead article described the causes and consequences of the trade in various cities, including New York, Los Angeles, Fort Lauderdale, and, at the heart of the piece, Detroit. It quoted Roy Hayes, who commented on how teens had come to dominate all aspects of the business. "They are being used to process, package, cut and distribute, to sell and even to enforce discipline in the ranks," he said, his knowledge gleaned from the Chambers case.

Hayes did not mention the case by name, but the magazine devoted a half-page sidebar to it. Entitled "I'm Going to Detroit," the story boiled down the saga of the Chambers brothers to seven paragraphs (and a color photograph of a pickup basketball game captioned: "Passing time outside a project in Marianna, Ark.").

"The hardscrabble town of Marianna, Ark. (pop. 6,200), near the Mississippi River, has no movie theater but plenty of boarded-up storefronts," the story began. "Summer work for teenagers can mean wrenching labor in the rice and soybean fields. Young black men know that if they want something better, they have to go elsewhere.

"Enter the four Chambers brothers—Larry, Billy Joe, Willie Lee and Otis—who blew into their old hometown driving gleaming BMWs and Camaros, sporting gold chains and fancy clothes. When they offered ambitious young men $2,000 a month to return with them to Detroit, they had no shortage of takers. Over four years, some 150 young men, most between the ages of 17 and 21, made the trip north."

Most of the remaining five paragraphs read like excerpts from a press release distributed by the U.S. attorney's office. "At the height of their empire, the Chambers gang controlled about half of Detroit's crack trade, running 200 drug houses, supplying some 500 more and raking in $3 million a week." (The authorities could never quite decide whether the three million dollar figure represented weekly or daily revenues; consequently it varied from article to article.)

The week the *Time* issue appeared on newsstands, Chief Birchler announced the Chambers brothers had targeted him for death. (He was quoted in the sidebar: "They ran everything on fear and intimidation.") Birchler called reporters to say that two informants told him they heard others threatening him. "I didn't place a lot of confidence in the information," he said at the time. That the tip was unsubstantiated was apparently irrelevant. As one city official put it, Birchler understood that there was "more milk to wring from this titty." The chief told reporters he and his twelve officers would not be intimidated. "I'm not scared, but I'm cautious," he said, modeling for reporters his new bulletproof vest.

On the morning of Wednesday, March 23, Roy Hayes, Larry Bunting, Tom McClain, and two other law enforcers flew to Memphis from Detroit. The group rented two Plymouths and drove west across Interstate 40 into Arkansas, turned south on U.S. 79, and followed the highway through Hughes (the town where Otis was arrested with nearly sixty thousand dollars stuffed in a Hefty bag) and into Marianna. They had come in search of potential witnesses, and, said Hayes, "to get firsthand information on what it's like here, and discuss things with local law enforcement." At ten-thirty A.M., the cars rolled to a stop on the brick pavement of the courthouse square in front of the police station.

Chief Birchler awaited the Detroiters. After pausing for a Memphis newsman to snap a photograph of Birchler and Roy Hayes, they retired to Birchler's inner office for a briefing. Birchler told Hayes that local missing persons reports indicated that at least one hundred youths, and perhaps as many as two hundred, traveled to Detroit to work for the Chambers brothers. He also said that no such reports were filed on many others who worked in the organization.

Meanwhile, the other agents fanned out across Lee County. Several went down to Hazel Chambers's house in La Grange to seize yet another car—a 1986 Dodge Daytona registered to Willie in Detroit. They interviewed a retired Marianna police officer named Bennie Foster who "knew the Chambers family well." He told them the Chamberses were "a farming family and had quiet boys." He said "the family started dealing drugs after the oldest boy came back from prison." (Actually, the oldest son, Curtis Jr., was a decorated and disabled Vietnam veteran with no criminal record.) He added that he "knew they were dealing drugs because they went away to a big city and came back driving fancy cars." More helpfully, Foster steered the agents toward several young men who worked in Detroit crack houses. He cautioned, though, that he doubted they would talk to the authorities for fear of retaliation.

One who did talk was a fellow named Stanford Coleman. Coleman said he had worked as a driver for Anthony Wilkins, Otis's high school classmate who was known as "23." Coleman said 23 was a Chambers recruiter. On three occasions, Coleman said, he drove five persons from Marianna to Detroit. Upon arriving, he and 23 and the recruits would meet with Marshall (Mario) Glenn, the Marianna native with a fondness for all things Cadillac. For each load of recruits they dropped on his doorstep, Mario paid 23 with "a thousand-dollar-sack of cocaine" and paid Coleman two hundred dollars, Coleman said.

In the aftermath of the indictment much was said and written about what the Chambers brothers did; very little about *why*. A notable exception was an opinion column by Deborah Mathis in the statewide *Arkansas Gazette*. "You must have heard about it," Mathis wrote. "Four brothers, natives of Marianna, charged with big-time drug running in Detroit, said to have come back home occasionally, flaunting flashy cars and other evidence of moneyed privilege and taking back with them young homeboys to man operations in their several crack houses."

Mathis compared this latter-day "exodus" of southern blacks to the North with Harriet Tubman's Underground Railroad for escaping slaves. But, she wrote, "where Tubman required courage for passport, the Detroit-bound train required recklessness." Still, she added, "the circumstances that made them so gullible begs our attention." And then:

"In Marianna, equal opportunity is often an empty slogan on the door. The town is in predominantly black Lee County, burdened with an unemployment rate second only to neighboring St. Francis County. Nearly a fourth of all working-aged residents are jobless. A car seat manufacturer, a garment factory and a Coca-Cola plant—all with low turnover—are the only games in town for local employment prospects, save for a few small businesses with limited payrolls. The school district's tax base is pitiably low. The social, cultural, and recreational options are, well, just not there. Deprivation *that* inclusive can be an awesome force to contend with—an armed and dangerous monster, fully able to direct decent people toward desperate actions."

Few other commentators recognized or acknowledged this "monster." One who did was the nationally unknown but ambitious governor of Arkansas, Bill Clinton. In July of 1988, in his infamously long nominating speech for presidential candidate Michael Dukakis at the Democratic National Convention, Clinton used an example from his home state to take a swipe at Nancy Reagan's vacuous public relations campaign against drugs.

"Not long ago, police in Detroit broke up the biggest crack ring in that city," Clinton told the delegates in Atlanta and a nationwide television audience. "It was being run by two brothers from the . . . Delta area of Arkansas. They had brought over one hundred other young men up from their home county to help them peddle dope. The news reports said these country boys were more reliable than the street-smart city kids. They gave a good day's work for a good day's pay.

"The unemployment rate in the county those boys fled is almost twenty percent. For black teenagers, it's more than twice that. Most farmers and businesspeople there are too broke to help get them off the street. Those kids could make more money in a month in Detroit than they could in a year back home.

"I wonder if their decision to deal misery for money would

have been different if President Dukakis had had eight years to make good on his commitment to good schools and good jobs for all our people in all our communities. I think they might have been able to say 'No to drugs' and 'Yes to life.' "

In Marianna, Mark Birchler, to his credit, was one of the few city officials to own up to the town's economic and social short-comings. (He also was one of the few non-natives; he had lived there only since 1983.) "Look," he explained to the *Detroit Free Press*, "we are one of the poorest counties in Arkansas. . . . When you consider just black males between eighteen and twenty-five—many of them dropouts with limited opportunities—the [unemployment] rate is about fifty percent. If they do get a job, it's three-thirty-five an hour. If somebody offers you two thousand a month for not very demanding work, it is *very* tempting."

Most other civic leaders were unable or unwilling to compre-hend this simple equation; most were perversely blind to the role of racism in creating and sustaining black poverty and deprivation. Representative was the comment of Sherry Benson, the executive director of the Marianna–Lee County chamber of commerce: "I guess it's just like blacks in any little town. They think the grass is always greener and they were out to make a fast buck. It's here for them if they want to find it."

Soon after the Chambers brothers went down, some of their recruits, rudderless in Detroit, returned home to Marianna bran-dishing their newly acquired skills. *It's here for them if they want to find it.* Crack had come to town. It arrived in the spring of 1988 as a high-priced novelty; residents paid as much as forty dollars a rock. Sales were confined to a couple of houses in a black neigh-borhood on the north side of town, and to the rundown Sands motel, across Highway 79 from the neighborhood.

In May, the police department began receiving complaints about the young entrepreneurs. Sergeant Bruce Page said people would stop him on the street, wondering, "When are you going to do something about this?"

In a midnight raid of the Sands on the first Sunday of August came the answer. Marianna police officers arrested seven persons, none older than twenty-two. Among those detained were Anthony Wilkins (aka 23), the alleged former recruiter, and his former driver, Stanford Coleman. News of the bust, which netted only fifteen rocks and a negligible amount of marijuana, was deemed worthy of a front-page story in the *Memphis Commercial Appeal*. Except for Chief Birchler, who garnered further accolades for his aggressive police work, mostly from himself—"Small agencies like ours have to take the initiative"—others in town were bitterly defensive about another big-city kidney punch. But the haymaker would come a day later.

On August 10 the paper published an editorial cartoon equating Marianna—depicted as a half-dozen tar-paper shacks—with the twin towers of Sodom and Gomorrah, the biblical symbols of evil and decadence. The angry citizenry struck back with an organized campaign that produced nearly fifty letters, almost half of which the *Commercial Appeal* printed on a full page of appeasement under the headline "MARIANNA: A GOOD TOWN WORKING TO GET BETTER." One reader scolded the cartoonist for his un-Christian "smear job." The Lee County judge declared a boycott: "We will not taint our homes with dirt from the devil's playground." Some correspondents invited the paper to send a reporter down to write about Marianna's strengths, others were less conciliatory. One suggested: "How about cleaning up your own backyard and staying out of ours?"

The Chambers brothers' trial would begin in a month, on September 12, in a federal courtroom in downtown Detroit. While their hometown convulsed over the shock waves of the latest unflattering media attention, and while federal investigators shuttled between Detroit and Marianna in the weeks remaining before the trial, searching for clues and interviewing prospective witnesses, three of the four Chambers brothers and six of their fellow defendants remained, bondless, in "the County"—the Wayne County

Jail. (Seven of the suspected co-conspirators, including Willie Chambers, were free on bail pending trial; four had yet to be arrested and were considered fugitives; one, Dennis Fayson, was in protective custody at the federal prison in Milan, Michigan.)

After more than five months of incarceration, Billy had settled into a routine. The first couple of months were "kinda rough," he recalls. "After that, it isn't so bad, because you start to get over your womens and your kids. And then you're okay." Billy lived in a two-man cell on a floor with a total of twenty inmates—a "twenty-man rock." His days began at six each morning, when the cell door was unlocked. Breakfast was a small "variety-pack size" box of cereal, a little milk, a little juice, and sometimes a doughnut or a bologna sandwich.

At nine A.M. the lone phone on the floor was activated. Much of his day was spent either with the receiver cradled between ear and shoulder or in negotiations with his floormates over phone usage. He was allotted an hour a day at the gym. Some guys rode the stationary bike, or played basketball, or lifted weights. Billy went to hang out. Lunch was at eleven. Usually it was "some kind of garbage you couldn't barely recognize"; sometimes pizza or chicken was served. Two or three times a week the commissary opened in the afternoon. Inmates could spend no more than thirty dollars a visit. The store carried general merchandise: cosmetics, moccasins, snack food. Dinner was at five, after which there were video movies shown in the classroom. Ten P.M. was lockdown.

Billy looked forward to the beginning of every week. At church on Sunday he might see Larry or Otis, depending on which floor his own "rock" had been assigned to attend with that week. And he might see Fats Wilkins there, or Paul Young, or "plenty other guys I knew on the street." Sundays were nice, but, says Billy, "I lived for my Mondays." Monday was visiting day (for inmates whose last name began with A, B, or C). Inmates were permitted up to six visitors during the day, thirty minutes a visit. Kela, with baby Sanchez, never missed a weekly visit, and sometimes she brought along Niece and her three kids. They would all crowd into a small booth, separated from Billy by a window and, near its base, a three-inch by three-inch metal sound grate. "You had to kind of stand hunchlike and yell when they was all jammed in there. It was chaos but it was real fun. They kept me real happy, right up to trial."

Jury selection began on schedule: Monday, September 12, 1988. Local citizens, law-abiding readers of the *Free Press* and the *News,* viewers of the sensational, blaring local TV news, had no doubt imagined the worst, their suburban paranoia spawning images of glowering red-eyed, shaven-headed killers. Then they saw the Chambers brothers on the nightly trial recaps, black guys off the farm in Arkansas, guys so short and sweet and country, so affable looking, that even the men who were prosecuting them nicknamed them the Smurfs, after a gang of endearing TV cartoon characters. If looks alone were any indication, these fellows were the most appealing drug lords around. "Nobody never called *me* no Smurf," Billy said later.

Because of the overheated pre-indictment and pretrial publicity surrounding the case, defense lawyers filed a motion asking the judge to move the trial away from Detroit. As they saw it, it was unlikely that any potential juror could not have heard about the case a little over a year earlier, when the "All in the Family" series aired on Channel 7. Larry's attorney contended that the home videos agents confiscated and released to reporter Chris Hansen for the series (and rebroadcast time and again on local and national TV) constituted a "trial by media . . . directed by the prosecution . . . [which] has resulted in a public conviction of Larry Chambers."

Prosecutors had already announced they would not use the tapes at the trial. The decision was tantamount to acknowledging that official control over the evidence was breached when the tapes were leaked to Hansen. But the defense contended the damage had already been done: it would be difficult to select jurors who had not been prejudiced by the tapes. Said Otis's lawyer, Thomas

Wilhelm: "I believe it's a strategic move on their [the government's] part to deprive the defense of an appealable issue. They tried to convict the Chambers in the minds of the public without a trial. And then they say, 'We're not going to use it [the tapes].' Give me a break. Where is due process?"

U.S. District Judge Richard F. Suhrheinrich (pronounced sir-HINE-rich) said he would wait until after the jury selection process began to rule on the motion. He wanted to see whether a twelve-person panel (and four alternates) could be seated from the pool of two hundred potential jurors. He ordered them to fill out a seven-page questionnaire on their background and knowledge of the case. He was concerned, he said years later, that the news media's "irresponsibility" made it harder for the Chambers brothers to obtain a fair trial. "I was watching television one evening and I think it was on Bill Bonds's newscast that a reporter stated how frightened he was of these people," recalls Judge Suhrheinrich. "Of course the Chamberses are only about five feet one and weigh maybe a hundred and twenty-five pounds soaking wet, so to be fearful of them is an absurdity. Plus, throughout the audience and near them there must have been ten or eleven United States marshals, so it's a little absurd.

"The real concern is that many people *were* frightened to be jurors," Suhrheinrich added. "And if our system of criminal law is to work you need jurors who are not afraid to come to court. And when you've got the media, for the sake of commercial theatrical bullshit, frightening viewers who might be prospective jurors, I think that's irresponsible. I mean, you would have thought this buffoon [the TV reporter] was on the Ho Chi Minh trail or something, instead of in a well-protected United States district court." In fact, early on in the jury selection process, thirty prospects were disqualified after a law clerk overheard one among them proclaim that serving on this jury could invite "a hole in the head."

The field was further winnowed to forty-one potential jurors. Of those, several who expressed racial prejudice were quickly dismissed. Under questioning by the judge, three persons said that they perceived blacks as more likely than whites to use and sell illegal drugs. These same persons also said they were more likely to believe the testimony of a white person than a black person. "I have a gut feeling that most crimes are committed by blacks," one woman said. Another, asked by Roy Hayes if she feared being a juror, said: "Not too much for myself, but I fear for my loved ones," adding, as she gazed over the long row of defendants, "All this seems too big."

Picking the jury was slow going. It would have taken longer still had not the judge sped up matters by limiting each defense lawyer to one dismissal of potential jurors and allowing the prosecution a total of only eight strikes. As it was, it took a week before the jury was seated. It was composed, including the four alternates, of three black men, two black women, seven white men, and four white women. They were referred to only by number; their names were sealed. The judge asked the artists sketching for the local TV stations to shield their features.

Fourteen of the twenty-two persons indicted were on trial. (With the jury seated, the judge formally denied the motion for a change of venue.) Four others had pleaded guilty: Rod Byrd and Dennis Fayson did so formally the previous week, and late on Wednesday, September 21, the night before opening statements, Perry Coleman and Charles Rhoades also pleaded out. They were expected to testify in exchange for lighter sentences. Four alleged co-conspirators were still fugitives: Carl Young, William Jackson, Albert Rucker, and Michael Lee. If caught, they would be tried separately. The remaining defendants were to be tried together by jury, with the exception of Willie Chambers, who, in the hope of distancing himself from his brothers, requested a bench trial. Judge Suhrheinrich would deliver his verdict.

The gathering of lawyers at the start of the trial looked like a trench-coat convention. There were sixteen of them: fourteen on the defense side, to the judge's right, and to his left the two prosecutors: Roy Hayes and his sidekick, Larry Bunting. Nine of the defense attorneys were court-appointed; each of their clients had proved his or her indigence. Of the Chambers brothers, only Willie and Billy hired attorneys. Willie's lawyer, a solo practitioner named Robert Mann, was a trim sixty-year-old ex–football star. As the trial wore on, though, Willie found that his attorney's competitive spirit had ebbed since his heyday with Michigan's victorious 1948 Rose Bowl team. "Mr. Mann couldn't even stay awake," Willie laments. "He just sat there and slept."

Billy's lawyer, Charles Lusby, was a tall, heavyset man with a large bald spot and a gruff, rumbling voice. Billy hired him—for twenty-seven thousand dollars—on the recommendation of a favored lawyer who, to his dismay, was not admitted to practice in federal court. From the start, though, there was something about Lusby Billy didn't trust. "My lawyer, Lusby, doesn't want to put his neck on the line," grumbles Billy. "He's got a family, big bills, getting ready to retire. Doesn't need the kind of publicity he'd get if he got this large-scale drug dealer cut loose."

The Honorable Richard Suhrheinrich was appointed to his lifetime job in 1984. A square-jawed man with a full head of armor-plated hair, he was born in the southern Indiana hamlet of Lincoln City. Hamlet may overstate the case: it's not on the map. "It was just a wide spot in the road, really," Suhrheinrich says, "a tavern, a church, and three houses." His parents moved to Detroit in 1936, just after he was born. A few months later, though, his father lost his factory job and the family returned to Lincoln City. By the late 1930s, his parents had divorced and Suhrheinrich and his mother were again in Detroit, living in a flat on Fairview, south of Jefferson, on the Lower East Side. Half a century later Billy Joe Chambers would establish a crack house on Fairview—across the street from Suhrheinrich's alma mater, Southeastern High School.

Suhrheinrich attended Wayne College (the forerunner to Wayne State University) and Detroit College of Law, where he finished third in his class and was voted class president. He joined an old-line Detroit firm that specialized in defending doctors against malpractice claims. He and a colleague left that firm to launch their own malpractice defense firm. The firm did well; by the early 1980s it was one of the ten largest in Michigan. Suhrheinrich, a staunch Republican, had become a regular contributor to the party. In 1984, nearing fifty years old, he says he "reached the age that I wanted to do something else. And so I got appointed [to the federal bench]."

Security surrounding the trial was tight. Protected witnesses were sequestered on the fourteenth floor of the Days Inn, across Lafayette Street from the Federal Building. Marshals escorted them to meals and ensured they were unseen in public. One evening, two of the witnesses stayed in for dinner. They ordered some sandwiches for delivery from an Arby's next door to the hotel. The deliveryman walked up the stairs instead of taking the elevator. He didn't know there were armed marshals and surveillance cameras everywhere. "The guy got up to the floor we were on and an agent put a gun in his face," recalls one of the witnesses, David Havard. "He thought the guy was a Chambers associate."

Precautions extended to the nine defendants who remained in custody at the Wayne County Jail. Each morning they were taken to court chained together in a van surrounded by police car escorts. They were deposited in an underground garage in the Federal Building and held in the "bull pen" downstairs, where they changed out of their jail garb. Each day Kela brought the marshals a change of clothes for Billy, nothing fancy like a suit, but a crisp, comfortable shirt and slacks. Before they left the bull pen, the defendants were again handcuffed and manacled together at the wrists. They were ushered into the elegant, blue-carpeted eighth-floor courtroom through a private entrance at the front, unshackled, and seated in a row of white plastic chairs against the marble wall. The five other defendants joined them, each sitting behind his or her respective lawyer, an arrangement born more of the necessity for order than allegiance. (Some of those on trial wished to fire their court-appointed attorneys even as the proceedings began.) And there were those ten marshals scattered throughout the courtroom, on both sides of the bar. Outside, marshals held vigil at both ends of the eighth-floor hallway and administered the metal detector through which all spectators were required to pass.

Shortly before nine o'clock on Thursday morning, September 22, 1988, the United States government, in the person of U.S. attorney Roy Hayes, stood in his "sincere blue suit" to introduce the case of *United States of America versus Larry Chambers (et al.)*. Hayes spoke evenly and competently; his manner was authoritative but warm; not low key, but not much higher up the scale. He was a compact man of forty-eight, a native Detroiter who moved away only to attend the University of Notre Dame. He returned home to earn his law degree from the University of Detroit and then spent a decade as a local prosecutor and seven years in private practice before he was appointed United States attorney for the eastern district of Michigan in November 1985. (Though Hayes tried many dozens of felony cases in his prosecutorial career, his résumé, given out five years after the Chambers trial, lists but two: the "Tenth Precinct Police Corruption Trial" in 1975, and the "Chambers Brothers Drug Conspiracy," the "Largest crack cocaine distribution network prosecuted.")

"Charles Dickens wrote a book called *A Tale of Two Cities*," Roy Hayes began. "It was about life in 1775. It begins with two statements: 'It was the best of times, it was the worst of times.' The evidence, the testimony, and what you will hear in this case could develop as well as a tale of two cities: Marianna, Arkansas, and Detroit, Michigan. Marianna . . . is a small rural town about an hour's drive from Memphis. . . . Like all places in our country it has greed, selfishness, courage, and honesty.

". . . Turning to the other city, this town, Detroit, we will prove to you that between 1983 and 1988 there was a migration, if you will, from Marianna, Arkansas; that initially Billy Joe Chambers came from Marianna, Arkansas, and opened up a party store on Kercheval Street in Detroit. We will prove that at that store he hired a young man from Arkansas by the name of Terry Colbert and that young man sold marijuana for him at that store." Hayes dropped Colbert's name to prepare the jury for a witness the government had pinned its hopes on.

Hayes rolled on with the official chronology. "[We will prove that] eventually Billy Joe Chambers opened a crack cocaine house on Gray Street in Detroit, that his brother Larry Chambers came and opened a crack cocaine house on Newport Street in Detroit. That at about that time Billy Joe Chambers and Larry Chambers formed a business and organization to work together and sell and deal in crack cocaine in the city of Detroit.

"We will then prove that they opened other locations, new locations . . . on East Grand Boulevard . . . on Knodell Street, on Kresge Street, on Martin Street, on Hamburg, on Gable, and various other locations. . . . That their business . . . proliferated through the east side of Detroit and on to the west side of Detroit."

Hayes sought to impress the jury that the Chambers brothers were no ordinary drug dealers, that they were a well-organized mass-marketing giant who had at least as much in common with "legitimate" business as with street gangs. "We will prove that their business, if you talk about making money, was a very successful business . . . and that there were three secrets to their success, that they were secrets that might be used in . . . legitimate business as well as a criminal enterprise . . . : recruiting, organization, and discipline."

As if he were conducting a business school seminar, Hayes lectured the jury on a case study of a successful start-up. He said the Chamberses' prosperity came from defying the prevailing wisdom. They recruited teenagers from Marianna, he said, because they "*weren't* streetwise or familiar with Detroit, [and because they] would not complain and would be less likely to try to rip them off."

Vital to their growth, Hayes told the jury, was putting in place a sound management structure. "Once they moved to more than two locations it was necessary for Larry and Billy . . . to develop a system of lieutenants, people who could help manage these houses, people who could be trusted to pick up the money and drop off the dope." Hayes unveiled a visual aid: an organizational chart mounted on an easel. The flowchart diagrammed the government's view of the Chamberses' hierarchy: under Billy and Larry's top nameplates, in white type on black background, Otis and Willie were listed side by side. Then the chart split in two, with six of the defendants grouped under Billy's direction (Jerry Gant, Marshall (Mario) Glenn, Paul Young, Dennis Fayson, Alvin (Frog) Chambers, and Morris (Gateman) Hampton), and five under Larry's (Belinda Lumpkin, Eric (Fats) Wilkins, Elayne Coleman, Charles Rhoades, and Rod Byrd). The alleged suppliers, Kevin (Hollywood) Duplessis and Perry Coleman, were depicted in the middle of the chart, as was the supposed recruiter, Romia Hall of Marianna. (The four fugitives were left off the chart.)

Like owners of any business, it was important to the Chamberses to hold down costs. Their steadily increasing market share necessitated more and more raw materials. As they graduated from dealing in "grams or ounces of cocaine" to "kilograms," their buying volume gave them the leverage to demand a lower purchase price. "In the early part of the conspiracy they paid forty thousand dollars" a kilo, Hayes said. "In the latter part . . . they paid between eighteen and twenty-six thousand dollars" a kilo. Their return on investment was impressive by any standard. The brothers "could sell fifty thousand five-dollar rocks" per kilo, Hayes pointed out. "If you do the math," he apprised the jury, "you will see that it is about a quarter of a million dollars, two hundred and fifty thousand, from one kilogram of cocaine."

The final secret to their success was discipline. To ensure that their employees "would not steal from them and not start their own business," Hayes said that "it was necessary" for Larry and Billy "to come up with rules." Here Hayes invoked the handwritten poster the No-Crack Crew discovered at Larry's house on Knodell. "Failing to follow instructions cost the worker a hundred dollars; stealing money from the group cost the worker three hundred; revealing secrets . . . cost the worker five hundred; bringing strangers to the house cost the worker five hundred."

"Well," Hayes went on, "the rules are empty unless there is a way to enforce those rules. . . . The Chambers brothers had what is called a wrecking crew or beat-up crew. The purpose . . . was to beat up or wreck people who worked for the Chambers or people who competed with the Chambers. . . . You will hear testimony the Wrecking Crew threatened people and beat people. They beat people with baseball bats, with hammers, with the legs of chairs. They either threw them out the window or forced them to jump out the windows and they shot people as well."

In the remainder of his opening statement, Hayes drew a thumbnail sketch of each defendant's role in the alleged conspiracy and catalogued the fifteen counts in the indictment. Then he tied up his remarks. "Let me say that this case, like life itself, is about accepting responsibilities. We intend to prove each one of the defendants accepted a responsibility to make the Chambers organization a success in order to achieve their own success, the money they would make from it."

Because the indictment named Larry Chambers as the primary defendant, his attorney assumed the role of lead counsel. Anthony T. Chambers, no relation to his client, worked for the Federal Defender Office in Detroit. He was one of four black attorneys in the case. Tall and lean, and with prematurely gray hair and glasses, he seemed older than twenty-eight. He was only three years out of law school, but he already held a wealth of courtroom experience, including a drug conspiracy case. He relished the idea of another. When Larry's case "came into the office," he says, "I frankly told the chief I was very interested in taking it on. I thought there would be some very interesting legal issues."

Tony Chambers's brief opening statement signaled the defense team's strategy: discredit the prosecution's witnesses at every turn. "The government," he said, "can meet their burden only by presuming one thing: credible, reliable, and believable testimony, information, and evidence. That is what this case is about. Credibility, believability, and reliability."

Eight of the other defense attorneys offered opening statements, all denouncing government impropriety, most so dry as to be a potential fire hazard. If one were the client of any of these attorneys, one would hope his oratorical skills were no match for his legal talents. There were some exceptions. Bernard Cohen, the lawyer for Morris (Gateman) Hampton, attacked Hayes's *Tale of Two Cities* analogy. He told jurors that by the end of the trial, "You will be reading a different book: *Much Ado About Nothing.*"

The next-to-last remarks were delivered by William Bufalino, Jr., the attorney for alleged supplier Kevin (Hollywood) Duplessis. Bufalino, the son and namesake of Jimmy Hoffa's personal lawyer, added color to the proceedings. In the sixteen years he had been practicing law, Bufalino, a stout, quiet-spoken (outside the court-room) forty-one-year-old, had defended his share of high-profile clients: from Hoffa, the disappeared Teamsters Union president, to assorted mobsters and beheaders, to White Boy Rick Wershe, the great white cocaine supplier.

Bill Bufalino countered the government's accusation that his client, Hollywood, was a weight dealer. He acknowledged that Hollywood had been convicted in Detroit Recorder's Court of possession of fourteen and a half grams of cocaine. (He had been arrested at Billy's Kresge Street house during the November 1986 raid.) But, Bufalino said, that small blemish on his client's record was no evidence that he supplied a major cocaine conspiracy. "If," Bufalino said, "we were to bring everyone in the city of Detroit who possesses cocaine into this case there wouldn't be enough room on Woodward Avenue from Jefferson to the end of Wood-ward . . . to have a courtroom big enough to seat the individual defendants."

After the last of the defense attorneys thanked the jury for listening to his opening statement, Judge Suhrheinrich instructed Roy Hayes to call the first government witness.

CHAPTER FOURTEEN

AS CLOSE AS BROTHERS GET

The government was not obliged to disclose beforehand the identity or order of its witnesses, and when Roy Hayes summoned Patricia Middleton, a short, plump, white woman with dark roots buried under an avalanche of big blond hair, the name and face confounded the defense. "Nobody recognized her, nobody knew who she was when she walked in the courtroom," recalls Timothy Patrick Murphy, one of the defense attorneys. "We thought she might be the keeper of some kind of records. We couldn't figure out why the government would be starting with that type of witness, starting so slowly. But then she starts talking: *bam bam bam!*"

Patricia Middleton was an excellent choice for first witness. She would testify about the lead defendant, Larry, and the location where Larry not only reached the pinnacle of his success but which was the single most spectacular crack house in all of Detroit—the quintessence of an efficient, *pumping* operation: 1350 East Grand Boulevard, the faded apartment building known as The Broadmoor and better known, once Larry commandeered it in early 1986, simply as "The Boulevard." Under one four-story-high roof customers could buy, smoke, drink, and have sex. *Marlow's One-Stop,* Billy joked. Middleton, followed by her boyfriend, David Havard, the building manager, would rivet the jury with her graphic description of Larry's management techniques: accounting and payroll, rules and regulations, quality control, retribution. Especially retribution. *You could look at him wrong and he'd shoot you.* In short, Patricia Middleton's direct testimony would amplify the "three secrets to success" Roy Hayes had let the jury in on: recruiting, organization, discipline.

She made for an odd, compelling witness. She was capable of weaving into the most sensational yarn the fiber of truth. Whether this skill came from years as an accomplished liar, as the defense would argue, or whether she actually was telling the whole truth, everyone understood to be irrelevant. Her convincing, credible manner, her luridly vivid tales from the front, her presentation as a buttoned-up, almost matronly (she was thirty-three now) white woman who consorted with ruthless black dopers—a fish-out-of-water if ever there was one—made for a dramatic presence.

It also made for a surprise. The defense assumed the government would first put Terry Colbert on the stand. It was he who knew nearly all the defendants, at least in passing, and he who could tie together the conspiracy. But Roy Hayes knew Terry Colbert was bound to be a difficult witness: he had lied to investigators about his crack habit since the day almost two years earlier he'd walked into the Fifth Precinct to snitch on Billy. In separate grand jury appearances, he had told conflicting stories about the same events; dates confused him. Certainly the defense would pounce on those weaknesses.

And Terry Colbert had been in trouble with the police even since he turned informant. Most recently, in the middle of an early June night, he was caught breaking into the office of a car wash on Gratiot. To get in, he had climbed on the roof, hammered and kicked open a skylight window, ripped out a wire-mesh screen. Inside, he kicked in the door of the outer office and ransacked the desk. Police found him hiding in the inner office. Asked by the arresting officer why he broke into the car wash, Terry replied: "I'm running from Willie Chambers's gang; I'm testifying as a grand jury witness against Chambers. They're trying to kill me. I was running for my life. The car wash was the only place I could think of to hide."

(Years later, Billy said of the incident: "Nobody never believed he was hiding from us. That's bullshit. He was fiending around and broke into the place." Billy was not the only one who thought Terry's explanation laughable; Terry himself, in an interview, succinctly dismisses his own defense of the time. "I was on that shit [crack] and needed some change.")

The breaking and entering charge was dropped because the owner of the car wash failed to attend the preliminary examination in Detroit Recorder's Court. But it was a close call for Terry Colbert, and a close call for federal prosecutors and investigators; they could ill afford the fresh stain of a felony conviction on one of their intended star witnesses.

The trial would not be held for three months after Terry's arrest—plenty of time for him to commit interim mayhem. No matter how short a leash the government had him on, as long as Terry was running the streets he was a threat to himself and—more important to the government—to its case. But how to protect Terry from himself, let alone the Chamberses, and from further criminal mischief before the trial? The government gave him a choice: Move out of town until you're needed to testify, or go to jail under "protective custody." If you move, Larry Bunting, the assistant U.S. attorney told him, we'll cover your expenses. The choice was not difficult. On June 22, Terry and a girlfriend packed their bags for Fort Lauderdale, Florida.

They were given a hotel room and spending money. And Terry was offered a job at the post office—as a snitch. A federal agent "come to see me about the job," Terry later recalled, "but all the time he want me to be an informant in the post office and buy cocaine from people in the post office, and I told him I'm not going to do that. And after I wasn't going to go along with them, and I was using cocaine in Florida too, and that just really upset him. And that's when he got in touch with them [DEA agents Crock and McClain] and told them he didn't need me no more, and they brung me back to Detroit."

Terry was in Florida for about six weeks. While there, he later testified under oath, he used crack for the first and only time.

The stakes were too high to gamble on Terry as the lead witness. He could be high on the stand, or change his mind about cooperating, or tangle himself up in lies—it wouldn't be the first time. Roy Hayes was a seasoned prosecutor; he knew the first witness would set the tempo for the trial. "Things either run uphill or downhill from there," he says. He felt Terry was too great a risk, that Pat Middleton was steadier, surer. "She's smart, quick on the uptake, with an excellent memory," Hayes says. "Plus, we thought she could take the heat. The defense was really shocked. They thought Terry would be our horse, that he would carry the mail," Hayes says. "Initially we thought he would be, but we decided to surprise them."

The move surprised Pat Middleton as well. She learned of the decision only the day before she was to testify. "I cried all night long," she recalls. "I was scared shitless. And when I got up on that stand in the courtroom the first thing I see is their [the Chamberses'] friends moving their index fingers across their throats, telling me I'm dead meat."

Roy Hayes began his questioning by having her acknowledge her criminal past; it was a tactic he hoped would cushion the later blows the defense would surely administer. Pat Middleton had a substantial record, including three felony convictions, of writing hot checks, forged checks, counterfeiting, and shoplifting, dating back to 1977, when she lived in Paw Paw, in southwestern Michigan. ("Let's face it," she said in an interview, "I'm not Snow White.") Hayes dispensed with that line of questioning quickly—

Middleton admitted only a small portion of her record—and went on to her experiences as a resident of 1350 East Grand Boulevard. (She was immunized from prosecution, as were the other civilian witnesses the government called.)

By asking her very short, unadorned questions—"What did he say?" "What did you see?" "What did you do?"—Hayes drew from Pat Middleton a powerful firsthand account of life as an unwilling, frightened employee of Larry Chambers's. She went to work as a money courier for him, she said, only after Larry threatened to harm her boyfriend. "He told me he would arrange for David to have an accident." She told the jury that after "seeing a lot of violence in the building—"I saw a gentleman carrying a body"—she had no reason to believe Larry was bluffing.

Hayes extracted from Middleton other choice examples of discipline meted out to miscreants in the building by Larry or his "Wrecking Crew": Larry beat one boy with a chair leg; he shoved another out a third-floor window; Eric (Fats) Wilkins took batting practice on another's head.

Hayes felt good about Middleton's testimony. With a witness who was tentative or who he felt lacked credibility, Hayes would ask a question and then position himself directly in front of the jury box to deflect attention from the floundering witness. (Like any good trial lawyer, he had learned over the course of his career to concentrate not only on what the witness was saying but on the jury's reaction to the testimony.) With Middleton on the stand, he found himself stepping back toward the rear of the jury box, out of the line of sight. "I wanted her to have their complete attention," he says.

The jury could not have been more attentive as Middleton recounted the morning in January of 1987 that she found Larry and Rod Byrd at her door. By then she had been talking regularly to Mick Biernacki and other members of the No-Crack Crew for nearly six months, since calling the 1-800-NO-CRACK hotline the previous August. Hayes asked his witness "what happened" when she opened the door. Middleton replied that Larry "pulled a gun and put it to my head and said if I talked to Biernacki again he would blow my—

Q: *What? Say it.*
A: Blow my fucking brains out.
Q: *What did you do?*
A: Peed in my pants.
Q: *Were you afraid?*
A: Still am.

The lawyer for Fats Wilkins, Tim Murphy, was the first to cross-examine Pat Middleton. He too had studied the jury intently as they listened to the witness's startling story. "From her first moment of testimony their eyes never got smaller than this," Murphy recalls, stretching both hands to maximum width. "It was pretty tawdry shit." As expected, he and the other defense lawyers attacked her character early and often. Murphy, at forty-two, was a balding walrus in gray pinstripes; a mustached Irish-American with slicked-back salt-and-pepper hair. He wore his heritage on his business card: his name was bracketed with green shamrocks. He was born and raised on the east side, near City Airport, and went to college and law school locally, at Wayne State. Larry Bunting was a law school classmate and good friend: Murphy attended both his weddings.

Murphy's was a demonstrative courtroom manner. A look of bemusement seemed etched on his well-fed face; it disappeared only when he was in the throes of protest. "I don't want to belabor the issue, Judge," he might begin, *"but..."* Then he would accent the point by waving his flippers exuberantly, as might a trained marine mammal anticipating a snack. Murphy sought to poke holes in a story regarding his client Middleton told on direct examination. She said that during the first week of December of 1986, Larry had ordered her and Fats to drive nearly the length of the country, to central Florida, to pick up a shipment of cocaine. She and Fats made it to their destination, the small town of Haines City, in two and a half days. She said they stopped only for gas, at rest areas, and at McDonald's, and overnight only once, in a Holiday Inn somewhere she could not recall. Once in Haines City, while Middleton waited at the wheel of their new Cadillac for a half hour, she said Fats entered a small house and emerged with two brown suitcases, each filled with twelve kilos. Middleton said she was paid two thousand dollars for the trip, plus two thousand for expenses.

On cross, Murphy asked which route she drove to Florida. "Do you recall taking I-75 south?" he asked. (That is the interstate that runs from Detroit directly through central Florida; it is, of course, the only practical route.)

"I think we got on [I-]94 to begin with and then we went toward Chicago, that's all I could tell you."

"You drove towards Chicago to get to Florida?" Murphy asked dryly.

"That is the way we went."

Court was recessed for the day at one o'clock, midway through Murphy's cross-examination. He and the other defense attorneys repaired to the Downtown Bar, a half-block south of the courthouse, to "lick our wounds." It was a place they would return to almost daily throughout the trial.

Tim Murphy led off Friday's session with rapid fire inquiries about Pat Middleton's checkered past—her criminal record, her various aliases, her failure to pay taxes on her eight-hundred-dollar weekly income from her work with Larry, her false statement on a state General Assistance fund application that she had no other source of income. (She received monthly welfare payments of some two hundred dollars plus seventy-two dollars worth of food stamps.)

Next to cross-examine was Tony Chambers. He too led Middleton through a series of questions concerning her felonious background. She admitted to him that while working for

Larry she illegally carried unregistered firearms—a .32-caliber and a .38-caliber pistol—and that she once spent thirty days in jail for writing a hot check while on probation. (She also served ninety days for a similar offense, she had conceded under questioning by Tim Murphy.)

Tony Chambers delved into Pat Middleton's psychiatric history. Chambers hoped that raising concerns about her mental health problems would further undermine the testimony, but the exchange may only have won her sympathy from the jury. "Have you ever been ordered to have mental health treatment?" he asked her.

"Years ago," she replied. "I'm talking about years ago." She said that in the 1970s she fled from an abusive husband. "I was married and when I got divorced I gave custody [of her three children] to my husband and at that time I did try to commit suicide and I checked myself into a mental health clinic."

Next up was Rudolph Wartella, the lawyer for Larry's girlfriend, Belinda Lumpkin. Rudy Wartella was not held in high esteem among most of his defense brethren; both his intellect and social skills were considered deficient. Wartella asked so many questions that were potentially damaging to the others' clients— questions such as, "Well, you weren't afraid of *my* client, were you?"—that the other attorneys honored him with a plaque they called the Golden Screw award. It was a railroad spike painted with gold leaf and mounted on a small piece of wood. At first, it wasn't intended that Wartella keep it; it would be presented daily to the lawyer who asked the most disastrous question. But Wartella won so consistently that he retired it.

Wartella pressed Patricia Middleton about the details of meetings she held with federal agents prior to the trial. Prosecutors were to have released to the defense copies of the statements Middleton gave at those meetings; they had not yet done so. When word of this violation of his order reached Judge Suhrheinrich during a bench conference (out of the hearing of the jury), the judge exploded.

"You tell those agents they can blow this case right out of the water if they don't obey my orders," he warned prosecutors Hayes and Bunting. "If you want to lose this case and have me flush it down the toilet I will do it very quickly if the agents play any more games by keeping out the statements. I'm not going to permit it."

"We will turn them over," Hayes replied.

"You impress upon them I won't have that," Suhrheinrich continued. "This is not a game and if they aren't bright enough to understand that, when this case gets dismissed and you people look crazy, then they may wake up."

The last to cross-examine Pat Middleton was David Goldstein, the pugnacious attorney who represented Marshall (Mario) Glenn.

"Do you care about the difference between the truth and a lie?"

"Yes, sir, I do," Middleton answered.

"You do?"

"I answered yes."

"Didn't you spend the last nine years of your life playing fast and loose with the truth?"

"No, sir."

"You weren't playing fast and loose with the truth on the eighth of October, 1979, when you wrote a check and had no account?"

There followed several minutes of objections, questions, and answers on variations of this theme. Goldstein asked the witness, for instance, if she did not find it "convenient to lie" about her income when she applied to the state for welfare?

Her reply was well taken. "Can you see me going in there telling them I got eight hundred dollars a week for crack?"

Pat Middleton stepped down on Friday afternoon, September 23. The trial was adjourned until the following Wednesday, when the government called its second witness, David Havard. His testimony about The Boulevard mirrored his girlfriend's. He described the first raid on the building—the only one in which he was caught. Although he and many others were detained, the police found no cocaine or cash. The raid drills Larry had put his crew through paid off: "Some of the guys threw the dope and money into the elevator shaft," Havard said. But that did not stop the No-Crack Crew from humiliating Havard and the others. As they were paraded outside past the hordes of customers—*it looked like a schoolhouse there were so many people in there*—they were made to loudly chant, over and over, "There's no hope in dope, there's no hope in dope, there's no hope in dope . . ."

Under cross-examination, he was asked about any arrangements he had made with the government prior to testifying. He said he had agreed to appear on the condition of a grant of immunity and the provision that the government pay to relocate him after the trial. Then he was asked about his future with Pat Middleton.

"At the moment," he said, "we don't have none."

The next witness was Richard Crock, the DEA special agent who had taken over the Chambers investigation from Tom McClain. Guided by questions from Larry Bunting, Crock introduced into evidence the spoils of eighteen months of raids: a warehouse full of guns, assorted paraphernalia, briefcases, beepers, all matter of lucre.

On cross, Crock was grilled about the timing and amount of payments to four informants. Was it a "coincidence," Tim Murphy asked him, that an informant was paid "on the same day he appeared before the grand jury?" Or was the money conditional on the value of the testimony? Murphy to Crock: "Isn't it a fact that you wouldn't authorize the payment unless he testified in the manner you anticipated . . . ?" Crock naturally denied the assertion: "No, sir."

But Crock acknowledged that three of the four paid informants had appeared before the grand jury at least once, and all three were paid on the day or days of their testimony. (He could not recall whether they were paid before or after their appearances, but Terry Colbert later confirmed that he, for one, was paid afterward.) By far the most DEA money went to Terry Colbert. He was paid—over eighteen months and forty-seven installments—a total of $12,699. (In addition to Colbert, Crock said the DEA paid Morris Killingham, the would-be infiltrator, $1,460; Dennis Fayson, whom the DEA forced into hiding when agent McClain revealed in open court he had snitched, $1,100; and Janice Davis Roberts, the former "rockette," $860.)

Janice Roberts followed Dick Crock on the witness stand. She took the jury on a guided tour of Larry's boiler-room operations. They peered into the basement of Larry's house on Buffalo Street, where Janice and her sister and several friends spent their after-school hours cutting five- and ten-dollar rocks under the watchful eye of William (Jack) Jackson. Jack was the fugitive co-conspirator who vanished after his scene-stealing cameo—*Money, money, money! We rich, goddammit!*—aired on Channel 7. The jury eavesdropped on conversations between Larry and Jack and the cut-up girls; they glimpsed the money-counting procedures; they tagged along with Janice on her shopping expeditions to the mall; and they overheard Belinda Lumpkin's threat after Janice quit the organization: *You don't know who you're messing with and you better watch yourself.*

Terry Colbert took the stand at around eight-thirty on the morning of Thursday, October 6. He had been staying at the Days Inn under "house arrest." Not, he later said, because government agents feared for his life, but because "they was afraid I was going to run." He said that his ready availability afforded the prosecution team—Hayes and Bunting, along with Agent Crock and Officer Biernacki—ample opportunity to prepare him for trial. They reviewed with him his grand jury appearances in May and December of 1987. They had him read the transcripts, Terry later said, "making sure that everything was in the same time frame, [drew] a picture of the courtroom, showing me where the defendants were sitting at, you know, things like that."

Many of the defendants had gone unmentioned since the day two weeks earlier the government and their attorneys had delivered opening statements. Willie Chambers, Otis Chambers, Jerry Gant, Marshall Glenn, Romia Hall, Kevin (Hollywood) Duplessis, Elayne Coleman, Alvin Chambers—none had yet to be linked to a conspiracy. Most of the testimony had concerned Larry; even scarce were references to Billy.

That would change over the course of Terry Colbert's testimony. During the sweep of a few hours of direct examination, Terry would implicate everyone who had remained unscathed. Roy Hayes had sat in the wings while his assistant, Larry Bunting, questioned the previous few witnesses. But Hayes was back again on center stage for Colbert, as if to flag the jury: Pay attention to this one, folks.

The prosecutor had Terry begin at the beginning: with his earliest days in Detroit in 1983 as a marijuana salesman for Billy at BJ's Party Store. After a few months, Terry said, Billy asked him to start selling crack from the house Willie Chambers owned at 1261 Newport. (Willie was renting it to Billy and his twin, Little Joe.)

The Newport house, as Terry would have it, was to the Chambers brothers what their original drive-in restaurant in California was to the McDonald brothers: a prototypical assembly line. Soon, Billy and company would mass-produce cocaine as McDonald's had mass-produced hamburgers, as Henry Ford had cars, as William Levitt had houses. It was at Newport, Terry said, that the conspirators first cooked up their recipe, first sold it, first hauled in such sums of cash that to hide it Willie drove large shipments down to Marianna. Willie did so, Terry testified, on the Fourth of July of 1983. Terry said he, Billy, Willie, and Jerry Gant counted out a hundred and fifty thousand dollars, put the money in two leather bags, and loaded them in the trunk of Willie's 1979 Seville.

But the story, like many of Terry's others, was implausible. For one thing, the details changed with every telling—from a briefing he gave federal agents in May of 1987 to his first grand jury testimony that month to this latest revision at the trial. Perhaps some alterations could be chalked up to lapses of memory—in one version the money was stuffed in paper bags rather than leather bags; in another the money was counted at and Willie left for Arkansas from a house on Charlemagne Street near Conner, not from 1261 Newport. But no memory lapse could account for a flaw fatal to all versions: that Willie could not have driven the nine hundred miles to Marianna on July 4—a fifteen-hour nonstop trip—and returned in time to work his mail route the following morning at 7:35. (Presented with Postal Service records, the government stipulated to the fact that Willie worked his regular shift on July 5, 1983.)

Terry spared nobody. Although he referred to Jerry Gant as his "uncle" (Jerry was raised as a foster son by Terry's grandmother in Lee County), Jerry's quasi-relative status did not exempt him from Terry's damaging testimony. He said Jerry was Billy's top associate, "like BJ's right-hand man." He told how he picked up money for the organization, brought it back to Newport, and gave it to Jerry.

Terry dropped other names. He said Otis, who turned sixteen in the summer of 1983, also worked as a drop-off/pickup man and that "he used to just be around." And he mentioned that he knew Marshall Glenn to be a drop-off/pickup man who worked for Billy.

There came a time, Terry said, when Billy moved his operations from Newport to a duplex on Gray Street. There, in the upstairs portion of the two-family flat, he saw Elayne Coleman, one of the two female defendants, sell crack. When was this? Roy Hayes asked his witness.

A: In August.
Q: *Of what year?*
A: Eighty-two.
Q: *August of what?*
A: This is August of eighty-four.

Terry's testimony about when he saw Elayne Coleman selling crack on Gray Street was no more credible than his tale about Willie's transcontinental driving heroics. Obviously he could not have seen her during 1982—neither Terry nor crack had yet to arrive in Detroit. Nor was it likely that Terry saw Elayne working on Gray Street in August of 1984. For as Terry told the jury, he was by then no longer employed by Billy; he had been laid off. "Approximately when was that?" Hayes inquired. "Around July," Terry answered. He added that he did not work again for Billy until the "early part" of 1985.

(Wanda Booker, the young woman who *did* sell crack for Billy from that flat during the summer of 1984, said in an interview that she knew Terry Colbert but never saw him on Gray Street. She also said she did not know Elayne Coleman, but that she knew one of her sisters, who back then was a regular user of crack. "If she was around there," Wanda Booker said of Elayne, "I would have known her.")

Elayne was a minor player, but the government used Terry's dubious testimony to corroborate police reports that she was a vested conspirator. She allegedly sold fifty dollars worth of crack to an undercover police officer from the upstairs flat of Gray Street on Labor Day of 1984. When the officer returned with his raiding crew ten or fifteen minutes later, Elayne supposedly led them on the wild chase that ended in the lower flat—where the officers found Billy and a house full of people with cocaine and money. As recounted earlier, the police did not have a search warrant for the downstairs flat. But because they say they chased Elayne into the apartment, there was no need for one.

Elayne was indicted for one reason: the government needed her to get Billy. Without her, the authorities had no case against Billy on Gray Street—it would have been an illegal entry and search of the downstairs apartment. And without that case, the government could not have charged Billy with supervising a continuing criminal enterprise. The government needed a minimum of three instances of narcotics activity for a CCE charge; Gray Street was one of the three. Without Gray Street—and therefore without the story that Elayne led the police to Billy in the downstairs apartment—the government had no conspiracy charge against Elayne, and no CCE case against Billy.

Roy Hayes went on to elicit from Terry reminiscences of the organization's violent tendencies. Terry told of the day Otis ordered him shot at his uncle's house on the west side. "I was standing in the corner and Otis and my uncle was arguing and Otis looked at me and said, 'You know, I don't like you no way.'" Terry said he also was assaulted once by Michael Curtis Lee, a co-conspirator who remained at large.

He pointed out incident after incident of violence against others: Fats belted a guy in the face with a baseball bat at a house on Chelsea Street; Larry directed four guys to do likewise to a guy on Montclair Street. Finally one defense lawyer could stand it no longer. At a bench conference out of the jury's hearing, William Swor, the attorney for Alvin Chambers, complained that Terry's testimony was becoming redundant and legally prejudicial (that is, outside the realm of the alleged conspiracy). "We already know and I am sure the jury is well aware this is a violent organization. There has been sufficient testimony it is violent and to keep adding violent incidents . . . it becomes cumulative."

"I can't help that," Judge Suhrheinrich replied. "This is the organization the people ran. I am sorry, it's not the boys school.

"Just to show you," the judge added, establishing his hard-knocks bona fides, "I lived in the projects, I wasn't born with a silver spoon, I lived in the projects."

Not to be outdone, lawyer Swor: "This house on Canton"—a street Terry mentioned in regard to a crack house Billy operated—"was only a block from where I was born."

"I can understand then," said the judge, appropriating the final word, "why the neighborhood went down."

The defense came out swinging. Lawyers for Fats, Otis, Elayne, Paul Young, Billy; one after the other, like tag-team wrestlers they bounded into the ring, each trying to bloody Terry Colbert's credibility. They clobbered him with repeated questions about his own family's drug-dealing history, attacked him as a liar who was testifying to protect himself and his father, Big Terry, from prosecution.

Tim Murphy, Fats's attorney, led the assault. "Your father is a dope dealer, isn't he?"

"Yes, sir," Terry replied.

"He sells cocaine in large amounts, is that correct?"

"Yes, sir."

"Has been doing that for how long?"

"A long time."

In answer to questions from Billy's attorney, Charles Lusby, Terry said that he moved to Detroit in 1983, when he was seventeen. "You came here to work selling dope for your father, is that right?" Lusby followed.

"Yes," Terry answered, adding that two of his three brothers also sold crack for their father. Then Lusby tried to position his client as an innocent uncorrupted until falling in with Big Terry. "In 1983, Billy Joe Chambers had just gotten here, practically?" Lusby asked.

"Yes."

"He didn't know what was happening in this city, did he?" Lusby withdrew the question following an objection by Roy Hayes.

"Your father, according to you, made Mr. Billy Joe Chambers aware of the drug traffic, isn't that true?"

"Yes, sir."

"So Billy Joe Chambers wasn't going down to Arkansas bringing anybody back. The Colbert family was bringing them back?" Lusby said, more an accusation than an inquiry. Terry denied the charge.

Lusby later challenged Terry's assertion during his direct examination that Billy once discussed with him the size of his operations. Terry had recalled for Roy Hayes that as early as the "summer of 1984" Billy told him that "he had about a hundred and fifty crack houses and about a hundred and seventy-five workers."

If this were so, Lusby wondered, if Billy had all those employees at his disposal, why, as Terry also told Roy Hayes, would Billy himself have performed some of the more mundane tasks of the drug business? "Did you ever consider that?" Lusby asked.

> A: Say what?
>
> Q: *You testified . . . Billy Joe Chambers would drop off and pick up with you, is that right?*
>
> A: Yes.
>
> Q: *You also testified he would do some rocking up himself, is that right?*
>
> A: Yes.
>
> Q: *Didn't it appear a bit strange to you with between a hundred and seventy-five and two hundred and seventy-five [a figure Terry had earlier provided the grand jury] workers that he would do this work himself?*
>
> A: No.

So it went for nearly a full day of cross-examination. The defense took its best shots, surely scoring some points, while Terry Colbert sat there stoically, a veritable punching bag of a witness who could absorb any blows, parry any and all inconsistencies and contradictions in his voluminous sworn testimony, no matter how obvious or brazenly fraudulent.

On the afternoon of Tuesday, October 11, following the long Columbus Day weekend and the morning testimony of four police officers who participated in the 1984 raid on Gray Street, the government called Morris Killingham to the stand. Killingham was the man Detroit police had hired to infiltrate Billy's crew in Marianna over the Fourth of July weekend of 1987. It was expected that his testimony would tie Marshall Glenn and Romia Hall to the conspiracy as recruiters.

Roy Hayes led Killingham through the biographical perfunc-
tories: that he was thirty-six, attended school through the eleventh
grade, was convicted of attempted armed robbery in 1971 and
breaking and entering in 1979 or 1980. Those were about the only
questions Killingham fielded successfully. Hayes asked him to
identify Marshall Glenn, whom he contended he spoke to about a
job while in Marianna. "I'm not sure," Killingham said, scanning
the row of defendants, "but I think it's the fourth from the end,
I'm not a hundred percent sure."

"You got to be sure," Hayes reproved. "The gentleman that
stood up there? Are you sure or not? Don't testify unless you are
sure."

"I'm not sure."

After Killingham also failed to pick out Billy—he confused
him with Otis—Hayes liberated his witness from further embar-
rassment to him and the government. "I have no further questions, Your Honor."

Court was recessed for the day. By the next morning, the
government had reevaluated its case. It had yet to present evidence
against at least two of the defendants, Alvin Chambers and Romia
Hall. Neither, it was by then clear, should have been indicted.
Alvin was the brothers' thirty-two-year-old cousin from Flint. His
only crime was finding himself in the lower flat on Gray Street the
day the house was raided four years earlier.

Alvin's case was dismissed in state court in 1985. And there
had been no testimony tying him to the federal conspiracy charges.
For twelve years, until he was arrested in April of 1988, he had
worked at a GM plant in Flint. By the time federal authorities released him on a fifty-thousand-dollar unsecured bond, he had been
fired. He was forced to go on General Assistance to support his
wife and four children. "I've done lost everything," he said at the
time.

Romia Hall was the Marianna man who had grown up with
Billy and Jerry Gant (he and Jerry were half-brothers). Romia and
his Detroit friends had remained close over the years. He had no

criminal record, had worked steadily as an emergency medical technician, but when the government needed a link to the Chamberses' hometown, needed to document the pipeline from Marianna to Detroit, it designated Romia as the organization's recruiter. Morris Killingham was to finger him. But because Killingham's unreliability had become apparent, Roy Hayes decided not to bother: as with Alvin Chambers, dismissing Romia Hall would not make or break the government's case.

The morning after Killingham's aborted testimony, Hayes moved to "dismiss all charges" against the pair.

"I take it," Judge Suhrheinrich polled both defendants' attorneys, "you have no objection to that motion?"

Neither did.

"That motion is granted."

There followed police testimony about incidents in which Billy, Larry, and Fats were arrested separately. And then the jury was to hear from a nineteen-year-old woman named Felicia Gilchrist. Felicia was to testify about Paul Young's role in the conspiracy, and about a murder of a young man that occurred at her house in May of 1987. Paul Young was one of three men convicted of the murder. The government argued that the murder "was perpetrated in furtherance of the conspiracy." But some of the defense lawyers, in a conference held without the jury present, objected that testimony about the murder in the presence of the jury would be unfair to their clients. "The prejudice would be overwhelming," argued Bernard Cohen, the lawyer for Morris (Gateman) Hampton. Cohen emphasized that Gateman was not alleged to have "handled drugs," only that he installed iron gates on Chambers crack houses and allowed his name to be attached to property actually owned by Larry.

Judge Suhrheinrich was unsympathetic. "Once he got stuck in the conspiracy, he is in part and parcel. If it's [the murder] in furtherance of the conspiracy, it's relevant."

"Not necessarily," Cohen retorted. "He is painted with the same miserable brush the other defendants are."

"Isn't it that he has a right not to join the conspiracy in the first place?" the judge replied. "Once he joins it he gets in bad with it." But then Suhrheinrich allowed that he had yet to hear any evidence that Cohen's client was part of the conspiracy. "I'm not sure the mere fact he sticks some gates up for people in and of itself makes him in any way responsible . . ."

Roy Hayes and Larry Bunting entered the discussion. They explained that another witness would implicate Morris Hampton in the purchase and sale of Larry's property in Detroit and Jamaica, and that the witness would testify that Hampton "erected gates" for Larry.

But Suhrheinrich told the prosecutors they had to prove that Hampton *knew* that Larry's money was "drug money." Otherwise, the judge implied, there would be a bottomless pool of potential co-conspirators. "The guy I buy my car from, which is a Mercedes, sold a car to one of these guys," Suhrheinrich explained. "Is he part of the conspiracy? This is a wild assumption on my part, but I imagine he ate three meals a day, the baker . . . that sold him bread . . . that they purchased with alleged drug money— does that make [*him*] part of the conspiracy?"

The government called Felicia Gilchrist to the witness stand midmorning on Thursday, October 13. Felicia wore her hair cropped nearly to her skull. Her bony body, vacant eyes, and, in Billy's words, her unkempt "dope-fiend hairstyle" gave her the look of someone in dire need of a good meal, a night's sleep, and a treatment program. She had been held in federal custody at the Days Inn for two days, and had apparently come down with a horrific cold. She also was suffering from withdrawal from crack.

On the stand, she coughed and spat incessantly, covering her mouth with her hands or T-shirt, and tucked her knees to her chest so that her body was curled almost in a fetal position. At times her language was incomprehensible. "I can't understand a word she is saying," Judge Suhrheinrich remarked. "I don't know if she is speaking English or what." Roy Hayes started to intervene, to advise his witness to take her time, talk slowly, but the judge was unconvinced such guidance would help. "I'm not sure you don't need an interpreter," Suhrheinrich said.

He called a ten-minute recess to allow a nurse to examine Felicia Gilchrist. During the break, in the judge's chambers, an anxious Suhrheinrich told the two prosecutors and two of the defense lawyers: "Gentlemen, I . . . was raised in this town and I am concerned she may be on something."

"I think she is on something," agreed Paul Young's lawyer, Lyle Russell.

"I think maybe she doesn't do crack cocaine but she has a heroin problem," Tony Chambers weighed in.

The nurse, though, examined Felicia and pronounced her competent. (In an interview years later, Felicia said it was fear and the forced withdrawal from crack rather than crack itself that hindered her performance. "I got on that stand and I was talking but I couldn't get my voice. Nothing would come out. I was just scared. Marlow"—the name she knew Larry by—"and them would all be looking at me so hard.")

Testimony resumed. Felicia recalled for jurors the exact day she began selling crack: March 23, 1987—a week after her second child was born. She said she sold five-dollar rocks out the back door of her mother's house on Linsdale Street, on the west side. "There was a little hole in the back door," she explained. "They stick their money through and I stick the rocks out." Her boss was Paul Young, who himself worked for Billy. She earned between $290 and $350 weekly, depending on how much crack or money was unaccounted for. She worked twenty-four/seven, sleeping only "when the traffic would slow down." The business became a family affair. After a while, she said, she began splitting shifts with her fourteen-year-old sister. Their uncle was paid to guard the house—he had previously worked some west-side houses for Larry—and their mother (a heavy user of crack to whom Felicia attributed the frequently irreconcilable balance sheets) also received weekly rental payments of two hundred and fifty dollars.

Roy Hayes was ready to question Felicia about the murder involving Paul Young that occurred at Felicia's house. In a bench conference, Hayes summarized his witness's anticipated testimony. He said that Felicia would tell jurors that in early May of 1987 a new drop-off/pickup man named Leonard Ruffin who worked for Paul had supposedly stolen close to two thousand dollars. One morning around five Felicia "happened to look outside" her window and saw a blue Trans Am with three men: Paul Young and two others. One of them shot Ruffin; all three were subsequently convicted of murder. (Paul was already serving a life sentence without parole in Michigan state prison for that conviction when he was indicted in the federal Chambers case.)

The defense again objected that the murder had nothing to do with "the overall conspiracy." The prosecution countered that the forthcoming testimony—that a worker came up short with money and violent retribution was exacted—was consistent with the organization's means of discipline. Back and forth it went until the judge stated that he disagreed with the government's theory that the organization would order the "assassination" of a new recruit for a relatively minor infraction. "If they want to discipline somebody, they could have shot this young lady [Felicia] because she was there every day," Suhrheinrich said. "They could have shot Paul Young if they wanted to—he was the pickup and drop-off man. Why pick a brand-new, never-mentioned name and say, 'Here, we are going to discipline somebody that never worked in our organization before to show you how serious we are about discipline'?"

After further exchange the judge ruled against the government. "This is an incident where it seems the prejudicial value outweighs the probative value," he concluded briskly.

Next to testify was Perry Coleman, the alleged supplier who pleaded guilty on the eve of the trial in exchange for a maximum five-year sentence. It was expected that his testimony would implicate the organization's other alleged main supplier, Kevin (Hollywood) Duplessis. The government also counted on Perry to provide the jury with further details about the size of Billy's operations—particularly the amount of cocaine he purchased weekly.

Billy and Perry had known each other for nine years, since Billy had run away from Lee County to Detroit to be with Perry's niece, Anita (Niece) Coleman. Perry introduced Billy to the streets, taught him the finer points of small-time hustling, hosted all-night card games, gave Billy a job at the party store he owned. It wasn't long before Billy eclipsed his tutor, finding success in the marijuana business through another mentor, Big Terry Colbert. Along the way to his early fortune, Billy always looked after Perry and his large extended family.

And now Perry Coleman, the man who had introduced a wary Billy Joe Chambers to crack—*BJ, I know what's wrong with you. You think you rich already. I'm gonna tell you. You ain't rich. You sell cocaine, you* really *gonna be rich*—was on the stand testifying against him. "It was real strange seeing him because we had no idea he'd be up there," Billy recalls. "All we knew is the marshals called him out of the bull pen [in the courthouse basement]. But we didn't know why. And when they called him to the stand he looked real sickly and pale, and kind of a little confused."

Perry was more than a little confused. He started lucidly enough, explaining the means by which Billy obtained his cocaine. When Billy ran low, Perry said, Billy beeped him. He in turn beeped the wholesaler "Art" [Derrick], who called him back to take the order. It might be for one kilo or as many as three keys, Perry said. Larry Bunting then set the stage for the heart of his witness's testimony. He posed the question nice and easy, a batting practice pitch: "If Art didn't have the cocaine, who else did you get it from?" The answer everyone in the courtroom anticipated was "Hollywood."

"I don't know," Perry replied.

The answer stunned the prosecutor as it would any director whose performer was ad-libbing. Bunting tried again: "Did Billy Chambers ever discuss with you who to get cocaine from?"

"Yes," Perry said.

"Who?"

"I can't remember."

And on it went. *I don't know, I don't remember, I can't remember:* Perry suddenly had the recall of an amnesiac.

Judge Suhrheinrich excused the jury and summoned the principal attorneys to the bench. "You have somebody else going to tie his client [Hollywood] in?" the judge asked a frustrated Bunting.

"Not until I get to the bottom [of Coleman's testimony]."

Suhrheinrich: "Don't yell at me. You do that once more and you will be going down there with them."

Bunting: "I wasn't yelling. I apologize."

Suhrheinrich: "You just be careful. This is a bench conference. I don't need you to yell at me or you'll be going down with the marshal. What else do you have?"

"I believe I would have this witness's testimony that Kevin Duplessis bought cocaine."

It was the end of a nightmarish day for the government. For whatever reasons, Perry Coleman did not deliver the agreed-upon goods; court was adjourned until the morning. Downstairs, in the marshals' office, Perry explained to an assistant U.S. attorney and an FBI agent that he froze on the stand because he feared for his family's safety. He said that during the week leading to his court appearance, "an unknown Chambers associate" (in the FBI's parlance) approached his brother-in-law to ask where his, Perry's, wife was staying. The government offered Perry a deal: we'll try to get you and your family into the Witness Protection Program, and you testify truthfully in the morning. The agents said they would apply to the program on his behalf, but that they could not promise admittance, that the ultimate decision would be made by the Justice Department in Washington. The assistant U.S. attorney, Ross Parker, left the meeting believing his witness was ready to cooperate. "We thought he was going to do the right thing," Parker recalls.

At eight-thirty the next morning, in the absence of the jury, Perry was back on the stand. And though he didn't clam up, he again completely defied the prosecutors' expectations—he recanted. "I've been lying on myself," he blurted tremblingly. "I don't remember what happened two years, four years. I've been scared." He added: "I ain't never sold anybody no three, four, or five keys, no week. I ain't done a lot of stuff they got on me."

Larry Bunting, naturally, had had enough of Perry Coleman. "It's our intention not to call him further as a witness," he told the court, making it clear also that perjury charges awaited. In short order, the judge struck Perry's testimony. "You are to disregard anything he has said," Suhrheinrich instructed jurors, "anything he has said whatsoever." And for the second time in three days, the government was left to move to dismiss charges against two defendants. Outside on Lafayette Street the sky was overcast and the temperature hovered only in the middle forties, but for Hollywood Duplessis and Morris Hampton (whom Perry also was to implicate), men loosed at last from the collar of indictment, it could not have been a finer, clearer fall morning.

Of the twenty-two persons indicted, there were now ten defendants on trial. Four had pleaded guilty, charges against four were dismissed, and four were fugitives. The government would take one week more to present its case. It would call only two more alleged former Chambers associates: James Lumpkin and James McKinney. James Lumpkin, twenty, took the stand to testify against his sister Belinda and her boyfriend, Larry Chambers. He described how he helped Larry hide assets—motorbikes, cars, real estate, cash—in Detroit and Jamaica. James McKinney, the eighteen-year-old from Marianna, was called to tie in Marshall (Mario) Glenn with Billy's wing of the business. McKinney said Mario recruited him with the promise that he would be paid two thousand dollars a month in Detroit. But he said that as far as he knew, he was working strictly for Mario. He had heard about Billy, but he never saw him in the "big-old apartment building" from which he sold five-dollar rocks, or even in the street. "I can't recognize him," he told the jury. "They all look alike."

The government paraded a small battalion of police officers and federal agents onto the stand. They testified about everything from the sixty-thousand-dollar garbage-bag bust of Otis in Arkansas, to sundry surveillance missions and raids, to a chemical analysis of cocaine seized, to the alleged attempt by Billy, Willie, and Larry to evade taxes. The agents' tax-count testimony was buttressed by that of auto dealers, bank managers, insurance agents, and a real estate agent, who were called upon to present bills of sale and receipts.

The prosecution was planning a lengthy tax case; it had subpoenaed many more record-keepers of businesses the Chamberses had patronized. During a recess, Larry and Billy pleaded guilty to the single count of tax evasion. They understood that a conviction on that count was inevitable, and rather than have the jury hear extended testimony about their assets—"my BMW this, his Caddy that," says Billy—they entered the pleas on the condition that their sentences would be no longer than two years, and that they would be served concurrently with any other sentences they might receive. ("We already had did all that time in the county [jail], so I wasn't too worried about no two years," Billy later said.)

With the tax matters resolved, the prosecution was finished. (There would be further testimony against Willie, who declined to plead guilty to tax charges and whose fate the judge rather than the jury would decide.) "All right," Judge Suhrheinrich intoned. It was the afternoon of Thursday, October 20, six weeks into the trial. "Does the government rest?"

"Yes, we do," Roy Hayes replied. "At this time we rest our case."

The defense mounted a minimal case. All but two of the ten attorneys refrained from calling witnesses. The others elected to stake their cases on final argument: to rely on the government's weak evidence, the inconsistencies in Terry Colbert's rambling testimony, and their clients' presumed innocence. They had little choice. As Tim Murphy later put it, "This was a case where you just had to sit there and take it. The proofs on these guys were overwhelming. They [the government] had everything: money, dope, all those raids . . ." With the defense's case closed, Judge Suhrheinrich announced that after a brief recess he would instruct the jury. Closing arguments, he said, would occur the following day.

His Honor began the ritual charge to the jury with the standard sermon. "The law does not permit jurors to be governed by sympathy, prejudice, or public opinion. Both the accused and the public expect that you will carefully and impartially consider all the evidence in the case, follow the law as stated by the court, and reach a just verdict, regardless of the consequences."

Suhrheinrich reminded jurors that "a defendant is never to be convicted on mere suspicion or conjecture"; that "the burden is always upon the prosecution to prove guilt beyond a reasonable doubt." The judge recited the indictment, defined its legal terms (aiding and abetting, conspiracy, continuing criminal enterprise, and so forth), and began his instructions. "What the evidence in this case must establish beyond a reasonable doubt is that the alleged conspiracy was knowingly formed, and that one or more of the means or methods described in the indictment were agreed upon to be used, in an effort to effect or accomplish some object or purpose of the conspiracy . . . ; and that two or more persons, including one or more of the accused, were knowingly members of the conspiracy. . . ."

Suhrheinrich instructed jurors that they were not to consider punishment—only guilt or innocence. Sentencing, were guilty verdicts returned, would be "a matter exclusively within the province of the court."

He told the jury to pick a "foreperson." He explained that the verdict "must represent the considered judgment" of each juror and that it must be unanimous. He had earlier told jurors they would be sequestered during deliberations. Just before dismissing them until the next day's closing arguments, he advised: "Bring your clothes for probably two or three days." Finally, he admonished them, as he had at the end of every single session since the trial commenced, to read nothing, see nothing, hear nothing. "We have come this far," he said, "and now tomorrow is the conclusion."

Larry Bunting did the first part of the summation for the government. As if he were pressing on after-dinner guests endless snapshots of a recent vacation, he revisited with the jury the highlights of the government's case: Here's James Lumpkin moving money around for Larry Chambers. And here's Pat Middleton watching Larry beat a boy with a chair, and there's Pat watching him push another boy out the window. And here's Billy teaching Terry Colbert how to rock cocaine, and Otis's wrecking crew shooting Terry . . .

Next Bunting told the jury why they should believe his paid informants. He cited the dangerous work Terry Colbert performed. "Is it wrong for the police to pay a man to go into [a crack house] and . . . make a buy?" he asked. "I submit it is not. Clearly it is not. The police aren't volunteers. They don't do their law enforcement work for nothing. I'm not a volunteer. I get a salary for what I do when I work. If you work for the police by making deals, going in and buying cocaine, you should get paid for it."

He asked and answered a crucial question the jury would have to address: Had the government proved there existed a single conspiracy? Or did the evidence show that the defendants operated separately, outside the sphere of a monolithic enterprise? "First," Bunting said, ". . . don't overlook the obvious. We have four young men from Marianna . . . who are now in Detroit. One of the witnesses testified it was about nine hundred miles away. Being in Detroit, there is nothing wrong with that, but not only to have four young men from an area nine hundred miles away and not only just in the dope business but in the crack cocaine business, and the operation runs identically.

"Are these people working together? Don't overlook the obvious on that. That speaks for itself."

Bunting recapped some testimony that spoke to the single-conspiracy theory. He said that witnesses from both wings of the business—Billy's and Larry's—"saw the same rules" and regulations. And he quoted Terry Colbert telling of an order Billy once gave Terry: "You are going to sell dimes, my brother is selling nickels."

"If they weren't the same organization," Bunting asked, "why price it so one half gets the [five-dollar] customers and the other half gets the ten-dollar-rock customers? . . . When Hudson's [the grand downtown department store] used to have the Rainbow Store in the basement, if you wanted something cheaper you go in the basement; if you wanted something more expensive you go on whatever floor it was, the fifth floor. It's the same organization; you price the shirts in the Rainbow Store a little cheaper than on the main floor."

Tim Murphy led the defense summations. He returned to the Dickensian analogy Roy Hayes had employed in his introduction to the trial more than a month earlier. "Mr. Hayes . . . said that the evidence would portray *A Tale of Two Cities,* and I agree," Murphy said. "One of those cities is Detroit, and one, I would argue to you, is Oz. Where the yellow brick road leads to where the wizard lives and where apparently much of the testimony from the government's witnesses comes."

Humor aside, Murphy knew the testimony against his client, Fats Wilkins, had been persuasive. Murphy's only defense, the only defense any of them really had, was to yet again remind the jury of the government witnesses' character flaws. He began with a potshot at the lead witness. He spoke of her felonious past, and her evasiveness on the stand about that past. "Would you," he asked jurors, "take a check from Patricia Middleton?"

Rudy Wartella grabbed the Middleton-bashing baton from Tim Murphy. Middleton had testified that his client, Belinda

Lumpkin, was the "paymaster" of The Boulevard. "You heard Mr. Murphy talk about Ms. Middleton's credibility, and there are a couple things that he forgot," Wartella reminded the jury, "specifically about her psychological problems."

Next Curtis Williams was up, on behalf of Jerry Gant. His duty was to defame the only witness who testified against his client. Williams's jibes echoed those of Tim Murphy: "Think for a minute whether you would buy a car from somebody like Terry Colbert."

Ronald Gold, trying to save Elayne Coleman, also proffered unflattering remarks about Terry Colbert, Elayne's prime accuser. "He is nothing more than the lowest of low. He is a snitch. . . . He is the same man [who] would tell you anything in return for some type of benefit. And what has he been promised in this case? He has been promised absolutely the moon."

Terry Colbert was the lone witness to link David Goldstein's man, Marshall Glenn, to any of the co-defendants. Goldstein joined the chorus of carpers. Terry "gets immunity, gets money, gets relocated, and all of a sudden the government tells you because he has been given immunity this guy who was out there doing criminal activity on a daily basis is suddenly on the side of the angels, [and] suddenly when Terry Colbert opens his mouth, out comes bouquets of the truth."

If there were an award given for least eloquent closing argument, it would have gone hands down to Billy's lawyer, Charles Lusby. His discourse was bombastic, disorganized, and witless; the performance so lackluster, so hard to follow, that even Lusby sensed it: he apologized several times for "boring" his listeners. He weaved through the case like a drunk driver, careening from one witness's testimony to another's, seldom braking to make a coherent point. His tendency to jumble dates and places and misstate names disabled his argument and doubtlessly confused jurors. His statement amounted to one long whine. Certainly his client was victimized by numerous falsehoods. But to seek to make that point without sufficient documentation—by merely griping that "he lied," "she lied," "they lied"—shows little more than mastery of the art of conjugation.

Finally, as if to ensure leaving a sour taste in jurors' mouths, Lusby departed from his legal brethren by not asking the jury to return a favorable judgment—rather, he *informed* them: "You are going to come back with a verdict of not guilty."

In contrast to Lusby, Lyle Russell, on behalf of Paul Young, offered a skillfully sculpted argument. He had only one witness to rebut, which made his task more manageable; he performed it clearly and engagingly. He spoke to the jury; he didn't harangue them.

He molded his statement around the uncorroborated testimony of Felicia Gilchrist, the woman who sold crack for Paul out of her mother's west-side house. Russell managed to cast Felicia as a sympathetic character who was forced to lie about his client to keep her family together. "Felicia Gilchrist has a need for money," Russell said. "She has a mother with a coke habit. She has a sister selling coke. She has at least one small child. One of the few [truthful] things I think she told you was, 'I was afraid if I was charged that I would lose my child.' "

Tom Wilhelm had a harder sell. He too argued that the government's case against his client, Otis, was based largely on the uncorroborated testimony of one witness, the ignominious Terry Colbert. No one else, Wilhelm said, confirmed that Otis was a drop-off/pickup man. "You cannot convict Mr. Otis Chambers just because [of] his last name . . . ," he cautioned.

As to the incident in Hughes, Arkansas, where police found sixty thousand dollars in the back of the Corvette in which Otis was a passenger and his girlfriend was at the wheel, Wilhelm had no recourse but disingenuousness. He insisted that the government's theory that "Otis knew the money was there and he brought it down from Detroit" defied "common sense." "If you were a passenger, let's say, in your neighbor's car, do you know everything that is in the trunk? . . . Do you go and inspect what is inside that trunk when you get in it? No."

It had been a wearisome day of final arguments. Tony Chambers, Larry's attorney and the de facto leader of the defense, knew jurors could bear only so much repetition and redundancy; all day he had been watching their heads nod and their eyes glaze over. Considering the deep hole in which his client had been entombed since Patricia Middleton's opening-day appearance, and considering the jury's late-afternoon near-catatonic state, Chambers deduced that a novel approach was in order. And so he eschewed garden variety narrative for a heavy-handed but entertaining theory of evolution.

"It was a stormy day back in August of 1986," Chambers began. "The wind was blowing, the rain was coming hard. There laid a rock out in the bushes against the trees. As it began to rain, as the water began to flow, there was, of course, the usual dirt and mud under this rock.

"This rock and this mud and this dirt got immensely wet, almost to the extent it was a flood. This mud, this dirt turned to slime, and this slime trickled down the hill through the flooding waters, and as it trickled down that hill, ladies and gentlemen of the jury, this slime began to ooze and pick up all the garbage it could. And this slime, this mud, oozed its way into the city of Detroit and into downtown Detroit. This slime, this mud, oozed its way to Lafayette Street and to this federal courthouse.

"This slime, this mud, oozed itself into the elevator up to the eighth floor and made a right turn. This slime, this mud . . . ended up in an office and into a chair and it said, 'Mr. Hayes, I got a story to tell you.' When there was an attempt to find out what this slime, this mud that oozed so badly and began to smell because of the garbage it picked up said, there was no name, no identification.

"So consequently, the government gave this slime and this mud and this garbage a name: key witness, star witness. And then this mud, this slime, oozed its way on to this witness stand and began to wail. . . . And when it got on the stand what was the name . . . of this slime and this mud? . . . Patricia Middleton."

Chambers had won the jury's attention. Upon returning from the land of allegory, he fixed on the specifics of Middleton's testimony, and that of the other key witnesses against Larry.

"These same people," Chambers said, "you can consider as if they are a foundation to a house. A house cannot stand without a foundation and this case must fall with these weak witnesses."

For the government's closing summation—its rebuttal to the day-long pounding by the defense—first-stringer Roy Hayes inserted himself back in the game. Before he delved into rebuttal Hayes spoke wistfully to the jury about the city he was born and raised in. "Sometimes," he said, "I look out the window early in the morning and I see the city of Detroit and I see houses, buildings, and cars, and if I look out to the east side I see generally the area where the Gray Street house might be, or 1350 East Grand Boulevard. . . . One of the days we were in trial I arrived back to my office there at quarter to seven or seven o'clock in the morning and I looked out my window and Detroit had vanished. It had vanished, it was gone."

It was a strong, if maudlin, opening, an unspoken appeal to jurors to broaden their perspective beyond the evidence table, past the familiar questions of reliability and credibility of witnesses, to look at the ten defendants who sat accused before them as emblematic of the terrible blight that befell their city.

For the next twenty minutes or so, Roy Hayes busied himself with refutation. Of Tony Chambers's characterization of Pat Middleton as "slime and ooze and mud," Hayes said: "It would be nice if we could bring in Rhodes scholars and teachers and all sorts of wonderful people to tell you about the narcotics business . . . but that can't be so. There is one thing about the [nonpolice] witnesses . . . that you haven't heard the defense say. They saw it. They heard it. They were part of it day to day, some for a short time and some for a long time. I'm not here to tell you they should be up for an award, but I am here to tell you they have had unique qualifications. They were there. They lived it."

Hayes emphasized that the case was "built on eyewitnesses, people who lived inside, as well as investigators and resources and work of the No-Crack Task Force." He summarized his witnesses's statements and asked jurors to discount any weak links in the entire chain of testimony. "It fits together and you have seen it. It happened before your eyes," Hayes said.

It was four o'clock on Wednesday, October 26, when Roy Hayes wrapped up. "The evidence and testimony you have has proven this case beyond a reasonable doubt and I ask you to return a verdict of guilty as charged against all defendants on all counts," Hayes concluded. "Thank you so much for your time and your attention."

Judge Suhrheinrich sent the jury to begin deliberations. After seventy-five minutes they broke for dinner; they would resume in the morning. Meanwhile, Suhrheinrich heard closing arguments regarding Willie Chambers, who had requested a bench trial. The judge promptly found Willie guilty of the tax count, of evading about twenty-one thousand dollars in taxes; as for the conspiracy charge he said, "I think there is a large drug conspiracy of which Willie Chambers was a part." But he added that unless the jury "finds a conspiracy exists between" Larry and Billy, there would be no one for Willie to have conspired with. "So," he said, "we have to wait . . ."

Around four o'clock on Thursday, after a night spent sequestered at the Days Inn and a full day of deliberations, jurors sent the judge a note: "Your Honor, sir, may we please be excused a little earlier today. Tempers are short, nerves are frazzled, if this is at all possible. Thank you."

Friday, October 28, noon. Judge Suhrheinrich read aloud another note from the jury. "Your Honor, sir, the jury reached their verdicts. Thank you." They had deliberated a total of only fourteen and a half hours, considerably less time than the rule of thumb in federal court: a day of deliberations per week of trial. Notice of such a quick decision made for little suspense.

The jury was escorted into the courtroom. The judge asked the foreperson to please rise. "Has the jury reached a unanimous verdict?"

"Yes it has."

"On all counts?"

"On all counts."

"On all the defendants?"

"Yes."

The foreman handed the verdict form to a law clerk, who passed it to the judge, who read it aloud.

"Count One, Conspiracy: Larry Chambers, guilty; Billy Joe Chambers, guilty; Otis Chambers, guilty; Belinda Lumpkin, guilty." The word echoes four times more: Jerry Gant, Marshall Glenn, Eric Wilkins, Elayne Coleman, all guilty. Only Paul Young, already serving a life sentence for murder, was acquitted. Of the defendants, who were surrounded by a dozen marshals, only Belinda, eighteen years old and pregnant with her first child, showed any emotion: she bowed her head and sobbed.

Judge Suhrheinrich then announced that the jury found guilty the defendants charged in the other counts: Elayne and Billy for aiding and abetting each other on Gray Street; Larry for possession of cocaine with intent to distribute; Larry for possession of a firearm in the course of a dangerous felony. The judge next read the inevitable verdicts on the continuing criminal enterprise charge, the "kingpin statute" that carried a possible life sentence for Billy and Larry. Guilty and guilty.

It was over. The jury was excused. Judge Suhrheinrich made official his finding of guilt in Willie's case. The judge revoked bond for Willie and Elayne and Belinda; he ordered all defendants returned to jail. "The court finds that this conspiracy is a threat, a serious one, to this community."

Then Suhrheinrich said he wanted to "see counsel in chambers." He invited them for cocktails to his swank watering hole, the Detroit Athletic Club. "He got us drunk after the verdict," says Tim Murphy. "Just the defense guys, he didn't take the prosecutors. Ran up a four-hundred-dollar bill."

At the start of the sentencing hearing five months later, in March of 1989, Judge Suhrheinrich indulged in a twenty-minute speech that made it clear those convicted should expect no leniency. Of crack, the judge told the packed courtroom, it is "doing to our poor people what no person could do. It's enslaving them, it's enslaving all economic groups that take this filth. It's doing what Hitler could never do to us. It's doing what no dictator, slave owner, or anyone else could do to us."

He then sentenced each of the Chambers brothers to lengthy prison terms and substantial fines, the most severe allowed under federal guidelines. Larry received the stiffest sentence—life in prison and a two-hundred-and-fifty-thousand-dollar fine. Billy was sentenced to forty-five years and a five-hundred-thousand-dollar fine; Otis and Willie each received twenty-seven years and three-hundred-and-fifty-thousand-dollar fines.

As for the other convicted defendants, Judge Suhrheinrich sentenced Jerry Gant and Marshall Glenn to terms of thirty years in prison; Belinda Lumpkin received a sentence of twenty-five years; Elayne Coleman, a sentence of ten years; and Eric Wilkins was slapped with thirty-four years, which was to run consecutively with the thirteen-and-a-half-year to twenty-year sentence he was already serving in Michigan state prison for an earlier possession charge.

The sentences remain in effect even though Terry Colbert recanted portions of his testimony after the trial, charging that the feds intimidated him and ordered him to lie on the witness stand. In a letter to the judge, Colbert wrote that "everything that [I] said in the trial was a lie. Two of the officers threatened me and held me against my will. . . . It was like my back was against the wall (and still is), but if it turns out for the better or for the worse I still want to come back and tell the whole truth, and nothing but the truth, so help me God."

When Colbert appeared in court in June of 1989 at a hearing on the motion for a new trial, his mumbled, murky statements seemed to puzzle and anger Judge Suhrheinrich. "Is there something physically or mentally wrong with you today?" he asked Colbert.

The defendants sat against the wall behind their attorneys at

the hearing, watching impassively as their former colleague meandered through his testimony, looking for all the world like a crackhead. The jury box was empty, save for a sketch artist.

On this day, a federal marshal motioned the brothers to
stand. They rose as one, four brothers in government fatigues, all
nearly the same height, their high foreheads bent slightly toward
the floor, their mouths identically firm and as sealed as their fates.
They were already handcuffed and bound by chains to one another's prison identification bracelets: Otis to Larry to Billy to Willie. In single file, like men in an indecorous conga line, they
marched toward a rear door, as close as brothers get. The future
was theirs together.

EPILOGUE

NOTHING TO LOSE

No new trial was granted. The defendants appealed to the
United States Court of Appeals for the Sixth Circuit, in Cincinnati.
The appeal was based largely on the recanted testimony of Terry
Colbert and Perry Coleman. In September of 1991, a three-judge
panel upheld the convictions of all but four of the appellants.

For Billy and Larry, and for Belinda Lumpkin and Eric (Fats)
Wilkins, the appeals court opened the door to the possibility of
some relief. In addition to their claim that two of the government's
witnesses, Colbert and Coleman, committed perjury, Billy and
Larry claimed that their convictions for supervising a continuing
criminal enterprise and conspiracy violated the double jeopardy
clause of the Fifth Amendment to the Constitution. They contended that because all of the elements of a conspiracy are sub-
sumed under the continuing criminal enterprise charge, they were,
in effect, convicted twice of the same crime.

The Sixth Circuit agreed with the brothers, remanding their
cases to the trial court for resentencing and ordering the court to
vacate one of the two convictions. The appeals court also re-
manded the cases of Belinda and Fats, each of whom had argued

that because they were under eighteen at the time of their offenses, they should not have been tried as adults. The appeals court was unsatisfied that the two had received a juvenile certification hearing at trial, and asked the district court to revisit its ruling.

On resentencing, District Court Judge Gerald E. Rosen vacated Larry and Billy's conspiracy convictions. (Judge Suhrhein-rich had since been appointed to the Sixth Circuit.) In December of 1992, Judge Rosen, a low-key, diminutive man, sentenced Billy on the continuing criminal enterprise count to twenty-seven years, a reduction of eighteen years. (A fifteen-year sentence for aiding and abetting is running concurrently.) For Larry the victory was hollow—the judge disposed of one of his two life sentences. And for Belinda and Fats, the narrow opening the appeals court had provided was slammed shut: Judge Rosen reinstated their convictions.

During the early stages of appeal, three of the four brothers—Billy, Willie, and Otis—were incarcerated at the federal medium-security prison in Milan, Michigan, a bucolic town about sixty-five miles southwest of Detroit. (Larry, whose record and life sentence mandated a more restricted facility, was returned to the maximum-security penitentiary at Leavenworth, Kansas.) In August of 1991, there surfaced a rumor that the brothers in Milan had offered a contract to murder police officer Gerard (Mick) Biernacki, the lead cop on many of the raids. Dick Crock of the DEA relayed the information to federal Bureau of Prison officials, who quickly separated the defendants. Billy was moved to a facility in Talladega, Alabama, a scenic town in the hills east of Birmingham. Willie was relocated to a prison in the Adirondack mountains of upstate New York. And Otis was sent to a unit in Indiana and then to south Texas.

The other convicted defendants were also separated from one another: Jerry Gant was sent to Atlanta; Marshall Glenn to Wisconsin; Belinda Lumpkin to Kentucky; Elayne Coleman to West Virginia (after a brief stay in Kentucky); and Eric Wilkins to a state prison in Michigan, where he was to serve out an earlier sentence.

Paul Young, the only defendant the jury acquitted, remains in a Michigan prison, where he is serving a life sentence for murder.

Within months of the trial, the authorities rounded up three of the four remaining fugitives: Carl Young, Michael Lee, and Albert (Baldy) Rucker. In separate trials, Young and Lee were convicted and sentenced to respective prison terms of nine years and twenty-one years. (Young's term was lighter because the only overt act he was charged with occurred in 1986, a year before federal mandatory sentencing guidelines went into effect.) The court accepted the guilty plea of Rucker; he agreed to a five-year sentence.

By the end of 1990, the lone fugitive was William (Jack) Jackson. Jack was the erstwhile star—*"Money, money, money! We rich, goddammit!"*—of Larry's home video. He had disappeared in July of 1987, on the night the video first aired on local television. He remained at large until the fall of 1992. During his years on the run, Jack received even more television exposure: his story aired on the program "America's Most Wanted." Jack had cut his hair and grown a beard; the resemblance to the man in the video was not obvious.

"I was laying up in a girlfriend's bed when the show came on," Jack recalls. "I tried to be cool. Told her, 'That guy a nut.' " His friend agreed. "Crazy nigger," she said, sharing a laugh.

Jack spent little time in Detroit during his four and a half years on the lam. He went first to Las Vegas, then to Chicago, returned briefly to Detroit. He used a variety of aliases, obtained credit cards and driver's licenses in those names. One day on the east side of Detroit, while driving his aunt's car, Jack was stopped by police and asked for identification. He produced an Ohio driver's license. The officer asked him why an Ohioan was driving a car registered in Michigan. Jack replied that he was visiting his aunt and that he was trying to find his way back to her house. "Get out of here," the officer cautioned. "It's a drug-infested area."

Jack took the officer's advice. He headed south, to Atlanta, and then to South Carolina. He left regular messages for his mother on her answering machine in Detroit. He always called from a pay phone immediately prior to relocating, and made sure to carry sufficient rolls of quarters. "This your baby, I'm fine," is all he'd say.

He bought full sets of credentials in two names: Willie Davis and Eddie Jackson. For fifty dollars a name, he received a Social Security card, driver's license, and birth certificate. At one point, he held driver's licenses from three states—California, Georgia, and South Carolina.

Jack never held a job during those years. He financed his travels through a healthy cash reserve, the bogus credit cards, and a talent for seducing well-off women. "I'd always wear the sharpest rags money could buy," Jack says. "Thousand-dollar alligator shoes, manicures, pedicures, go to the nicest clubs. Women would ask what I do, and I'd tell them, 'I'm here on a confidential government experiment.' I'd let them take me to their fifteen-hundred-a-month apartment.

"But I couldn't get close to them. I'd call this girl, 'Hey baby, this is Dave'; I'd call that girl, 'This is Eddie.' Not that I'm nobody special, but I broke a lot of hearts because I'd leave after two or three months."

By late summer of 1992, Jack was running low on cash. He headed to Akron, Ohio, where some friends were running a crack house. Jack says the house gave him a "nervous feeling right from the start." His instincts were sound; the house was under surveillance. He left there shortly after he arrived, and drove to a hotel, where police arrested him. The officers found no outstanding warrants for "Willie Davis," the name that matched Jack's photo on his driver's license. He thought he might be off the hook. "But when they took me down for fingerprints," Jack recalls, "my heart was beating like a cartoon." Sure enough, the prints matched those of William Jackson—wanted by the FBI. Jack was convicted in state court in Ohio of two counts: aggravated trafficking and conspiracy to commit aggravated trafficking. He was sentenced to ten to thirty years in state prison. Then he was brought back to Detroit to face federal conspiracy charges in the Chambers case. In early 1994, Judge Rosen sentenced William Jackson to thirty years in federal prison. He will begin serving that time after he fulfills his state sentence in Ohio.

Prosecutors also saw to it that Perry Coleman and Terry Colbert, the government's treasonous witnesses, did not escape prosecution. Perry, a supplier of Billy's, had agreed to testify against him and to implicate another alleged supplier, Kevin (Hollywood) Duplessis, in exchange for a prison sentence of no more than five years. After Perry froze in terror on the witness stand and subsequently recanted his testimony, the government charged him with perjury.

Perry served a little more than four years in prison. He was illiterate when he arrived, which was especially frustrating because his wife, Gail, had taken to writing him faithfully. During his second year in prison, in Duluth, Minnesota, Gail wrote him a final letter, to announce she was leaving him. Perry says he suffered a "nervous breakdown," and ended up in a prison psychiatric hospital in Rochester, Minnesota. There he enrolled in a reading program. "They taught me to learn the sounds with those flash cards," he says. "You got to understand every letter means something. And then you learn syllables. And then you read and read and read. And then you write." He and his sister Elayne, imprisoned in Kentucky at the time, wrote each other every week. "I was there five months," he says of his stay in the psychiatric unit, "and that was the best thing to happen to me."

Perry Coleman was released from prison in the summer of 1992. He returned to Detroit, where he found work as a janitor at Cobo Hall, the downtown arena and convention center.

Hollywood Duplessis and Morris Hampton resumed their lives. Hollywood owned several small businesses on the east side, including a car wash, record store, and promotions firm. He lost the businesses, and today works odd jobs when he can find them, sometimes for a building-contractor friend. Though he has been down on his luck for some time, the formerly flashy entrepreneur manages to maintain a healthy ego. His house is a shrine to himself: on the few walls that aren't mirrored (the bathroom walls and ceiling, for instance, are entirely mirrored) are reminders of his minor celebrity, from the days when he modeled men's clothing and sang R&B. There are assorted publicity shots autographed by popular local singers and deejays, and, most prized, a photo of Hollywood with the boxer Thomas (Hit Man) Hearns. "I still have nightmares," Hollywood says years later of his close brush with the law. "I'm broke and having problems, but I know one day I'll regain my throne again."

Along with Willie Chambers, who supported his wife and two children, Morris (Gateman) Hampton stood the most to lose of any defendant. Morris was forty-one at the time he was indicted, with a wife and four children. He is a licensed Baptist lay minister, and prior to his arrest had been a Greyhound driver for seventeen years. He also moonlighted with two iron companies in Detroit, installing security gates and burglar bars; it was on a call for one of those firms that he met Larry Chambers.

Following the trial, Morris Hampton went back to college part-time. After his practical exposure to the subject, he decided to study criminal justice; the subject of his thesis was "Gangs and Crime in the United States of America." He continues to preach and is employed as a counselor at a boys' correctional facility.

Alvin Chambers, the brothers' first cousin, went home to Flint. The ordeal cost him his job at GM. He is unemployed and living with a sister.

Dennis Fayson, the arsonist and wrecking crew member who cooperated with the government, was sentenced to two years in prison. In 1989, he was paroled to Austin, Texas, where he had lived previously and where he had family. Fayson's value on the street had been as an enforcer, but he was only useful in that capacity when he was high. (It was to him Larry once said: "My friend, I hear you can wake up, throw six rocks in the pipe, and be ready to beat up the world.")

Dennis had not smoked crack since his arrest. But when he arrived in Texas in the summer of 1989 he found a thriving market, and once again was drawn to the drug. He had found construction work in Austin, but his habit was consuming most of his income. By December, he had fallen far enough behind on his rent that the apartment-building manager had sought to evict him.

One night Dennis had been smoking heavily and went to the manager's apartment, ostensibly to use the telephone. When the manager, a sixty-eight-year-old woman, let him in, Dennis began fatally stabbing her with a kitchen knife. He stabbed her twenty-seven times. Dennis Fayson is serving a life sentence without possibility of parole in the Texas Department of Corrections.

Arthur Derrick, the flamboyant "weight dealer," pleaded guilty to supplying Billy and White Boy Rick Wershe. He was released from prison in 1994, after serving about half of a ten-year sentence.

Patricia Middleton, the government's surprise leadoff witness, and David Havard, the manager of the apartment building Larry took over, married shortly after the trial. They declined an offer to enter the federal witness protection program, but accepted train fare away from Detroit. They headed west, to Arizona and then to California, where Havard had lived as a child. By 1991, they had divorced but had returned together to the Detroit area. Middleton, who goes by a different name, works as a waitress at an all-night restaurant; Havard drives a city bus.

Janice Davis Roberts, the cut-up girl who testified before the grand jury that Belinda Lumpkin had threatened her baby son, relocated to Ohio. On Christmas day of 1992, her son, then five years old, was killed by a hit-and-run driver. Janice's younger sister, Cindy, who was fourteen when she went to work for Larry, lives with her boyfriend and baby in Detroit.

Trouble followed Terry Colbert like a storm cloud. Within days of the trial's conclusion, Terry was arrested for carrying a concealed weapon; six months later he robbed a Payless shoe store on Gratiot Avenue. He was caught a week later—in a stolen 1981 Buick Regal. Among the items police seized from the stolen car were two letters Larry had written Terry from Leavenworth. The letters contained portions of Terry's grand jury testimony and some DEA investigative reports. The prosecutors believed the letters to be evidence of Terry's willingness to assist the defendants in their attempts to overturn their convictions.

The government began monitoring the defendants' phone calls from prison. In one late-night call to Terry Billy placed from Milan, Terry asked for money. "I'm broke," he pleaded, "I need some cash, dog. . . . I'm starving." Billy agreed to help out. The two exchanged notes on Billy's girlfriend, Kela, whose phone had recently been disconnected. Billy was frustrated that he had been unable to talk to her; rumor had it she was seeing another man. Billy had asked Terry to check it out. Terry and his younger brother Terrence had driven by Kela's house in the middle of the night several days earlier. Terry confirmed the rumor: he had seen the new boyfriend's car there.

"Shit," Billy replied. "Three o'clock in the motherfuckin' morning first day, first day the phone gets cut off. This nigger over all motherfuckin' night."

In another call, during the time Billy was preparing a motion for a new trial based on newly discovered evidence—affidavits he'd obtained from Janice Roberts, Terry, and two other government witnesses—Billy advised Terry on how to act on the witness stand. "Play your role to the max with them," Billy counseled. "Then, when you get on the stand, break on them like, you know, know what I'm talking about now?"

The government, of course, was livid that Terry was carrying water for the Chamberses. He had to be stopped. On October 24, 1990, a federal grand jury indicted Terry Colbert on eight counts of perjury, each of which carried a potential five-year sentence. The charges resulted from "irreconcilably contradictory" statements Terry made at the trial and at the hearing on the motion for a new trial in June of 1989, when he recanted in full his damning trial testimony.

The indictment was only the beginning of an extraordinary month of tragedy for Terry Colbert. The day after he was indicted,

Terry's father, L. C. (Big Terry) Colbert, Jr., was murdered in a drug deal gone bad. He was forty-one years old. Three weeks later, Terry's thirty-eight-year-old uncle, Tommie Colbert (in whose house Otis Chambers had ordered Terry shot in 1987), was killed. And down in Memphis, where Terry's mother lived with his step-father, his stepfather died of a heart attack.

In March of 1991, Terry, then twenty-five years old, was con-victed on all eight counts of perjury. He was sentenced to eleven years and three months. (The trial judge spared Terry decades in prison by ordering the sentencing on various of the counts to run concurrently.) During his second year in prison, at a medium-secu-rity facility in Memphis, Terry learned that his brother Terrence, age twenty-three, had been killed in Detroit in a drive-by shooting.

Many of those who worked on the case for the government have moved on. Judge Richard Suhrheinrich, as noted, was pro-moted to the Sixth Circuit Court of Appeals. He has lectured before the Rotary Club and chamber of commerce in Lansing and elsewhere on the significance of the Chambers brothers case. Roy C. Hayes left the U.S. attorney's office for private practice; he worked first for a large Detroit firm and is now a solo practitioner in Charlevoix, a small town on the shores of northern Lake Michi-gan. Larry Bunting, the assistant U.S. attorney, returned to his former position as an assistant prosecutor in Oakland County, Michigan. Tom McClain of the DEA went home to Pittsburgh to practice law and raise a family with Cynthia Stock, a former IRS undercover agent whom he met on assignment to the Chambers task force. Dick Crock, the DEA's point man on the street, is still at work for the agency in Detroit. His partner on the task force, Mick Biernacki, retired from the Detroit Police Department with medi-cal disability benefits.

Crack sales in Detroit continued to flourish, despite the highly publicized demise of the Chambers brothers' enterprise. If law enforcement officials believed in theory that the Chamberses' conviction would deter others from entering the field, in fact the huge profits the Chamberses earned had smaller dealers jostling to replace them as kings of the hill.

Six weeks after the trial, the *Detroit Free Press* analyzed the city's then year-long "Crackdown on Crack." The police had arrested record numbers of alleged drug offenders, the newspaper found, but the arrests were self-defeating: the city and state's courts and prisons had become so overloaded that most of those charged found themselves quickly back on the street. Of 1,015 people arrested in the first three months of the crackdown, nearly 80 percent were free nine months later. And with the knowledge that small-time dealers faced little risk of long prison sentences, most returned to their profitable trade.

The crack war's only measurable impact seems to have been on overworked police officers, judges, prosecutors, probation officers, and jailers. One former user told the *Free Press* that buying crack remained "as easy as it is to buy a loaf of bread."

Not only in Detroit and other cities was crack easily obtainable; by the late 1980s, crack had transformed countless small towns, the tranquil but vulnerable places emblematic of post-agricultural rural America. Crack and the relative crime wave that accompanied it brought to poor towns a new despair. One such place was Marianna, Arkansas.

In the way that rural southern migrants once imbued northern cities with their ways, the reverse was happening. When the Chamberses were operational, they made it a point while visiting Marianna never to mix business with pleasure. But once the brothers were indicted and there were no longer jobs for those who had followed them to Detroit, many of their displaced workers, almost all of them still in their teens, naturally came home. Some straightened out, returning to Lee Senior High; others, sensing a ready, untapped market, were eager to apply the retail and marketing techniques they had learned on the job up north.

"I got a helluva crack problem down here," Marianna police chief Mark Birchler said in March of 1989. "And it all goes right back to those damn Chambers brothers." Birchler said that his department had made twelve arrests for drug-dealing since the previous March. He estimated that there were probably about a dozen dealers still on the streets of Marianna. "That may not sound like a lot in Detroit, but we've never had drug arrests like this before. Two years ago we didn't have any."

To the dismay of its residents, Marianna, which boosters decades ago christened "The City Beautiful," has become best known as "Crack City"—the hometown of the infamous Chambers brothers. Many Mariannans report that when they travel they are routinely asked about the case and whether they know the Chambers family. "Our problems are no better or worse than elsewhere," says Sheriff Bobby May, Jr. "But all the attention we get sure makes it seem like things here are worse. A book like yours," he adds, "is another weight on a drowning man."

Chief Birchler, who to Sheriff May's chagrin slurped more than his share of the credit for exposing the Marianna-Detroit connection, complains that the city fathers would rather sweep the problem under the rug than clean it up. "We're not the crack capital of Arkansas," Birchler says. "We just happen to be doing something about it." Birchler says some city officials warned him to keep his mouth shut. "I've been getting pressured not to talk to you." (The local newspaper editor at the time was also instructed by her publisher not to "sensationalize" the case.)

Crime is also big business for Lee County. Its second largest employer, after the schools, is a state prison at Brickeys, a crossroads in the county's northeastern portion. The five-hundred-bed facility opened in 1992. It employs 175 people with an annual payroll of three million dollars. Though Marianna has attracted other industry in recent years, including a hair-care products plant and a door manufacturer, it is the prison that is seen as the primary hope for economic growth, what with the "multiplier effect," as the county administrator puts it, of nearby service stations, mobile home parks, and motels and restaurants serving the inmates' visitors. When a county is as poor as Lee—its per capita income in

1990 was $6,387, the lowest in the state—there is little room for discussion of the morality and politics of the nationwide prison expansion boom and the ever-rising prison population.[1] "People are thrilled," County Judge Kenneth Hunter said when the county learned of its successful bid. "It's going to cause a completely different outlook on life here."

Marianna and Lee County lean heavily on government transfer payments—"a first-of-the-month town," says a service station operator whose business slumps markedly toward the end of every month. "Once a month they love me," says a rural letter carrier. "Nobody goes anywhere on the day the checks are supposed to come. Everyone's waiting around the mailbox for their AFDC [Aid to Families with Dependent Children] and food stamps and Social Security."

For many there is nowhere to go anyway. The storied and fertile cotton fields of the Delta that once provided livelihoods today offer few jobs. Family farms have become corporate farms. Corporate farms, owned largely by absentee investors, have become ever more mechanized and less dependent on labor. In the fall of 1988, at the time Billy Joe and his brothers were convicted, more than 20 percent of Lee County's workforce was unemployed. In all of Arkansas, only in neighboring St. Francis County was a higher percentage of people without work.

As the jobs disappeared, so have the people. Lee County lost more people in the last fifty years than it has remaining. Between 1980 and 1990 alone, one of every four people who lived in the county moved away. "Sometimes it looks like it's going to be, 'Last person turn out the lights,' " says a local official from nearby Helena, in Phillips County.

If the lights are to remain on, the Delta must attract secure,

---

[1] More prisons have not made for safer streets. Despite the fact that the United States incarcerates a higher percentage of its citizens than does any other country, the rates of murder, violent crime, and drug-related crime persist at record levels.

skilled jobs for its residents. (Of the few jobs available, many pay so little that full-time workers qualify for food stamps.) To do so requires an educated workforce. But to the generations of white farmers who ruled the county, education was a dirty word: it spoiled good field hands. And there is the rub: much of the present workforce is uneducated because there are few jobs, and there are few jobs because the workforce is uneducated.

Most people in the county know that the schools must be improved if the county is to prosper. There are two major barriers: a tax base insufficient to improve the public schools; and the all-white private school, Lee Academy, which drains the public system of valuable resources. "We have a racial tug-of-war going on with the Jim Crow academy," says Charles Robinson, the principal of the public Lee Senior High. "I call it a Bedford Forrest institution." Nathan Bedford Forrest (for whom neighboring Forrest City was named) was a founder of the Ku Klux Klan.

Jim Crow, of course, is long buried. But as the dual school systems suggest, in place of official racism stands de facto segregation. Most governmental and quasi-governmental institutions are still viewed as the territory of whites. Every Fourth of July the chamber of commerce sponsors a block party downtown. The chamber always hires a country-and-western band, and the audience is nearly all white. The city and county maintain a local historical museum, but the exhibits are largely devoid of black contributions. There is no mention, in either the museum or in a companion history book, published in 1986, of the defining moment in contemporary Lee County life: the economic and school boycotts of the early 1970s. And the Rotary Club, which in Marianna, as in many small towns, is composed of the town's movers and shakers, is virtually all white. (In the late 1980s, the Rotarians recruited two black men who had recently moved to town for professional reasons. None of the county's homegrown black leaders, including State Senator Bill Lewellen and Circuit Judge Olly Neal, who helped found the Lee County Cooperative Clinic, has yet been invited to join.)

White leaders insist that the races peaceably coexist, and on the surface, at least, they appear to be correct. Robert Shearon, the genial editor of the weekly *Courier-Index* (and a past president of both the chamber of commerce and the Rotary Club), wrote in his column that living in Marianna compares favorably to life in Mayberry, the idyllic hometown of television's Andy Griffith. For one thing, Shearon wrote, "the races get along in Marianna better than anyplace I've ever lived." "Marianna is just a friendly small town, and a neat place to live. It's not Mayberry," he concluded, "but it's closer than some might think."

Shearon's weekly version of Marianna is as realistic a portrait of a small town as was Mayberry. There is the Yard of the Week, the report on the guest speaker at the Monday Rotary Club luncheon, the roundup of the public and private schools' sporting news, the social news ("Mr. and Mrs. John Burchardt of Tallulah, La. were the weekend guests in the home of Mrs. Owen Dell Moore . . ."), the shots of the biggest fish and the biggest cucumber and the first deer of the season; the innumerable grip-and-grin photos of the mayor with some worthy citizen.

In Shearon's Marianna, there is no human wreckage. Nobody goes hungry, or without adequate health care or housing or education or transportation. Shearon's ability to ignore the county's crushing problems could perhaps be dismissed as journalistic Babbittry if it didn't perpetuate matters and if it wasn't shared by his fellow civic leaders. It was Sherry Benson, the executive director of the chamber of commerce, who could not understand why so many young black men flocked to Detroit. "It's here for them if they want to find it," she said in 1989.

A year earlier Congress had certified the Delta as the poorest region in America. It created a commission, the Lower Mississippi Delta Development Commission, to devise a ten-year economic plan to fight the region's staggering poverty. Its chairman was then-governor Bill Clinton of Arkansas. In its initial report, published in 1989, the commission noted that 21 percent of Delta residents live in poverty, as compared to 12 percent nationally.

And more than half the blacks in the region have incomes below the national poverty level.

Behind the statistics lies the burden of Delta history. "The Delta's economic, social and cultural structure of life has often reinforced tensions between ethnic groups and worsened the economic subjugation of African-Americans," the report stated. The commission's final report, released in May of 1990, offered more than four hundred recommendations, many of them sound, but only a few of which even hinted at restructuring the region's economy. "Band-Aids for a gaping wound," wrote one critic.

The Delta Commission report was a start. It recognized, at least implicitly, that life in the Delta has always been based on inequality. And it recognized that the political and economic equation must change if the poverty cycle is to be broken. It acknowledged that government, too long neglectful, must play a key role. Government can create economic opportunities for disenfranchised, poorly educated young blacks—those who remain afflicted by the stubborn consequences of historical segregation and inequality. Congress can enact a fair minimum-wage standard and national public works program; it can revive the right of workers to organize and join labor unions; it can pass federal mandates for minority contracts; it can ensure compensation to towns when industrial employers desert them; it can pressure private, segregated academies, through tax reform and other means, to close their doors.

As important as federal money to saving ravaged counties like Lee are self-help initiatives. Poor people must organize, take power over their own fate, as they did around the issue of health care in the late 1960s and early 1970s, when they established the Lee County Cooperative Clinic.

As for crime, until there are more attractive and practical options for young people mired in urban and rural ghettos, until their life prospects amount to more than serving or cleaning up after other people, it takes little reflection to see that selling drugs and gang-banging will continue to be rational career choices.

*　*　*

His years in prison have left Billy Joe Chambers with plenty of time for reflection. He thinks of his twin, Little Joe, who died in 1986, on Easter Sunday, trying to outrace the train to a crossing. Billy feels cursed, unduly persecuted. "They just blowed this case up," he says. "Everybody in the streets was dealing." He sat there in his prison khakis, his hair cropped to within a quarter inch of his scalp, a man whose world had been reduced to a six-by-eight cubicle in a barrackslike dormitory. He and his brothers had been perhaps Detroit's most successful entrepreneurs of the eighties, making the automotive companies look like flimsy, if legal, endeavors, and now he was earning all of five dollars a month in the kitchen of a federal prison. His financial decisions are simple: what magazines to subscribe to, what to buy through the prison commissary. He'd already run through a lifetime's supply of regrets and dreams. There are those rumors of cash buried somewhere in the fields of Lee County, money he could avail himself of, if he was lucky, in 2015. He would be fifty-three years old.

ACKNOWLEDGMENTS

The substantive reporting for this book began as I suspect few do: over lunch with a source who was on the lam and dressed in drag. It was late April of 1989. I had been trying for weeks to make contact with Billy Joe and Larry, who were incarcerated in federal prison at Milan, Michigan. Letters went unanswered, as did messages left with relatives and friends. I had spent ten days in Detroit, poring over the voluminous court record, interviewing cops and federal agents, neighborhood activists, government and defense lawyers. I was filling notebooks like a diarist, but I had made no inroads with the defendants themselves. One Saturday morning at seven the phone rang.

Hushed tones: "You wanna meet the government's star witness?"

It was Terry Colbert, calling from a phone booth downtown. I was startled to hear from him. I hadn't tried to find him; I'd heard, in fact, that he was on the run from the DEA. (Terry had just recanted his trial testimony in a letter to the judge.) Terry told me Billy had given him my phone number. We arranged to meet at the Arby's restaurant near the federal courthouse.

An hour past the appointed meeting time. No sign of Terry. Two hours. It's now late on a rainy and raw Saturday afternoon. Arby's, like the rest of downtown Detroit, is all but deserted. Two young women enter, eye me. One walks out. She returns a minute later with an odd-looking third. It's Terry, wearing a woman's wig and overcoat.

"Feds lookin' for me," he mumbles, extending his hand. "Gotta keep it *low.*"

The interview yielded scant information, but subsequent conversations with Terry were more revealing. Most important, the meeting opened the door to Billy and his brothers. For that I thank Terry Colbert.

This book obviously could not have been written without the cooperation of Billy Joe Chambers. For five years, we met repeatedly in jails and prisons all over the central United States. We spoke countless times on the telephone. He provided introductions to dozens of people, most of whom—even if I had been able to find them on my own—would otherwise have been unreceptive to a stranger's queries. Billy trusted me to tell his story accurately and honestly; I have tried to do so.

Larry Chambers, whom I also interviewed extensively, and who is a prolific correspondent, was vital to my reporting. Willie Chambers was very helpful, as were many of the brothers' co-defendants and their families. I am indebted to them all.

Among the many others to whom I am grateful for help:

In Marianna: Carrie Baker, Jenny Ann Boyer, Becca Daggett, Susan Daggett, Helen Funk, Romia Hall, Pinky Hill, Hope Howard, Adrienne Lewellen, Doris Lewellen, Roy Lewellen III, Earnestein McLilly, Harold Meins, Olly Neal, Wilbur Peer, Robert Shearon and the staff of the *Courier-Index,* Derwin Sims, Grif Stockley, Pat Zachary.

Elsewhere in Arkansas: Earl Anthes, Diana Blair, Becky Haynie, Ken Hubbell, Jan Meins, Gordon Morgan, Jay Salvest, Marvin Schwartz, Jim Youngdahl.

In Detroit: Ron Alpern, Gary Baumgarten, George Best, Rob Brinkman, Beatrice Buck, Bill Bufalino, Jr., Zev Chafets, John Cichowicz, Bill Coonce, Dick Crock, Bob DeFauw, Brian Dickerson, Victor Hall, Allan Lengel, Paul Lindsay, Carole McCabe, John Minock, Lillie Richards, Tricia Serju, Carl Taylor.

Special thanks to Bill Lewellen in Marianna, for teaching me about catfish and courage, and Dave Riddle in Detroit, for leaving the light on.

Thank you to David Hirshey, who assigned me to write about the Chambers brothers for *Esquire;* to Eric Bates and Bob Hall at *Southern Exposure;* and to the Dick Goldensohn Fund, which bankrolled an extended visit to Marianna.

I thank the librarians and archivists who assisted me at the following institutions:

Special Collections Department of the Riley-Hickingbotham Library, Ouachita Baptist University, Arkadelphia, Arkansas.

Arkansas Archives, University of Central Arkansas, Conway.

Special Collections Division of Mullins Library, University of Arkansas at Fayetteville.

Arkansas History Commission, Little Rock.

Marianna–Lee County Museum, Marianna.

The Martin Luther King, Jr., Center for Nonviolent Social Change, Atlanta.

Harry S. Truman Presidential Library, Independence, Missouri.

Mississippi Valley Collection, Memphis State University, Memphis.

Bentley Historical Library, University of Michigan, Ann Arbor.

Burton Historical Collection, Detroit Public Library, Detroit.

Walter Reuther Labor and Urban Archives, Wayne State University, Detroit.

I thank the wardens and their executive assistants who assisted me at the following institutions: Wayne County Jail, Detroit; Ryan Road Correctional Facility, Detroit; federal correctional institutions at Milan, Michigan, El Reno, Oklahoma, and Talladega, Alabama; U.S. penitentiaries at Atlanta, Leavenworth, Kansas, and Terre Haute, Indiana; Federal Medical Center, Lexington, Kentucky; CCA West Tennessee Detention Facility, Mason, Tennessee; Stiles Unit, Texas Department of Corrections, Beaumont, Texas.

I am indebted to my agent, Geri Thoma, for her critical intelligence, enduring grace and warmth, and assistance far beyond the call of duty.

I thank Anton Mueller, my editor at Atlantic Monthly Press, who inherited the manuscript late in life and generously endowed it with his keen sense of what the book needed, and what it did not.

I thank those who weathered early drafts of the manuscript, perceptive critics and great Americans all: Dave Denison, Bob Elder, Jody Jenkins, and Monica Reeves. Monica, a skilled editor in her own right, was of particular help in smoothing some rough spots.

I am grateful to many teachers, formal and informal: Peter Decker, for waiting until the cows came home to leave the classroom; Bob Caro, for steady encouragement; Bill Ferris, for helpful discussions in the early stages of research; Gary Grant, Maurine Hedgepeth, Nat Wilkins, and the late Lucy Taylor, for fundamental lessons in perseverance. Thanks, too, to David Rosenthal, for the initial vote of confidence.

Thanks to relations and friends: Teri Havens propped me up and talked me down, more than once; Cliff Olofson, Lou Dubose, Stefan Wanstrom, Jim Cullen, and all the ships in the *Texas Observer* sea were constant companions; and Jim Magnuson, whose lunchtime haunts may have wavered, but not his enthusiasm for this project.

My appreciation also to Phil Banks, Mike Binstein, Ken Case, Jodie Chase, Tom Curtis, John Dugan, Allan Freedman, Suzanne Hershey, Mark Kyle, Dick Lavine, Rich Lee, Rick Levy, Christina

Lowery, Linda Rocawich, Sandra Rose, John Scibal, Mort Williams, and the elusive and estimable Gilmer P. Woods.

My deepest gratitude goes to Charlotte Katzin. If I have never told her how much her support and encouragement have meant to me, I do so now.

NOTES

Abbreviations

AD	*Arkansas Democrat*
AG	*Arkansas Gazette*
AHQ	*Arkansas Historical Quarterly*
C-I	*(Marianna, Ark.) Courier-Index*
DFP	*Detroit Free Press*
DN	*Detroit News*
DPD	Detroit Police Department
FGJT	Federal grand jury transcripts
MCA	*Memphis Commercial Appeal*
NYT	*New York Times*
USAvLC	*USA v. Larry Chambers et al.*, federal trial transcript No. 88-80250, U.S. District Court, Eastern District of Michigan, Southern Division
WSJ	*Wall Street Journal*

INTRODUCTION HOMECOMING

Sources

Newspaper Articles

"Poverty and Prejudice," *AD*, June 19–27, 1988.
"Crack: So Cheap, So Costly," *DFP*, Nov. 15, 1987.

Isabel Wilkerson, "Detroit Crack Empire Showed All Earmarks of Big Business," *NYT,* Dec. 18, 1988.

Document
"Drug Abuse Problems, Programs, and Policy Recommendations for Metropolitan Detroit," a report of the Skillman Foundation, Detroit, Nov. 1991.

Interviews
Billy Joe Chambers, Larry Chambers, Willie Lee Chambers, Clifton Collier, Keith Crawford, Lillie Perry, Charles Robinson, Derwin Sims.

Notes
Limousine scene: Based on interviews with most of those inside the Cadillacs, including Billy Joe, Larry, and Willie Lee Chambers, as well as with many observers.

"Wads in both pockets": Crawford.

"Throwing money out the windows!": Perry, Otis's ninth-grade English teacher.

Admitted to treatment clinics: *DFP,* Nov. 15, 1987. **Emergency-room admissions:** *DFP,* undated clipping, 1988. **Cocaine-related deaths:** *DFP,* undated clipping. **Detroit's murder rate:** "Drug Abuse Problems." **Half the murder victims:** *DFP,* undated clipping.

The New York Times: NYT, Dec. 18, 1988.

Any legal privately held business: According to *Michigan Business* magazine for May 1988 (pp. 38–39), the state's largest private firm, based in Lansing, grossed ninety-one million dollars in 1987. The second largest firm, in Birmingham, grossed forty-five million dollars that year. No Detroit company approached the Chambers brothers' fifty-five million dollars, a figure reached by multiplying average sales of nearly thirty thousand a week at each of thirty-five houses.

Crushing poverty in Arkansas: For a fine overview of the county's and the region's social and economic problems, see *AD,* June 19–27, 1988.

"The certainty of nothing": Collier.

1 LAND OF COTTON

Sources

Books
Arsenault, *Wild Ass of the Ozarks;* Chapman, ed., *Black Voices;* McMillen, *Dark Journey;* Sandford, *Poverty in the Land of Opportunity;* Sherrill, *Gothic Politics in the Deep South.*

Newspaper Articles

"Study Ordered On Rights Claim," *AG*, Oct. 20, 1963.

"Segregationists Defend 'Rides,' " *Christian Science Monitor*, May 28, 1962.

"Faubus Speaks to Large Crowd Here," *C-I*, July 19, 1962; Aug. 2, 1962.

Documents

Divorce Decree, No. E-76-36, Chancery Court of Lee County (Ark.), Oct. 19, 1976.

Faubus Papers, Special Collections Division, Mullins Library, University of Arkansas, Fayetteville.

Last Will and Testament of Fritz Schreiber and Order Admitting Will to Probate, No. P-76-47, Lee County (Ark.) Probate Court, July 20, 1976.

Marianna Centennial, Lee County, Ark., 1970, in the Lee County Library.

Interviews

A. J. Atkins, Pat Audirsch, Barney L. Buford, Edward Buford, Billy Joe Chambers, Curtis Chambers, Danny Chambers, Francis Chambers, John L. Chambers, Willie Lee Chambers, Anita Coleman, L. E. Coleman, Lorraine Jones, Sterling King, Jr., Robert May, Jr., Wilbur Peer, Geneva Robinson, Leonard Sims, C. Calvin Smith, Louise Chambers Stewart.

Notes

Porch scene: Described to the author by Billy Joe Chambers.

Curtis's father: Curtis Chambers and his siblings, John L. Chambers and Louise Chambers Stewart.

Blacks constituted: U.S. Bureau of the Census, *Characteristics of the Population: Arkansas,* Washington, D.C., 1960.

"Kill a mule": Quoted in William R. Ferris, "Black Folklore from the Mississippi Delta" (Ph.D. diss., University of Pennsylvania, 1969), p. 68, and cited in McMillen, p. 224.

"Whose nigger are you?": McMillen, p. 205.

Farmers obtained driver's licenses: Audirsch, director of the Lee County Literacy Council.

"Every time you educate": Davis made the remark during his 1904 campaign for reelection, a campaign that amounted to a crusade against black education. Quoted in Arsenault, p. 205.

A sea of friendly faces: The scene is drawn from the *C-I*, July 19, 1962, and from a tape recording of Faubus's speech filed with the Faubus Papers.

Faubus had deftly used: For the single best explanation of Faubus's political career, see Sherrill, pp. 79–124.

"It's two more hands": "The Young Ones," Chapman, pp. 413–14.

"The whole campus would freeze": Biographical information on Anna Strong comes from "Anna Strong Was Moving Force in Marianna Education

System," *Marianna Centennial*. Additional information comes from interviews with former students Smith, Robinson, and King.

Faubus was renominated: *C-I,* Aug. 2, 1962.

A German man showed up: Barney L. Buford, Billy Joe Chambers, Francis Chambers, Sims. **He actually had emigrated:** Last Will and Testament.

"Like a show horse": One of Mrs. Chambers's closest friends, who asked that her name not be used. **"That hot-girl twitch":** Anita Coleman.

Schreiber's relationship with Hazel Chambers: Described by six individuals, none of whom would speak for attribution.

A small café on their land: Atkins, Barney L. Buford, Curtis Chambers, Sims.

"My little boy": Billy Joe Chambers.

"She sold herself": The source refused to be named. His story was confirmed by three others, all of whom were also "in a position to know" and insisted on anonymity.

According to other Mt. Perion members: Again, these sources, some of whom were also privy to Mrs. Chambers's relationship with Schreiber, spoke on condition that they not be identified.

"Doing what I need to do": Hazel frequently confided in this person, who refused to be named.

"Mr. Curt whipped her": The front-yard brawls were "commonplace," said another former bus rider who works in the Lee County school system.

The nation's sixth poorest county: Sandford, p. 160.

He was awarded the Purple Heart: "It Happened in Lee County 20 Years Ago," *C-I,* June 27, 1991.

His parents were divorced: In her petition (Divorce Decree No. E-76-36), Hazel Chambers wrote that her husband had "rendered indignities . . . that have resulted in a settled hate, estrangement, and alienation."

Curtis moved off the land: Curtis Chambers, John L. Chambers. **Amounted to less than $6,500:** Order Admitting Will to Probate.

Friday evening "entertainments": Edward Buford, Billy Joe Chambers, Willie Lee Chambers, Wilbur Peer.

2 WASHING WINDOWS IN A BLIZZARD

Sources

Books

Babson, *Working Detroit;* Darden et al., *Detroit;* Lacey, *Ford;* Lemann, *The Promised Land;* Meier and Rudwick, *Black Detroit and the Rise of the UAW;* Woodford and Woodford, *All Our Yesterdays.*

Newspaper Articles

"Kettering High Works to Get Graduates Jobs," *DN,* Mar. 20, 1979; "Kennedy Briefed on City's Plight," *DN,* Nov. 21, 1983.

"Detroit to Lay Off 348 Employees," *NYT,* Dec. 28, 1978; "Detroiters Ponder Life After Chrysler," *NYT,* Oct. 14, 1979.

Magazine Article
Bill Kellerman, "The Angel of Detroit," *Sojourner's,* Oct. 1989.

Document
FGJT, No. 87-4-59, U.S. District Court, Eastern District of Michigan, Southern Division.

Interviews
Diana Alexander, Alvin Chambers, Billy Joe Chambers, Danny Chambers, Larry Chambers, Willie Lee Chambers, Willie Mae Colbert, Anita Coleman, Cynthia Coleman, Wagie Farris, Jerry Gant, William Hamilton, Wally Harkins, Grace Harris, Roy Leinweber, Henry R. McKee, Junior Smith.

Notes

The world's largest manufacturing complex: Woodford and Woodford, p. 287. For more on Ford and his legacy see especially Lacey, *Ford.*
"I'm goin' to Detroit": Cited in Meier and Rudwick, p. 5.
To "do for teenagers": Lemann, p. 151.
A "weird urban stalagmite": *Sojourners,* Oct. 1989.
The sign beamed a healthy glow: Harris, a librarian at *Automotive News* in Detroit.
Forty-two auto-related plants would be shuttered: Babson, p. 211.
The Goodyear scoreboard was so anemic: Leinweber, an official with Gannett Outdoor, Inc., in Detroit.
He was laying off 348 workers: *NYT,* Dec. 28, 1978. **Fully a third of its local workforce:** *NYT,* Oct. 14, 1979. **More than *half* the city's blacks:** *DN,* Mar. 20, 1979. **Before the decade was over:** Darden, p. 27.
The school's dropout rate: The figures were furnished by McKee, the current Kettering principal.
The company had replaced: Babson, p. 228.
"A crisis unparalleled": *DN,* Nov. 21, 1983.
The real estate market: The figures are cited in Darden, p. 183.
"Selling weed for him": FGJT, No. 87-4-59, Terry Colbert, Dec. 17, 1987, p. 5.

3 HEAVEN DUST

Sources

Books
Berquist, Sanchez, and Penaranda, *Violence in Colombia;* Byck, ed., *Cocaine Papers* by Sigmund Freud; Lewis Cole, *Never Too Young to Die;* Dinges, *Our Man in Panama;* Eddy with Sabogal and Walden, *The Cocaine Wars;* Gugliotta

and Leen, *Kings of Cocaine;* Inciardi, *The War on Drugs* and *The War on Drugs II;* Kahn, *The Big Drink;* Morgan, *Drugs in America;* Musto, *The American Disease;* Nicholl, *The Fruit Palace;* Sabbag, *Snowblind;* Shannon, *Desperados;* Woodford and Woodford, *All Our Yesterdays.*

Newspaper Article
"Caribbean Exodus: U.S. Is Constant Magnet," *NYT,* May 6, 1992.

Magazine Articles
Michael Massing, "Crack's Destructive Sprint Across America," *New York Times Magazine,* Oct. 1, 1989.

Gordon Witkin, "The Men Who Created Crack," *U.S. News & World Report,* Aug. 19, 1991.

Interviews
Arthur Derrick, James A. Inciardi.

Notes

The void was filled: Details of the cartel's origins come primarily from Gugliotta and Leen, pp. 18, 84–90; Shannon, pp. 98–106.

Almost a billion dollars: Inciardi, *The War on Drugs,* p. 195. **"Latin America's only successful multinational":** Dinges, p. 124. **"To buy vacuum cleaners":** Shannon, p. 25.

Some two hundred exotic animals: Gugliotta and Leen, p. 112.

Thoroughly engaged in the business: See, for example, Dinges on Manuel Noriega.

"A form of cultural genocide": Shannon, p. 73, quoting from testimony before the U.S. Senate Subcommittee on Foreign Assistance, May 9, 1978. **"Stab a piece of mercury":** Shannon, p. 72.

The Colombian marijuana fields: Nicholl, pp. 6–7. **Colombia supplied 75 percent:** Shannon, p. 73, citing a 1979 federal government study.

"I prefer a life": Quoted in Eddy, Sabogal, and Walden, p. 39.

Heartened by what he read: The cover of the first article on cocaine that the *Detroit Therapeutic Gazette* published, in September 1880, is reprinted in Byck, p. 14. In *The Life and Work of Sigmund Freud,* excerpted in the same volume, Ernest Jones, M.D., writes that Freud's interest in cocaine was prompted by reading articles in the *Detroit Therapeutic Gazette* of its use for the purpose of curing morphine addiction (Byck, p. 6). **Parke, Davis & Company:** For a brief history of the company's origins, see Woodford and Woodford, p. 206. **"An exceptionally enthusiastic producer":** Musto, p. 7. **"To say that I am surprised":** Quoted by David F. Musto, M.D., in Chapter 23, "Sherlock Holmes and Sigmund Freud," of Byck, p. 359. **A "magical drug":** quoted by Ernest Jones, M.D., in Byck, p. 7, from an unpublished letter Freud wrote to his fiancée on May 25, 1884. **"Damage to the heart":** In a paper Freud wrote in 1887, reprinted in Byck, pp. 171–76, he defended cocaine against its critics, saying it was not addictive but that in "long continued use" damage to vital organs "may be expected."

An 1885 pitch to doctors: The promotional brochure, "Coca Erythroxylon and Its Derivatives," was compiled by the Scientific Department of Parke, Davis. It is excerpted in Byck, pp. 127–50. The quotation is on p. 128.

"Heaven dust": Morgan, p. 92. **"In syrups, tonics, liqueurs":** Sabbag, p. 65. **An entrepreneurial chemist:** Kahn, pp. 55–56. **"Not only a delicious . . . beverage":** Inciardi, *The War on Drugs,* p. 8.

"Undiluted fraud": Cited ibid., p. 13. **Addicts were plentiful:** Musto, p. 5, and see p. 253*n*13 for an explanation of the derivation of this figure.

"Many of the horrible crimes": The *Tribune* story, of June 21, 1903, is cited in Musto, p. 254*n*15.

A black man reportedly under the influence: *NYT,* Dec. 6, 1907, cited in Morgan, p. 93. **"Ordinary shootin' ":** *Everybody's Magazine,* quoted in Morgan, p. 93.

Harrison Anti-Narcotic Act: For an informed discussion of the act and the events and legislation preceding it, see especially Chapters 1–3 of Musto. **A 1939 Treasury Department report:** Cited in Inciardi, *The War on Drugs,* pp. 18–19.

"Like high-quality caviar": Sabbag, p. 59.

The World Bank: Interview with Inciardi.

Chile's flyspeck cocaine trade: Gugliotta and Leen, p. 22.

Colombian health officials counted: Figure cited in Shannon, p. 147, from a U.S. State Department report, "International Narcotics Control Strategy, 1985."

Lehder was born: Eddy, Sabogal, and Walden, Chapter 10; Shannon, pp. 100–101; Gugliotta and Leen, pp. 28–29.

In just seven flights: Dinges, p. 127.

Limit the exports to Colombia: Gugliotta and Leen, pp. 119–28. **The cartel began shipping:** *U.S. News & World Report,* Aug. 19, 1991.

According to researchers: Ibid. **"A local cop":** Ibid.

Lehder bought virtually every asset: Gugliotta and Leen, p. 44. **"When the world tastes this":** *U.S. News & World Report,* Aug. 19, 1991.

A 1977 study: Cited in Inciardi, *The War on Drugs II,* p. 109.

An exodus greater: *NYT,* May 6, 1992.

Base rock spread rampantly: Interview with Inciardi.

The cost of a kilo: Derrick. These figures were corroborated by Melvin Turner, undersheriff of Wayne County. **High school seniors would try the drug:** Cole, p. 65.

4 "BJ, WHY DON'T YOU START SELLING CRACK?"

Sources

Interviews

Diana Alexander, Edna Alexander, Celeste Appleby, John Autrey, Charles Bailey, Jimmy Bohn, Wanda Booker, Alvin Chambers, Billy Joe Chambers, Willie Lee Chambers, Cynthia Coleman, Elayne Coleman, Perry Coleman, Willie

Driscoll, Barbara Foster, Jerry Gant, Devona Hunter, Gale E. Nicholas, Lillie Richards.

Notes

"Allowing marijuana possession": Cited in Affidavit in Support of Seizure Warrant, July 24, 1990, in *USA v. PC Palace, Inc.,* U.S. District Court, Eastern District of Michigan, Southern Division, Case No. 90–CR–72149. **Perry was urging Billy:** Billy Joe Chambers.

Willie was arrested: As noted in the DPD records of Willie Lee Chambers and Jerry Gant; in the author's possession.

Silver four-door Saab 900: The transaction record was obtained by the Criminal Investigation Division of the IRS and cited in *USAvLC,* p. 1964.

Detroit Receiving Hospital: Billy Joe's emergency room record for Aug. 15, 1984; in the author's possession.

"Watch our butts": The police description of the Aug. 23, 1984, raid on Gray Street is drawn from the DPD Investigator's Report and Investigator's Report Supplement, the search warrant for the premises, and the DPD Preliminary Complaint Record, all Aug. 23, 1984.

Flipped him the keys: Biographical information on Elayne Coleman and her pre-raid activities of Sept. 3, 1984, are drawn from interviews with her and Richards and from the Presentence Report, Dec. 6, 1988, prepared by U.S. Probation Officer Timothy Kozak.

The time of Elayne's arrest: Autrey's estimate is included in his testimony at the Preliminary Examination of Sept. 11, 1984, in the Thirty-sixth District Court for the City of Detroit, p. 22: "It was approximately five to ten minutes before we came right back and executed it." **He found an additional one hundred and thirty dollars:** Autrey noted in the DPD Preliminary Complaint Record that he "confiscated . . . $130.00 of Narcotic proceeds of which none was the pre-recorded secret service funds."

Elayne was charged with two counts: *State of Michigan v. Elayne Coleman, Billy Joe Chambers, Alvin Jerome Chambers, Danny Carl Chambers,* No. 84-64187, Thirty-sixth District Court, City of Detroit.

5 COOL HAND LARRY

Sources

Book
Williams et al., *A Documentary History of Arkansas.*

Newspaper Articles
Camden (Ark.) News, January 3, 5, 1970.

Documents
Larry Chambers, criminal case files in Lee County Circuit Court, Marianna, Arkansas.

Interviews

Edward Buford, Billy Joe Chambers, Larry Chambers, Romia Hall, Peggy Stiles.

Notes

Larry was sentenced: *Camden News,* January 3, 5, 1970.

"An isolated remnant": Quoted in Williams, p. 254. **"The inmate would be taken":** Quoted ibid., p. 255.

"I've been classified": Letter filed at Lee County Circuit Court, Jan. 31, 1980.

"May try to harm me": Letter filed at Lee County Circuit Court, Apr. 22, 1980.

6 MOVING LIKE LIGHTNING

Sources

Documents

DEA Form 6, Interview of Dennis Fayson, Dec. 30, 1987, prepared Jan. 3, 1988.

FGJT, No. 87-4-59, U.S. District Court, Eastern District of Michigan, Southern Division.

State of Michigan v. One JetStar N420G et al., No. 88-803290, Wayne County Circuit Court.

Interviews

Tony Alexander, Billy Joe Chambers, Larry Chambers, Perry Coleman, Arthur Derrick, Jerry Gant, Melvin Turner, Von Williams.

Notes

"Art wants to get married": *State of Michigan v. One JetStar N420G et al.,* deposition of Marvin Knecht, Aug. 17, 1988, p. 11.

James was putting himself through school: FGJT, No. 87-4-59, James Lumpkin, Nov. 3, 1987, p. 24.

7 MARLOW'S ONE-STOP

Sources

Documents

DEA Form 6, interview of Dennis Fayson, Dec. 30, 1987.

FGJT, No. 87-4-59, U.S. District Court, Eastern District of Michigan, Southern Division.

USAvLC, beginning Sept. 16, 1988.

Interviews

Diana Alexander, Tony Alexander, Mark Birchler, Lawrence J. Bunting, Billy Joe Chambers, Danny Chambers, Francis Farris Chambers, Larry Chambers, Willie Lee Chambers, Anita Coleman, Cindy Davis, Wagie Farris, Dennis Fayson, David Havard, Devona Hunter, Robert May, Jr., Patricia Middleton, Lillie Perry, Ronald Scott, Michael (Pork Chop) Williams.

Notes

"ADDICTIVE NEW 'CRACK' COCAINE": *DN*, Jan. 5, 1986.

"I knew he was lying": *USAvLC*, pp. 337–38.

"We would like to hire your services": *USAvLC*, p. 339.

Havard had learned general maintenance skills: Biographical material is drawn from interviews with Havard.

Pat Middleton was born in Indiana: Biographical material is drawn from interviews with Middleton.

"Arrange for David to have an accident": *USAvLC*, pp. 121–22.

"I was white and chunky": Middleton. "Over on Helen and Canton": *USAvLC*, p. 126.

"Clean" of crack: Larry Chambers.

An unqualified success: Larry Chambers provided the figures.

"It was like a merry-go-round": *USAvLC*, p. 118. He would send his driver in: Middleton.

He established these rates: DEA Form 6, interview with Dennis Fayson. "For three dime bags": Havard. "Everything I could": Ibid.

Danny would often linger: Danny Chambers, Larry Chambers, and Havard.

"When a crackhead comes to you": DEA Form 6, interview with Dennis Fayson.

The customer was asked: Michael Williams. Havard tacked up a sign: *USAvLC*, p. 358.

"Like he was J. Edgar Hoover": Fayson.

"Looked like a schoolhouse": Havard.

"I bought trunk loads of food": Middleton.

"In-house first!": Ibid.

"Go on home": Ibid.

"Ass-kicking clothes": Havard.

"No one will ever sell soap for crack": *USAvLC*, pp. 111–12.

"His head was all busted": FGJT, No. 87-4-59, Terry Colbert, May 20, 1987, p. 44.

"Instead of killing her": Havard.

"You roll your sleeves up": Janice (Davis) Roberts is in the Federal Witness Protection Program. All direct quotations are drawn from grand jury and trial testimony.

"**Making their mama happy**": Francis Farris Chambers.

"**They're Hazel's sons**": The author heard this line or a variation of it spoken by Sheriff Bobby May, Jr., Wagie Farris, and two anonymous sources, one of whom is related to Hazel Chambers.

They happened upon a prostitute: The person who told the author this story requested anonymity, but it was substantially confirmed by Larry Chambers. He says, though, that he didn't "stuff" the money in her blouse; he "threw it at her."

"**He always kept me**": Interview with anonymous source.

"**Your son just got killed**": Details of Joe's death are from interviews with Hunter, Willie Lee Chambers, and Billy Joe Chambers.

"**They pasted him back together**": Coleman. **Larry and Billy bought new cars**: Testimony of Wayne Youngblood, sales manager of Bavarian Motor Village, in *USAvLC*.

"**The Chambers boys are back**": Ronald Scott, a classmate of Otis Chambers's.

Rare was the Lee Senior High student: Based on a wholly unscientific but sizable sampling of students, teachers, and administrators. **Marianna police estimated**: Birchler.

Many of those youngsters were brought forcibly: Birchler and newspaper stories.

8 "GOOD-BYE, DIXIE LAND"

Sources

Books

Apple and Keasler, *Lee County History;* Ashmore, *Arkansas;* Barnes, *Farmers in Rebellion;* Caro, *The Years of Lyndon Johnson: The Path to Power;* Conot, *American Odyssey;* Cortner, *A Mob Intent on Death;* Drake and Cayton, *Black Metropolis;* Goodwyn, *The Populist Moment;* Gregory, *American Exodus;* Heard, *A Two-Party South?;* Henri, *Black Migration;* Kester, *Revolt Among the Sharecroppers;* Key, *Southern Politics in State and Nation;* McCullough, *Truman;* Marks, *Farewell;* Rawick, *The American Slave: A Composite Autobiography;* Tucker, *Arkansas;* Williams, et al., *A Documentary History of Arkansas;* Woodward, *The Strange Career of Jim Crow.*

Newspaper Articles

"Reported Riot," *AD,* Sept. 28, 1891; "Marianna Today, with About 5,000 Inhabitants, Fully Awake," *AD,* Sept. 10, 1910; "Marianna," *AD,* Oct. 16, 1916.

"Desperate Fighting Between Whites and Negroes Occurs in Southern Section of Phillips," *AG,* Oct. 2, 1919; "Negroes Have Been Aroused by Propaganda," and "Federal Troops Have Situation Under Control," *AG,* Oct. 3,

1919; "Vicious Blacks Were Planning Great Uprising," *AG,* Oct. 4, 1919; "Thurmond Bids for Arkansas Democrats Aid," *AG,* Aug. 27, 1948.

"Arkansas State News: The Floods in the Valley," *Arkansas Mansion,* Apr. 19, 1884.

"Lured by Schools and Jobs, Negroes Flock North to Flee Racial Tension," *Atlanta Journal,* Aug. 15, 1956.

"Lee County Invites You," *C-I,* Apr. 17, 1941; "John L. Daggett Replies to Article Published in Batesville Daily Guard," *C-I,* Oct. 24, 1946; "Thurmond-Wright to Appear Here," *C-I,* Aug. 19, 1948; "City Receives National Publicity," *C-I,* Sept. 9, 1948; "About Marianna and Lee County," *C-I,* July 1, 1976 (bicentennial ed.).

"Blacks in Detroit," *DFP* reprint, Dec. 1980.

"A True Report of the Riot," *Lee County Courier,* Oct. 3, 1891; "A Word to Our Farmers," *Lee County Courier,* Oct. 10, 1891.

Magazine and Journal Articles

Willard B. Gatewood, Jr., "Arkansas Negroes in the 1890s: Documents," *AHQ* 33 (1974); William F. Holmes, "The Arkansas Cotton Pickers Strike of 1891 and the Demise of the Colored Farmers Alliance," *AHQ* 32 (summer 1973); Gail Murray, "Forty Years Ago: The Great Depression Comes to Arkansas," *AHQ* 33 (1974); C. Calvin Smith, "From 'Separate but Equal to Desegregation': The Changing Philosophy of L. C. Bates," *AHQ* 42 (1983).

"Blood in the Delta: The Elaine Race Riots of 1919," *Arkansas Times,* April 1983.

"Board Undertakes Negro Survey," *Detroiter,* July 16, 1923, p. 1.

Elaine Moon, "Paradise Valley," *Detroit Discovery,* May–June 1974, pp. 13–19.

"What Is the Arkansas Free Enterprise Assn?" *Free Enterpriser* (Little Rock, Ark.) Oct. 1950.

"Our Immigrant, the Negro," *Iron Trade Review,* Sept. 13, 1923.

"Drought: Field Report," *New Republic,* Feb. 25, 1931, pp. 40–41.

Walter F. White, "The Race Conflict in Arkansas," *Survey,* Dec. 13, 1919.

Dissertations

Moyers, "Arkansas Progressivism"; Rison, "Arkansas During the Great Depression."

Documents

Birth certificate of Hazel Chambers, May 31, 1931.

Marianna Centennial, Lee County, Ark., 1970, in the Lee County Library.

Urban League of Detroit, Papers, Carter G. Woodson Collection, Library of Congress, Washington, D.C.

Interviews

A. J. Atkins, Jenny Ann Boyer, Barney L. Buford, Curtis Chambers, Jesse Chambers, John L. Chambers, Clifton Collier, Joseph Cooper, Elijah Council,

Wagie Farris, Geneva Robinson, Leonard Sims, Queen Ester Smith, Louise Chambers Stewart.

Notes

A native of Macon: Birth certificate of Hazel Chambers. **Who came from Mississippi:** John L. Chambers and Louise Chambers Stewart. **"Little in advance of pauperism":** *Arkansas Mansion,* April 19, 1884. **Its population of eighteen thousand:** The county's population for 1990 was 14,500, according to the U.S. Bureau of the Census.

"Sweet potatoes grew": Tucker, p. 46. **"Hogs were just laying around"** . . . **"picking cotton off the stalk":** Henry "Happy Day" Green quoted in Rawick, vol. 9, pt. 3, pp. 98–99.

No "finer prospect": *C-I* of Apr. 17, 1941, reprinted the story from which this quote was extracted. It appeared originally in the first edition of the *Marianna Index,* published in 1874. **Blacks held considerable local political power:** Tucker, p. 44.

"Arkansas is destined": The *Freeman* dispatch of Jan. 5, 1889, was written by Bishop Henry M. Turner of the African Methodist Episcopal Church; it is quoted in *AHQ* 29 (1970), p. 296.

"The lands along the Nile": *AD,* Oct. 16, 1916. **Barely enough to cover the costs:** See Barnes, p. 52, for a table showing declining prices and the note on p. 199 for production costs.

"Our grand old country": *Lee County Courier,* Oct. 10, 1891.

"Most elaborate example of mass insurgency": Goodwyn, p. xvii.

"Before the black man could worry": Ibid., p. 121. **The Colored Alliance claimed a membership:** Goodwyn believes the figure is grossly inflated. He estimates the membership at around 250,000 (p. 120).

"They are in the ditch": quoted in Woodward, p. 61.

"Engender a race feeling": Most of the information regarding the strike is from *AHQ* 32 (summer 1973), pp. 107–19. Also useful was the *Lee County Courier,* Oct. 3, 10, 1891.

"A total failure": *(Houston) Daily Post,* Sept. 13, 1891; cited in *AHQ* 32 (summer 1973), p. 114.

"Dancing resumed": Description from the *Lee County Courier,* n.d., cited in *Marianna Centennial.*

Some only two weeks old: For further discussion of the hardships endured by sharecropping families during this period, see Kester, especially p. 47.

"Assumed a sanguinary aspect": *AD,* Sept. 28, 1891.

"Too much praise": *Lee County Courier,* Oct. 3, 1891; *Appeal-Avalanche* and *American Citizen* quotes from *AHQ* 32 (summer 1973), p. 117.

The legislature repealed the Civil Rights Act: For more on the formation of Jim Crow laws in Arkansas, see Moyers.

"To come in contact with such live wires": Quoted in *Marianna Centennial.* **"The people of the city":** *AD,* Sept. 10, 1910.

The sawmills whined: *C-I,* July 1, 1976.

"Boll weevil got half the crop": Quoted in Marks, p. 59; and see p. 58 for a map of the boll weevil's invasion. The floods destroyed: *C-I,* July 1, 1976.

"Come up to Detroit": The character, Alexander Kynance, appears in *Dodsworth,* by Sinclair Lewis (New York: Harcourt Brace, 1929; reprint, New York: New American Library, 1982, p. 24). The city's black population swelled: Henri, p. 69, puts the city's population increase for the decade at 36,240. In 1910, according to U.S. Census figures cited by the Urban League of Detroit in a 1917 report, there were 6,000 blacks living in Detroit.

White-owned newspapers: Drake and Cayton, p. 59.

"Turn a deaf ear": Editorial of Oct. 7, 1916, quoted ibid.

"Due consideration": Cortner, p. 32. "Like a hungry mule grabs fodder": Marks, p. 28. "Thrown into a crowd of Negroes": ibid.

More than 360,000 had served their country: Woodward, p. 114.

"The greatest period of interracial strife": Quoted ibid.

"DESPERATE FIGHTING": *AG,* Oct. 2–4, 1919.

It was officially announced: *Survey,* Dec. 13, 1919. "Like wild beasts": Quoted in an NAACP press release of Jan. 14, 1925, cited in Cortner, p. 30.

"No juryman could have voted": Holmes's opinion in *Moore v. Dempsey,* 261 U.S. 86 (1923), is included in Cortner. Forced to prepare: *Arkansas Times,* April 1983.

A three-room shotgun shack: Biographical information on Curtis Chambers's childhood is from interviews with Curtis and his siblings John L. Chambers, Jesse Chambers, and Louise Chambers Stewart and from lifelong La Grange residents Buford and Sims.

The price of cotton dropped: Tucker, p. 78.

One hundred and forty-three banks failed: Rison, p. 25. "From twenty percent to grand larceny": Leland Duvall, a writer for *AG,* quoted in Ashmore, p. 120.

Twenty-two qualified: *New Republic,* Feb. 25, 1931. "Would weaken the national character": Caro, p. 244. The Red Cross was feeding: *AHQ* 33 (1974), p. 299, and recollections of Atkins and Sims. "Actual starvation": Quoted in Rison, p. 26. A dollar a person: *AHQ* 33 (1974), p. 299.

"Thousands of colored farmers": Rison, p. 12.

Haywood ran out: Biographical information on Hazel Chambers's childhood is largely from interviews with Curtis Chambers, Cooper, and Atkins.

An endless cycle of field work: Description of daily chores is from interviews with Atkins, Curtis Chambers, Council, Farris, and Smith. Also useful was "Remember Back When," an essay by Zella Lee Mathews in Apple and Keasler, pp. 31–32.

"Nigger Row": Many recall those Saturday afternoons with fondness. Most helpful were Atkins, Boyer, and Robinson.

Hazel wanted to follow: Curtis Chambers.

"Two main reasons why": Quoted in the *WSJ* and reprinted in the *Atlanta Journal*, Aug. 15, 1956.

"Everyone writes back": Gregory, p. 27. **Any of the six other states:** Tucker, p. 82, and Williams, et al., p. 222, from an *AG* article of Oct. 25, 1955. **Almost twenty-five hundred people evacuated Lee County:** U.S. Bureau of the Census, 1950.

Swelled and swelled: *Detroit Discovery,* p. 13. **Two hundred thousand by 1943:** Conot, p. 483. **"Negro immigrants":** Urban League of Detroit, "Brief Outline of Housing Conditions Among the Negroes of Detroit Michigan," May 2, 1917.

"Filthy, smelly, teeming slum": *Detroiter,* July 16, 1923.

"Hot and heavy work": *Iron Trade Review,* Sept. 13, 1923, p. 733.

" 'Turn the corner, baby' ": Betty DeRamus, "Innocence and Vice on Hastings Street," *DFP* reprint, Dec. 1980.

The alarm was sounded: The Supreme Court, in *Smith v. Allwright,* wrote that "the great privilege of choosing his rulers may not be denied a man by the state because of his color." **"A private association":** For further description of the state's efforts to circumvent the ruling, see *AHQ* 42 (1983).

"Our first goal": Quoted in McCullough, p. 586.

"There's not enough troops": Quoted ibid., p. 667.

Support for the Dixiecrats: For more on the Dixiecrats, see Key, Chapter 15, and Heard, pp. 26–27.

"Nefarious and insidious encroachments": *C-I,* Oct. 24, 1946. "No. 1 labor-baiter": *Batesville Guard,* cited ibid.

"Preserve, protect, and defend": *(Little Rock, Ark.) Free Enterpriser,* Oct. 1950.

Heralded Thurmond's arrival: *C-I,* Aug. 19, 1948. **"Pictures and stories":** *C-I,* Sept. 9, 1948.

"In the eyes of the nation": *AG,* Aug. 27, 1948.

Thurmond won only: Heard, p. 26.

9 TOO WINDY FOR TEAR GAS

Sources

Books

Couto, *Ain't Gonna Let Nobody Turn Me Round;* Morris, *Yazoo;* Schwartz, *In Service to America;* Tucker, *Arkansas.*

Newspaper Articles

"Poverty and Prejudice: The Delta—A Special Report," *AD,* June 19–27, 1988.

"The War on Poverty: Arkansas's Role," *AG,* July 12, 1964; "SNCC Will Open Its Project Today," *AG,* June 21, 1965; "A Test at Marianna," (editorial),

AG, Nov. 19, 1969; "Marianna," (letter to the editor), *AG,* Nov. 29, 1969; "Fire Damages Three Stores at Marianna; County Judge Fined," *AG,* Aug. 12, 1971; "About the Racial Unrest at Marianna," *AG,* Aug. 15, 1971; "17 Found Guilty in Marianna Case," *AG,* May 25, 1972; "Black Boycott, After 'Ruining' Downtown Marianna, Apparently Backfiring," *AG,* June 18, 1972; "Many Factors Could be Linked to Results of Basic Skills Test," *AG,* Aug. 18, 1985; "Tests Unsettling for Marianna," *AG,* Dec. 22, 1985.

"Investigation of School Disruption Underway by State Department of Education; Blacks Boycott," *C-I,* Jan. 20, 1972.

"Medical Society Locks Out Physician to Poor," *MCA,* Nov. 14, 1969; "Marianna School Attendance Off as Curfew Quietens Pupil Unrest," *MCA,* Jan. 15, 1972; "Charges and Denials Fly in Furor Over Lee Clinic," *MCA,* Mar. 7, 1972.

"Black Vs. White: A Boycott Devastates Little Southern Town Bypassed by the 60s," *WSJ,* Feb. 24, 1972.

Magazine and Journal Articles
Arkansas Business and Economic Review 22, No. 2 (summer 1989).

"Olly's Law," *Arkansas Times,* Oct. 1990; "Leveling the Playing Field," *Arkansas Times,* Nov. 1990.

"Medicine on the Firing Line," *Hospital Practice,* Mar. 1972.

"I'm Going to Detroit," *Time,* May 9, 1988.

Dissertation and Manuscripts
Daggett, "Marianna, Arkansas."

Richard J. First and Joan D. First, "Political Impact of the Lee County Health Clinic," Mar. 1974; copy in the author's files.

Michael F. Sylva, "Black Population in Arkansas, 1900–1970," unpublished Master's thesis, University of Arkansas, 1981.

Video Recordings
CBS News, "Don't Get Sick in America," documentary broadcast Dec. 13, 1969 (transcript, Nashville: Aurora Publishing, 1970).

Lee County White Citizens Council, *The Marianna Story,* film, 1972.

Documents
"Blacks in the Arkansas Delta," a report of the Arkansas State Advisory Committee to the U.S. Commission on Civil Rights, Washington, D.C., Mar. 1974.

Campbell v. Lee County Election Commission, No. H-C-86-48, U.S. District Court, Eastern District of Arkansas, Eastern Division.

Papers of Senator John L. McClellan, Special Collections Department, Riley-Hickingbotham Library, Ouachita Baptist University, Arkadelphia, Arkansas.

"On Arkansas in General," a report of the Student Nonviolent Coordinating Committee, Feb. 1965.

Interviews

A. J. Atkins, Pat Audirsch, James Banks, Daniel Blumenthal, David Cahoon, Martin Chaffin, Clifton Collier, Yvette Glenn, Marilyn Goins, Pinky Hill, Andrea Hope Howard, Lorraine Jones, Sterling King, Jr., Roy C. Lewellen, Jr., Lon Mann, James McKinney, Harold Meins, Franklin Montgomery, Olly Neal, Jr., Marzella Robins, Quency Tillman, Jan Wrede, Judy Wright, Patricia Zachary.

Notes

"Negroes have met the most harassment": *AG*, June 21, 1965.

A two-row picking machine: Tucker, p. 77.

"Worse in Arkansas": *AG*, July 12, 1964.

The sixth poorest county: Schwartz, p. 191. The median family income: *AG*, July 12, 1964. Black men earned: "On Arkansas in General." Without indoor plumbing: *WSJ*, Feb. 24, 1972. Its black infant mortality rate: *WSJ*, Feb. 24, 1972, and Schwartz, p. 191.

"Suffer it out": "Don't Get Sick in America," p. 34.

"Had no objection at first": Quoted in *The Marianna Story*.

"That's enough for me": *MCA*, Nov. 14, 1969.

"The situation at Marianna": *AG*, Nov. 19, 1969. "We should wear this label": *AG*, Nov. 29, 1969.

"With a clipped mustache": Quoted in Morris, p. 122.

More than 150 telegrams: Press release, March 9, 1972, McClellan Papers. The OEO awarded the clinic: *MCA*, Mar. 7, 1972. The clinic's annual budget: *Hospital Practice*, Mar. 1972.

"Negroes in Memphis": *Arkansas Times*, Oct. 1990.

Expelled from school: *Arkansas Times*, Oct. 1990.

" 'You just gotta admit' ": Quoted in Couto, p. 55.

"Damn the book": quoted in Nov. 1971 testimony included in "Blacks in the Arkansas Delta." The sheriff, Courtney Langston, in an Aug. 30, 1972, letter to the commission (appended to the report), "emphatically" denied making the statement.

"Fell into the Mississippi River": Couto, p. 61.

One retailer complained: *The Marianna Story*.

"It's made a ghost town": *The Marianna Story*.

"I run the courthouse": Quoted in Nov. 1971 testimony included in "Blacks in the Arkansas Delta."

"It was definitely arson": *AG*, July 28, 1971. "Go the violence route": First and First.

Judge Adams pleaded no contest: *AG*, Aug. 12, 1971.

"You reporters": Quoted ibid.

"Since the Game and Fish Commission": Paul Buchanan in the *Batesville Daily Guard*, quoted in *AG*, Aug. 15, 1971.

"Off the top of my head": *AG*, Aug. 12, 1971.

"If we let them": *MCA,* Jan. 15, 1972.

The well-known "Nigra" author: Howard. "Then she sprayed the seats": Zachary.

"Don't let anyone in or out": The chronology of the confrontation is taken from the *C-I,* Jan. 20, 1972, and from several students and teachers who were present.

"We had no choice": Quoted in *WSJ,* Feb. 24, 1972.

A misdemeanor offense: *AG,* June 18, 1972; for the specifics of the verdicts, see *AG,* May 25, 1972.

The boycott "ruined" Marianna: *AG,* June 18, 1972. "I ain't got no business": Quoted in *WSJ,* Feb. 24, 1972.

No blacks belonged: *Campbell v. Lee County Election Commission,* deposition of Mayor Martin Chaffin, July 13, 1988, pp. 56–57, and interviews with Chaffin and Lewellen. Sat in the visitors' section: Banks, coach of the Lee Senior High basketball team.

"We might lose our jobs": Goins, wife of the minister of the First Christian Church, Marianna. "People wouldn't feel comfortable there": Mann.

"They're messing around": *Campbell v. Lee County Election Commission,* deposition of Rabon H. Teague Cheeks, July 13, 1988, p. 13. "It's taken a while": Quoted in *AD,* June 19–27, 1988, p. 12.

The poorest county: *Arkansas Business and Economic Review,* p. 39. The highest percentage lost: Sylva, p. 70. "Eight black teenagers": Quoted in *Time,* May 9, 1988, p. 27.

Only one in five: *Arkansas Times,* Nov. 1990, p. 22. Functionally illiterate: Audirsch, director of the Lee County Literacy Council. Basic skills test: *AG,* Dec. 22, 1985. Average achievement test: *AG,* Aug. 18, 1985. "Make more money": Wright, a former Marianna teacher.

Had invited Mario: Biographical details on Marshall Glenn are from interviews with Robins, his aunt, and Glenn, his sister.

"The certainty of nothing": Collier.

10 "WE RICH, GODDAMMIT!"

Sources

Books
Babson, *Working Detroit;* Inciardi, *The War on Drugs II.*

Newspaper Articles
"Blacks in Detroit," *DFP* reprint, Dec. 1980; "Deadly Cocaine: Local Authorities Describe Use as Near-Epidemic," *DFP,* July 1, 1986; "First Rally Against Crack Has Students Dancing in the Aisles," *DFP,* Oct. 4, 1986; "Drug Deaths Skyrocket, Study Shows," *DFP,* 1988; "Judge Tosses Arguments for Police in Barney Case," *DFP,* Sept. 25, 1993.

"Clout for Crack Crackdown," *DN*, Oct. 3, 1986; "No Crack Week Rally Draws 2,000," *DN*, Oct. 4, 1986.

"Poster Outlines Do's and Don't's," *MCA*, Sept. 29, 1988.

Documents

"The Crack Cocaine Crisis," report of a joint hearing before the U.S. House Select Committee on Narcotics Abuse and Control and the U.S. House Select Committee on Children, Youth, and Families, Washington, D.C., July 15, 1986.

FGJT No. 87-4-59, U.S. District Court, Eastern District of Michigan, Southern Division.

USAvLC, beginning Sept. 16, 1988.

USA v. Carl Young, federal trial transcript No. 87-80933-06, U.S. District Court, Eastern District of Michigan, Southern Division, Dec. 19, 1988.

Interviews

Stanley Barnes, Gerard Biernacki, Richard J. Crock, Robert J. DeFauw, Arthur Derrick, Jerry Gant, Frank Heaney, Robert (Bobby) May, Jr., Thomas McClain, Patricia Middleton, Greg Woods, Carl Young.

Notes

"Without telling every kid in town": Details of the meeting are from an interview with DeFauw.

A telephone hotline: Crock, DeFauw, McClain; *DN*, Oct. 14, 1986.

The number of deaths: *DFP,* undated report on National Institute for Drug Abuse study, in author's files. **All property crimes:** *DFP,* July 1, 1986. **The "most dangerous substance":** Inciardi, p. 81.

Gilliam told the members: "The Crack Cocaine Crisis," p. 71. **"A shadowy adversary":** Ibid , p 73.

No-Crack Crew, as it came to be known: FGJT, No. 87-4-59, McClain, Aug. 20, 1987, p. 8.

A police unit called STRESS: *DFP,* Dec. 1980. **The department's uniformed officers:** Babson, p. 199.

"They just want to do raids": McClain interview.

"They call him BJ": Middleton. **Biernacki had Middleton fill out the forms:** Testimony of Biernacki, *USAvLC,* p. 1766.

"I've been copping cocaine": Affidavit for Search Warrant for 12575 Glenfield, Detroit, Aug. 25, 1986; in author's files.

"What's up?": Billy Joe Chambers.

"This chicken-shit lawyer": McClain interview.

"Just get off the watermelon truck": May.

"I couldn't help noticing": Barnes and interview with Western Union operator, who asked that her name not be used.

Carl eventually became a truck driver: Biographical material on Carl Young comes from a telephone interview and from Young's Rule 35 Motion for

Reduction of Sentence, included in *USA v. Carl L. Young*, No. 87-80933-06, Jan. 1991.

"I just dove into the insulation": Young trial transcript, p. 190.

"RAIDED CRACK DEN": *DN*, Sept. 19, 1986.

There had been 204 calls: Michigan Bell records obtained by DPD; copies in author's files.

"Crack was readily available": *DN*, Oct. 3, 1986.

Room 327 of the Regency Inn: Details of the Nov. 14, 1986, raid are from Johnston's DEA Form 6 report filed Nov. 24, 1986.

"No Crack Week": DeFauw; *DFP*, Oct. 4, 1986; and *DN*, Oct. 4, 1986. **Barney himself**: *DFP*, Sept. 25, 1993.

"P-Boy!": Derrick.

A great deal of gold: James Lumpkin describes the house in FGJT, No. 87-4-59, Nov. 3, 1987, p. 42, and in *USAvLC*, pp. 1648–56.

A video tour: Parts of this and other tapes that the No-Crack Crew found on Albion were broadcast in July 1987 on a local television station.

They found no drugs: Biernacki testimony, *USAvLC*, p. 1756. **Very little cash**: DPD Preliminary Complaint Record for 17204 Albion, Oct. 13, 1986. **Under Michigan law**: Quoted in Petition for Forfeiture, *Michigan v. $181,310.94 U.S. Currency, Misc. Items of Jewelry, and One Pager, Defendant*, Wayne County Circuit Court, Detroit, Dec. 1, 1986.

A handwritten poster: Crock testimony, *USAvLC*, pp. 442–46, and *MCA*, Sept. 29, 1988.

11 "FUCK IT, I'LL FIX HIM"

Sources

Video Recordings
Chambers family home videotapes.

Chris Hansen, WXYZ, Channel 7, "All in the Family," five-part news series broadcast July 27–31, 1987.

Documents
FGJT, No. 86-5-66, U.S. District Court, Eastern District of Michigan, Southern Division; FGJT, No. 87-4-59, U.S. District Court, Eastern District of Michigan, Southern Division.

USAvLC, beginning Sept. 16, 1988.

USA v. Terry Colbert, perjury trial transcript No. 90-80894, U.S. District Court, Eastern District of Michigan, Southern Division, Mar. 26, 1991.

USA v. Carl L. Young, federal trial transcript No. 87-80933-06, Dec. 19, 1988.

Various internal DEA and FBI memoranda.

Interviews

Tony Alexander, Gerard Biernacki, Lawrence J. Bunting, Billy Joe Chambers, Larry Chambers, Terry Colbert, Perry Coleman, Richard J. Crock, Romia Hall, Morris Hampton, Patricia Middleton, Herbert Neighbors, Greg Woods, Paul Young.

Notes

"I was using every day": Colbert interview.

His father shunned him: Ibid. Terry was paid either fifteen or twenty: In his testimony in *USA v. Carl Young*, p. 44, Biernacki says the amount was twenty dollars; in *USA v. Terry Colbert*, vol. 6, p. 14, Colbert says it was fifteen dollars. On p. 15 is Colbert's quote on how he spent the money. Terry told Biernacki: Biernacki testimony in *USAvLC*, p. 1771. "A drop-off and pickup man": Colbert testimony in *USAvLC*, p. 904. Reported to Billy: Colbert testimony in *USAvLC*, p. 905.

Five hundred dollars a month: Coleman.

"Police outside, y'all": Young.

"We're on his ass": Billy Joe Chambers.

GOOD $10 BOULDER: "All in the Family."

"Brought to my attention": Best letter to Gilliam, Dec. 11, 1986; in the author's possession.

"Ladies and gentlemen": FGJT, No. 86-5-66, Dec. 18, 1986, pp. 2–7.

"Build an underground house": Hampton.

"Perfecto": Chambers family home video; in the author's possession.

Titled in James's name: Testimony of James Lumpkin in *USAvLC*, pp. 1656–62, and Memorandum of Interview, Nov. 3, 1987, with Lumpkin conducted by IRS agents in the Federal Building, Detroit.

Every other week: Larry Chambers.

"They were treating us pretty good": FGJT, No. 87-4-59, Janice (Davis) Roberts, Sept. 2, 1987, pp. 27–28.

"I wasn't going" and "Better watch yourself": Testimony of Janice (Davis) Roberts in *USAvLC*, p. 685.

"I stood there": Middleton.

"He borrowed it from a friend": Neighbors.

"Reluctant to provide information": FBI report of incident of Apr. 24, 1987; in author's possession.

Surma testified: Surma testimony in *USAvLC*, pp. 1330–33, and Terry Colbert testimony in *USAvLC*, pp. 1284–87.

"Just be careful": DPD Witness Statement of Terry Colbert, taken by Crock and Biernacki, May 3, 1987.

"It may end up being a RICO": FGJT, No. 86-5-66, May 20, 1987, p. 4.

Operated "over about two hundred": Ibid., p. 23. "Get his ass": Ibid., p. 31.

In an internal memo: DEA Form 6, Deactivation of SI7-87-0030," June 9, 1987.

"Gettin' paid": Colbert interview.

"The major source of cocaine": DEA Form 6, Investigation in Marianna, July 7, 1987.

"Lay the groundwork": Ibid. The DEA form does not name Melvin Brown; his name, however, was disclosed during Killingham's grand-jury and trial testimony.

A two-time felon: Biographical details are from Killingham's testimony in *USAvLC,* p. 1267, and DEA Form 6, Initial Debriefing, July 3, 1987.

"Partying and getting high": FGJT, No. 87-4-59, Oct. 22, 1987, p. 6.

"Would be less trouble": Ibid., p. 8.

"I don't like you": Colbert recounts the incident in *USAvLC,* pp. 906–10, and in interviews. The author also possesses a copy of the DPD Preliminary Complaint Record, July 7, 1987.

12 ALL IN THE FAMILY

Sources

Newspaper Articles
"Suspected Smugglers' Transportation," *DN,* March 5, 1988.
"When Life in the Projects Was Good," *NYT,* July 31, 1991.
"Detroit TV Anchor Is Quite Outrageous, and Quite Popular," *WSJ,* June 19, 1991.

Magazine Article
"White Boy Rick," *Detroit Monthly,* March 1988.

Video Recording
Chris Hansen, WXYZ, Channel 7, "All in the Family," five-part news series broadcast July 27–31, 1987.

Documents
FGJT, No. 86-5-66, U.S. District Court, Eastern District of Michigan, Southern Division; FGJT, No. 87-4-59, U.S. District Court, Eastern District of Michigan, Southern Division.

Interviews
Billy Joe Chambers, Larry Chambers, Willie Lee Chambers, Arthur Derrick, Dennis Fayson, Chris Hansen, William Jackson, Sharena Jasper, Thomas McClain.

Notes

"If this is supposed to be a secret": FGJT, No. 86-5-66, July 29, 1987, pp. 4–5.

"Mad as hell": *WSJ,* June 19, 1991.

"This is a tough town": Ibid.

"He didn't show me the same respect": Jackson.

"Good evening, everybody": Transcription of "All in the Family" by the author, from videotape DEA made available.

"Out to kill people": Bunting's and McClain's comments are from FGJT, No. 87-4-59, Aug. 20, 1987.

"Unfortunately they are": Ibid., p. 92.

"I know of him": FGJT, No. 87-4-59, Abbott, Hurt, and Roberts, Sept. 2, 1987.

He was "seizing the vehicle": DEA Report of Investigation, Seizure of 1987 Jeep from Hazel Chambers, Dec. 9, 1987.

White Boy Rick guilty: *Detroit Monthly,* Mar. 1988.

The flamboyant supplier: Derrick, and *DN,* Mar. 5, 1988.

"All for show": Willie Lee Chambers and DPD Preliminary Complaint Record, Dec. 1, 1987.

She was living with her husband: FGJT, No. 87-4-59, Dec. 17, 1987.

Larry offered the hit: DEA Form 6, Interview of Derrick Lee Poole, June 17, 1988.

Alive and limping: FGJT, No. 87-4-59, Janice (Davis) Roberts, Dec. 17, 1987, pp. 6–7.

One of the nation's first experiments: *NYT,* July 31, 1991. "Baby Saigon": Fayson.

"I'm back friends with Belinda": FGJT, No. 87-4-59, Janice (Davis) Roberts, Dec. 17, 1987, p. 11. The DEA paid Janice: DEA Form 356, Informant Payment Record re Informant SI7-88-0013, n.d.

A good haul: DPD Preliminary Complaint Record, 11060 E. McNichols, Apt. 106, Dec. 3, 1987.

George C. Dahl later claimed: Statement of George C. Dahl, BATF memorandum 33910-88-1018R, June 20, 1988. *"In the hallway":* DPD Preliminary Complaint Record, 11060 E. McNichols, Apt. 106, Dec. 3, 1987.

Dennis Fayson agreed to cooperate: Fayson, McClain, and DEA Form 6, Interview of Dennis Fayson, Dec. 30, 1987, prepared Jan. 3, 1988. "Oh my God": DEA Form 6, Assessment of Threat to Dennis Fayson, Mar. 7, 1988.

13 A TALE OF TWO CITIES

Sources

Newspaper Articles

"Two Arkansas Youths Worked Undercover in Drug Ring Inquiry," *AD,* Mar. 4, 1988.

"Hope Lives in Marianna, Despite the Detroit Railroad," *AG,* Apr. 3, 1988;

"Targeted for Death, Marianna Chief Told," *AG,* May 4, 1988; "Expressions of Bias Slow Jury Selection in Chambers Drug Case," *AG,* Sept. 15, 1988; "Potential Jurors Cite Fear in Drug Trial in Detroit," *AG,* Sept. 16, 1988.

"Authorities: Crack Ring Employed 275," *DFP,* Mar. 2, 1988; "Crack Trade Drains Town of Its Youth," *DFP,* Mar. 6, 1988.

"Arkansas Teens Sought Dreams in Detroit Drug Dens," *DN,* Mar. 6, 1988.

"Suspects in Ring to be Prosecuted by U.S. Attorney," *MCA,* Mar. 16, 1988; "Pretrial Visit Paid in Crack Case," *MCA,* Mar. 24, 1988; "Threats Dog Police in Drug Probe," *MCA,* May 5, 1988; "Motel Raid Halts Sale of Crack, Police Say," *MCA,* Aug. 9, 1988; "Jury Will Not See Video Drug Tapes," *MCA,* Sept. 4, 1988; "Jury Selection Is Completed in Chambers Brothers' Trial, *MCA,* Sept. 21, 1988.

Isabel Wilkerson, "Detroit Crack Empire Showed All Earmarks of Big Business," *NYT,* Dec. 18, 1988; "Ex-Police Chief Gets a 10-Year Sentence in Detroit Graft Case," *NYT,* Aug. 28, 1992.

Magazine Articles

"From Rocks to Riches," *Esquire,* Jan. 1990.

"I'm Going to Detroit," *Time,* May 9, 1988.

Documents

USAvLC, beginning Sept. 16, 1988.

Interviews

Sherry Benson, Mark Birchler, William Bufalino, Lawrence J. Bunting, Anthony T. Chambers, Billy Joe Chambers, Willie Lee Chambers, Terry Colbert, Bennie Foster, David Havard, Roy Hayes, Roy C. Lewellen, Jr., Robert Mann, Robert May, Jr., Patricia Middleton, Kela Nealis, Richard F. Suhrheinrich.

Notes

"Does he have": Preliminary Examination, *USAvLC,* No. 87-80933, U.S. District Court, Eastern District of Michigan, Southern Division, Dec. 29, 1987.

"Nobody gets hurt too bad": Unger testimony, *USAvLC,* p. 1318.

Prosecutors waited until Tuesday afternoon: Hayes.

"About four hundred": DEA Form 6, Arrest of Billy Joe Chambers and Otis Chambers on Mar. 1, 1988.

"That's what I figured": Ibid.

Three others had been rounded up: Times and details of arrests are from DEA Form 6 reports of investigation.

A forest of microphones: Hayes.

"The most significant case": Quoted in *DFP,* Mar. 2, 1988.

The indictment would curb the flow: Ibid.

He would be sentenced: *NYT*, Aug. 28, 1992.

State agents seized sixty-eight vehicles: Figures cited are from *NYT*, Dec. 18, 1988; *DFP*, Mar. 2, 1988; and *DN*, Mar. 2, 1988.

"The dominant crack distribution network": Hayes. The first time in six years: *MCA*, Mar. 16, 1988.

Thundered the Gannett paper: *DN*, Mar. 2, 1988. Echoed the Gannett paper: *AG*, Mar. 3, 1988.

"Here they come": *DN*, Mar. 6, 1988.

"Michigan vehicles": *AD*, Mar. 4, 1988. "Tips from disaffected Marianna youths": *Time*, May 9, 1988.

"Mark's first involvement": May.

The Chambers brothers had targeted him for death: *AG*, May 4, 1988, and *MCA*, May 5, 1988.

"To get firsthand information": *MCA*, Mar. 24, 1988.

Birchler told Hayes: The discussion was summarized in DEA Form 6, Interview of Marianna, Ark., P.D. Chief, Mar. 31, 1988.

"A thousand-dollar-sack of cocaine": DEA Form 6, Investigation in Marianna, Mar. 26, 1988.

Mathis wrote: *AG*, Apr. 3, 1988.

Clinton used an example: From the transcript of his speech, July 20, 1988.

"It is *very* tempting": *DFP*, Mar. 6, 1988.

"The grass is always greener": Benson.

"When are you going": *MCA*, Aug. 9, 1988.

A full page of appeasement: *MCA*, Aug. 21, 1988.

"Trial by media": Supplemental Memorandum in Support of Change of Venue, *USAvLC*, July 27, 1988.

"Where is due process?": *MCA*, Sept. 4, 1988.

"On the Ho Chi Minh trail": Suhrheinrich. "Hole in the head": *MCA*, Sept. 21, 1988.

"A gut feeling": *AG*, Sept. 15, 1988. "All this seems too big": *AG*, Sept. 16, 1988.

Armor-plated hair: The author, whose own best hair days are behind him, used this description of Suhrheinrich in an earlier published piece (*Esquire*, Jan. 1990). In a subsequent interview, the judge needled: "At least I've got hair."

They ordered some sandwiches: Havard.

"*A Tale of Two Cities*": Hayes's opening statement, *USAvLC*, pp. 33–48.

The defense team's strategy: Anthony Chambers's opening statement, *USAvLC*, pp. 50–53.

"*Much Ado About Nothing*": Cohen's opening statement, *USAvLC*, p. 86.

"There wouldn't be enough room": Bufalino's opening statement, *USAvLC*, pp. 98–99.

14 AS CLOSE AS BROTHERS GET

Sources

Documents
USAvLC, beginning Sept. 16, 1988.
USA v. Terry Colbert, perjury trial transcript No. 90-80894, U.S. District Court, Eastern District of Michigan, Southern Division, Mar. 26, 1991.

Newspaper Articles
"Nine Guilty in Chambers Gang Drug Case," *DN,* Oct. 29, 1988.
"Life Resumes for Two Cleared Men," *MCA,* Oct. 13, 1988.

Interviews
Billy Joe Chambers, Terry Colbert, Felicia Gilchrist, Morris Hampton, Roy Hayes, Patricia Middleton, Timothy Patrick Murphy, Ross Parker.

Notes

"I'm running from Willie Chambers's gang": DPD Interrogation Record of suspect Terry Colbert, June 1, 1988.

The owner of the car wash: In an affidavit administered by DEA Special Agent Crock, dated June 21, 1988, the owner, Yousif E. Thomas, swore that the government did not "threaten, intimidate, or coerce" him.

"They brung me back to Detroit": *USA v. Terry Colbert,* vol. 6, p. 35.

He used crack for the first and only time: *USAvLC,* p. 823.

"I cried all night long": Middleton.

Three felony convictions: *USAvLC,* p. 256. **A small portion of her record:** *USAvLC,* pp. 103–4.

"He would arrange for David": *USAvLC,* p. 122. **"A gentleman carrying a body":** *USAvLC,* p. 108.

"Their complete attention": Hayes.

"Blow my fucking brains out": *USAvLC,* p. 148.

Plus two thousand for expenses: *USAvLC,* pp. 139–45.

"That is the way we went": *USAvLC,* pp. 190–91.

"Lick our wounds": Murphy.

Monthly welfare payments: *USAvLC,* p. 233.

A .32-caliber: *USAvLC,* pp. 234–35. **For writing a hot check:** *USAvLC,* p. 248. **She also served ninety days:** *USAvLC,* p. 165.

"I did try to commit suicide": *USAvLC,* p. 247.

The Golden Screw award: Conceived and designed by Tom Wilhelm, Otis's lawyer.

"This is not a game": *USAvLC,* p. 305.

"Can you see me": *USAvLC,* pp. 312–14.

"Some of the guys": *USAvLC*, p. 358. "No hope in dope": *USAvLC*, p. 359.

A grant of immunity: *USAvLC*, p. 363. The government pay to relocate him: *USAvLC*, p. 402.

"We don't have none": *USAvLC*, p. 401.

Crock was grilled: *USAvLC*, p. 526.

Terry Colbert later confirmed: *USAvLC*, p. 939. A total of $12,699: *USAvLC*, pp. 531, 629. In addition to Colbert: *USAvLC*, pp. 500–501.

Larry's boiler-room operations: *USAvLC*, pp. 654–85.

"They was afraid": *USA v. Colbert*, vol. 6, p. 47. "Making sure that everything": *USA v. Colbert*, ibid., p. 48.

Counted out a hundred and fifty thousand dollars: *USAvLC*, pp. 832–35.

Driven the nine hundred miles: *USAvLC*, p. 832. The government stipulated: *USAvLC*, p. 2121.

"Like BJ's right-hand man": *USAvLC*, p. 830. Gave it to Jerry: *USAvLC*, p. 851.

"He used to just be around": *USAvLC*, p. 847. He knew Marshall Glenn: *USAvLC*, pp. 918–19.

"This is August of eighty-four": *USAvLC*, p. 855.

"Around July": *USAvLC*, p. 862. Did not work again: *USAvLC*, p. 863.

" 'I don't like you no way' ": *USAvLC*, p. 909. He also was assaulted once: *USAvLC*, p. 911.

Chelsea Street: *USAvLC*, p. 890. Montclair Street: *USAvLC*, p. 888. "We already know": *USAvLC*, p. 895.

"With a silver spoon": *USAvLC*, pp. 895–96.

"I can understand then": *USAvLC*, p. 896.

"A long time": *USAvLC*, pp. 927–28.

"You came here to work": *USAvLC*, pp. 1048–49.

About a hundred and fifty crack houses: *USAvLC*, p. 872.

"Didn't it appear a bit strange": *USAvLC*, pp. 1108–9.

Attempted armed robbery: *USAvLC*, p. 1267.

"You got to be sure": *USAvLC*, p. 1268.

"No further questions": *USAvLC*, p. 1269.

"I've done lost everything": *MCA*, Oct. 13, 1988.

"Dismiss all charges": *USAvLC*, p. 1281.

"That motion is granted": *USAvLC*, p. 1282.

"Was perpetrated in furtherance": *USAvLC*, p. 1429.

Hampton "erected gates": *USAvLC*, pp. 1431–33.

"The guy I buy my car from": *USAvLC*, p. 1433.

"You don't need an interpreter": *USAvLC*, p. 1471.

"She has a heroin problem": *USAvLC*, p. 1473.

"When the traffic would slow down": *USAvLC*, p. 1464.

"The overall conspiracy": *USAvLC*, p. 1491. " 'How serious we are about discipline'?": *USAvLC*, pp. 1504–5.

"The probative value": *USAvLC*, p. 1506.

He started lucidly enough: Perry lost his memory on *USAvLC*, p. 1564.

"I wasn't yelling": *USAvLC*, p. 1567.

Offered Perry a deal: Letter from Assistant U.S. Attorney Parker to Perry Coleman, Oct. 13, 1988; in the author's possession. "He was going to do the right thing": Parker.

"I ain't never sold": *USAvLC*, p. 1592.

Suhrheinrich instructed jurors: *USAvLC*, p. 1604.

How he helped Larry hide assets: *USAvLC*, pp. 1638–71. "Big-old apartment building": *USAvLC*, p. 1613. "I can't recognize him": *USAvLC*, p. 1626.

"My BMW this": Billy Joe Chambers.

"We rest our case": *USAvLC*, pp. 2013–14.

"Sit there and take it": Murphy.

"Beyond a reasonable doubt": *USAvLC*, p. 2304. "Knowingly members of the conspiracy": *USAvLC*, p. 2314.

"The province of the court": *USAvLC*, p. 2323.

"Tomorrow is the conclusion": *USAvLC*, p. 2331.

He revisited with the jury: *USAvLC*, pp. 2342–52.

"Is it wrong": *USAvLC*, pp. 2359–60.

"Don't overlook the obvious": *USAvLC*, p. 2372.

"The Rainbow Store in the basement": *USAvLC*, p. 2374.

"The yellow brick road": *USAvLC*, p. 2388.

"Take a check from Patricia Middleton": *USAvLC*, p. 2391.

"Her psychological problems": *USAvLC*, p. 2404.

"Somebody like Terry Colbert": *USAvLC*, p. 2424.

"He is a snitch": *USAvLC*, pp. 2428–29.

"Bouquets of the truth": *USAvLC*, p. 2453.

"A verdict of not guilty": *USAvLC*, p. 2475.

A skillfully sculpted argument: *USAvLC*, pp. 2477–85.

"You cannot convict": *USAvLC*, pp. 2511–12.

"If you were a passenger": Ibid.

"It was a stormy day": *USAvLC*, pp. 2486–88.

"A house cannot stand": *USAvLC*, p. 2497.

"I look out the window": *USAvLC*, pp. 2514–28.

"We have to wait": *USAvLC*, p. 2542.

"Tempers are short": *USAvLC*, p. 2550. "The jury reached their verdicts": *USAvLC*, p. 2551.

"Has the jury reached": Ibid.

She bowed her head: *DN*, Oct. 29, 1988.

"**The court finds that this conspiracy**": *USAvLC*, p. 2555.

"**Doing to our poor people**": *USAvLC*, Remarks of the Court Before Sentencing Defendants, Mar. 24, 1989, pp. 5–6.

"**So help me God**": Letter of Apr. 13, 1989; in the author's possession.

"**Something physically or mentally wrong**": *USAvLC*, Motion for New Trial, June 14, 1989, p. 8.

EPILOGUE **NOTHING TO LOSE**

Sources

Newspaper Articles

"500-Bed Prison Will Be 'Boost' for Lee County," *AG*, Aug. 8, 1990. "Delta Has a Lot of Empty," *AG*, Apr. 28, 1991.

"Off the Cuff," *C-I*, July 14, 1994.

"Sales Flourish Despite Arrests, *DFP*, Dec. 4, 1988.

Magazine Articles

"Crime Time Live," *In These Times*, Dec. 27, 1993.

"Down and Out in the Delta," *Nation*, July 9, 1990.

Documents

"Body of the Nation," interim report of the Lower Mississippi Delta Development Commission, Memphis, TN, Oct. 16, 1989.

Transcript of Phone Call 7, Oct. 27, 1989, Government Exhibit 4-A, *USA v. Terry Colbert*, perjury trial transcript No. 90-80894, U.S. District Court, Eastern District of Michigan, Southern Division.

Interviews

Mark Birchler, Alvin Chambers, Billy Joe Chambers, Terry Colbert, Perry Coleman, Richard J. Crock, Cindy Davis, Kevin Duplessis, Dennis Fayson, Morris Hampton, David Havard, Roy Hayes, William Jackson, Roy C. Lewellen, Jr., Thomas McClain, Patricia Middleton, Olly Neal, Jr., Charles Robinson.

Notes

The defendants' phone calls: Government Exhibit 4-A, *USA v. Terry Colbert*.

"**Buy a loaf of bread**": *DFP*, Dec. 4, 1988.

More prisons have not made: *In These Times*, Dec. 27, 1993, p. 15.

"**People are thrilled**": *AG*, Aug. 8, 1990.

More than 20 percent: "Jobless rate by county for March 1988," *AG*, n.d.

One of every four people: *AG*, Apr. 28, 1991. " 'Turn out the lights' ": State Representative Ernest Cunningham quoted in *AG*, Apr. 28, 1991.

"It's not Mayberry": *C-I,* July 14, 1994.

"Has often reinforced tensions": "Body of the Nation" (interim report of the Lower Mississippi Delta Development Commission, Oct. 16, 1989), Appendix A, II. "Band-Aids": *Nation,* July 9, 1990, p. 50.

SELECTED BIBLIOGRAPHY

Alexander, Donald Crichton. *The Arkansas Plantation, 1920–1942.* New Haven, Conn.: Yale University Press, 1943.

Apple, Nancy, and Keasler, Susie, eds. *Lee County History.* Dallas: Curtis Media, 1986.

Arsenault, Raymond. *The Wild Ass of the Ozarks.* Philadelphia: Temple University Press, 1984.

Ashmore, Harry S. *Arkansas: A Bicentennial History.* New York: W. W. Norton, 1978.

Babson, Steve. *Working Detroit.* New York: Adama Books, 1984.

Barnes, Donna A. *Farmers in Rebellion: The Rise and Fall of the Southern Farmers Alliance and People's Party in Texas.* Austin: University of Texas Press, 1984.

Bartley, Numan V. *The Rise of Massive Resistance: Race and Politics in the South During the 1950's.* Baton Rouge: Louisiana State University Press, 1969.

Berquist, Charles, Gonzalo Sanchez, and Ricardo Penaranda, eds. *Violence in Colombia: The Contemporary Crisis in Historical Perspective.* Wilmington, Del.: SR Books, 1991.

Blair, Diane D. *Arkansas Politics and Government: Do the People Rule?* Lincoln and London: University of Nebraska Press, 1988.

Byck, Robert, M.D., ed. *Cocaine Papers,* by Sigmund Freud. New York: Meridian Books, 1975 (paperback ed.).

Caldwell, Erskine, and Margaret Bourke-White. *You Have Seen Their Faces.* Arno Press, 1975.

Caro, Robert A. *The Years of Lyndon Johnson: The Path to Power.* New York: Alfred A. Knopf, 1982.

Chapman, Abraham, ed. *Black Voices: An Anthology of Afro-American Literature.* New York and Toronto: New American Library, 1968.

Cole, Lewis. *Never Too Young to Die: The Death of Len Bias.* New York: Pantheon Books, 1989.

Conot, Robert. *American Odyssey.* New York: William Morrow, 1974.

Conrad, David Eugene. *The Forgotten Farmers: The Story of Sharecroppers in the New Deal.* Urbana: University of Illinois Press, 1965.

Cortner, Richard C. *A Mob Intent on Death: The NAACP and the Arkansas Riot Cases.* Middletown, Conn.: Wesleyan University Press, 1988.

Couto, Richard A. *Ain't Gonna Let Nobody Turn Me Round: The Pursuit of Racial Justice in the Rural South.* Philadelphia: Temple University Press, 1991.

Daggett, Susan D. "Marianna, Arkansas: A Study of Small Town Race Relations." Undergraduate thesis, Mount Holyoke College, 1986.

Daniels, Jonathan. *A Southerner Discovers the South.* New York: Macmillan, 1938.

Darden, Joe T., Richard Child Hill, June Thomas, and Richard Thomas. *Detroit: Race and Uneven Development.* Philadelphia: Temple University Press, 1987.

Dinges, John. *Our Man in Panama.* New York: Random House, 1990.

Dollard, John. *Caste and Class in a Southern Town.* 3rd ed. New York: Doubleday, Anchor Books, 1957.

Drake, St. Clair, and Horace R. Cayton. *Black Metropolis: A Study of Negro Life in a Northern City.* 2 vols. New York: Harcourt, Brace & World, 1945.

Dunbar, Tony. *Our Land Too.* New York: Pantheon Books, 1969, 1971.

———. *Delta Time.* New York: Pantheon Books, 1990.

Eddy, Paul, with Hugo Sabogal and Sara Walden. *The Cocaine Wars.* New York and London: W. W. Norton, 1988.

Ferris, William. *Blues from the Delta.* New York: Da Capo Press, 1978.

Fletcher, John Gould. *Arkansas.* Chapel Hill: University of North Carolina Press, 1947.

Gatewood, Willard B., Jr.. "Arkansas Negroes in the 1890s: Documents." *Arkansas Historical Quarterly* 33 (1974).

———. "The Ark. Delta: Land of Gifts and Trials" (manuscript), n.d.

Goodwyn, Lawrence. *The Populist Moment: A Short History of the Agrarian Revolt in America.* Oxford: Oxford University Press, 1978.

Gregory, James N. *An American Exodus.* New York and Oxford: Oxford University Press, 1989.

Grubbs, Donald H. *Cry from the Cotton: The Southern Tenant Farmers' Union and the New Deal.* Chapel Hill: University of North Carolina Press, 1971.

Gugliotta, Guy, and Jeff Leen. *Kings of Cocaine.* New York: Simon & Schuster, 1989.

Havard, William C., ed. *The Changing Politics of the South*. Baton Rouge: Louisiana State University Press, 1972.

Heard, Alexander; *A Two-Party South?* Chapel Hill: University of North Carolina Press, 1952.

Henri, Florette. *Black Migration: Movement North, 1900–1920*. Garden City, N.Y.: Doubleday, Anchor Press, 1975.

Holmes, William F. "The Arkansas Cotton Pickers Strike of 1891 and the Demise of the Colored Farmers Alliance." *Arkansas Historical Quarterly* 32 (summer 1973): 107–19.

Hubbell, Ken, and Janis Kearney Lunon. *The Arkansas Delta: A Historical Look at Our Land and People*. Little Rock: Department of Arkansas Heritage, 1990.

Inciardi, James A. *The War on Drugs*. Palo Alto, Calif.: Mayfield, 1986.

———. *The War on Drugs II*. Palo Alto, Calif.: Mayfield, 1992.

Johnson, Charles S., Edwin R. Embree, and W. W. Alendander. *The Collapse of Cotton Tenancy*. Chapel Hill: University of North Carolina Press, 1935.

Kahn, E. J., Jr. *The Big Drink: The Story of Coca-Cola*. New York: Random House, 1960.

Kester, Howard. *Revolt Among the Sharecroppers*. New York: Covici Friede, 1936.

Key, V. O., Jr. *Southern Politics in State and Nation*. New York: Alfred A. Knopf, 1949.

Lacey, Robert. *Ford: The Men and the Machine*. New York: Ballantine Books, 1986.

Lemann, Nicholas. *The Promised Land*. New York: Alfred A. Knopf, 1991.

Lester, Jim. *A Man for Arkansas: Sid McMath and the Southern Reform Tradition*. Little Rock, Ark.: Rose, 1976.

McCullough, David. *Truman*. New York: Simon & Schuster, 1992.

McMillen, Neil R. *The Citizens' Council: Organized Resistance to the Second Reconstruction, 1954–64*. Urbana: University of Illinois Press, 1971.

———. *Dark Journey: Black Mississippians in the Age of Jim Crow*. Urbana: University of Illinois Press, 1989.

Marks, Carole. *Farewell—We're Good and Gone*. Bloomington: Indiana University Press, 1989.

Meier, August, and Elliott Rudwick. *From Plantation to Ghetto*. 3rd ed., New York: Hill & Wang, 1976.

———. *Black Detroit and the Rise of the UAW*. New York: Oxford University Press, 1979.

Mellon, James, ed. *Bullwhip Days: The Slaves Remember*. New York: Weidenfeld & Nicolson, 1988.

Mitchell, H. L. *Mean Things Happening in This Land*. Montclair, N.J.: Allanheld, Osmun, 1979.

Morgan, H. Wayne. *Drugs in America: A Social History, 1800–1980.* Syracuse, N.Y.: Syracuse University Press, 1981.

Morris, Willie, ed. *The South Today: 100 Years After Appomattox.* New York: Harper & Row, 1965.

Morris, Willie. *Yazoo.* New York: Harper's Magazine Press, 1971.

Moyers, Michael David; "Arkansas Progressivism: The Legislative Record." Ph.D. diss., University of Arkansas, 1986.

Musto, David F., M.D. *The American Disease: Origins of Narcotic Control.* New Haven, Conn., and London: Yale University Press, 1973.

Myrdal, Gunnar. *An American Dilemma.* New York: Harper & Row, 1945.

Nicholl, Charles. *The Fruit Palace.* New York: St. Martin's Press, 1985.

Rawick, George P., general ed. *The American Slave: A Composite Autobiography.* Westport, Conn.: Greenwood Publishing Co., 1972.

Richards, Eugene. *Few Comforts or Surprises: The Arkansas Delta.* Cambridge, Mass.: MIT Press, 1973.

Rison, David Ellery. "Arkansas During the Great Depression." Ph.D. diss., University of California, Los Angeles, 1974.

Rosengarten, Theodore. *All God's Dangers.* New York: Alfred A. Knopf, 1974.

Sabbag, Robert. *Snowblind: A Brief Career in the Cocaine Trade.* New York: Vintage Books, 1990 (paperback ed.; originally published 1976).

Sanford, Juanita. *Poverty in the Land of Opportunity.* Little Rock, Ark.: Rose, 1978.

Schwartz, Marvin. *In Service to America: A History of VISTA in Arkansas, 1965–1985.* Fayetteville: University of Arkansas Press, 1988.

Shannon, Elaine. *Desperados.* New York: Viking, 1988.

Shannon, Jasper Berry. *Toward a New Politics in the South.* Knoxville: University of Tennessee Press, 1949.

Sherrill, Robert. *Gothic Politics in the Deep South.* New York: Ballantine, 1968.

Stockley, Grif. "Race Relations in Arkansas: Thank God for Mississippi" (manuscript), n.d.

Tucker, David M. *Arkansas: A People and Their Reputation.* Memphis, Memphis State University Press, 1985.

Waskow, Arthur I.: *From Race Riot to Sit-In, 1919 and the 1960s.* Garden City, N.Y.: Doubleday, 1966.

Whisenhunt, Donald M., ed. *The Depression in the Southwest.* Port Washington, N.Y.: Kennikat Press, 1980.

Williams, C. Fred, S. Charles Bolton, Carl H. Moneyhon, and Leroy T. Williams, eds. *A Documentary History of Arkansas.* Fayetteville: University of Arkansas Press, 1984.

Woodford, Frank B., and Arthur M. Woodford. *All Our Yesterdays: A Brief History of Detroit.* Detroit: Wayne State University Press, 1969.

Woodward, C. Vann. *The Strange Career of Jim Crow*. 2nd rev. ed. Oxford: Oxford University Press, 1966.

Wright, Richard. *12 Million Black Voices*. rev. ed. New York: Thunder's Mouth Press, 1988.